CITIES FOR PEOPLE, NOT FOR PROFIT

The worldwide financial crisis has sent shock waves of accelerated economic restructuring, regulatory reorganization, and sociopolitical conflict through cities around the world. It has also given new impetus to the struggles of urban social movements emphasizing the injustice, destructiveness, and unsustainability of capitalist forms of urbanization. This book contributes analyses intended to be useful for efforts to roll back contemporary profit-based forms of urbanization, and to promote alternative, radically democratic, and sustainable forms of urbanism. The contributors provide cutting-edge analyses of contemporary urban restructuring, including the issues of neoliberalization, gentrification, colonization, "creative" cities, architecture and political power, sub-prime mortgage foreclosures, and the ongoing struggles of "right to the city" movements. At the same time, the book explores the diverse interpretive frameworks – critical and otherwise – that are currently being used in academic discourse, in political struggles, and in everyday life to decipher contemporary urban transformations and contestations. The slogan, "cities for people, not for profit," sets into stark relief what the contributors view as a central political question involved in efforts, at once theoretical and practical, to address the global urban crises of our time.

Drawing upon European and North American scholarship in sociology, politics, geography, urban planning, and urban design, the book provides useful insights and perspectives for citizens, activists, and intellectuals interested in exploring alternatives to contemporary forms of capitalist urbanization.

Neil Brenner is Professor of Urban Theory at the Graduate School of Design, Harvard University. He formerly served as Professor of Sociology and Metropolitan Studies at New York University. He is the author of *New State Spaces: Urban Governance and the Rescaling of Statehood* (Oxford University Press, 2004); co-editor of *Spaces of Neoliberalism* (with Nik Theodore; Blackwell, 2002); and the co-editor of *The Global Cities Reader* (with Roger Keil; Routledge, 2006). His research interests include critical urban theory, sociospatial theory, state theory, and comparative geopolitical economy.

Peter Marcuse, a planner and lawyer, is Professor Emeritus of Urban Planning at Columbia University. He is the co-editor of *Globalizing Cities* (Blackwell, 2000) as well as *Of States and Cities: The Partitioning of Urban Space* (Oxford University Press, 2002) and *Searching for the Just City* (Routledge, 2009). His fields of research include city planning, housing, homelessness, the use of public space, the right to the city, social justice in the city, globalization, urban history, the relation between cultural activities, and urban development, and, most recently, solutions to the mortgage foreclosure crisis. He is beginning work on a book on critical planning, and a companion volume including analytic cases culled from past writings.

Margit Mayer teaches comparative and North American politics at the Freie Universität Berlin. Her research focuses on comparative politics, urban and social politics, and social movements. She has published on various aspects of contemporary urban politics, urban theory, and (welfare) state restructuring, much of it in comparative perspective. She is the co-editor of *Politics in European Cities* (with Hubert Heinelt; Birkhäuser, 1993), *Urban Movements in a Globalising World* (with Pierre Hamel and Henri Lustiger-Thaler; Routledge, 2000), and *Neoliberal Urbanism and its Contestations – Crossing Theoretical Boundaries* (with Jenny Künkel; Palgrave, 2011).

CITIES FOR PEOPLE, NOT FOR PROFIT

Critical urban theory and the right to the city

Edited by
Neil Brenner, Peter Marcuse,
and Margit Mayer

Routledge
Taylor & Francis Group

LONDON AND NEW YORK

First published 2012
by Routledge
2 Park Square, Milton Park, Abingdon, Oxon OX14 4RN

Simultaneously published in the USA and Canada
by Routledge
711 Third Avenue, New York, NY 10017

Routledge is an imprint of the Taylor & Francis Group, an informa business

British Library Cataloguing in Publication Data
A catalogue record for this book is available from the British Library

Library of Congress Cataloging in Publication Data
Cities for people, not for profit : critical urban theory and the right to the
city / edited by Neil Brenner, Peter Marcuse and Margit Mayer.
p. cm.
Includes bibliographical references and index.
1. Sociology, Urban. 2. Urbanization. 3. City planning. I. Brenner, Neil.
II. Marcuse, Peter. III. Mayer, Margit.
HT151.C5684 2012
307.1'21601--dc22
2011014122

ISBN: 978-0-415-60177-1 (hbk)
ISBN: 978-0-415-60178-8 (pbk)
ISBN: 978-0-203-80218-2 (ebk)

Typeset in Bembo
by GreenGate Publishing Services

CONTENTS

List of figures   vii
Contributors   viii
Preface and acknowledgments   xi

1 Cities for people, not for profit: an introduction   1
   Neil Brenner, Peter Marcuse, and Margit Mayer

2 What is critical urban theory?   11
   Neil Brenner

3 Whose right(s) to what city?   24
   Peter Marcuse

4 Henri Lefebvre, the right to the city, and the new
   metropolitan mainstream   42
   Christian Schmid

5 The "right to the city" in urban social movements   63
   Margit Mayer

6 Space and revolution in theory and practice: eight theses   86
   Kanishka Goonewardena

7 The praxis of planning and the contributions of critical
   development studies   102
   Katharine N. Rankin

8 Assemblages, actor–networks, and the challenges of
   critical urban theory   117
   Neil Brenner, David J. Madden, and David Wachsmuth

9 The new urban growth ideology of "creative cities"   138
   Stefan Krätke

10 Critical theory and "gray space": mobilization of the colonized   150
    Oren Yiftachel

11 Missing Marcuse: on gentrification and displacement   171
    Tom Slater

12 An actually existing just city? The fight for the right to
    the city in Amsterdam   197
    Justus Uitermark

13 A critical approach to solving the housing problem   215
    Peter Marcuse

14 Socialist cities, for people or for power?   231
    Bruno Flierl in conversation with Peter Marcuse

15 The right to the city: from theory to grassroots alliance   250
    Jon Liss

16 What is to be done? And who the hell is going to do it?   264
    David Harvey with David Wachsmuth

    Afterword
    Peter Marcuse   275

Index   *276*

FIGURES

2.1	Four mutually constitutive propositions on critical theory	15
10.1	Hussein al-Rafi'yah, Head of the RGUV, speaking to local community, Wadi al-Na'am, January 2009	151
10.2	Rebuilding the mosque, Wadi al-Na'am, January 2009	151
10.3	Chashem Zaneh, an unrecognized Bedouin locality with the city of Beersheba in the background, August 2008	155
10.4	Human and Municipal Geography Beersheba region, 2005	155
10.5	Day of Nakbah commemoration, al-Krein, May 2008	164
12.1	Social housing in the Nieuwmarkt neighborhood	198
12.2	Social housing of the 1980s in the Oosterparkbuurt in Amsterdam East	205
12.3	Income segments and housing market segments compared	208
14.1	Stalinallee in Berlin; built 1952–7	238
14.2	Marzahn residential area in Berlin in the 1980s	239
14.3	Project for the East German governmental high-rise, 1951	240
14.4	City center of the East German capital in Berlin, 1990	241
14.5	Castle design, 2008	243
14.6	Castle design, 2008	243
14.7	Governmental quarter of the Federal Republic in Berlin. The old Reichstag and the new buildings near the Spree	244
14.8	High-rises on Potsdamer Platz	245
14.9	High-rises on Potsdamer Platz	245
14.10	High-rises for the unrealized Alexanderplatz Project of architect Hans Kollhoff, 1993	246

CONTRIBUTORS

Neil Brenner is Professor of Urban Theory at the Graduate School of Design, Harvard University. He formerly served as Professor of Sociology and Metropolitan Studies at New York University. He is the author of *New State Spaces: Urban Governance and the Rescaling of Statehood* (Oxford University Press, 2004); the co-editor of *Spaces of Neoliberalism* (with Nik Theodore; Blackwell, 2002); and the co-editor of *The Global Cities Reader* (with Roger Keil; Routledge, 2006). His research interests include critical urban theory, sociospatial theory, state theory, and comparative geopolitical economy.

Bruno Flierl, PhD, is a freelance scholar specializing in the theory, history, and critical analysis of architecture, urbanism, and city planning in East Berlin and (after 1990) the united Berlin.

Kanishka Goonewardena trained as an architect in Sri Lanka and now teaches urban design and critical theory at the University of Toronto.

David Harvey is Distinguished Professor of Anthropology at the CUNY Graduate Center in New York City and the author of, among many other works, *The Limits to Capital* (Chicago, 1982), *The Urban Experience* (Johns Hopkins, 1989), *The Condition of Postmodernity* (Blackwell, 1989), and *The New Imperialism* (Oxford, 2004). His most recent book is *The Enigma of Capital* (Oxford, 2010).

Stefan Krätke is Professor of Economic and Social Geography at the Europa University Viadrina, Frankfurt an der Oder, Germany. His newest book, *The Creative Capital of Cities: Interactive Knowledge Creation and the Urbanization Economies of Innovation*, published in 2011 with Blackwell-Wiley in the Studies in Urban and Social Change (SUSC) book series.

Jon Liss has been community organizing in Virginia for almost 30 years. He was a founding member and is currently the Executive Director of Tenants and Workers United and Virginia New Majority and a co-founder and steering committee member of the Right to the City Alliance.

David J. Madden holds a PhD from Columbia University and is currently Visiting Assistant Professor of Sociology at Bard College in Annandale-on-Hudson, NY. His research is focused on urban studies, political sociology, and social theory.

Peter Marcuse, a planner and lawyer, is Professor Emeritus of Urban Planning at Columbia. He is the co-editor of *Globalizing Cities* (Blackwell, 2000) as well as *Of States and Cities: The Partitioning of Urban Space* (Oxford, 2002) and *Searching for the Just City* (Routledge, 2009). His fields of research include city planning, housing, homelessness, the use of public space, the right to the city, social justice in the city, globalization, urban history, the relation between cultural activities, and urban development, and, most recently, solutions to the mortgage foreclosure crisis. He is beginning work on a book on critical planning, and a companion volume including analytic cases culled from past writings.

Margit Mayer teaches American and comparative politics at the Freie Universität Berlin. Her research focuses on comparative politics, urban and social politics, and social movements. She has published on various aspects of contemporary urban politics, urban theory, and (welfare) state restructuring, much of it in comparative perspective. She is the co-editor of *Politics in European Cities* (with Hubert Heinelt; Birkhäuser,1993), *Urban Movements in a Globalising World* (with Pierre Hamel and Henri Lustiger Thaler; Routledge, 2000), and *Neoliberalizing Cities and Contestation* (with Jenny Künkel; Palgrave, 2011).

Katharine N. Rankin is Associate Professor and Director of Planning in the Department of Geography and Program in Planning at the University of Toronto. Her broad research interests include the politics of planning and development, comparative market regulation, feminist and critical theory, and social polarization. She is the author of *The Cultural Politics of Markets: Economic Liberalization and Social Change in Nepal* (Pluto Press and the University of Toronto Press, 2004), and is currently conducting research on commercial gentrification in Toronto and political subjectivity and post-conflict transition in Nepal.

Christian Schmid is a geographer and teaches urban sociology at the Faculty of Architecture at ETH Zurich. His research interests include urbanization processes in comparative perspective and theories of the urban and of space. He is the author of *Stadt, Raum und Gesellschaft: Henri Lefebvre und die Theorie der Produktion des Raumes* (Steiner, 2005), a critical reconstruction of Henri Lefebvre's theory of the production of space; the co-author of *Switzerland: an Urban Portrait* (together with Roger Diener, Jacques Herzog, Marcel Meili, and Pierre de Meuron; Birkhäuser, 2005); and the co-editor of *Space, Difference, Everyday Life: Reading Henri Lefebvre* (together with Kanishka Goonewardena, Stefan Kipfer, and Richard Milgrom; Routledge, 2008).

Tom Slater is Senior Lecturer in Human Geography at the University of Edinburgh. He has published many articles and books on the theme of gentrification and displacement, and is currently writing a book entitled *Fighting Gentrification* (Wiley-Blackwell Studies in Urban and Social Change (SUSC series)). His more recent work is concerned with urban marginality and territorial stigmatisation, funded by The Leverhulme Trust.

Justus Uitermark is Assistant Professor at the Sociology Department of the Erasmus University of Rotterdam. He completed his PhD thesis "Dynamics of Power in Dutch Integration Politics" in 2010. Currently he is working on research projects on gentrification, cyber politics, and integration politics.

David Wachsmuth was trained as an urban planner in Toronto and is now a PhD candidate in sociology at New York University, where he studies urban political economy.

Oren Yiftachel is Professor of political geography and urban planning at Ben-Gurion University, Beersheba. He is part of the planning team at the Regional Council for Unrecognized Bedouin Villages (RCUV), and a co-chair of B tselem, the Israeli information center for human rights in the occupied territories. He is working as co-author on a forthcoming volume, *Indigenous (In)Justice: Land and Human Rights among the Bedouins in Southern Israel/Palestine* (Harvard Human Rights Press).

PREFACE AND ACKNOWLEDGMENTS

Early versions of most of the chapters in this book were presented at an international conference titled, "Cities for people, not for profits," held in November 2008 at the Center for Metropolitan Studies (CMS), Berlin (see Horlitz and Vogelpohl 2009). Linking debates in critical urban theory and conjunctural analyses of ongoing urban struggles, this conference attracted 250 participants, including 30 speakers, principally from North America and western Europe. The event was made possible by a primary grant from the German Research Association (DFG). Both the DFG and the Transatlantic Graduate Program Berlin–New York (housed at the Berlin CMS) also generously supported a co-teaching arrangement for a graduate seminar convened jointly by the three editors of this volume in the Department of Sociology, New York University and the Graduate School of Architecture and Urban Planning, Columbia University in Fall 2006. Many of the ideas behind this volume were forged through our discussions in that seminar and in follow-up workshops in the CMS Transatlantic Graduate Program; we thank both our New York and Berlin students for the seriousness of their engagement with our evolving ideas. We are grateful to the DFG for supporting our intellectual collaboration and for contributing essential funding towards the Berlin conference. We owe a special debt of gratitude to Katja Sussner of the Berlin CMS for her invaluable work in organizing the conference. Without her expert assistance and organizational support, this project would have been an impossible undertaking. Additionally, we thank Prof. Dr Heinz Reif of the CMS for his steadfast support of our work and, more generally, for his visionary organizational work in the field of transnational urban studies. We also thank the Rosa Luxemburg Stiftung for contributing crucial additional funding towards the Berlin conference.

The argument and form of this book have been shaped foundationally through our ongoing dialogue with Bob Catterall and his energetic editorial board at the journal *CITY*. Earlier versions of many of the chapters included here appeared in a special issue of that journal (13, 2–3, 2009). We are grateful to the editorial committee of *CITY*, particularly Bob Catterall, Paul Chatterton, Dan Swanton, and Martin Woessner, for supporting our collective work both in the journal and, in revised and expanded form, in this volume.

CITY proved to be an ideal forum for discussion of the problematic developed in this book because of its long-standing commitment to bringing together, in readable form, theoretical reflections on the contemporary urban condition, analyses of practical experiences in contemporary urban conflicts, and perhaps most crucially, explorations of their necessary, if constantly evolving, interrelationships. It has been a privilege and a pleasure to contribute to *CITY*'s work and to engage in critical yet always comradely dialogue with its energetic team of editors.

Finally, we would like to thank Alex Hollingsworth and Louise Fox at Routledge for their support, expertise and – it must be said – patience as we worked to complete this book.

References

Horlitz, S. and Vogelpohl, A. (2009) "Something can be done! A report on the conference 'Right to the City: Prospects for Critical Urban Theory and Practice'," *International Journal of Urban and Regional Research*, vol. 33 (1), pp. 1067–72.

1

CITIES FOR PEOPLE, NOT FOR PROFIT

An introduction

Neil Brenner, Peter Marcuse, and Margit Mayer

The unfolding effects of the global economic recession are dramatically intensifying the contradictions around which urban social movements have been rallying, suddenly validating their claims regarding the unsustainability and destructiveness of neoliberal forms of urbanization. Cities across Europe, from London, Copenhagen, Paris, and Rome to Athens, Reykjavik, Riga, and Kiev, have erupted in demonstrations, strikes, and protests, often accompanied by violence. Youthful activists are not alone in their outrage that public money is being doled out to the banks even as the destabilization of economic life and the intensification of generalized social insecurity continues. The Economist Intelligence Unit (2009) offered the following observation: "A spate of incidents in recent months shows that the global economic downturn is already having political repercussions … There is growing concern about a possible global pandemic of unrest … Our central forecast includes a high risk of regime-threatening social unrest." Similarly, the US director of national intelligence presented the global economic crisis as the biggest contemporary security threat, outpacing terrorism (Schwartz, 2009). Preparations to control and crush potential civil unrest are well underway (Freier, 2008).

In light of these trends, it appears increasingly urgent to understand how different types of cities across the world system are being repositioned within increasingly volatile, financialized circuits of capital accumulation. Equally important is the question of how this crisis has provoked or constrained alternative visions of urban life that point beyond capitalism as a structuring principle of political-economic and spatial organization. Capitalist cities are not only sites for strategies of capital accumulation; they are also arenas in which the conflicts and contradictions associated with historically and geographically specific accumulation strategies are expressed and fought out. As such, capitalist cities have long served as spaces for envisioning, and indeed mobilizing towards, alternatives to capitalism itself, its associated process of profit-driven urbanization, and its relentless commodification and re-commodification of urban spaces.

It is this constellation of issues that we wish to emphasize with the title of this book, "Cities for people, not for profit." Through this formulation, we mean to underscore the urgent political priority of constructing cities that correspond to human social needs rather than to the capitalist imperative of profit-making and spatial enclosure. The demand for "cities for people, not for profit" has been articulated recurrently throughout much of the history of capitalism. It was, for instance, expressed paradigmatically by Engels (1987 [1845]) as he analyzed the miserable condition of the English working class in the dilapidated housing districts of nineteenth-century Manchester. It was articulated in yet another form by writers as diverse as Jane Jacobs (1962) and Henri Lefebvre (1996 [1968]) as they polemicized against the homogenizing, destructive, and anti-social consequences of postwar Fordist urban renewal projects. It has been explicitly politicized and, in some cases, partially institutionalized by municipal socialist movements in diverse contexts and conjunctures during the course of the twentieth century (Boddy and Fudge, 1984; MacIntosh and Wainwright, 1987). Of course, both negative and positive lessons can also be drawn from the experience of cities under real-existing socialism, in which top-down, centralized state planning replaced commodification as the structuring process of sociospatial organization (Flierl and Marcuse, this volume). And finally, the limits of profit-based forms of urbanism have also been emphasized in the contemporary geoeconomic context by critics of neoliberal models of urban development, with its hypercommodification of urban land and other basic social necessities (housing, transportation, utilities, public space, health care, education, even water and sewage disposal) in cities around the world (see, for instance, Smith, 1996; Harvey, 1989; Brenner and Theodore, 2003).

The contributors to this book seek to extend reflection on this same problematic in the current moment, in which the worldwide financial crisis starting in 2008–10 and its consequences continue to send shock waves of instability and conflict throughout the global urban system. One of our goals in this collection is to contribute intellectual resources that may be useful for those institutions, movements, and actors that aim to roll back the contemporary hypercommodification of urban life, and on this basis to promote alternative, radically democratic, socially just, and sustainable forms of urbanism. Writing over thirty years ago, Harvey (1976: 314) succinctly characterized this challenge as follows:

> Patterns in the circulation of surplus value are changing but they have not altered the fact that cities [...] are founded on the exploitation of the many by the few. An urbanism founded on exploitation is a legacy of history. A genuinely humanizing urbanism has yet to be brought into being. It remains for revolutionary theory to chart the path from an urbanism based

in exploitation to an urbanism appropriate for the human species. And it remains for revolutionary practice to accomplish such a transformation.

Harvey's political injunction remains as urgent as ever in the early twenty-first century. In Harvey's view, a key task for critical or "revolutionary" urban theory is to "chart the path" toward alternative, post-capitalist forms of urbanization. How can this task be confronted today, as a new wave of "accumulation by dispossession" (Harvey, 2008) and capitalist enclosure (De Angelis, 2007) washes destructively across the world economy?

The need for critical urban theory

Mapping the possible pathways of social transformation – in Harvey's (1976: 314) terms, "charting the path" – involves, first and foremost, *understanding* the nature of contemporary patterns of urban restructuring, and then, on that basis, analyzing their implications for action. A key challenge for radical intellectuals and activists, therefore, is to decipher the origins and consequences of the contemporary global financial crisis and the possibility for alternative, progressive, radical, or revolutionary responses to it, at once within, among, and beyond cities. Such understandings will have considerable implications for the character, intensity, direction, duration, and potential results of resistance.

The field of critical urban studies can make important contributions to ongoing efforts to confront such questions. This intellectual field was consolidated in the late 1960s and early 1970s through the pioneering interventions of radical scholars such as Henri Lefebvre (2003 [1970]), 1996 [1968]), Manuel Castells (1977 [1972]), and David Harvey (1976). Despite their theoretical, methodological, and political differences, these authors shared a common concern to understand the ways in which, under capitalism, cities operate as strategic sites for commodification processes. Cities, they argued, are major basing points for the production, circulation, and consumption of commodities, and their evolving internal sociospatial organization, governance systems, and patterns of sociopolitical conflict must be understood in relation to this role. These authors suggested, moreover, that capitalist cities are not only arenas in which commodification occurs; they are themselves intensively commodified insofar as their constitutive sociospatial forms – from buildings and the built environment to land-use systems, networks of production and exchange, and metropolitan-wide infrastructural arrangements – are sculpted and continually reorganized in order to enhance the profit-making capacities of capital.

Of course, profit-oriented strategies of urban restructuring are intensely contested among dominant, subordinate, and marginalized social forces; their outcomes are never predetermined through the logic of capital. Urban space under capitalism is therefore never permanently fixed; it is continually shaped and reshaped through a relentless clash of opposed social forces oriented, respectively, towards the exchange-value (profit-oriented) and use-value (everyday life) dimensions of urban sociospatial configurations (Lefebvre, 1996 [1968]; Harvey, 1976; Logan and Molotch, 1987). Moreover, strategies to commodify urban space often fail dismally, producing devalorized, crisis-riven urban and regional landscapes in which labor and capital cannot be combined productively to satisfy social needs, and in which inherited sociospatial configurations are severely destabilized, generally at the cost of considerable human suffering and massive environmental degradation. And, even when such profit-making strategies do appear to open up new frontiers for surplus-value extraction, whether within, among, or beyond cities, these apparent "successes" are inevitably precarious, temporary ones – overaccumulation, devalorization, and systemic crisis remain constant threats. Paradoxically, however, the conflicts, failures, instabilities, and crisis tendencies associated with capitalist urbanization have led not to its dissolution or transcendence, but to its continual reinvention through a dynamic process of "implosion–explosion" (Lefebvre, 2003 [1970]) and "creative destruction" (Harvey, 1989). Consequently, despite its destructive, destabilizing social and environmental consequences, capital's relentless drive to enhance profitability has long played, and continues to play, a powerful role in producing and transforming urban sociospatial configurations.[1]

These analytical and political starting points have, since the 1970s, facilitated an extraordinary outpouring of concrete, critically oriented research on the various dimensions and consequences of capitalist forms of urbanization – including patterns of industrial agglomeration and inter-firm relations; the evolution of urban labor markets; the political economy of real estate and urban property relations; problems of social reproduction, including housing, transportation, education, and infrastructure investment; the evolution of class struggles and other social conflicts in the spheres of production, reproduction, and urban governance; the role of state institutions, at various spatial scales, in mediating processes of urban restructuring; the reorganization of urban governance regimes; the evolution of urbanized socio-natures; and the consolidation of diverse forms of urban social mobilization, conflict, and struggle (for oveviews, see Dear and Scott, 1980; Soja, 2000; Heynen et al., 2006). Such analyses in turn contributed to the elaboration of several distinct strands of critical urban research that have inspired generations of intellectual and political engagement with urban questions. These research strands include, at various levels of abstraction: (a) *periodizations* of capitalist urban development that have linked (world-scale) regimes of capital accumulation to changing (national and local) configurations of urban space; (b) *comparative* approaches to urban studies that have explored the place- and territory-specific forms of urban sociospatial organization that have crystallized within each of the latter configurations; and (c) *conjunctural* analyses that attempt to decipher ongoing, site-specific processes of urban restructuring, their sources within the underlying crisis-tendencies of world capitalism, their ramifications for the future trajectory of urban development, and the possibility of subjecting the latter to some form of popular democratic control.

This is not, however, to suggest that critical urban studies represents a homogeneous research field based on a rigidly orthodox or paradigmatic foundation. On the contrary, the development of critical approaches to the study of capitalist urbanization has been fraught with wide-ranging disagreements about any number of core theoretical, methodological, and political issues (for overviews see Katznelson, 1993; Saunders, 1984; Soja, 2000; see also Brenner et al., this volume). Even though their form, content, and stakes have evolved considerably in relation to the continued forward-movement of worldwide capitalist urbanization, such controversies remain as intense in the late 2000s as they were in the early 1970s.

Nonetheless, against the background of the past four decades of vibrant theorizing, research, debate, and disagreement on urban questions under capitalism, we believe it is plausible to speak of a broadly coherent, "critical" branch of urban studies. This critical branch can be usefully counterposed to "mainstream" or "traditional" approaches to urban questions (for further elaboration on the specificity of "critical" urban theory, see the contributions to this volume by Brenner, Marcuse, Goonewardena, and Rankin, respectively). In the most general terms, critical approaches to urban studies are concerned: (a) to analyze the systemic, yet historically specific, intersections between capitalism and urbanization processes; (b) to examine the changing balance of social forces, power relations, sociospatial inequalities and political–institutional arrangements that shape, and are in turn shaped by, the evolution of capitalist urbanization; (c) to expose the marginalizations, exclusions, and injustices (whether of class, ethnicity, "race," gender, sexuality, nationality, or otherwise) that are inscribed and naturalized within existing urban configurations; (d) to decipher the contradictions, crisis tendencies, and lines of potential or actual conflict within contemporary cities; and on this basis, (e) to demarcate and politicize the strategically essential possibilities for more progressive, socially just, emancipatory, and sustainable formations of urban life.

Cities in crisis: theory ... and practice

This book is concerned with each of these issues, and in this sense it represents a sustained collective engagement with the project of critical urban studies. The initial versions of most contributions were presented in November 2008, at a conference held at the Center for Metropolitan Studies, Berlin, in honor of Peter Marcuse's birth 80 years earlier in the same city. The conference was framed broadly around some of the key issues to which Marcuse has devoted his academic career as a critical urbanist and planner – the transformation of cities and urban space under contemporary capitalism; the role of the state and urban planning in mediating those transformations; the politics of urban sociospatial exclusion and polarization along class and ethnoracial lines; and the possibilities for progressive or radical interventions and mobilizations to produce more socially just, radically democratic, and sustainable urban formations.

These themes are well represented in the contributions below, which span from reflections on the nature of critical urban theory and the concept of the right to the city (Marcuse, Brenner, Schmid, Goonewardena, Mayer), through analyses of historical alternatives to the commodification of urban space (Mayer, Flierl and Marcuse, Uitermark, Marcuse), discussions of how best to interpret the contemporary moment of worldwide urban restructuring (Marcuse, Mayer, Krätke, Yiftachel, Harvey with Wachsmuth), critical engagements with established bodies of knowledge on urban questions (Rankin, Brenner/Madden/Wachsmuth, Krätke, Slater), concrete investigations of various contemporary patterns of urban sociospatial restructuring and exclusion (Yiftachel, Uitermark), and critical accounts of contemporary mobilizations that contest currently dominant patterns of urbanism (Mayer, Schmid, Harvey with Wachsmuth).

All of the contributions to this book insist on the centrality of commodification as an intellectual and political reference point for any critical account of the contemporary urban condition. But they approach this problematic through various theoretical and methodological lenses, and they assess its implications for concrete urban configurations from diverse thematic standpoints. The majority of the contributions focus on patterns of urban restructuring and their associated contradictions during the past decade, with particular reference to the hypercommodified urban spaces of western Europe and North America, but also, in some contributions, with reference to urbanization processes in the Middle East (Yiftachel) or in the global South (Mayer, Rankin).

Several contributions engage with Lefebvre's (1996 [1968]) classic concept of the "right to the city," which has recently been rediscovered by radical academics and activists alike (in this volume, see the chapters by Marcuse, Schmid, Mayer, and Harvey with Wachsmuth). This slogan represents one important rallying cry and basis for transformative political mobilization in many contemporary cities, and it also resonates with earlier calls to create "cities for citizens" through the reinvigoration of participatory urban civil societies (Douglass and Friedmann, 1998). However, as Mayer points out in her chapter, this potentially radical political slogan, much like that of "social capital," is also being used ideologically by state institutions, which have co-opted it into a basis for legitimating existing, only weakly participatory forms of urban governance, or for exaggerating the systemic implications of newly introduced forms of citizen participation in municipal affairs (see also Mayer 2003). Lefebvre (2009 [1966]) himself grappled with an analogous problem in the 1960s and 1970s, when the Eurocommunist concept of *autogestion* – literally, "self-management," but perhaps best translated as "grassroots democracy" – was being pervasively misappropriated by various interests to legitimate new forms of state bureaucratic planning. In contrast to such tendencies, Lefebvre insisted that "limiting the world of commodities" was essential to any project of radical democracy, urban or otherwise, for this would "give content to the projects of democratic planning, prioritizing the social needs that are formulated, controlled, and managed by those who have a stake in them" (Lefebvre, 2009 [1966]: 148). While several contributions explore the challenges and dilemmas associated with such an urban politics of grassroots participation (Marcuse, Schmid, Mayer, Rankin, Harvey with Wachsmuth), others also advocate its construction, extension, or reinvention in the wake of restructuring processes that are intensifying the marginalization, exclusion, displacement, disempowerment, or oppression of urban inhabitants (Yiftachel, Marcuse, Slater, Uitermark, this volume; see also Purcell, 2008).

Clearly, since the Fordist–Keynesian period, urban social movements have had their ups and downs. On occasion, they have succeeded in producing major changes, but in other cases their radical promise has been aborted, co-opted or "mainstreamed." Of course, as the above remarks indicate, not all such movements actually sought systemic change.[2] But from the perspective of the field of critical urban studies, one may venture the following conjecture regarding the current situation: the transformative potential of social movement mobilizations will depend on two basic factors – the objective position, power, and strategies of those currently established in positions of domination; and the objective position, power, and strategies of those who are mobilizing in opposition to established forms of urbanism.

As indicated above, the objective position in which both elements currently find themselves is *crisis*. Initially, that crisis appears to be rooted in the economic structure, but it has also been extended to forms of governance, regulation, and political consciousness. The strategy of those in power is unfortunately quite clear, and can be summarized under the rubric of neoliberalism and its various permutations. This forms the backdrop for many of the contributions to this book, which examine various ways in which the social power relations of capitalism – along with imperialism, colonialism, racism, and other modalities of social disempowerment – are inscribed within urban sociospatial landscapes around the world. But what about the forces of resistance to domination, those suffering due to the current crisis and, indeed, the longer-term relations of exploitation of which the current situation is a consequence and part? What is their future, and what kind of change, if any, will they produce?

The nature of the groups that are adversely affected by existing arrangements and contemporary restructuring processes is likewise addressed in several of the chapters. For instance, Marcuse distinguishes between the *deprived* – those who are immediately exploited, unemployed, impoverished, discriminated against in jobs and education, in ill health and uncared for, or incarcerated; and the *discontented* – those who are disrespected, treated unequally because of sexual, political, or religious orientation, censored in speech, writing, research, or artistic expression, forced into alienating jobs, or otherwise constrained in their capacity to explore the possibilities of life. Members of both of these partially overlapping groups have considerable cause to oppose the existing system of capitalism and contemporary forms of urbanism. But they are a heterogeneous group, and their common interest is not always obvious, nor is concerted action easy. The events of 1968 are mentioned recurrently in several of the contributions here as manifesting, simultaneously, the transformative potential and the endemic difficulty of united, collective action across diverse constituencies. The possibility for such action is further constrained by the potent force of the corporate media, the daily, routinized language of politics, and the perceived need to deal with everyday crises before long-term, systemic issues can be addressed. And, above all, transformative action is constrained by the propaganda of market fundamentalism, the induced appeal of mass consumerism, the technically instrumentalized educational system, the oppressive weight of bureaucracy, and through it all, the overwhelming force of dominant ideologies of exclusion and supremacy (for instance, nationalism, racism, Eurocentrism, Orientalism, heteronormativity, speciesism, and so forth).

Several different approaches to resistance and change are, however, possible. The overwhelming reaction to the collapse of the prevailing private market financial system, whose trivial public regulation is itself in the hands of the dominant institutions and corporations of the private world, is popular outrage. That outrage could well be directed against the system as a whole; it could take a radical turn, in the spirit of Lefebvre. The argument could be made that the present crisis exposes the vices of the capitalist system as a whole, and that the realization of a genuine right to the city requires the abolition of the rule of private finance, and thus with it the rule of private capital, over the urban economy, and indeed, that of the world economy as a whole. That would be a radical response, one oriented precisely towards the construction of an "urbanism appropriate for the human species," as envisioned by Harvey (1976: 314).[3]

A liberal-progressive or reformist response, on the other hand, would focus on individual and "excessive" greed, whether of bankers or financiers or politicians, as the villains that have produced the current crisis. Such a response would, accordingly, focus on regulating the activities of such power-brokers more thoroughly than existing regulations permit. It would direct outrage not at the system as a whole, but at the bonuses which executives get from it, the Ponzi schemes which some have perpetrated, or the abuses of political power that have likewise been implicated in the current crisis. To the extent that this response thematizes nationalization at all, it sees this as a step towards restoring the banks to "health," that is, renewed profitability, and then returning them to their private, corporate owners, perhaps now sheltered from excessive "risk" through "better" regulation. Thus, the outrage is eviscerated, and the right to the city shrivels to a right to unemployment benefits and public investment in urban infrastructure (needed anyway to keep businesses "competitive"), with massive bail-outs for banks being offset by some minimal protections for small and middle-class borrowers of "viable" mortgages.

Will contemporary urban social movements be thus co-opted, as they were during the austerity, roll-out phase of neoliberal restructuring in the 1980s? Will they be content with reforms that merely reboot the system, or will they attempt to address the problem of systemic change as did the militant student and labor movements of 1968? As of this writing (March 2011), both increased militancy, as in the squatting of foreclosed homes, and co-optation, as in the endless debates about mortgage regulation, appear possible. Prediction is hazardous, not least because urban space continues to serve simultaneously as the arena, the medium, and the stake of ongoing struggles regarding the future of capitalism. It is, in Harvey's (2008: 39) formulation, the "point of collision" between the mobilizations of the deprived, the discontented and the dispossessed, on the one side, and on the other, ruling class strategies to instrumentalize, control, and colonize social and natural resources, including the right to the city itself, for the benefit of the few. As such struggles over the present and future shape of our cities intensify, we hope that this volume will contribute to clarifying what needs to be understood and what needs to be done in order to forge a radical, if not revolutionary, alternative to the dismal, destructive *status quo* of worldwide capitalist urbanization. The slogan, "Cities for people, not for profit" is thus intended to set into stark relief what we view as a central political objective for ongoing efforts, at once theoretical and practical, to address the crises of our time.

Notes

1 Exploration of the nexus between cities and commodification had, of course, already been initiated in the mid-nineteenth century by Engels in his classic study of industrial Manchester (1987 [1845]). However, this constellation of issues was subsequently neglected by most mainstream twentieth-century urbanists, who opted instead for some combination of transhistorical, technocratic, or instrumentalist approaches and tended to interpret cities as the spatial expressions of purportedly universal principles of human ecology or civilizational order (for a partial exception see Mumford's [1961: 446–81] revealing account of "coketown").
2 While Castells (1977 [1972]) limited his definition of social movements to those that succeeded in producing systemic change, we embrace a broader conceptualization. The issue of success or failure is contested, particularly on a systemic level, and it may vary according to whether it is assessed under, for example, genuinely emancipatory criteria or those of mainstream power politics. Both are relevant.
3 If the election of Obama expressed the power of the people to use the political process to achieve some change, it also underscored the intrinsic limitations of election-based, parliamentary-democratic strategies of social transformation. When the centers of economic power remain in the hands of multinational corporations and unaccountable financial institutions, elections will have only a limited impact on the actual operations of global capitalism.

References

Boddy, M. and Fudge, C. (eds) (1984) *Local Socialism?* London: Macmillan.

Brenner, N. and Theodore, N. (eds) (2003) *Spaces of Neoliberalism*, Cambridge, Mass.: Blackwell.

Castells, M. (1977 [1972]) *The Urban Question: A Marxist Approach*, London: Edward Arnold.

De Angelis, M. (2007) *The Beginning of History: Value Struggles and Global Capital*, London: Pluto.

Dear, M. and Scott, A. J. (eds) (1980) *Urbanization and Urban Planning in Capitalist Society*, London: Methuen.

Douglass, M. and Friedmann, J. (eds) (1998) *Cities for Citizens*, New York: Wiley.

Economist Intelligence Unit (2009) "Governments under pressure: how sustained economic upheaval could put political regimes at risk," *The Economist*, [online] [accessed March 19, 2009], available at: http://viewswire.eiu.com/index. asp?layout=VWArticleVW3&article_id=954360280&rf=0.

Engels, F. (1987 [1845]) *The Condition of the Working Class in England*, trans. by V. Kiernan, New York: Penguin.

Freier, N. P. (2008) "Known unknowns: unconventional 'strategic shocks' in defense strategy development," *Strategic Studies Institute U.S. Army War College*, [online] [accessed June 29, 2011], available at: http://www.strategicstudiesinstitute.army.mil/pubs/display. cfm?PubID=890.

Harvey, D. (2008) "The right to the city," *New Left Review*, no. 53, 23–40.

Harvey, D. (1989) *The Urban Experience*, Baltimore: Johns Hopkins University Press.

Harvey, D. (1976) *Social Justice and the City*, Cambridge, Mass.: Blackwell.

Heynen, N., Kaika, M., and Swyngedouw, E. (eds) (2006) *In the Nature of Cities*, New York: Routledge.

Jacobs, J. (1962) *The Death and Life of Great American Cities*, New York: Vintage.

Katznelson, I. (1993) *Marxism and the City*, New York: Oxford University Press.

Lefebvre, H. (2009 [1966]) "Theoretical problems of autogestion," in H. Lefebvre, *State Space, World*, N. Brenner and S. Elden (eds), Minneapolis: University of Minnesota Press, 138–52.

Lefebvre, H. (2003 [1970]) *The Urban Revolution*, trans. by R. Bononno, Minneapolis: University of Minnesota Press.

Lefebvre, H. (1996 [1968]) "The right to the city," in H. Lefebvre, *Writings on Cities*, E. Kofman and E. Lebas (eds), Cambridge, Mass.: Blackwell, 63–184.

Logan, J. and Molotch, H. (1987) *Urban Fortunes*, Berkeley: University of California Press.

MacIntosh, M. and Wainwright, H. (eds) (1987) *A Taste of Power: The Politics of Local Economics*, London: Verso.

Mayer, M. (2003) "The onward sweep of social capital," *International Journal of Urban and Regional Research*, vol. 27, no. 1, 110–32.

Mumford, L. (1961) *The City in History*, New York: Harcourt.

Purcell, M. (2008) *Recapturing Democracy*, New York: Routledge.

Saunders, P. (1984) *Social Theory and the Urban Question*, 2nd edition, New York: Routledge.

Schwartz, N. (2009) "Rise in jobless poses threat to stability worldwide," *The New York Times*, February 15.

Smith, N. (1996) *The New Urban Frontier*, New York: Routledge.

Soja, E. (2000) *Postmetropolis*, Cambridge, Mass.: Blackwell.

2

WHAT IS CRITICAL URBAN THEORY?

Neil Brenner

Introduction

What is *critical* urban theory? This phrase is generally used as a shorthand reference to the writings of leftist or radical urban scholars during the post-1968 period – for instance, those of Henri Lefebvre, David Harvey, Manuel Castells, Peter Marcuse, and a legion of others who have been inspired or influenced by them (Katznelson, 1993; Merrifield, 2002). Critical urban theory rejects inherited disciplinary divisions of labor and statist, technocratic, market-driven, and market-oriented forms of urban knowledge. In this sense, critical theory differs fundamentally from what might be termed "mainstream" urban theory – for example, the approaches inherited from the Chicago School of urban sociology, or those deployed within technocratic or neoliberal forms of policy science. Rather than affirming the current condition of cities as the expression of transhistorical laws of social organization, bureaucratic rationality, or economic efficiency, critical urban theory emphasizes the politically and ideologically mediated, socially contested and therefore malleable character of urban space – that is, its continual (re)construction as a site, medium, and outcome of historically specific relations of social power. Critical urban theory is thus grounded on an antagonistic relationship not only to inherited urban knowledges, but more generally, to existing urban formations. It insists that another, more democratic, socially just, and sustainable form of urbanization is possible, even if such possibilities are currently being suppressed through dominant institutional arrangements, practices, and ideologies. In short, critical urban theory involves the critique of ideology (including social–scientific ideologies) *and* the critique of power, inequality, injustice, and exploitation, at once within and among cities.

However, the notions of critique, and more specifically of critical theory, are not merely descriptive terms. They have determinate social–theoretical content that is derived from various strands of Enlightenment and post-Enlightenment social philosophy, not least within the work of Hegel, Marx, and the western marxian tradition (Koselleck, 1988; Postone, 1993; Calhoun, 1995; Callinicos 2006; Sayer 2009). Moreover, the focus of critique in critical social theory has evolved significantly during the course of the past two centuries of capitalist development (Benhabib, 1986; Therborn, 1996). Given the intellectual and political agenda of this book, it is worth revisiting some of the key arguments developed within the aforementioned traditions, particularly that of the Frankfurt School, which arguably provide a crucial, if often largely implicit, reference point for the contemporary work of critical urbanists.

One of the main points emphasized in this chapter is the historical specificity of any approach to critical social theory, urban or otherwise. The work of Marx and the Frankfurt School emerged during previous phases of capitalism – competitive (mid- to late nineteenth century) and Fordist–Keynesian (mid-twentieth century), respectively – that have now been superseded through the restless, creatively destructive forward motion of capitalist development (Postone, 1999, 1993, 1992). A key contemporary question, therefore, is how the conditions of possibility for critical theory have changed today, in the early twenty-first century, in the context of an increasingly globalized, neoliberalized, and financialized formation of capitalism (Therborn, 2008).

Such considerations also lead directly into the thorny problem of how to position *urban* questions within the broader project of critical social theory. With the significant exception of Walter Benjamin's *Passagen-Werk*, none of the main figures associated with the Frankfurt School devoted much attention to urban questions. For them, critical theory involved the critique of commodification, the state, and the law, including their mediations, for instance, through family structures, cultural forms, and social-psychological dynamics (Kellner, 1989; Jay, 1973; Wiggershaus, 1995). This orientation had a certain plausibility during the competitive and Fordist–Keynesian phases of capitalist development, insofar as urbanization processes were then generally viewed as a straightforward spatial expression of other, purportedly more fundamental social forces, such as industrialization, class struggle, state regulation, and the culture industry. I argue below, however, that such an orientation is no longer tenable in the early twenty-first century, as we witness nothing less than an *urbanization of the world* – the "urban revolution" anticipated nearly four decades ago by Henri Lefebvre (2003 [1970]; see also Schmid, this volume; Brenner, Madden, and Wachsmuth, this volume). Under conditions of increasingly generalized, worldwide urbanization (Lefebvre, 2003 [1970]; Schmid, 2005; Soja and Kanai, 2007), the project of critical social theory and that of critical urban theory have been mutually intertwined as never before.

Critique and critical social theory

The modern idea of critique is derived from the Enlightenment and was developed most systematically in the work of Kant, Hegel, and the Left Hegelians (Benhabib, 1986; Habermas, 1973; Marcuse, 1954; Jay, 1973; Calhoun, 1995; Therborn, 1996). But it assumed a new significance in Marx's work, with the development of the notion of a critique of political economy (Postone, 1993; Benhabib, 1986). For Marx, the critique of political economy entailed, on the one hand, a form of *Ideologiekritik*, an unmasking of the historically specific myths, reifications, and antinomies that pervade bourgeois forms of knowledge. Just as importantly, Marx understood the critique of political economy not only as a critique of ideas and discourses about capitalism, but as a critique of capitalism itself, and as a contribution to the effort to transcend it. In this dialectical conception, a key task of critique is to reveal the contradictions within the historically specific social totality formed by capitalism.

This approach to critique is seen to have several important functions. First, it exposes the forms of power, exclusion, injustice, and inequality that underpin capitalist social formations. Second, for Marx, the critique of political economy is intended to illuminate the landscape of ongoing and emergent sociopolitical struggles: it connects the ideological discourses of the political sphere to the underlying (class) antagonisms and social forces within bourgeois society. Perhaps most crucially, Marx understood critique as a means to explore, both in theory and in practice, the possibility of forging alternatives to capitalism. A critique of political economy thus served to show how capitalism's contradictions simultaneously undermine the system, and point beyond it, towards other ways of organizing material life, social capacities, and society/nature relations.

During the course of the twentieth century, Marx's critique of political economy has been appropriated within diverse traditions of critical social analysis, including the traditional Marxism of the Second International (Kolakowski, 1981) and the alternative strands of radical thought associated with Western Marxism (Jay, 1986). It was arguably within the Frankfurt School of critical social theory, however, that the concept of critique was explored most systematically as a methodological, theoretical, and political problem. In confronting this issue, the major figures within the Frankfurt School also developed an innovative, intellectually, and politically subversive research program on the political economy, social-psychological dynamics, evolutionary trends, and inner contradictions of modern capitalism (Arato and Gebhardt, 1990; Bronner and Kellner, 1989; Wiggershaus, 1995).

It was Max Horkheimer (1982 [1937]) who, writing from exile in New York City in 1937, introduced the terminology of "critical theory." The concept was subsequently developed and extended by his associates Theodor Adorno and Herbert Marcuse, and later, in very different directions, by Jürgen Habermas, up through the 1980s. In the Frankfurt School conception, critical theory represented a decisive break from the orthodox forms of Marxism that prevailed under the Second International, with its ontology of labor and its invocation of proletarian class struggle as the privileged basis for social transformation under capitalism. Additionally, during the course of the mid-twentieth century, the Frankfurt School of critical theory was animated by several other contextually specific concerns and preoccupations – including the critique of fascism in Germany and elsewhere; the critique of technology, mass consumerism, and the culture industry under postwar capitalism in Europe and the USA; and, particularly in the later work of Herbert Marcuse, the critique of suppressed possibilities for human emancipation latent with present institutional arrangements.

The Frankfurt School notion of critical theory was initially elaborated as an epistemological concept. In Horkheimer's classic 1937 essay "Traditional and critical theory," it served to demarcate an alternative to positivistic and technocratic approaches to social science and bourgeois philosophy (Horkheimer, 1982 [1937]: 188–252). This line of analysis was famously continued by Adorno in the 1960s, in the *Positivismusstreit* (positivism dispute) with Karl Popper (Adorno et. al., 1976), and again in a totally different form in his philosophical writings on dialectics and aesthetic theory (for a sampling, see O'Connor, 2000). The notion of critical theory was developed in yet another new direction by Habermas in his debate on technocracy with Niklas Luhmann in the early 1970s (Habermas and Luhmann, 1971), and in a still more elaborate, mature form in his magnum opus, *The Theory of Communicative Action*, in the mid-1980s (Habermas, 1987, 1985).

The most politically charged vision of Frankfurt School critical theory was arguably presented by Herbert Marcuse in the mid-1960s, above all in his 1964 classic book, *One-Dimensional Man*. For Marcuse, critical theory entailed an immanent critique of capitalist society in its current form: it is concerned, he insisted, with "the *historical alternatives* which haunt the established society as subversive tendencies and forces" (Marcuse, 1964: xi–xii; italics added). There is thus a direct link between Marcuse's project and a central aspect of Marx's original critique of political economy – the search for emancipatory alternatives latent within the present, due to the contradictions of existing social relations (as emphasized systematically by Postone, 1993).

Key elements of critical theory: four propositions

There are, of course, profound epistemological, methodological, political, and substantive differences among writers such as Horkheimer, Adorno, Marcuse, and Habermas. Nonetheless, it can be argued that their writings collectively elaborate a core, underlying conception of critical theory (for an alternative but compatible reading, see Calhoun, 1995). This conception can be summarized with reference to four key propositions: critical theory is theory; it is reflexive; it involves a critique of instrumental reason; and it is focused on the disjuncture between the actual and the possible. These propositions should be understood

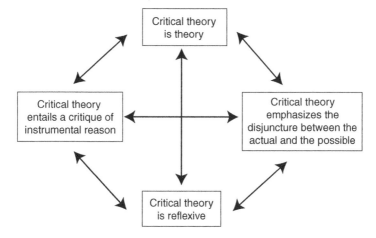

FIGURE 2.1 Four mutually constitutive propositions on critical theory

as being inextricably intertwined and mutually constitutive; the full meaning of each can only be grasped in relation to the others (Figure 2.1).

Critical theory is theory

In the Frankfurt School, critical theory is unapologetically abstract. It is characterized by epistemological and philosophical reflections; the development of formal concepts; generalizations about historical trends; deductive and inductive modes of argumentation; and diverse forms of historical analysis. It may also build upon concrete research, that is, upon an evidentiary basis, whether organized through traditional or critical methods. As Marcuse (1964: xi) writes, "In order to identify and define the possibilities for an optimal development, the critical theory must abstract from the actual organization and utilization of society's resources, and from the results of this organization and utilization." It is, in this sense, a *theory*.

Critical theory is thus not intended to serve as a formula for any particular course of social change; it is not a strategic map for social change; and it is not a "how to" style guidebook for social movements. It may – indeed, it *should* – have mediations to the realm of practice, and it is explicitly intended to inform the strategic perspective of progressive, radical, or revolutionary social and political actors. But, at the same time, crucially, the Frankfurt School conception of critical theory is focused on a moment of abstraction that is analytically prior to the famous Leninist question of "What is to be done?" It was Adorno (1998 [1969]: 267, 268) who most sharply summarized this position, as follows: "The requirement that theory should kowtow to praxis dissolves theory's truth content and condemns praxis to delusion [It is …] through its difference from immediate, situation-specific action, i.e. through its autonomization [that] theory becomes a transformative and practical productive force."

Critical theory is reflexive

In the Frankfurt School tradition, theory is understood to be at once enabled by, and oriented toward, specific historical conditions and contexts. This conceptualization has at least two key implications. First, critical theory entails a total rejection of any standpoint – positivistic, transcendental, metaphysical, or otherwise – that claims to be able to stand "outside" of the contextually specific time/space of history. All social knowledge, including critical theory, is embedded within the dialectics of social and historical change; it is thus intrinsically, endemically contextual. Second, Frankfurt School critical theory transcends a generalized hermeneutic concern with the situatedness of all knowledge. It is focused, more specifically, on the question of how oppositional, antagonistic forms of knowledge, subjectivity, and consciousness may emerge within an historical social formation.

Critical theorists confront this issue by emphasizing the fractured, broken, or contradictory character of capitalism as a social totality. If the totality were closed, non-contradictory, or complete, there could be no critical consciousness of it; there would be no need for critique; and indeed, critique would be structurally impossible. Critique emerges precisely insofar as society is in conflict with itself, that is, because its mode of development is self-contradictory. In this sense, critical theorists are concerned not only to situate themselves and their research agendas within the historical evolution of modern capitalism. Just as crucially, they want to understand what it is about modern capitalism that enables their own and others' forms of critical consciousness.

Critical theory entails a critique of instrumental reason

As is well known, the Frankfurt School critical theorists developed a critique of instrumental reason (analyzed at length in Habermas, 1987, 1985). Building on Max Weber's writings, they argued against the societal generalization of a means-ends rationality oriented towards the purposive-rational (*Zweckrationale*), an efficient linking of means to ends, without interrogation of the ends themselves. This critique had implications for various realms of industrial organization, technology, and administration, but most crucially here, Frankfurt School theorists also applied it to the realm of social science. In this sense, critical theory entails a forceful rejection of instrumental modes of social scientific knowledge – that is, those designed to render existing institutional arrangements more efficient and effective, to manipulate and dominate the social and physical world, and thus to bolster current forms of power. Instead, critical theorists demanded an interrogation of the ends of knowledge, and thus, an explicit engagement with normative questions.

Consistent with their historically reflexive approach to social science, Frankfurt School scholars argued that a critical theory must make explicit its practical–political and normative orientations, rather than embracing a narrow or technocratic vision. Instrumentalist modes of knowledge necessarily presuppose their own separation from their object of investigation. However, once that separation is rejected, and the knower is understood to be embedded within the same practical social context that is being investigated, normative questions are unavoidable. The proposition of reflexivity and the critique of instrumental reason are thus directly interconnected.

Consequently, when critical theorists discuss the so-called theory/practice problem, they are *not* referring to the question of how to "apply" theory to practice. Rather, they are thinking this dialectical relationship in exactly the opposite direction – namely, how the realm of practice (and thus, normative considerations) always already inform the work of theorists, even when the latter remains on an abstract level. In Adorno's (1998 [1969]: 278) terms, "Praxis is a source of power for theory, but cannot be prescribed by it." Or, in Habermas' formulation (1973: 210–11), "The dialectical interpretation [associated with critical theory] comprehends the knowing subject in terms of the relations of social praxis, in terms of its position, both within the process of social labor and the process of enlightening the political forces about their goals."

Critical theory emphasizes the disjuncture between the actual and the possible

As Therborn (2008) argues, the Frankfurt School embraces a dialectical critique of capitalist modernity – that is, one that affirms the possibilities for human liberation that are opened up by this social formation while also criticizing its systemic exclusions, oppressions, and injustices. The task of critical theory is therefore not only to investigate the forms of domination associated with modern capitalism, but equally, to excavate the emancipatory possibilities that are embedded within, yet simultaneously suppressed by, this very system. Callinicos (2006: 1) summarizes this point concisely with reference to the question of transcendence: "How," he asks, "are we able to go beyond the limits set by existing practices and beliefs and produce something new?"

In much Frankfurt School writing, this orientation involves a "search for a revolutionary subject," that is, the concern to find an agent of radical social change that could realize the possibilities unleashed yet suppressed by capitalism. However, given the Frankfurt School's abandonment of any hope for a proletarian-style revolution, their search for a revolutionary subject during the postwar period generated a rather gloomy pessimism regarding the possibility for social transformation and, especially in the work of Adorno and Horkheimer, a retreat into relatively abstract philosophical and aesthetic concerns (Postone, 1993).

Marcuse, by contrast, presents a very different position on this matter in the "Introduction" to *One-Dimensional Man* (1964). Here he agrees with his Frankfurt School colleagues that, in contrast to the formative period of capitalist industrialization, late-twentieth-century capitalism lacks any clear "agents or agencies of social change"; in other words, the proletariat was no longer operating as a class "for itself." Nonetheless, Marcuse (1964: xii) insists forcefully that "the need for qualitative change is as pressing as ever before [...] by society as a whole, for every one of its members." Against this background, Marcuse proposes that the rather abstract quality of critical theory, during the time in which he was writing, was organically linked to the absence of an obvious agent of radical, emancipatory social change. He argues, moreover, that the abstractions associated with critical theory could only be blunted or dissolved through concrete-historical struggles: "The theoretical concepts," Marcuse (1964: xii) suggests, "terminate with social change." This powerful proposition thus returns us to the idea of critical theory *as* theory. Just as the *critical* thrust of critical theory is historically conditioned and historically oriented, so too is its *theoretical* orientation continuously shaped and reshaped through ongoing social and political transformations.

Marcuse's position is reminiscent of Marx's famous claim in Volume 3 of *Capital* that all science would be superfluous if there were no distinction between reality and appearance. Similarly, Marcuse suggests, in a world in which radical or revolutionary social change were occurring, critical theory would be effectively marginalized or even dissolved – not in its critical orientation, but *as theory*: it would become concrete practice. Or, to put the point differently, it is precisely because revolutionary, transformative, emancipatory social practice remains so tightly circumscribed and constrained under contemporary capitalism that critical theory remains critical *theory* – and not simply everyday social practice. From this point of view, the so-called theory/ practice divide is an artifact not of theoretical confusion or epistemological inadequacies, but of the alienated, contradictory social formation in which critical theory is embedded. There is no theory that can overcome this divide, because, by definition, it cannot be overcome theoretically; it can only be overcome in practice.

Critical theory and the urbanization question

While Marx's work has exercised a massive influence on the post-1968 field of critical urban studies, few, if any, contributors to this field have engaged directly with the writings of the Frankfurt School. Nonetheless, I believe that most authors who position themselves within the intellectual universe of critical urban studies would endorse, at least in general terms, the conception of critical theory that is articulated through the four propositions summarized below:

- they insist on the need for abstract, theoretical arguments regarding the nature of urban processes under capitalism, while rejecting the conception of theory as a "handmaiden" to immediate, practical, or instrumental concerns;
- they view knowledge of urban questions, including critical perspectives, as being historically specific and mediated through power relations;
- they reject instrumentalist, technocratic, and market-driven forms of urban analysis that promote the maintenance and reproduction of extant urban formations; and
- they are concerned to excavate possibilities for alternative, radically emancipatory forms of urbanism that are latent, yet systemically suppressed, within contemporary cities.

Of course, any given contribution to critical urban theory may be more attuned to some of these propositions than to others, but they appear, cumulatively, to constitute an important epistemological foundation for the field as a whole. In this sense, critical urban theory has developed on an intellectual and political terrain that had already been tilled extensively not only by Marx, but also by the various theoreticians of the Frankfurt School. Given the rather pronounced, even divisive character of methodological, epistemological, and substantive debates among critical urbanists since the construction of this field in the early 1970s (see, for instance, Saunders, 1985; Gottdiener, 1985; Robinson, 2006; Brenner and Keil, 2005; Soja, 2000; see also Brenner, Madden, and Wachsmuth, this volume), it is essential not to lose sight of these broad areas of foundational agreement.

However, as the field of critical urban studies continues to evolve and diversify in the early twenty-first century, its character as a putatively "critical" theory deserves to be subjected to careful scrutiny and systematic debate. In an incisive feminist critique of Habermas, Fraser (1989) famously asked, "What's critical about critical theory?" Fraser's question can also be posed of the field of study under discussion in this book: what's critical about critical *urban* theory? Precisely because the process of capitalist urbanization continues its forward-movement of creative destruction on a world scale, the meanings and modalities of critique can never be held constant; they must, on the contrary, be continually reinvented in relation to the unevenly evolving political–economic geographies of this process and the diverse conflicts it engenders. This is, in my view, one of the major intellectual and political challenges confronting critical urban theorists today, and it is one that the contributors to this volume grapple with quite productively.

As indicated above, the concept of critique developed by Marx and the vision of critical theory elaborated in the Frankfurt School were embedded within historically specific formations of capitalism. Consistent with their requirement for reflexivity, each of these approaches explicitly understood itself to be embedded within such a formation, and was oriented self-consciously towards subjecting the latter to critique. This requirement for reflexivity, as elaborated above, must also figure centrally in any attempt to appropriate or reinvent critical theory, urban or otherwise, in the early twenty-first century. However, as Postone (1999, 1993) has argued, the conditions of possibility for critical theory have been thoroughly reconstituted under postfordist, post-Keynesian capitalism. The nature of the structural constraints on emancipatory forms of social change, and the associated imagination of alternatives to capitalism, have been qualitatively transformed through the acceleration of geoeconomic integration, the intensified financialization of capital, the crisis of the postwar model of national welfare state intervention, the still ongoing neoliberalization of state forms, the onslaught of new forms of capitalist enclosure at all spatial scales, and the deepening of planetary ecological crises (Harvey, 2005; Albritton et al., 2001; De Angelis, 2007). The most recent global financial crisis – the latest expression of a "roller coaster" of catastrophic regional crashes that have been rippling across the world economy for at least a decade (Harvey, 2008) – has generated a new round of worldwide, crisis induced restructuring that has still further rearticulated the epistemological, political, and institutional conditions of possibility for any critical social theory (Gowan, 2009; Brand and Sekler, 2009; Peck et al., 2010). While the four aforementioned elements of critical theory surely remain urgently relevant in the early twenty-first century, their specific meanings and modalities need to be carefully reconceptualized. The challenge for those committed to the project of critical theory is to do so in a manner that is adequate to the continued forward-motion of capital, its associated crisis-tendencies and contradictions, and the struggles and oppositional impulses it is generating across the variegated landscapes of the world economy.

Confronting this task hinges, I submit, on a much more systematic integration of urban questions into the analytical framework of critical social theory as a whole. As mentioned above, the problematic of urbanization received relatively scant attention within classical Frankfurt School analyses; and it is only relatively recently that Benjamin's (2002) wide-ranging sketches on the capitalist transformation of nineteenth-century Paris have engendered significant scholarly interest (Buck-Morss, 1991). Even during the competitive and Fordist–Keynesian phases of capitalist development, urbanization processes – manifested above all in the formation and expansion of large-scale urban regions – figured crucially in the dynamics of capital accumulation and in the organization of everyday social relations and political struggles. Under present geohistorical conditions, however, the process of urbanization has become increasingly generalized on a world scale (see also Schmid, this volume; Brenner, Madden, and Wachsmuth, this volume). Urbanization no longer refers simply to the expansion of the "great towns" of industrial capitalism, to the sprawling metropolitan production centers, suburban settlement grids and regional infrastructural configurations of Fordist–Keynesian capitalism, or to the anticipated linear expansion of city-based human populations in the world's "mega-cities." Instead, as Lefebvre (2003 [1970]) anticipated nearly four decades ago, this process now increasingly unfolds through the uneven stretching of an "urban fabric," composed of diverse types of investment patterns, settlement spaces, land use matrices, and infrastructural networks, across the entire world economy. Urbanization is, to be sure, still manifested in the continued, massive expansion of cities, city-regions and megacity regions, but it equally entails the ongoing sociospatial transformation of diverse, less densely agglomerated settlement spaces that are, through constantly thickening inter-urban and inter-metropolitan infrastructural networks, being ever more tightly interlinked to the major urban centers. We are witnessing, in short, nothing less than the intensification and extension of the urbanization process, via processes of capitalist enclosure, at all spatial scales and across the entire surface of planetary space (Lefebvre, 2003 [1970]; Schmid, 2005; De Angelis 2007).

As during previous phases of capitalist development, the geographies of urbanization are profoundly uneven – but their parameters are no longer confined to any single type of settlement space, whether defined as a city, a city-region, a metropolitan region, or even a megacity-region. Consequently, under contemporary circumstances, the urban can no longer be viewed as a distinct, relatively bounded site; it has instead become a generalized, planetary condition in and through which the accumulation of capital, the continuous enclosure of "common" spaces and realms, the regulation of political–economic life, the reproduction of everyday social relations, and the contestation of the earth and humanity's possible futures are simultaneously organized and fought out. In light of this, it is increasingly untenable to view urban questions as merely one among many specialized sub-topics to which a critical theoretical approach may be applied – alongside, for instance, the family, social psychology, education, culture industries, and the like. Instead, each of the key methodological and political orientations associated with critical theory, as discussed above, today requires sustained engagement with contemporary worldwide patterns of capitalist urbanization and their far-reaching consequences for social, political, economic, and human/nature relations.

This is an intentionally provocative assertion, and this chapter has offered no more than a modest attempt to demarcate the need for such an engagement and some of the broad intellectual parameters within which it might occur. Clearly, the effective elaboration of this "urbanistic" reorientation of critical theory will require further theoretical reflection, extensive concrete, and comparative research, as well as creative, collaborative strategizing to nourish the institutional conditions required for an effervescence of critical knowledges about contemporary urbanization. I argued above that critical urbanists must work to clarify and continually redefine the "critical" character of their theoretical engagements, orientations, and commitments in light of early twenty-first century processes of urban restructuring. Given the far-reaching transformations associated with such processes, the time seems equally ripe to integrate the problematic of urbanization more systematically and comprehensively into the intellectual architecture of critical theory as a whole.

References

Adorno, T. (1998 [1969]) "Marginalia to theory and praxis," in T. Adorno, *Critical Models: Interventions and Catchwords*, New York: Columbia University Press, 259–78.

Adorno, T., Albert, H., Dahrendorf, R., Habermas, J., Pilot, H., and Popper, K. (1976) *The Positivist Dispute in German Sociology*, trans. by G. Adey and D. Frisby, London: Heinemann.

Albritton, R., Itoh, M., Westra, R., and Zuege, A. (eds) (2001) *Phases of Capitalist Development: Booms, Crises, Globalizations*, New York: Palgrave.

Arato, A. and Gebhardt, E. (eds) (1990) *The Essential Frankfurt School Reader*, New York: Continuum.

Benhabib, S. (1986) *Critique, Norm and Utopia*, New York: Columbia University Press.

Benjamin, W. (2002) *The Arcades Project*, R. Tiedemann (ed.), trans. by H. Eiland and K. McLaughlin, Cambridge, Mass.: Harvard University Press.

Brand, U. and Sekler, N. (eds) (2009) "Postneoliberalism: a beginning debate," special issue of *Development Dialogue*, 51, 3–211.

Brenner, N. and Keil, R. (eds) (2005) *The Global Cities Reader*, New York: Routledge.

Bronner, S. and Kellner, D. (1989) *Critical Theory and Society: A Reader*, New York: Routledge.

Buck-Morss, S. (1991) *The Dialectics of Seeing: Walter Benjamin and the Arcades Project*, Cambridge, Mass.: MIT Press.

Calhoun, C. (1995) "Rethinking critical theory," in C. Calhoun, *Critical Social Theory*, Cambridge, Mass.: Blackwell, 1–42.

Callinicos, A. (2006) *The Resources of Critique*, London: Polity.

De Angelis, M. (2007) *The Beginning of History: Value Struggles and Global Capital*. London: Pluto.

Fraser, N. (1989) *Unruly Practices*, Minneapolis: University of Minnesota Press.

Gottdiener, M. (1985) *The Social Production of Urban Space*, 2nd edition, Austin: University of Texas Press.

Gowan, P. (2009) "Crisis in the heartland: consequences of the new Wall Street system," *New Left Review*, 55, 5–29.

Habermas, J. (1987) *The Theory of Communicative Action, Volume 2*, trans. by T. McCarthy, Boston, Mass.: Beacon.

Habermas, J. (1985) *The Theory of Communicative Action, Volume 1*, trans. by T. McCarthy, Boston, Mass.: Beacon.

Habermas, J. (1973) *Theory and Practice*, trans. by J. Viertel, Boston, Mass.: Beacon.

Habermas, J. and Luhmann, N. (1971) *Theorie der Gesellschaft oder Sozialtechnologie – was leistet Systemforschung?* Frankfurt: Suhrkamp Verlag.

Harvey, D. (2008) "The right to the city," *New Left Review*, 53, 23–40.

Harvey, D. (2005) *The New Imperialism*, New York: Oxford University Press.

Horkheimer, M. (1982 [1937]) "Traditional and critical theory," in M. Horkheimer, *Critical Theory: Selected Essays*, trans. by M. J. O'Connell, New York: Continuum, 188–243.

Jay, M. (1986) *Marxism and Totality*, Berkeley: University of California Press.

Jay, M. (1973) *The Dialectical Imagination*, Boston, Mass.: Little, Brown and Company.

Katznelson, I. (1993) *Marxism and the City*, New York: Oxford University Press.

Kellner, D. (1989) *Critical Theory, Marxism and Modernity*, Baltimore, MD: Johns Hopkins University Press.

Kolakowski, L. (1981) *Main Currents of Marxism, Volume 2: The Golden Age*, Oxford: Oxford University Press.

Koselleck, R. (1988) *Critique and Crisis*, Cambridge, Mass.: MIT Press.

Lefebvre, H. (2003 [1970]) *The Urban Revolution*, trans. by R. Bononno, Minneapolis: University of Minnesota Press.

Marcuse, H. (1964) *One-Dimensional Man*, Boston, Mass.: Beacon.

Marcuse, H. (1954) *Reason and Revolution: Hegel and the Rise of Social Theory*, London: Humanities Press.

Merrifield, A. (2002) *Metro-Marxism*, New York: Routledge.

O'Connor, B. (ed.) (2000) *The Adorno Reader*, Oxford: Wiley-Blackwell.

Peck, J., Theodore, N., and Brenner, N. (2010) "Postneoliberalism and its malcontents," *Antipode*, 41, 1, 94–116.

Postone, M. (1999) "Contemporary historical transformations: beyond postindustrial theory and neo-marxism," *Current Perspectives in Social Theory*, 19, 3–53.

Postone, M. (1993) *Time, Labor and Social Domination: A Re-interpretation of Karl Marx's Critical Social Theory*, New York: Cambridge University Press.

Postone, M. (1992) "Political theory and historical analysis," in C. Calhoun (ed.) *Habermas and the Public Sphere*, Cambridge, Mass.: MIT Press, 164–80.

Robinson, J. (2006) *Ordinary Cities*, London: Routledge.

Saunders, P. (1985) *Social Theory and the Urban Question*, 2nd edition, New York: Routledge.

Sayer, A. (2009) "Who's afraid of critical social science?" *Current Sociology*, 57, 6, 767–86.

Schmid, C. (2005) "Theory," in R. Diener, J. Herzog, M. Meili, P. De Meuron, and C. Schmid, *Switzerland: An Urban Portrait*. Basel: Birkhäuser Verlag, 163–224.

Soja, E. (2000) *Postmetropolis*, Cambridge, Mass.: Blackwell.

Soja, E. and Kanai, M. (2007) "The urbanization of the world," in R. Burdett and D. Sudjic (eds), *The Endless City*, London: Phaidon Press, 54–69.

Therborn, G. (2008) *From Marxism to Post-marxism?* London: Verso.

Therborn, G. (1996) "Dialectics of modernity: on critical theory and the legacy of 20th century Marxism," *New Left Review*, I/215, 59–81.

Wiggershaus, R. (1995) *The Frankfurt School*, trans. by M. Robertson, Cambridge, Mass.: MIT Press.

3

WHOSE RIGHT(S) TO WHAT CITY?

Peter Marcuse

The main concern of this chapter is what I take to be the ultimate purpose of critical urban theory: implementing the demand for a right to the city. But that is a demand, a goal, that needs definition. Whose right is it about, what right is it, and to what city? The chapter begins with a look at the actual problems that people face today, and then looks at them in their historical context, focusing on the difference between the crisis of 1968 which produced the demand for the right to the city, and the crisis we confront today. The question, then, is: how do we understand the right to the city today, and how can a critical urban theory contribute to implementing it? The chapter suggests an approach to action that relies on three steps a critical theory could follow: exposing, proposing, and politicizing. The conclusion presents a perhaps far-fetched idea of what the possibilities for large-scale and enduring social change might actually be today. Is another world not only possible, but realistically attainable?

A word on the use of terms. "Critical," "urban," "theory," and "practice" are four important words and concepts. (One might argue that "theory and practice" are really only one word in this context, but that's truer in theory than in practice.)

"Critical" I take to be, among other things, shorthand for an evaluative attitude towards reality, a questioning rather than an acceptance of the world as it is, a taking apart and examining and attempting to understand the world. It leads to a position not only necessarily critical in the sense of negative criticism, but also critically exposing the positive and the possibilities of change, implying positions on what is wrong and needing change, but also on what is desirable and needs to be built on and fostered.

"Urban" I take to be shorthand for the societal as congealed in cities today, and to denote the point at which the rubber of the personal hits the ground of the societal, the intersection of everyday life with the socially created systemic world about us In Lefebvre's hands, it is a normative concept, incorporating the positively desirable organization of space and time (see Schmid, this volume).

"Theory" I take to be the attempt to understand, to explain, and to illuminate the meaning and possibilities of the world in which practice takes place. It is, in a sense, the conscious and articulated aspect of practice, of action. It is developed through action, and in turn informs understanding and undergirds practice.

"Practice" is often spoken of as if it were the Siamese twin of theory, because it is needed for theory and because theory should lead to practice if it is taken seriously. The image is of a theory and a practice that are linked organically, that a critical theory depends on a critical practice and a critical practice depends on a critical theory. But it is not so simple. The Paris Commune, a classical example of critical practice, relied on no "theory," and leading exponents of critical theory saw their work as *Flaschenpost*, in Adorno's words, analysis written down and put in a bottle thrown in the ocean hoping it would someday be retrieved and be useful. But it may have been one of the failings of some of the mainstream of critical theory that it saw itself evolving independently of practice, and it may similarly have been a weakness of some forms of critical action that they proceeded uninformed and even rejecting critical theory, as in the *We Are the Poors* approach (Desai 2002) and in some forms of anarchist and communitarian action.[1]

In any event, as used here, critical urban theory is taken as analysis that flows from the experience of practice in developing the potentials of existing urban society, and critical theory is intended to illuminate and inform the future course of such practice.

The reality today and its history

Today

When this chapter was first written, two developments shaped the context for this analysis: the election of Barack Obama as president of the United States, and the deepening economic crisis globally.

The election of Obama was seen as a dramatic event, not only in the United States but in the world. What did it in fact mean? What did it change, and what did it leave unchanged? Answering the question requires exactly critical theory. For the answer is, some things did and some did not change – and it is the ability of critical theory to illuminate this issue that entitles it to an important place in our thinking and action. What Obama's election changed is that the use of racism as a support for economic and social policies that exploit and oppress has become more questionable, as racism is rejected by more and more people (although not by all) as contrary to their own experiences and values. And we still have institutional racism, so that for every dollar of wealth held by the typical white family, the African–American family has only one dime (Lui 2009: A15). What it did not change is the underlying structure of the society in which the election took place, either politically – this was the most expensive campaign in the history of the United States, and the media's role in it was enormous – or economically – the Goldman Sachs crew who are running the national treasury, and their economist academic minions, is running the Federal government's economic role after Obama's election as it did before, and the proposed $700 billion bail-out for the financial sector has been fully implemented. Even the staid *New York Times* writes, "Goldman's presence in the [US Treasury] department is so ubiquitous that other bankers and competitors have given the star-studded firm a new nickname; Government Sachs" (Creswell and White 2008: 1).

Another aspect of the US presidential election campaign that led up to the election result is noteworthy, and ties in with a major argument I want to make here. Both parties ran under the slogan of "Change"; Obama's was "Change you can believe in," McCain highlighted his maverick, non-conformist record every chance he got. Close to 50 percent saw the change needed as being in one direction, close to 50 percent saw it in another, but hardly anyone was satisfied with things as they are. If critical urban theory is able to expose the roots of that dissatisfaction, and show both almost equal halves that their dis satisfaction is with the same features of the economy, the politics, the society, it will have done its job.

The other development around which this chapter is framed, which was already unfolding as the election took place, is the economic crisis. I focus here on the United States, but the picture is similar globally. In the United States today, over six million households (Credit Suisse 2008) face mortgage foreclosure, unemployment is rising to a several decades-long high, homeless use of emergency shelters is at an all-time high in New York City, real wages are falling way behind increases in productivity, the gap between rich and poor is growing. The financial crisis seems to be spreading, to engulf more and more people, to cause more and more unemployment, insecurity, hunger, and want, a greater and greater dissatisfaction with conditions as they are, with inequality, luxury in the midst of poverty, illiteracy, substantive as well as linguistic, selfishness in place of solidarity, isolation in place of love. But I think it is not a financial crisis spreading to other parts of the economy that we confront, but an economy whose contradictions are erupting in a very visible manner in the financial sector, but only as manifestations of much more deep-seated contradictions which we should not allow to be concealed in the focus on issues of regulation or deregulation in one small excrescence of a fundamentally flawed system as a whole. The problem is not in unregulated credit default swaps or out of control hedge funds; the problem is in exploitation, domination, repression system-wide.

Fundamentally, the crisis comes from a system that both necessarily produces gross material inequality and at the same time produces gross insecurity and emotional discontent and distortions. Greed is not an aberration of the system; it is what makes the system go. Calling greed "the profit motive" is a euphemism that tries to justify a system that relies on greed to produce growth at the expense of all other values, and that stifles creativity that does not serve profit. Anti-abortion activists, religious fundamentalists, defenders of "family values," are as much a reflection of emotional impoverishment as hunger and homelessness are of material deprivation. A society one-dimensional in its driving force produces one-dimensional people, and struggles to be supported by them. The victims of the system include both the materially deprived and the intellectually and socially alienated, as is explored below.

The notion of the right to the city as a slogan dealing with such problems came into widespread usage largely out of the events – the theory and the practice – of May 1968 in Paris, and their parallels worldwide. Further discussion requires a look at that history, what preceded it, how it compares to the events of today.

History: before and after 1968

"Crisis?" Capitalism has always been a system with deep internal contradictions. Marxism has had the investigation of crises at the center of its concerns, and its conclusions are hardly likely to be disproven by current events. In the twentieth century, five major crises, five periods of deep-going social turmoil, can be identified. They differ in their severity and consequences in the respective strengths and weaknesses of both the system's critics and of its defenders – a critical point. The five crises are:

1917: The crisis after the end of World War I, and the victory of the Russian revolution, the Weimar Republic.
1929: The Great Depression, the triumph of fascism, the New Deal.
1968: The Civil Rights Movement, the new left, the student protests, the Vietnam war.
1990: The crisis of really existing socialism in Eastern Europe and the Soviet Union.
2008: Today's more-than-financial crisis.

I mention three of these, 1917, 1929, and 1990, only to make an often forgotten point: the range of resolutions of crisis is a broad one, not confined to the kinds of questions that seem to pre-empt public discourse today: do we regulate speculation or not, do we increase welfare benefits of not, do we end this war or not, do we bail out this bank or this business or not, do we put up trade barriers or take them down? Historically, the choices are much broader. As these earlier crises have shown, at the extremes there lie, and have always lain, communism on the one side, barbarism, in the modern form of fascism, on the other. Neither extreme seems imminent today, if for different reasons – not communism, for lack of a base that presses for it or might bring it about, and not fascism, because the forces of domination have found subtler and more insidious means of holding on to power than naked violence.[2] In each crisis, the outcome has depended, not simply on the strength or weakness of the critical forces (and not the quality of their critical theory) but also on the strength and weaknesses of the established system. Indeed, one key function of critical theory may well be to expose and evaluate both the strengths and weaknesses of the existing system and the ultimate nature of its crises, thus informing practice as to what its strategic potential actually is, as well as analyzing the strategies that that practice might adopt.

After 1917, none of these crises involved more than sporadic violence, and all but 1929 in Europe seemed in reality (if not always in the minds of the participants) remote from the extremes of communism and fascism. But the crises of 1968 and 1990 were different from the earlier ones in one key regard: they did not rest on the material breakdown of the existing system, on the depth of poverty or oppression or material want, but on the combined dissatisfaction of broad elements of the population with the frustrated potentials that they saw society might frustrate – in a sense, resting on injustice rather than, or in addition to, want. The contradiction between the reality and the potential for greater progress undermined really existing socialism in the Stalinist period, but the potential was even clearer in May 1968, in Paris most prominently, but in April of that year in universities in the United States and elsewhere also. In each case critical action represented a new element in the oppositional protest. For the first time on a significant scale, the agitation resulting from the aspirations of the alienated were linked, if tenuously and in constant tension, with the demands of the materially exploited: the claims of the students to the claims of the workers (see Marcuse 2008). Workers as a whole were not uniformly supportive, and the institutionalized organs of the working class opposed the protests; yet worker support on the ground was strong.

On the other hand, the state against which the protests were directed, the rulers, the capitalists, and the underwriters of the establishment, were strong. The context was not of economic crisis; the system was still, in Herbert Marcuse's phrase, producing the goods. And the goods it produced satisfied the majority; those aspiring to something more than those goods remained a minority. The protest was defeated.

Today, in 2011, we have, in a sense, the reverse situation. The system is shaky in its production of the goods, whose delivery relies today more and more on financial arrangements rather than direct home production within the national economy. Foreclosures are up dramatically, with close to 4,000,000 threatened, unemployment is rising, local tax revenues and thus local governmental services are shrinking, public education is endangered, the security of retirements is threatened as pension funds lose large percentages of their value. And things are expected to get worse.

The establishment's response has been widely and deeply unpopular. The largest financial institutions have taken over the national treasury quite directly in private hands, have in effect privatized the government (quite a reversal of the nationalization of the banks of which Marx wrote in *The Communist Manifesto*). Goldman Sachs, one of the largest of the private financial banking and speculation firms, now has its members ruling the national treasury as well, distributing multiple billions of dollars to the biggest banks and financial institutions, those precisely that are universally recognized as having caused the immediate crisis to which they are supposed to be responding. Insecurity is widespread and deep, and the rulers and their lackeys are almost apologetic in their response; Alan Greenspan has admitted that he "overestimated the market."

Yet the protest has been subdued. Life on the campuses barely notices the crisis. Labor unions confine themselves to asking for limits on CEO pay. Bernie Sanders, the one socialist member of Congress (elected as an independent – socialist is not a label that can get you elected) speaks of nationalizing the banks; no one listens. The media denounce the "greed" of the bankers; no one blames the banking system and its driving force, the accumulation of profit, and expansion of capital. The left intelligentsia speaks to itself, trying to figure out how deep the crisis is; the media erects a wall against fundamental questioning of the system. Socialism remains a bad word in US electoral politics, in which the contenders shy away from it in unquestioning condemnation and speak only of regulation and renewed economic growth.

Critical urban theory can provide some illumination on why this situation exists. It has to do with the question of whose right to the city is involved, who the potential actors, the "agents of change," are, and what moves them either to propose or to oppose basic change.

Right to the city

The right to the city is both an immediately understandable and intuitively compelling slogan, and a theoretically complex and provocative formulation. What does the right to the city mean? More specifically: Whose right are we talking about? What right is it we mean? What city is it to which we want the right?

Henri Lefebvre popularized the slogan in 1968, but he was more provocative than careful in its usage. The best definition he gave is:

> the right to the city is like a cry and a demand. This right slowly meanders through the surprising detours of nostalgia and tourism, the return to the heart of the traditional city, and the call of existent or recently developed centralities.

> (Lefebvre 1967: 158)

In other places he has it meandering through:

> the right to information, the rights to use of multiple services, the right of
> users to make known their ideas on the space and time of their activities in
> urban areas; it would also cover the right to the use of the center.
>
> (Lefebvre 1991: 34)

So: *whose right*, *what right*, and *to what city*?

Whose right?

"Whose right" is a more complex question, and one as to which I think an
expansion of the existing discussion would be worthwhile – useful both theoretically and in practice.

The question is a long-standing one. Herbert Marcuse (1969) struggled with
it. David Harvey (2009) recently called attention to it in today's context:

> I don't think we are in a position to define who the agents of change will
> be in the present conjuncture and it plainly will vary from one part of the
> world to another. In the United States right now there are signs that ele-
> ments of the managerial class, which has lived off the earnings of finance
> capital all these years, is getting annoyed and may turn a bit radical. A lot
> of people have been laid off in the financial services – in some instances
> they have even had their mortgages foreclosed. Cultural producers are
> waking up to the nature of the problems we face and in the same way
> that the 1960s art schools were centers of political radicalism, you might
> find something like that re-emerging. We may see the rise of cross-border
> organizations as the reductions in remittances spread the crisis to places like
> rural Mexico or Kerala.

On the other hand, Harvey (2010) has indirectly formulated a possible
approach: "a co-revolutionary movement" that would bring together the traditional working class, the anti-imperialist, or anti-globalization movement,
those opposed to sexism and racism, and the environmental movement.[3]

The analysis following is new, but I think it is consistent with Lefebvre's,
and certainly with my father's. Lefebvre's right is both a cry and a demand, a
cry out of necessity and a demand for something more. Those are two separate
things. I would reformulate them to be an exigent demand by those deprived
of basic material and legal rights, and an aspiration for the future by those discontented with life as they see it around them and perceived as limiting their
potentials for growth and creativity.

The demand comes from those directly in want, directly oppressed, those
for whom even their most immediate needs are not fulfilled: the homeless, the
hungry, the imprisoned, the persecuted on gender, religious, racial grounds.

It is a demand of those whose work injures their health, those whose income is below subsistence, those excluded from the benefits of urban life. The aspiration comes rather from those superficially integrated into the system and sharing in its material benefits, but constrained in their opportunities for creative activity, oppressed in their social relationships, guilty perhaps about an undeserved prosperity, unfulfilled in their lives' hopes. The discussion of the role of art, and of an aesthetic revulsion against the results of the existing order of things, is relevant (Miles, forthcoming). For both, their enforced one-dimensionality eats away at their humanity, and from the same source, but it does it in different ways.

So that there is no misunderstanding, those deprived even of the material necessities of life are as entitled to, and in need of, the fuller life to which the alienated aspire as are the alienated, and the sources of dissatisfaction for both arise out of equally organic and essential human needs. "Erst kommt das Fressen, dann kommt die Morale,"[4] as Brecht said; but both are necessary for a human and humane life. Where choices must be made, the demands of the deprived are entitled to priority over the fulfillment of the aspirations of the alienated, but they should be seen not as in conflict, but as complementary.

To return to whose rights are our concern, the demand is of those who are excluded, the aspiration is of those who are alienated; the cry is for the material necessities of life, the aspiration is for a broader right to what is necessary beyond the material to lead a satisfying life. But to make the discussion clearer, let me digress briefly to a schematic definition of terms.[5]

An analysis in terms of material interests, in somewhat traditional class terms (see, for instance, in urban terms: Marcuse 1989) along the lines of position in the relations of production (somewhat modernized), might be:

- The *excluded* (not in fact an accurate term, for they are in fact a part of the system, without the protections won by the working class for labor, but they operate at its margins).
- The *working class,* the materially exploited (including what is euphemistically called the middle class, i.e. white- as well as blue-collar workers, skilled as well as unskilled, service as well as manufacturing workers, but underpaid and producing profit for others) – together with the excluded, we may speak of these two groups as the *deprived.*
- The *small business people* (the individual proprietor, the small entrepreneurs, the craftsmen).
- The *gentry* (including the more successful small business persons, professionals, the highly paid servants of the multi-nationals).
- The *capitalists* (owners and decision-making managers of large business enterprises).
- The *establishment intelligentsia* (including much of the media, academics, artists, and others active in the ideological aspect of the production processes).

- The *politically powerful* (including most of those in or aspiring to high public office).

Looked at economically, the cry for the right to the city here comes from the most marginalized and the most underpaid and insecure members of the working class, not from most of the gentry, the intelligentsia, the capitalists.

An analysis in "cultural" terms, along lines of relation to the dominant cultural, ethnic, and gendered society and ideology, might be:

- The *directly oppressed* (oppressed along lines of race, ethnicity, gender, life style, often called the excluded, but excluded only in this "cultural" sense, often included in an economic sense).
- The *alienated* (of any economic class, many youth, artists, a significant part of the intelligentsia, in resistance to the dominant system as preventing adequate satisfaction of their human needs).
- The *insecure* (a shifting group, varying with conjunctural changes, e.g. level of crisis, prosperity, including much of the working class and periodically some of the gentry).
- The *hapless lackeys* of power (including some of the gentry and some of the intelligentsia).
- The *underwriters* of the established cultural and ideological hegemonic attitudes and beliefs.

Looked at from this point of view, the demand for the right to the city comes from the directly oppressed, the aspiration comes from the alienated.

Demand and aspiration, deprivation, and discontent. The demand led to the Russian Revolution, the aspiration led to the fall of the Berlin wall. The demand and the aspiration both surfaced, rather independently, in 1968 (see above), but failed to come fully together; the distance between the deprived and the alienated remained. The description of the World Social Forum's meeting in Belem in 2009 as "The Gathering of the Distressed" (Ramirez and Cruz 2009) can be interpreted as covering both material and cultural or intellectual distress. Overcoming that distance, with due priority for the deprived and attention to the alienated, is high on what needs to be done today.

It is crucially important to be clear that that it is not everyone's right to the city with which we are concerned, but that there is in fact a conflict among rights that needs to be faced and resolved, rather than wished away. Some already have the right to the city, are running it now, have it well in hand (although "well" might not be just the right word, today!). They are the financial powers, the real estate owners and speculators, the key political hierarchy of state power, the owners of the media.

It is the right to the city of those who do not now have it with which we are concerned. But that is not a useful answer. It is necessary to know who is most deeply affected, who is likely to lead the fight, who will be most likely to support it, what will their reasons be? Contributing to understanding exactly who that is is a contribution critical urban theory should attempt to make. I suggest here it is a combination of the deprived and the discontent who will lead the push for the right to the city, but the issue can use a lot more attention.

Specifically, I would argue that discontent, and for that matter deprivation, does not automatically lead to support for the claim to the right to the city for all deprived and alienated. The threat of discontent, especially when coupled with fear of unrest from the deprived and the working class, has always worried those on top ("A specter is haunting Europe…"). The effort to channel that discontent has been a chief task for the lackeys of power, the manipulators of ideology, with the media, the schools, religious institutions, and a variety of business and civic organizations as their allies/targets. The results are seen in a variety of wide-spread emotional group-based phenomena, circling around issues such as:

- anti-abortion and right to life
- the right to hold guns
- anti-tax measures
- homophobia
- racism
- anti-immigrant sentiment
- religious fundamentalism
- family values
- chauvinist war-mongering
- false patriotism
- elements of sports fanaticism.

And, I would argue:

- home ownership as the American Dream.

It is tempting to use Freudian terms for the process, repression of discontent, and its sublimation in these emotional phenomena, a cathexis in which emotion is attached to these issues and removed from more dangerous discontents, or even realization of discontent (Marcuse 1955; Žižek 2008). A direct confrontation with this repression/sublimation may have to be a very concrete part of any practical political action to achieve real change.

So I would argue people affected by these phenomena are also among the deprived and the discontent, but their direction of their reaction is quite opposite. It is the basis for the old formulation that the future lies between socialism and barbarism – it is that they provide the base for the barbarism, the "national socialism," but it is a base that can also be addressed in a progressive manner.

The battle thus becomes ever more a battle of ideology, understanding, grounded in material oppression but not limited to it, combining the demands of the oppressed with the aspirations of the alienated.

The organizational form of that opposition needs exploration. Clearly the view that it will be the proletariat that, as a single class, leads the struggle with the aid of some intellectuals is outdated. If, in the process of struggle, *social blocs, à la* Gramsci, can develop, something solid will have been achieved. The present debates in the World Social Forum, strikingly at its meeting in Belem about the nature of that gathering, suggest that a broad theoretical understanding along the above lines might help clarify that it is a single conflict in which all participating groups are engaged, with a single objective, even though the immediate form may be only that of a *forum* (where sympathetic groups around varying issues come together to exchange experiences and debate), or of a *coalition* (a temporary coming together around specific temporally and spatially limited issues), or of an *alliance* (a more permanent coalition), or of a *movement* (less organized, less clear in its ultimate goals but very clear in its solidarity and concerned with multiple issues), an *assembly* (a single, or many single, coming togethers of multiple groups for varying levels of common thinking, sharing, action). There are other formulations: *networks, cross-network convergence, network of networks* (Costello and Smith 2009), but these are formulations that beg the question of what kind of coming together a "network" is – convergence on what, around what? The argument here is that there is a convergence of all groups, coalitions, alliances, movements, assemblies around a common set of objectives, which see capitalism as the common enemy and the right to the city as their common cause.

What right?

The answer to "what right?" on first blush seems simple. And the answer to what rights in the city are claimed by the deprived and the discontent is indeed simple. What they are, or should be, can be itemized: the right to clean water, clean air, housing, decent sanitation, mobility, education, health care, democratic participation in decision making, etc. – the necessities for a decent life. And that answer, the demand for those rights, must have priority; they are immediate, indeed existential, needs.

But that answer is not enough. For the demand for the right to the city is a demand for a broad and sweeping right, a right not only in the legal sense of a right to specific benefits, but a right in a political sense, a claim not only to a right or a set of rights to justice within the existing legal system, but a right on a higher moral plane that demands a better system in which the potential benefits of an urban life can be fully and entirely realized. Speaking of rights in this sense does not contradict a claim of rights in an immediate and legal sense, rights ready to be implemented individually and separately. But the right to the city is a unitary right, a single right that makes claim to a city in which all of the separate and individual rights so often cited in charters and agendas and platforms are implanted. It is *The* right to the city, not *rights* to the city. It is a right to social justice, which includes but far exceeds the right to individual justice.

The right to the city does not demand all rights for all people. Mayor Bloomberg, the leaders of multinational corporations, the rich and the powerful, already have all the rights they need, and within the existing legal system, more than they need or can justly claim. The point is important, both theoretically and strategically. To gain rights for those that do not have them will involve eliminating some rights for those that do: the right to dispossess others, to exploit, to dominate, to suppress, to manipulate the conduct of others. No one should be deprived of the right to the city as it is socially defined, including those individual rights necessary for a decent life referred to above; but to secure them for all means no one may have the right to deny them to any. In the long run, winning the right to the city for all may be a win–win game for all, but in the shorter run it will involve conflict, many winners, but also some losers. To pretend otherwise is deceptive and strategically misleading.

The right to the city is a moral claim, founded on fundamental principles of justice. "Right" is not meant as a legal claim enforceable through a judicial process today (although that may be part of the claim); rather, it is multiple rights that are incorporated here: not just one, not just a right to public space, or a right to information and transparency in government, or a right to access to the center, or a right to this service or that, but the right to a totality, a complexity, in which each of the parts is part of a single whole, to which the right is demanded. The homeless person in Los Angeles has not won the right to the city when he is allowed to sleep on a park bench in the center of the city. Much more is involved, as the concept refers to a set of rights, not individualistic rights. An intuitively analogous concept might be that of citizenship: citizenship involves a set of rights, and the claim to citizenship is not a claim to the right to vote, or to protection of the law, or to a right of entry, but to a status that provides all of these rights as a right to the single status of citizenship.

What city?

Lefebvre is quite clear on this: it is not the right to the existing city that is demanded, but the right to a future city, indeed not necessarily a city in the conventional sense at all, but a place in an urban society in which the hierarchical distinction between the city and the country has disappeared. The demand of the landless farmer in the Amazon in Brazil is not met by giving him entrée to a favela in the middle of Rio de Janeiro. As Lefebvre (1967: 158) has it, "The right to the city cannot be conceived of as a simple visiting right or as a return to traditional cities." And in fact not a city at all, but a whole society. The "urban" is only a synecdoche and a metaphor, in Lefebvre (1967: 45, 158), "[The right to the city] can only be formulated as a transformed and renewed right to urban life … thus from this point on I will no longer refer to the city but to the urban."

Harvey (2003) formulates well what such a city/society might be in principle; he uses Robert Park's phrase "the city of heart's desire." Can we paint a picture of what such a city would look like, a city where material and aspirational needs are met, the needs of the deprived and of the alienated? Yes, but only up to a point. The principles that such a city would incorporate can be set forth in general terms. They would include concepts such as justice, equity, democracy, beauty, accessibility, community, public space, environmental quality, support for the full development of human potentials or capabilities, to all according to their needs, from all according to their abilities, the recognition of human differences. They would include terms such as sustainability and diversity, but these are rather constraints on the pursuit of goals rather than goals in themselves.

But there is a limit to how much benefit can be gained from trying to spell those principles out in detail today. The form such a city might take cannot be foretold in detail, as Lefebvre often said (indeed, following Marx and Engels, in opposition to the early utopians – see Engels 1880 [1970]), "To the extent that the contours of the future city can be outlined, it could be defined by imagining the reversal of the current situation, by pushing to its limits the converted image of the world upside down" (Lefebvre 1967: 172).

A conceptual note: the right to the city appears initially as a right of consumption – a right to consume what the city, and city life, has to offer. It should also, perhaps stretching it grammatically but clearly in Lefebvre's spirit, include the right to produce the city as well as to enjoy it, and the two are integrally linked. It is not only the right to a choice of what is produced after it is produced, but a right to determine what is produced and how it is produced and to participate in its production, that is important. Fulfilling work, work providing an opportunity for creativity, work whose result is socially valued, is an important part of a decent life. The depression of the unemployed and programs such as welfare to work in the United States, reveal in painful detail the consequence of long-term unemployment and underemployment, over and above the simple insecurity of access to the necessities of life.

Solutions: expose, propose, politicize

How can a right to the city be achieved, if indeed it can? More specifically for purposes of this discussion, what is the contribution that critical urban theory can make to those solutions? How can theory inform and help practice – for, while in theory, theory and practice are one, in practice there are real differences, if only that the development of theory and leadership in practice largely reside in different people, different occupations, different life histories. Our common task, those privileged (to be honest about it) to work in the realm of theory, and those differently privileged to be able to lead in the realm of practice, is to make that link between theory and practice and to make it productive. In other words, how do we go from critical urban theory to radical urban practice?

First, and vitally important, critical theory can systematically, logically, and even dramatically show that alternatives to the undesired present are indeed possible. It can ground that conclusion through critical examination of history, study of economics, knowledge of political science, the use of methods honed in the service of countless struggles for a better world. The simple knowledge that there *is* an alternative, and the convincing demonstration that it is so, can be a strongly empowering force in practice, and has been found to be so repeatedly – the slogan of the World Social Forum movement, "Another World is Possible," can be undergirded by the use of critical theory.

In my own field, urban planning, an examination of what planning in New Orleans was doing in the aftermath of hurricane Katrina led to a suggestion for an approach I called Critical Planning which is composed of three steps: *Expose, Propose,* and *Politicize* (Marcuse 2007). *Expose* in the sense of analyzing the roots of the problem and making clear and communicating that analysis to those that need it and can use it. *Propose,* in the sense of working with those affected to come up with actual proposals, programs, targets, strategies, to achieve the desired results. Critical urban theory should help deepen the exposé, help formulate responses that address the root causes thus exposed, and demonstrate the need for a politicized response. *Politicize,* in the sense of clarifying the political action implications of what was exposed and proposed and the reasoning behind them, and supporting organizing around the proposals by informing action. Politicizing includes attention to issues of organization strategy and potentials. And where appropriate, it includes supporting organization directly with interventions in the media and sometimes raising issues within the critic's peer groups themselves, often academics. In each case, the focus on alternatives, what the situation could have been and what it still can be, is a constant theme injected by critical theory into the process.

The goal of the right to the city?

If this is the strategy for action using critical urban theory and practice, what exactly is its ultimate goal? Most immediately, the goal suggested in the discussion here, running through all contributions to this book, is to a totality, to something whole and something wholly different from the existing city, the existing society. Lefebvre and most of those on the streets of Paris and in the occupied buildings of Columbia University in 1968 might call it socialism or communism, but it has various names: a democratic society (Purcell 2008), or a society supporting strivings for life, liberty, and the pursuit of happiness, as in the US Declaration of Independence, or for liberty, equality, fraternity, as in the French Revolution, or a just society (Fainstein 2010) or a humane one or one allowing for the full development of the human capabilities (Nussbaum 1999, also developed by Fainstein 2010), or to fulfilling the potentials of humans as a species being (Marx 1844). What all of these formulations must imply, if the analysis of critical urban theory is correct, is a fundamental rejection of the prevailing capitalist system. What all but the most old-fashioned utopian proposals also have in common is a rejection of the idea that the most desirable future can be spelled out, designed, defined, now, in advance, except in most broad principles. Only in the experience of getting there, in the democratic decisions that accompany the process, can a better future be formed. It is not for lack of imagination or inadequate attention or failing thought that no more concrete picture is presented, but because, precisely, the direction for actions in the future should not be preempted, but left to the democratic experience of those in fact implementing the vision.

Can an alternative to capitalism really be accomplished, given the proven power of the established system?[6] Not only is the end product hard to imagine, but the steps leading there are hard to see; anything now on the agenda seems trivial in such a long-term perspective. Many believe that spaces of hope, in David Harvey's (2000) formulation, can be found, and many such spaces indeed move in the direction of broader change. There is perhaps general agreement, by Marx, Lefebvre, my father, Harvey, and most thinking people, that the seeds of the future must be found in the present. But what does that, apart from the spatial conceptualization, exactly mean?

A spatial image for the seeds of the future can be helpful (Pinder 2005; Miles 2007) and whatever is done will surely also have a spatial aspect.[7] But a spatial focus has its dangers too: most problems have a spatial aspect, but their origin lies in economic, social, political arenas, the spatial being a partial cause and an aggravation, but only partial. It might be better to see the seeds of the future as sectors. It is clearly possible to have sectors of everyday life that are free of capitalist forms, operating within the capitalist system but not of it, not dominated by it. For short-hand, those are the sectors of the economy and of daily life that are not operated on the profit system, that are within it but not of it, that are not motivated by profit but rely on solidarity, humanity, the flexing of muscles, and the development of creative impulses, for their own sake. They will need to draw resources from the for-profit sector, preferably democratically and openly through government, but their own driving force will be found in general principles that are radically different from those motivating the for-profit economy, and principles that can have increasingly wider visibility and appeal.

Such sectors, such areas of activity, already exist, are well known, are sought after. The aspirations of those who are alienated from capitalism lead in this direction. Artists create, teachers teach, inventors invent, philosophers think, young people volunteer, not for profit, but because they believe that is what life is for, that is what they want to do. They come up against the same constraints that make people homeless, hungry, sick, impoverished, people whose demands thus naturally link with the aspirations of the alienated. The ultimate goal of most social movements, and certainly of the right to the city movement, necessarily leads in this direction: they are not after profit, but seek a decent and supportive living environment. Profit, if a concern at all, is a means to an end, which is not high consumption, social status, or further accumulation, but rather decent living conditions for all. Thus the culturally alienated and the immediately deprived have a common enemy. And that is increasingly recognized, even if its name is not always the same: capitalism, neoliberalism, greed, multinationals, power elite, the bourgeoisie, the capitalist class. Above all, eliminating profit as means and motivation in the political sector, eliminating the role of wealth and the power linked to it from public decisions, is a key requirement for both the immediately oppressed and the alienated.

The logic of attempting to expel that enemy from everyday life, one sector at a time, is appealing. We are moving in that direction, although the present leadership is only being dragged there reluctantly, in health care and in education, to sectors in which the conflict over private versus public has turned, if only slightly, in favor of public. The opportunity is there in housing (see Marcuse, this volume). The economic crisis has certainly expanded the government's role in finance, banking, real estate, if always within conservative ideological limits. It has certainly made the question of the appropriate role of government high in the minds of vast numbers. The extent of deprivation and discontent is now widely apparent.

A critical urban theory, dedicated to supporting a right to the city, needs to expose the common roots of the deprivation and discontent, and to show the common nature of the demands and the aspirations of the majority of the people. A critical urban theory can develop the principles around which the deprived and the alienated can make common cause in pursuit of the right to the city. How to politicize most effectively that common ground? We already have sectors of society where the commonality is visible, where action for people, not for profit, is the rule. Think of (unfortunately only some) education. Think of (unfortunately only some) health care. Think of (unfortunately only some) the arts. Think of space exploration. Think of the environmental movement. Think of the nonprofit and cooperative sector in housing. Think of the effort to deepen democracy and expand participation in public decisions, and limit or abolish the role of money in elections and governmental decisions. In each of these, the slogan of *Cities for People, not for Profit,* resonates. Let that be the political cry that embodies the nature of the city to which the right is being claimed. Let it be the cry that forms a noose about one part of the capitalist system after another. Rudi Dutschke, at the peak of the 1968 movement in Germany, spoke of the "long march through the institutions." Let us pick them off, separately or together. Let us tighten the noose around the housing system, and move to squeeze the profit out of it, one sector at a time. The subprime mortgage crisis, for example, could be an opportunity to move again in that direction (Marcuse, this volume), as social housing was before it. Let us not be afraid to name the common enemy and spell out the common goal.

A critical urban theory, internally linked to practice, might help get us there.

Notes

1 I am aware that the school known as critical theory comes at the critical from a different direction, but it is one which, I believe, inevitably leads to this position. I suspect that the root of the differences between my father and Adorno in the Vietnam era was in Adorno's unwillingness to deal with the issue of the seeds and movements for change, which had become my father's major concern.
2 Underneath, violence still plays a role, as the level of incarceration in the United States shows, as does right-wing violence against opposition, including both left-wing and cultural non-conformists, shows.
3 These are my interpretations – Harvey formulates his argument in terms of positions: bringing together "the traditional working-class critique of capital, the critique of imperialism, the critiques of patriarchy and racism, and the critique of ecologically destructive growth, and their respective mass movements" (Harvey 2010: 228–35).
4 "First comes eating, then comes morality."
5 Iris Marion Young's "five faces of oppression" may provide an alternate basis for the analysis I am proposing.
6 For a recent honest, thoughtful, approach to an answer, see Ehrenreich and Fletcher 2009.
7 See the new journal from Nanterre, France: *Justice spatiale | Spatial Justice*: http://www.jssj.org.

References

Costello, T. and Smith, B. (2009) "WSF: is another world possible?" *The Nation* [online]. [Accessed February 13, 2009]. Available at: http://www.thenation.com/article/wsf-another-world-possible.

Credit Suisse (2008) "Credit Suisse sees 6.5 million loans in foreclosure by 2012" The Orange County Register [online]. [Accessed June 1, 2011]. Available at: http://mortgage.ocregister.com/2008/04/24/credit-suisse-sees-65-million-loans-in-foreclosure-by-2012/1064.

Creswell, J. and White, B. (2008) "The guys from 'government Sachs'," *The New York Times* [online]. [Accessed October 19, 2008]. Available at: http://www.nytimes.com/2008/10/19/business/19gold.html?pagewanted=all.

Desai, A. (2002) *We Are the Poors: Community Struggles in Post-Apartheid South Africa*. New York: Monthly Review Press.

Ehrenreich, B. and Fletcher, B. (2009) "If we are in the death spiral of capitalism, can we still use the 'S' word?" *The Nation* [online]. [Accessed March 6, 2009]. Available at: http://www.alternet.org/story/130365.

Engels, F. (1880 [1970]) *Socialism: Utopian and Scientific*, Moscow: Progress Publishers.

Fainstein, S. (2010) *The Just City*. Ithaca, NY: Cornell University Press.

Harvey, D. (2000) *Spaces of Hope*, Berkeley: University of California Press.

Harvey, D. (2003) "The right to the city," *International Journal of Urban and Regional Research*, vol. 27, no. 4, pp. 939–41.

Harvey, D. (2009) "Is this *really* the end of neoliberalism?" *Counterpunch*, March 13–15 [online]. [Accessed June 1, 2011]. Available at: http://www.counterpunch.org/harvey03132009.html.

Harvey, D. (2010) *The Enigma of Capital*. New York: Oxford University Press.

Lefebvre, H. (1967) "The right to the city," in E. Kofman and E. Lebas (eds) (1996), *Writings on Cities*, London: Blackwell, pp. 63–184.

Lefebvre, H. (1991) "Les illusions de la modernite," *Manieres de voir 13, Le Monde Diplomatique*, in Kofman, E. and Lebas, E. (eds) (1996) *Henri Lefebvre: Writings on Cities*, London: Blackwell, p. 34.

Lui, M. (2009) "The wealth gap gets wider," *The Washington Post* [online]. [Accessed March 23, 2009]. Available at: http://www.washingtonpost.com/wp-dyn/content/article/2009/03/22/AR2009032201506.html.

Marcuse, H. (1955) *Eros and Civilization*, Boston, MA: Beacon Press.

Marcuse, H. (1969) *An Essay on Liberation*, Boston, MA: Beacon Press.

Marcuse, P. (1989) "Dual city: a muddy metaphor for a quartered city," *International Journal of Urban and Regional Research*, vol. 13, no. 4, pp. 697–708.

Marcuse, P. (2007) "Social justice in New Orleans: planning after Katrina," *Progressive Planning*, Summer, pp. 8–12.

Marcuse, P. (2008) "In defense of the 60s," *In These Times*, vol. 32, no. 8 , pp. 33–5.

Marx, K. (1844) *Economic and Political Manuscripts*, Moscow: Progress Publishers.

Miles, M. (2007) *Urban Utopias*, London: Routledge.

Miles, M. (forthcoming) *Herbert Marcuse: An Aesthetics of Liberation*, London: Pluto.

Nussbaum, M.C. (1999) *Sex and Social Justice*, New York: Oxford University Press.

Pinder, D. (2005) *Visions of the City*, Edinburgh: Edinburgh University Press.

Purcell, M. (2008) *Recapturing Democracy*, New York: Routledge.

Ramirez, M. and Cruz, O. (2009) "Looking back: the 2009 world social forum," *Council on Hemispheric Affairs* [online]. [Accessed March 20, 2009]. Available at: http://www.coha.org/2009/03/looking-back-the-2009-world-social-forum.

Žižek, S. (2008) *Violence*. New York: Picador Books.

4

HENRI LEFEBVRE, THE RIGHT TO THE CITY, AND THE NEW METROPOLITAN MAINSTREAM

Christian Schmid

Translated by Christopher Findlay

The phrase "the right to the city" has been making a comeback as a rallying cry in recent years. In cities of the North and the South alike, it is used by urban social movements, by political alliances, by international organizations, and also at academic conferences. A closer look reveals, however, that its usage varies considerably. It often serves just as a kind of conceptional umbrella for all types of political and social demands that generally address the problems arising in urban areas today (see also Mayer, this volume; Marcuse, this volume).

The renaissance of the slogan is remarkable, as it hearkens back to the late 1960s, a specific moment in the history of urbanization. At the time, it was coined by French philosopher Henri Lefebvre in response to the urban crisis of that period. However, the situation then was quite different from the one today. The resurgence of this rallying cry therefore raises some important questions: Are we experiencing a new urban crisis? What are its specific traits and characteristics? What distinguishes it from earlier phases of urbanization? In order to clarify these questions, it is useful to return to the original conception of the term and explore its (potential) meanings for urbanization today.

The urban crisis and the right to the city

The crisis of the city

Lefebvre's concept of the "right to the city" is based on his investigation of urbanization in France during the 1960s (Stanek, 2011). Like most of the Western industrialized nations, France was marked by the ascent of Fordism and the expansion of the Keynesian welfare state. This development was accompanied by massive migration from rural to urban areas and a fundamental change in spatial structures. Functionalist urban planning led to a restructuring of inner city areas; the margins of the cities were dominated by mass production of social housing as well as by an extensive proliferation of single-family detached housing units.

These urban transformations also entailed a fundamental modernization of everyday life. Contemporary critics conceptualized this specific aspect of urbanization as a "crisis of the city."[1] For Lefebvre, this crisis consisted primarily of a tendency towards the homogenization of lifestyles and an engineering and colonization of daily life. In middle-class suburbs and in working-class housing estates, analogous conditions prevailed – the monotony of the labor process, the order of functionalized and bureaucratized cities, and the normative constraints of the modernized urban everyday life (Lefebvre, 1996).

The right to the city

The "crisis of the city" was also an important departure point for the manifold social movements of the late 1960s. They were not only aimed against Western imperialism and the Vietnam war, or against various forms of discrimination and marginalization. They were also directed against alienation in daily life, against the modernization of cities and the destruction of their specific qualities, and against exclusion from urban life. They were struggles for a different city.

Lefebvre regarded these events, especially those of May 1968 in Paris, as parallels to those of the Paris *Commune* of 1871. Programmatically, he demanded a "right to the city": the right not to be displaced into a space produced for the specific purpose of discrimination.

> In these difficult conditions, at the heart of a society which cannot completely oppose them and yet obstructs them, rights which define civilization [...] find their way. These rights which are not well recognized, progressively become customary before being inscribed into formalized codes. They would change reality if they entered into social practice: right to work, to training and education, to health, housing, leisure, to life. Among these rights in the making features the *right to the city*, not to the ancient city, but to urban life, to renewed centrality, to places of encounter and exchange, to life rhythms and time uses, enabling the full and complete *usage* of these moments and places, etc.
>
> (Lefebvre, 1996: 178)

Thus, Lefebvre's concern was not to propose a new comprehensive slogan demanding the right to the basic needs. It was about something more – a specific urban quality, which had hitherto been neglected in public debate: access to the resources of the city for all segments of the population, and the possibility of experimenting with and realizing alternative ways of life.[2]

Struggles for the city

Demands for a new and renewed urban life were raised repeatedly during subsequent years in many places and in multiple forms. For many of these urban actions, urban movements, and also urban revolts, documentation is fragmentary; their history has yet to be written.[3] In these struggles, different demands and frontlines can be identified (see also Mayer, this volume).[4]

In many places, mainly young people protested against the lack of urban life and demanded fulfillment of the "urban promise" that cities were constantly offering and yet constantly breaking: the promise of liberty, opportunities for encounter, urban culture, and appropriation of public space. These struggles entailed efforts to create alternative cultural venues and community centers as well as squatting, resistance to large-scale projects, and struggles against the diverse forms of gentrification. In the late 1970s and early 1980s, many cities in Italy, Western Germany, the Netherlands, and even Switzerland experienced urban revolts: they were expressions of a palpable lack of urban lifestyles; the focus was on alternative culture, but also on the struggle for public life, for tolerance, and for openness. Many other urban moments could be mentioned in this context, such as the battles against gentrification in Manhattan's Lower East Side in the mid 1980s, the Toronto metropolitan strike of 1996 or the uprisings that flared up in Athens in 2008. In recent years, moreover, there have been increasing instances of urban movements in major East Asian cities such as Hong Kong, Beijing, and Seoul.

Quite different strategies of contestation were adopted in struggles to enhance the participation of less privileged and socially disadvantaged groups: especially in the neglected inner-city districts and suburbs of the West, which in some cases developed into "territorial traps," there were many waves of struggle against social exclusion. There has been a long history of resurging revolts and clashes in the French *banlieues*, especially in and around Paris. Other countries also experienced uprisings in neglected neighborhoods, such as in 1981 in London's Brixton district, mainly populated by an African–Caribbean community, or in 1992 in South Central LA, to mention only two examples.

Even longer is the list of urban struggles in the exploding megacities of the global South. In particular, these include social movements in informal settlements and shantytowns against displacement and neighborhood destruction as well as often successful struggles for improved living conditions and infrastructure. In Latin America during the 1980s and 1990s, urban movements were formed that have in some cases become significant political forces, including at the national level. For instance, major urban social movements developed in Mexico City after the devastating earthquake of 1985, or in São Paulo during the same period.

Despite the many differences, there are obvious similarities among these urban struggles: they can be understood, in the most general sense, as struggles against social exclusion and marginalization, and they articulate a demand for centrality, for access to the material and immaterial resources of a city. In this sense, they address the spatial dialectics of center and periphery, and of appropriation and domination.

Complete urbanization and the specificity of the urban

Urban social movements

Against the background of these manifold urban struggles, the crucial question is how the urban dialectic can be conceptualized. In Paris in the early 1970s, Manuel Castells and his colleagues developed the concept of "urban social movements."[5] However, this concept encompasses only a small segment of urban reality, and it mainly takes into account those movements that are oriented towards "collective consumption" (see Mayer, this volume). This reflects a very narrow conception of the city as a unit for the daily reproduction of labor power and a narrow political perspective that is focused mainly on organized forms of protest and ignores many spontaneous actions and revolts.

Conversely, Lefebvre's reflections were based on a far more open and radical notion of the urban.[6] He did not, however, develop a definitive theory of the urban, but embarked on a quest that continued to produce new insights into the phenomenon of urbanization. Therefore, the excavation of isolated passages from his work cannot fully represent the fluidity and openness of his reflections; their significance often only unfolds in the context of his complete works.

Tellingly, Lefebvre's first major statement of his emergent urban ideas and concepts, entitled *Le droit à la ville* [*The right to the city*], was presented in the "mythical" year 1968 (Lefebvre, 1996). Only two years later, however, he subjected this first approach to a fundamental review and extension in another major book, *La révolution urbaine* [*The urban revolution*] (Lefebvre, 2003). The main critique in this latter work concerns precisely the notion of the "city" itself: his search for the urban had led Lefebvre to a radical shift in his perspective, from the analysis of a *form*, the city, to a *process* – urbanization.

Complete urbanization

The point of departure of this new understanding of the urban is Lefebvre's famous thesis of the complete urbanization of society. This thesis states that contemporary social reality can no longer be grasped with the categories "city" and "countryside," but must be analyzed in terms of an emerging urban society. The epistemological shift involved here cannot be overestimated. Lefebvre's theory constitutes a radical break with the traditional Western conception of the city. The classic definitions of this notion were based on the assumption that the city is a clearly identifiable unit that provides the environment for a distinctively "urban" way of life. For instance, Simmel (1971 [1903]) regarded the city as a cultural form and postulated a nexus between urban morphology and the social organization of coexistence. Similarly, Wirth (1938) famously defined the city as a "way of life" built upon three specific material factors of coexistence: size, density, and heterogeneity.

Against these definitions, Lefebvre's thesis of complete urbanization points towards a long-term conception of urban transformation. As Friedrich Engels in *The condition of the working class in England* (2009 [1844]) had already recognized, the Industrial Revolution marked the beginning of a massive migration from rural areas to the cities in conjunction with the spatial concentration of factories and workers under industrial capitalism. Lefebvre proceeds to conceptualize the process of industrialization in a general sense as the extension of the industrial logic to society as a whole. Industrialization and urbanization, he states, form a highly complex and conflictual unit. Industrialization supplies the conditions and means of urbanization, while urbanization results from the spread of industrial production across the entire globe. From this point of view, Lefebvre derives his understanding of urbanization as a reshaping and colonization of rural areas by an urban fabric as well as a fundamental transformation of historic cities.

The crucial consequence of this transformation is the dissolution of the city itself: for Lefebvre, the city can no longer be understood as an object or as a definable unit. It is instead a historical category that is disappearing as urbanization progresses. This also means, however, that the term "city" itself becomes problematic:

> The concept of the city no longer corresponds to a social object [...] However, the city has a historical existence that is impossible to ignore. Small and midsize cities will be around for some time. An image or representation of the city can perpetuate itself, survive its conditions, inspire an ideology and urbanist projects. In other words, the "real" sociological "object" is an image and an ideology!
>
> (Lefebvre, 2003: 57)

The question thus arises as to how the urban can still be theoretically grasped under conditions in which society as a whole has been urbanized. Lefebvre's inquiry into this question yields three core concepts: mediation, centrality, and difference (see also Schmid, 2005; Kipfer et al., 2008).

The urban level: mediation

In a first approximation, Lefebvre identifies the urban as a specific level or order of social reality. It is an intermediary and mediating level situated between two others – on the one hand, the private level, the proximate order, everyday life, and dwelling; on the other hand, the global level, the distant order, the world market, the state, knowledge, institutions, and ideologies. This intermediate level has a decisive function: it serves as a relay and as mediation, connecting the global and the private levels.

In urbanized society, however, the urban level is in danger of being whittled away between the global and the private levels. On the one hand, industrialization and the logic of the global market produce a universal rationale shaped by technology, and thus a tendency towards homogenization. The unique traits of the place and its location thus seem to disappear. On the other hand, space is parceled out and submitted to a corporate, individual logic. In this attack from "above" and "below," the city is threatened with attrition. The result is the dissolution of urban units, which disintegrate into countless disconnected fragments, leading in turn to the proliferation of overflowing, apparently indistinguishable urban landscapes.

Thus, the complete urbanization of society tends to eliminate the urban level of mediation. However, it is only in the most extreme thesis of the disappearance of the city that the importance of the urban becomes visible for Lefebvre. In this context, he suggests, the city must be seen as a social resource. It constitutes an essential device for the organization of society, it brings together diverse elements of society, and thus it becomes productive.

The urban form: centrality

These considerations enable Lefebvre to arrive at a new definition of the city – the city as a center. In this sense, the city creates a condition in which heterogeneous elements no longer exist in isolation. As a place of encounter, communication, and information, the city is also a place in which constraints and normality are dissolved, and are joined by the elements of the playful and unpredictable:

> The urban is defined as the place where people walk around, find themselves standing before and inside piles of objects, experience the intertwining of the threads of their activities until they become unrecognizable, entangle situations in such a way that they engender unexpected situations.
>
> (Lefebvre, 2003: 39)

For Lefebvre, the space–time vector converges to zero in urban space; every point can become a focal point that attracts all, a privileged place upon which everything converges. The city is thus the virtual nullification, the negation of distances in time and space: "the cancellation of distance haunts the occupants of urban space. It is their dream, their symbolized imaginary, represented in a multiplicity of ways" (Lefebvre, 2003: 39).

Centrality therefore does not refer to a concrete geographic situation, but to a pure form. Its logic represents the synchronicity of objects and people that can be assembled around a given point. What is it that comes together in urban space? Centrality as a form does not entail a concrete content, but merely defines the possibility of an encounter. It constitutes itself both as an act of thought and as a social act. Mentally, it is the synchronicity of events, of perceptions, and of the elements of a whole. Socially, it amounts to the convergence and combination of goods and activities. Centrality can thus also be understood as a totality of differences.

Urban space–time: difference

This leads to the third marker of the urban – the city is a place of difference. Differences are points of active connection and should be clearly distinguished from particularities that remain isolated from one another. Particularities are derived from nature, location, and natural resources; they are bound to local conditions and are thus derived from rural society. They are isolated, external, and can easily revert into antagonisms. However, in the course of history, such particularities come into mutual contact. Out of their confrontation arises a mutual "understanding" and thus difference. The instant of confrontation is always a decisive one. Transformed by the confrontation, the elements no longer assert themselves in isolation from one another. Instead, they can only present and re-present themselves in and through their interactions. This gives rise to the concept of difference. The concept emerges not just from logical thought, but along a variety of paths – the trajectories of history and of multiple dramas in everyday life.

Therefore, the specific quality of urban space arises from the simultaneous presence of very different worlds and value-systems, of ethnic, cultural, and social groups, activities, and knowledge. Urban space creates the possibility of bringing together these different elements and making them productive. At the same time, however, they have a constant tendency to separate themselves from one another. The decisive question therefore is how these differences are experienced and lived in actual everyday life.

As Kipfer (2008) reminds us, there is an important distinction between minimal and maximal difference. Minimal or induced difference tends towards formal identity, which fragments everyday life and pushes social groups into the periphery. Maximal or produced difference implies a fundamental social transformation. The concept of difference as defined by Lefebvre must therefore be clearly distinguished from other, postmodern definitions. For Lefebvre, difference is a multidimensional concept that arises from gaps in the fabric of everyday life and from political struggles. It must be understood as an active element.

The urban as concrete utopia

Lefebvre's notion of the urban thus differs fundamentally from the classic conceptions in urban theory. Criteria such as size, density, or heterogeneity as once defined by Wirth can hardly be applied to analyze the reality of the contemporary city. Thus, the size of a city can no longer be determined unambiguously, and the significance of that criterion is quite limited – smaller cities can also attain a high degree of urbanity. The density of a city has a limited influence on the quality of everyday life either. And finally, heterogeneity is a necessary, but not a sufficient condition of urban life. Rather, the decisive question is whether productive differences arise between the heterogeneous elements. Therefore, the essence of the city is determined not by size, density, or heterogeneity, but by the quality of active, everyday processes of interaction.

In a Lefebvrian framework, the city can thus be defined as a place where differences encounter, acknowledge, and explore one another, and affirm or cancel out one another. Distances in space and time are replaced with opposites, contrasts, and superimpositions, and with the coexistence of multiple realities. Lefebvre's positive conception of the urban as differential space–time should be understood as referring to a concrete utopia (Stanek, 2011). It points towards a possibility, a promise, not an already achieved reality. It must constantly be produced and reproduced (Lefebvre, 2003: 38).

This also means, however, that the term "city" itself becomes problematic. Accordingly, Lefebvre himself amended the term "the right to the city" with other terms: "the right to centrality" (Lefebvre, 2003: 194), "the right to difference" (Lefebvre, 1991: 64), and finally "the right to space" (Lefebvre, 1978: 317).

The production of urban space

A three-dimensional dialectic

As has become clear, Lefebvre opened up a new pathway towards defining the urban in *La révolution urbaine*. First of all, it constitutes the level of mediation between the global and the private. Secondly, its form is centrality, assembly, encounter, and interaction. Finally, the urban is characterized by difference; it is a place where differences come together and generate something new. This leads to the question of how these different aspects are related to each other, and how they are socially produced. It gives rise to a new radical shift in analytical perspective. It requires a more general term and a more general theory – the term "space" and the theory of production of space, which Lefebvre elaborated in *La production de l'espace* [*The production of space*] in 1974 (Lefebvre, 1991).

This theory rests on the assumption that the production of space can be split analytically into three dialectically linked dimensions or processes. These dimensions – which Lefebvre also refers to as "formants" or "moments" in the production of space – are defined in duplicate. The first is the triad of "spatial practices," "representations of space," and "spaces of representation"; the second is the "perceived," "conceived," and "lived" space. This duplicate string of terms points to a twofold approach to space: a phenomenological approach on the one hand, and a linguistic or semiotic approach on the other (Schmid, 2005, 2008, 2010).

Urban practice

Space has, first of all, a perceptible component that can be grasped with the five senses. It relates directly to the materiality of the elements that constitute a space. Spatial practice combines these elements into a spatial order, an order of synchronicity. Urban space is therefore a place of material interaction and of physical encounter. This practical aspect of mediation, centrality, and difference can be seen as the superimposition and interlacing of networks of production and of communication channels, as a combination of social networks in everyday life, as places of encounter and exchange that are amenable to surprises and innovations.

This means that urban space can be empirically observed. What is happening in the streets? Who is present, who encounters whom? What resources are available, and who has access to them? Primarily, what is meant here is the physical presence of people in urban space. Very often, in urban research only the residents of an urban area are considered. But urban space also includes those who work there, visitors, street vendors, and diverse types of places. Shops, restaurants, meeting places, and venues for cultural and social exchange set the stage for urban life. These may be permanent facilities or ephemeral occasions — events or celebrations that create opportunities and chances for interaction.

Opportunities for social interaction are, however, unequally distributed across urban space. In certain places, urban resources are concentrated, while in other areas they are thinly scattered and diffuse. The question of access to these resources is immediately linked to their distribution. The struggle for the right to remain within urban space has always been among the central questions provoked by urban revitalization programs, gentrification, or projects for slum improvement.

Due to the huge expansion of urban areas today, though, this issue is no longer confined to the traditional urban core areas. The classic model of urbanity based on the examples of metropolises such as Berlin, Paris, or Chicago has long been overtaken by worldwide urbanization processes. In the overflowing cityscapes of the North and the South, manifold new forms of centrality have evolved. While these new urban configurations have long been discussed (Soja, 1996; Sieverts, 2002), such discussions have yet to shed concrete light on the particular question of what new forms of urbanity are emerging and evolving in these areas. In order to make some progress in this direction, it would be necessary to demarcate new definitions of "urbanity" or "urban quality" based on the effects of interaction processes in urban space. For the mere presence of different social groups and networks is not sufficient for the emergence of an urban culture. What matters, rather, is the way they interact and the quality of these interaction processes. Differences must always be understood dynamically. Is the outcome an open exchange, or are differences curtailed and domesticated? Such questions also pertain to the immaterial conditions of communication – the rules and norms governing urban spaces. This brings us to the second moment in the production of urban space – the conception of space.

The definition of the urban

As Lefebvre noted, a space cannot be perceived without having first been conceived in the mind. A conceived space is therefore a depiction that reflects and defines a space and thus also represents it. The combination of individual elements into a whole that is subsequently regarded as space requires a mental effort. Constructions or conceptions of space are supported by social conventions that define which elements are related to one another and which ones are excluded – conventions that are not immutable, but often contested, and which are negotiated in discursive (political) practice. This is a social production process that is connected to the production of knowledge and power structures. In a broader sense, the representations of space also include social rules and ethics.

Our conception of the "city" therefore depends on society's definition of the urban and thus on the idea of the city, the design, the map, the concept, or the scientific theory that attempts to define and demarcate the urban. As a representation of space, the urban initially remains undefined in an urbanized world. Since the city no longer forms a distinct social or economic unit, or a discrete mode of production or way of life, there are many ways of defining and demarcating a city. Such definitions of the city always contain mechanisms of inclusion and exclusion and thus become battlegrounds for a variety of strategies and interests. All kinds of political and economic actors, urban specialists, and intellectuals intervene in this field, and urban movements may also have considerable impact.

These definitions do not mark the end point; they immediately translate into political questions, for they are directly connected to rules and norms that define who and what is admissible or prohibited and what is included or excluded in urban space. Often, implicit distinctions and invisible boundaries play important roles here that are hidden to the outside observer. Thus, if the "right to the city" is once again demanded today, the question immediately arises as to which "city" this right refers to. Does the demand relate to old or inherited conceptions and images? Is it a demand to reconstitute the "classic" city? Or are new forms of the urban being sought?

The urban experience

The third dimension in the production of space is what Lefebvre calls "spaces of representation." These are spaces that signify "something." They refer not to space itself, but to a third, other aspect – for instance, a divine power, *logos*, the state, or the male or female principle. This dimension of the production of space refers to the process of signification, which is expressed in (material) symbolism. The production of significance imparts symbolic meaning to spaces and thus turns them into spaces of representation. This aspect of space is encountered or experienced by people in their everyday life, which is why Lefebvre also calls it "*espace vécu*," a space that is lived or experienced. A lived, practical experience cannot be fully grasped by theoretical analysis. "Something" always remains, an ineffable residue that defies analysis and that can only be expressed by artistic means.

The city is thus always also a concrete, practical experience, a place of its residents who use it and appropriate it in their everyday practices. The nature of a "city" is something that its inhabitants learn from infancy – and something they combine with their memories. These worlds of experience and processes of socialization also give rise to implicit value systems. Whether a city is perceived as a refuge of civilization, or as a dangerous and unpredictable place, is due mainly to such experiences.

It is therefore crucial in this context which experiences are inscribed in space and in the collective consciousness. Such experiences contain both collective and individual aspects; they include positive and negative values; they may be banal and commonplace or spectacular and far-reaching. Struggles for the city themselves are constitutive elements of such urban experiences. They facilitate concrete processes of appropriation and the recognition that urban spaces can be used in different ways than were previously envisaged. Thus, urban "moments" such as May 1968 in Paris are crucial reference points whose effects persist many years later, influencing contemporary debates and urban practices in distinctive ways.

Urbanization and urbanity

The theory of production of space therefore includes, at core, a three-dimensional production process – first, material production; second, the production of knowledge; third, the production of meaning. These three dimensions of the production of space form a contradictory, dialectic unity. The determination is a threefold one; space is only produced through the interaction among all three elements.

Space is the result of production processes that take place in time. This basic presupposition leads to a dynamic conception of urban space as being constantly produced and reproduced. Urban qualities do not appear automatically as the result of urbanization. Urbanization lays the groundwork for generating urban situations, but the latter are created only as the result of multiple actions. This also implies a constant struggle over the content of the urban. Concrete, "lived" urbanity is the outcome of continuous conflicts and contestations. "The city" is not a general category, but a concrete, historical one that is perpetually being renewed and redefined – both in theory and in practice.

From this point of view, the "right to the city" may be redefined as the "right to (urban) space" – that is, as the right to participate at the transformation of space and to control investment into space (Lefebvre, 1978: 317).

The new metropolitan mainstream and the commodification of the urban

The rediscovery of the urban

Based on the theoretical reflections sketched above, it is possible to decipher some key aspects of global urbanization during the last few decades. Indeed, the history of recent urban struggles reveals a remarkable set of trends. While urbanization has accelerated and generalized, there is also strong, albeit diffuse, evidence in many places that urban spaces are being reclaimed. This process has been shaped and advanced in manifold ways. Urban social movements have resisted the transformation and modernization of their cities, fought against commercialization and displacement, and demanded old and new forms of urbanity, mixed districts in the city centers, street life, and public spaces. At the same time, they have created many kinds of concrete urban spaces and alternative, oppositional everyday practices, often based on cultural, ethnic, or sexual differences. During the course of the 1970s and 1980s, these "urban values" were increasingly embraced by broader social strata. This marked the beginning of a long history of a "rediscovery of the urban," a trend which is sometimes also labeled an "urban renaissance" (Porter and Shaw, 2008).

This rediscovery of the urban was also closely intertwined with the dynamics of globalization, which has been closely associated with new forms of centrality and agglomeration.[7] Two aspects are essential here. On the one hand, centrality plays a key role for global economic control and command functions and for certain forms of innovation, especially those that require a wide variety and multiplicity of inputs for the development and creation of complex products. On the other hand, metropolitan centers became privileged spaces for the new urban elites that had formed under the neoliberal development model (Sassen, 1994; Scott, 1998).

The "other side" of centrality was now revealed – the resurgence of the city as a center of decision making and control. Long before the proliferation of scholarly interest in "global cities" and "world cities," Lefebvre had already predicted the consolidation of new forms of global centrality:

> Despite countervailing forces [...] the centre continues effectively to concentrate wealth, means of action, knowledge, information and "culture." In short, everything. These capacities and powers are crowned by the supreme power, by the ability to concentrate all powers in the power of decision.
> (Lefebvre, 1991: 332–3)

At the same time, the metropolitan centers are becoming high-grade consumer products, and indeed manage to survive due to their simultaneous role as places of consumption and as consumable places. The urban cores are thus turned into citadels of power, while their population becomes an elite (Lefebvre, 1996: 73; Lefebvre, 2003: 79). Lefebvre's clear-sighted analysis sketched a development whose full effects are only today becoming widespread – the global city model has now become generalized, as "metropolitan" values, cultures, and lifestyles are widely accepted and sought after. A corresponding set of urban strategies and policies have come to form the new general guidelines of urban development – the metropolitan has become mainstream.

The new metropolitan mainstream

The term "new metropolitan mainstream" was developed to decipher a broad range of phenomena that have recently emerged in cities around the world.[8] Initially, this mainstream is articulated as a norm that defines what is to be regarded as urban or metropolitan while also presenting certain standards and processes for urban planning and design. Richard Florida's theses on the "creative class" (2005), which have had a significant ideological impact in urban policy in cities around the world, only mark the tip of the iceberg in this regard (see Peck 2005; as well as Krätke's chapter in this volume). These and other relatively banal ideas about how to ignite urban "growth" have been diffused among municipal governments and city councils around the world. The promotion of "soft" location factors, of "quality of life" for elites, and of a prestigious blend of cultural amenities and offerings for luxury consumption is today part of the standard policy repertoire for attracting capital investment and highly qualified workers. Accordingly, many contemporary cities both in the global North and in the global South have been equipped with skyscrapers, flagship projects, and "star" architecture. The "standard metropolitan architecture" is becoming the new fuel of global urbanization. In this context, a remarkable shift in the role models for the "urban future" has occurred. Today, "new" metropolises such as Dubai, Shanghai, or Singapore are much more likely to be seen as exemplars for the future of urban development than the "old" Western metropolises such as Paris or New York (Roy, 2010).

The consequences of these local development strategies for local populations are obvious. The longstanding debates on gentrification and the vociferous criticism of urban regeneration and urban revitalization projects do not need to be revisited here (see Slater, this volume; Smith, 2002; Porter and Shaw, 2008). Nevertheless, it should be pointed out that processes of gentrification and displacement have spread tremendously in recent years while also becoming more differentiated. First, private and public strategies are increasingly intertwined, with urban policies now actively promoting gentrification and the attendant displacement of marginalized populations. Second, many of these strategies are actually proposed and implemented by left-wing and liberal political coalitions.

Closely linked to this development are the manifold processes by which selected segments of erstwhile oppositional milieus are integrated and co-opted into the new metropolitan mainstream. Third, the various forms of urban upgrading are also now increasingly spreading on a global scale, into the cities of the South, into suburban areas, and even into smaller cities. Fourth, these trends also entail a significant rescaling of urban development. Processes of gentrification and displacement are no longer limited to individual neighborhoods; rather, entire intra-urban areas and even large parts of metropolitan regions are upgraded and transformed into zones of reproduction for metropolitan elites. A massive increase of land and real estate prices and the accompanying housing crisis have already imposed heavy restrictions on access to these areas for less privileged parts of the population.

In the current debate, such strategies and policies are often equated with neoliberalism. Indeed, cities and metropolitan regions have become places of strategic importance for neoliberal policies, and key institutional arenas in and through which neoliberalism is itself evolving (Brenner and Theodore, 2002; Leitner et al., 2007). Nevertheless, we must remember that such processes should be regarded as elements of long-term tendencies in capitalist urbanization. Urbanization leads not only to the dissolution of historic forms of the city and to urban sprawl, but also to the formation of new centralities. Centrality is always ambivalent in this context, since on the one hand it creates possibilities for unexpected encounters, while conversely, it is also susceptible to economic exploitation. This ambivalence brings us to yet another process – the commodification of urban life.

The commodification of the urban

This development, of course, is not a new one. The city has long been the place where the market has installed itself and flourished, and it also constitutes the privileged arena in which the world of commodities unfolds – as Walter Benjamin (1995 [1955]) analyzed so brilliantly for the late-ninteenth century metropolis of Paris. What is new, however, is the systematic economic exploitation of urban space. The city itself, urban life, becomes a commodity. This process can be described as the commodification of the urban (Kipfer and Schmid, 2004; Kipfer et al., 2008).

As Lefebvre noted, this strategy goes far beyond simply selling space, bit by bit. Space itself, and not only the land and real estate, becomes exchange value. As a consequence, urban space becomes the very general object of production, and hence of the formation of surplus value:

> The deployment of the world of commodities now affects not only objects but their containers, it is no longer limited to content, to objects in space. More recently, space itself has begun to be bought and sold. Not the earth,

the soil, but social space, produced as such, with this purpose, this finality
(so to speak).

(Lefebvre, 2003: 154)

The commodification of the urban has not yet been grasped adequately in all
of its dimensions and implications. This process encompasses not only the sale
of parcels of land, and the reservation of exclusive locations for certain population groups. At stake, more generally, is the process by which urban space as
such is exploited. The entire space is sold – including the people living in it, as
well as the social resources and the economic effects produced by them. Urban
life itself is implicated in the economic process of valorization and is thereby
transformed.

This means that the qualities of urban space – difference, encounter, creativity – become part of the economic logic and of systematic exploitation of
productivity gains. Such processes have long been visible in the occupation
and control of public space by private actors – shopping malls, entertainment
centers, or private railway and metro stations constitute quasi-public spaces
that are controlled by private interests. Their *raison d'être* consists exclusively
in generating added value. Accordingly, they are designed to channel urban
life into commercially exploitable avenues and to prioritize market-oriented
and consumption-oriented practices. These forms of economic domination are
today beginning to spread across entire urban areas. In the process, the people,
residents and visitors alike, are reduced to mere "extras" in the great urban
spectacle.

Appropriation and domination

At a general level, the question of center and periphery is thus transformed
into the antagonism between productive and non-productive ways of con-
suming space, between capitalist "consumers" and collective "users." The
contradiction between exchange value and use value, when transferred to
space, thus becomes the contradiction between capitalist domination and the
self-determined appropriation of space (Lefebvre, 1991: 356, 359).

This implies the question of both economic and political control. This aspect
of control is ultimately decisive in the privatization of public space and in the
creation of manifold forms of privately controlled space, from demarcated and
segregated districts to gated communities. Access to the urban arena with its
opportunities and possibilities is controlled and economically exploited. Thus,
certain social groups succeed in reserving urban spaces for themselves and limiting access for others. It is often forgotten that these spaces do not exist in
isolation, but are part of a concrete historical and geographic context, and positioned strategically within their respective urban regions. Thus, the entirety of
urban life is transformed (Eick et al., 2007).

Centralization and peripheralization

Another aspect of centralization must be mentioned in this context – displacement and exclusion from centrality. The dialectics of center and periphery must today be reconsidered. It has long ceased to be determined in geographic terms, and neither does it always follow the logistical principles that are the basis of transportation infrastructure (Veltz, 1996). Rather, centrality today implies the availability of manifold possibilities and access to social resources. Conversely, peripheralization stands for dispersion, demarcation, and exclusion from urban life. This was already problematized in the debates on world cities and global cities in the 1980s and 1990s – it inspired the metaphor of "citadel and ghetto" (Friedmann and Wolff, 1982), the "dialectics of centrality and marginality" (Sassen, 1994), and also the concept of the "quartered city" (Marcuse, 1989). Today, this dialectics is articulated in a new form insofar as the less controlled, relatively non-commercialized interstitial spaces within the metropolitan cores are now almost completely disappearing.

From a general point of view, this is a manifestation of the fundamental contradiction within the dialectic of the urban. On the one hand, the social potential of urban space lies precisely in its capacity to facilitate contacts and mutual interaction between the various parts of society. On the other hand, access to urban resources is increasingly controlled and appropriated by global metropolitan elites. This not only limits access to urban space but also imposes limits on its social productivity. In this process, urban space loses some of its essential elements, but especially its most important characteristic – the possibility of unexpected, unplanned encounters and interactions.

The urban as concrete utopia

Theory and practice

In contemporary society, the urban always remains ambiguous, as it is determined by a twofold dialectical movement between centralization and peripheralization on the one hand, and between appropriation and domination on the other.

This theoretical determination must be translated into concrete terms. Theory is a construction that should not be confused with reality. While theory follows the laws of logic, practice is determined by the development of society in everyday life. Therefore, the relationship between theory and practice is always complex and contradictionary (see Brenner, this volume; and Marcuse, this volume). As Lefebvre stated succinctly, theory must be steeped in practice in order to become effective. In practical terms, this means that theoretical analysis must be confronted with practice. Doing so is always a social act and an intervention in social reality, and thus also a confrontation, an exchange, and an encounter where theory itself is transformed.

As Lefebvre indicates, the point of departure of critical social theory should always be everyday life, the banal, the ordinary. Changing everyday life: this is the real revolution! Everyday life is today marked by urbanization, and we must therefore study its potential. With complete urbanization, the city is becoming virtually omnipresent, and any point has the potential to become central and be transformed into a place of encounter, difference, and innovation. This means viewing urbanization from a different point of view. Urbanization creates the possibility of an urban society. But it must be realized. There is no automatism involved. This is precisely the historic lesson that Lefebvre is communicating.

The right to the city today

Forty years ago, Lefebvre observed the rise of a new *problematique* and introduced the slogan "the right to the city." Obviously, the situation today is no longer the same, and we are living in a completely different urban world. Nevertheless, it is precisely in this situation that this call is heard anew, in the "global West" as well as in the "global South." In this context, the call for a right to the city also acquires new importance and a new content. Three tendencies are particularly noticeable here.

First, the focus today is once again on basic needs such as access to shelter, food, clean water, health, and education. This is due largely to the massive urbanization of the global South, but also due to increasing levels of socioeconomic polarization in major parts of the world. As the dramatic example of the destruction of New Orleans has shown, there are situations in which the fulfillment of even the most basic needs is no longer guaranteed. In this context, the notion of the right to the city acquires a new significance.

Second, the call for a right to the city also represents a response to the withdrawal of the (national) state from many areas of social life. Significant tasks are today delegated to the regional or local levels. This has not only imparted new importance to the local, but has also caused increased fragmentation, segregation, and inequality. The various alliances that have coalesced around the rallying cry of the right to the city demand – and, through their practice, in fact constitute – a new unity in the splintered and fragmented urban regions.

Third, such alliances also today facilitate the formation of new collective moments. Even if many alliances appear, at first glance, to be pursuing a rather pragmatic course (see Mayer, this volume), they contain the potential to reframe the urban question, to discover new, self-determined definitions of the urban in the sprawling urban landscapes, and to open up possibilities for conceiving and living different forms of urban life.

Over a decade ago, John Friedmann (1993: 139) stated in his text *The Right to the City* that "a city can truly be called a city only when its streets belong to the people". More recently, David Harvey's influential text with the same title defined the right to the city as the right to control the urbanization process and to institute new modes of urbanization (Harvey, 2008: 40). Although he was writing in an earlier moment, Lefebvre's analysis actually went one step further by postulating a generalized form of self-management (*autogestion généralisée*) as the basis and expression of that right (Lefebvre, 2003: 150). Ultimately, this means the rearticulation, in a radically new context, of the long-standing demand for the right to self-determination – a right that is indispensible for the creation of a different society.

Possible urban worlds

Today, the world is being jolted by a major economic crisis. Many of the issues identified by Lefebvre have apparently been relegated to the background. Nevertheless, it should be clear that even under these new conditions, the right to the city must include more than merely the right to exist and to satisfy basic needs. This "more," this additional aspect, is precisely what defines urban society. The urban is a constant reinvention, it may assume very diverse forms, and the purpose here is not to propose yet another range of normative models. This, however, implies viewing the contemporary urban crisis as an opportunity to imagine alternatives and to create new possible urban worlds.[9]

Thus, the same old issues are at stake, albeit in a new context: What is a city, and what does urban living mean? Who is to determine the urban future? Lefebvre opened up a new pathway towards understanding urbanization. In his analysis, urban society is not an already achieved reality, but a potential, an open horizon. The quality of this analysis is that it transcends mere criticisms of urbanization, and proceeds to explore its inherent possibilities and potentials. However, they can only be realized through a fundamental social transformation – an urban revolution.

The grand theoretical and practical project that Lefebvre envisioned consists of exploring possible pathways towards an urban world where unity no longer positions itself in opposition to difference, where the homogenous no longer battles the heterogeneous, and where assembly, encounter, and interaction replace – though not without conflicts – the struggle of individual urban elements that have been turned into antinomies by segregation. Such an urban space would constitute the social basis for a transformation in everyday life that is open for manifold possibilities – for a radically different world.

Notes

1 Compare e.g. Jacobs, 1961, or the polemical critiques of urbanism published in *Internationale Situationiste*.
2 For a discussion of Lefebvre's conception of the right to the city, see also Purcell, 2002; Gilbert and Dikeç 2008; and Schmid, 2010.
3 Until recently, there have been relatively few books dealing with urban social movements – see, for example, Mayer et al., 1978; Castells, 1983, INURA, 1998; Hamel et al., 2000; Leitner et al., 2007.
4 For the following paragraphs, see Maggio, 1998; Schmid, 1998; Uitermark in this volume; Smith, 1996; Kipfer, 1998; Tang, 2009; Eckstein, 2001; Moreira Alves, 2004.
5 See Castells, 1973, Castells et al., 1978, Castells 1983.
6 In many respects, Castells' and Lefebvre's conceptions of the urban and of urban struggle can be understood as representing two competing approaches. Whereas Castells followed a form of structural Marxism derived from the work of Louis Althusser, Lefebvre developed a heterodox and open critical theory inspired by many sources, especially by the German dialectics of Hegel, Marx, and Nietzsche and by French phenomenology (see Schmid, 2010).
7 In this context, it is interesting to note that mainstream economic analysis has long neglected this aspect of urban development. It was not until the late 1990s that neoclassical economics rediscovered space and centrality (Fujita et al., 1999).
8 See Schmid and Weiss, 2004. The International Network for Urban Research and Action (INURA) started a collective mapping project which traces the various elements of the new metropolitan mainstream in more than 30 cities. Initial results have been presented at an exhibition in conjunction with the twentieth INURA conference held in Zurich in 2010 (see www.inura.org).
9 The phrase is from Harvey, 1996. See also INURA, 1998; Lehrer and Keil, 2006.

References

Benjamin, W. (1995 [1955]) "Paris: capital of the nineteenth century," in P. Kasinitz (ed.) *Metropolis*, New York: NYU Press, pp. 46–57.
Brenner, N. and Theodore, N. (eds) (2002) *Spaces of Neoliberalism*, Oxford: Blackwell.
Castells, M. (1973) *Luttes urbaines et pouvoir politique*, Paris: F. Maspero.
Castells, M. (1977) *The Urban Question: A Marxist Approach*, London: Edward Arnold.
Castells, M. (1983) *The City and the Grassroots*, Berkeley and Los Angeles: University of California Press.
Castells, M., Cherki, E., Godard, F., and Mehl, D. (1978) *Crise du logement et mouvements sociaux urbains*, Paris: Mouton.
Eckstein, S. (2001) "Poor people versus the state and capital: anatomy of a successful community mobilization for housing in Mexico City," in S. Eckstein (ed.) *Power and Popular Protest*, Berkeley and Los Angeles: University of California Press, pp. 329–50.
Eick, V., Sambale, J., and Töpfer, E. (eds) (2007) *Kontrollierte Urbanität*, Berlin: Transcript Verlag.
Engels, F. (2009 [1844]) *The Condition of the Working Class in England*, London: Penguin.
Florida, R. (2005) *Cities and the Creative Class*, New York: Routledge.
Friedmann, J. (1993) "The right to the city," in M. Morse and J. Hardoy (eds) *Rethinking the Latin American city*, Baltimore: Johns Hopkins University Press, pp. 135–51.
Friedmann, J. and Wolff, G. (1982) "World city formation: an agenda for research and action," *International Journal of Urban and Regional Research*, 6 (1), pp. 309–44.

Fujita, M., Krugman, P., and Venables, A.J. (1999) *The Spatial Economy*, Cambridge, Mass. and London: MIT Press.

Gilbert, L. and Dikeç, M. (2008) "Right to the city: politics of citizenships," in K. Goonewardena, S. Kipfer, R. Milgrom, and C. Schmid (eds) *Space, Difference, Everyday Life: Reading Henri Lefebvre*, New York: Routledge, pp. 250–63.

Hamel, P., Lustiger-Thaler, H., and Mayer, M. (eds) (2000) *Urban Movements in a Globalising World*, London: Routledge.

Harvey, D. (1996) *Justice, Nature and the Geography of Difference*, Cambridge, Mass.: Blackwell.

Harvey, D. (2008) "The right to the city," *New Left Review*, vol. 53, pp. 23–40.

INURA (ed.) (1998) *Possible Urban Worlds*, Basel: Birkhäuser.

Jacobs, J. (1961) *The Death and Life of Great American Cities*, New York: Random House.

Kipfer, S. (1998) "Urban politics in the 1990s: notes on Toronto," in INURA (ed.) *Possible Urban Worlds*, Basel: Birkhäuser, pp. 172–9.

Kipfer, S. (2008) "How Lefebvre urbanized Gramsci: hegemony, everyday life, and difference," in K. Goonewardena, S. Kipfer, R. Milgrom, and C. Schmid (eds) *Space, Difference, Everyday Life: Reading Henri Lefebvre*, New York: Routledge, pp. 193–211.

Kipfer, S. and Schmid, C. (2004) "Right to the city/bourgeois urbanism," paper prepared for the International Network of Urban Research and Action, Toronto.

Kipfer, S., Schmid, C., Goonewardena, K., and Milgrom, R. (2008) "Globalizing Lefebvre?" in K. Goonewardena, S. Kipfer, R. Milgrom, and C. Schmid (eds) *Space, Difference, Everyday Life: Reading Henri Lefebvre*, New York: Routledge, pp. 285–305.

Lefebvre, H. (1978) *De l'État, tome IV: les contradictions de l'État moderne*, Paris: Union Générale d'Editions.

Lefebvre, H. (1991 [1974]) *The Production of Space*, Oxford: Blackwell.

Lefebvre, H. (1996 [1968]) "The right to the city," in H. Lefebvre, *Writings on Cities*, E. Kofman and E. Lebas (eds), Cambridge, Mass.: Blackwell, pp. 63–184.

Lefebvre, H. (2003 [1970]) *The Urban Revolution*, Minneapolis: University of Minnesota Press.

Lehrer, U. and Keil, R. (2006) "From possible urban worlds to the contested metropolis: urban research and activism in the age of neoliberalism," in H. Leitner, J. Peck and E. Sheppard (eds) *Contesting Neoliberalism*, London: Guilford Press, pp. 291–310.

Leitner, H., Peck, J., and Sheppard, E.S. (eds) (2007) *Contesting Neoliberalism*, New York and London: Guilford Press.

Marcuse, P. (1989) "Dual city: a muddy metaphor for a quartered city," in *International Journal of Urban and Regional Research*, 13 (4), pp. 697–708.

Maggio, M. (1998) "Urban movements in Italy: the struggle for sociality and communication," in INURA (ed.) *Possible Urban Worlds*, Basel: Birkhäuser, pp. 232–7.

Mayer, M., Brandes, V., and Roth, R. (eds) (1978) *Stadtkrise und soziale Bewegungen*, Köln: Europäische Verlagsanstalt.

Moreira Alves, M.H. (2004) "São Paulo: the political and socioeconomic transformations wrought by the new labour movement in the city and beyond," in J. Gugler (ed.) *World Cities Beyond the West*, Cambridge: Cambridge University Press, pp. 299–327.

Peck, J. (2005) "Struggling with the creative class," *International Journal of Urban and Regional Research*, 29 (4), pp. 740–70.

Porter, L. and Shaw, K. (eds) (2008) *Whose Urban Renaissance?* London: Routledge.

Purcell, M. (2002) "Excavating Lefebvre: the right to the city and its urban politics of the inhabitant," *GeoJournal*, 58, pp. 99–108.

Roy, A. (2010) "The 21st century metropolis: new horizons of politics," paper presented at the 20th INURA conference in Zurich, June 27–30.

Sassen, S. (1994) *Cities in a World Economy*, Thousand Oaks, Calif.: Pine Forge Press.

Schmid, C. (1998) "The dialectics of urbanisation in Zurich: global city formation and urban social movements," in INURA (ed.) *Possible Urban Worlds*, Basel: Birkhäuser, pp. 216–25.

Schmid, C. (2005) "Theory," in R. Diener, J. Herzog, M. Meili, P. de Meuron, and C. Schmid *Switzerland – an Urban Portrait*, Basel: Birkhäuser, pp. 163–223.

Schmid, C. (2008) "Henri Lefebvre's theory of the production of space: towards a three-dimensional dialectic," in K. Goonewardena, S. Kipfer, R. Milgrom, and C. Schmid (eds) *Space, Difference, Everyday Life: Reading Henri Lefebvre*, New York: Routledge, pp. 27–45.

Schmid, C. (2010) *Stadt, Raum und Gesellschaft: Henri Lefebvre und die Theorie der Produktion des Raumes*, 2nd ed., Stuttgart: Franz Steiner Verlag.

Schmid, C. and Weiss, D. (2004) "The new metropolitan mainstream," in INURA and R. Paloscia (eds) *The Contested Metropolis*, Basel: Birkhäuser, pp. 252–60.

Scott, A.J. (1998) *Regions and the World Economy*, Oxford: Oxford University Press.

Sieverts, T. (2002) *Cities Without Cities*, London: Routledge.

Simmel, G. (1971 [1903]) "The metropolis and mental life," in D.N. Levine (ed.) *Georg Simmel on Individuality and Social Forms*, Chicago: University of Chicago Press, pp. 324–39.

Smith, N. (1996) *The New Urban Frontier*, London: Routledge.

Smith, N. (2002) "New globalism, new urbanism: gentrification as global urban strategy," in N. Brenner and N. Theodore (eds) *Spaces of Neoliberalism*, Oxford: Blackwell, pp. 80–103.

Soja, E.W. (1996) *Thirdspace*, Oxford and Cambridge, Mass.: Blackwell.

Stanek, L. (2011) *Henri Lefebvre on Space: Architecture, Urban Research, and the Production of Theory*, Minneapolis: University of Minnesota Press.

Tang, W.S. (2009) "When Lefebvre meets the East: a case of redevelopment in Hong Kong," paper presented at the conference "Urban research and architecture: beyond Henri Lefebvre," ETH Zurich, November 24–5, 2009.

Veltz, P. (1996) *Mondialisation, villes et territoires*, Paris: PUF.

Wirth, L. (1938) "Urbanism as a way of life," *American Journal of Sociology*, 44 (1), pp. 1–24.

5

THE "RIGHT TO THE CITY" IN URBAN SOCIAL MOVEMENTS

Margit Mayer

The movements currently gathering under the claim for the "right to the city" could mark a new phase in the development of urban social movements – one where a novel type of coalition across the city appears to have the potential to unify a multiplicity of urban demands under one common banner and thus to create a real challenge to neoliberal planners, politicians, and developers. The claim for the right to the city has turned into a viral slogan across Europe, North America as well as Latin America, because it fuses and expresses a variety of issues that have become highly charged over years of neoliberal urban development and even more so through the effects of the financial and economic crisis. They have made the loss of social, economic, and political rights painfully tangible not just for traditionally disadvantaged and marginalized groups, but increasingly also for comparatively privileged urban residents, whose notion of the good urban life is not realized by increasing privatization of public space, in the "upgrading" of their neighborhoods, or the subjection of their everyday lives to the intensifying interurban competition.

At the same time, the "right to the city" has also developed traction with international NGOs and advocacy organizations, some of whom have taken to work on formal covenants and even a world charter for the right to the city.[1] Additionally, a host of governments on different scales have incorporated a "right to the city" in their legislation or in various urban reform projects. However, the substance of the "right to city" as defined in such legal instruments and guidelines[2] is not necessarily identical with what local movements are aiming at when they take to the streets to protest gentrification and displacement, the imposition of urban mega-projects in their neighborhoods, the closing of local public service institutions, or the intensifying surveillance of urban space – even if all of these forms of activism invoke Lefebvre and envision a city that is more just, sustainable, and democratic.

In order to explain this multifaceted emergence of the "right to the city" motto in local as well as global contexts, the first part of this chapter contextualizes this slogan in relation to the historical development of urban social movements. Seen in this context, the contemporary movements directed against neoliberal urban development appear significantly distinct from earlier phases that urban movements have gone through since the crisis of Fordism. In the current period, urban protests and the claims made on urban development correspond with specifically neoliberal designs and enclosures that they address, more and less radically – while they are also shaped by the legacies of prior phases of urban struggles. Thus, in order to understand the novelty and specificity of contemporary movements assembling under the slogan of the "right to the city," they are here interpreted within the framework of a phase model of the development of urban movements. This will allow us, in the second part of the chapter, to identify relevant differences in the practice and goals of the broad spectrum of "right to the city" movements – on one end of the spectrum, groups and organizations working to get charters passed seek to protect *specific* rights (plural) in order to secure participation for all in the city (as it exists); on the other end of the spectrum, more activist movements seek to create *the* right to a (more open, genuinely democratic) city through social and political agency.

This distinction allows, in a third, final step, a critical analysis of actually existing "right to the city" movements in first world metropoles, i.e. of those coalitions of leftist and alternative movements, artists and creative professionals, minority and community-based organizations, and the sundry citizens initiatives that mobilize, often successfully, against the restructuring of their neighborhood. What on first glance looks like a successful convergence of different protest groups under the banner of the "right to the city" may be problematized against the background of the transformed role of metropoles of the global North within the new international division of labor. Even though these coalitions do frequently succeed in preventing, or at least modifying, crass neoliberal urban development projects, their struggles often end up saving some oases and protected spaces only for the comparatively privileged protagonists, spaces which increasingly become instrumentalized in creative city branding efforts in the competitive entrepreneurial urban policy game. The chapter thus raises the question whether "right to the city" movements in the global North need not relate more directly to the struggles of groups that have been excluded from the model of the neoliberal city. Such struggles include those of the dispossessed at the peripheries of this model in the global North (whether in banlieues or ghettos), and the urban struggles taking place in the global South – even if the conflicts struggled over and the everyday practices of these movements differ vastly.

Stages of urban movements from the crisis of Fordism to neoliberalism

The macro trends of the past 40 years have fundamentally transformed both the environment – the cities and political milieus – in which movements operate, as well as the movements themselves, at first slowly, almost imperceptibly, but in hindsight rather drastically. It is crucial to understand the impacts of these trends on the trajectory of urban resistance, if we are to develop the potential of the "right to the city" as a "working slogan and political ideal" (Harvey 2008). To this end, this section traces, in a first step, the shifting mottos of urban social movements (limited to the Euro–North American core) from Fordism through the various neoliberal regimes. These rallying cries stand as shorthand memos for the respective collective identity of the actors, their target, and their concerns, i.e. the particular forms of urban exclusion or oppression prevalent within each period. On this basis, it becomes possible to appreciate what is new and different about the current conjunction and about the contemporary slogan "right to the city."

In the reactions to the crisis of Fordism, since the 1970s, urban development patterns have become increasingly similar across the advanced capitalist countries, and forms of urban governance have converged so much that it is not surprising that the movements challenging and resisting them, across the global North anyway, have gone through similar cycles.

Crisis of Fordism and politicized opposition of the 1970s

The first wave of broad urban mobilizations, in the wake of the 1960s movements, reacted, as so many of the mobilizations of the era, to the crisis of Fordism. Struggles around housing, rent strikes, campaigns against urban renewal (which drastically restructured cities and displaced many, particularly poor residents), against what the German psychologist Alexander Mitscherlich back then aptly called "the inhospitality of our cities"[3] (referring to the barrenness which Fordist zoning of urban space and suburbanization had brought about), and struggles for youth and community centers were all politicized in a progressive manner by the wider "threat context" which the student, anti-war, and leftist mobilizations of the 1960s and early 1970s had created, and by the political openings which governments (generally in the mold of a social-democratic compromise) allowed at that time. The protests, even those around public transport, schools, child care, and other public services, all contested the cultural norms of the institutions of collective consumption, their price, their quality, and the limited options to participate in their design.

Many of the European movements at that time were influenced by the motto "Let's take the city!" (Lotta 1972),[4] whereas most of the North American movements were more pragmatically oriented: the prevailing slogan here was for "Community control" (Fainstein and Fainstein 1974). In Europe, the movements were mostly spearheaded by youth, students, and migrants, whereas in the US the rebellions were led by those most excluded from Fordist prosperity, especially by Afro-Americans. Central for the movements in all these western cities was the "reproductive sphere" (class struggle had shifted from the factory to the neighborhoods) and "collective consumption" – demands focused on public infrastructures and services, challenging both the cultural norms and the price and quality of public infrastructures. The movements demanded not only improved institutions of collective consumption, but also more participation in the decision making of their design. Additionally, the movements developed progressive alternative projects of their own, which, in many cities, generated a vibrant infrastructure of community and youth centers, alternative and feminist collectives, autonomous media, and other self-managed projects. Overall, the movements challenged the "Keynesian city," in which the state takes over a large part of social reproduction, and which represents the climax of a very direct relationship between the urban scale and social reproduction. This is what led many authors at the time to define "the urban" explicitly in categories of collective consumption.[5] In spite of the breadth of the mobilizations and the vibrancy of movement cultures, it was not possible during this period to join the movements made up of the culturally and politically alienated, primarily young activists with those discriminated by or excluded from the blessings of the Fordist model (see Marcuse, Chapter 3 in this volume).[6]

Roll-back neoliberalization – re-emergence of "old" topics and the transformation of relations between urban movements and the (local) state (1980s)

The second phase of urban social movements was induced by the austerity politics of the 1980s. This politics initiated a global shift toward a neoliberal paradigm, which in its initial roll-back phase[7] ground away at Keynesian-welfarist and social-collectivist institutions. These had provided, during the previous phase, a material base for much of the alternative movement activities – even if this was not widely admitted at the time. The neoliberalization of policies brought the so-called "old" social issues back on the agenda of urban movements. Increasing unemployment and poverty, a "new" housing need, riots in housing estates, and new waves of squattings changed the make-up of the urban movements. Meanwhile, local governments were confronted with intensifying fiscal constraints while expenditures were growing, and became interested in innovative ways to solve their problems.

These pressures led to a reconfiguration in the relations between movements and local states: what had so far been a rather antagonistic relationship of opposition between movements and municipalities transformed into a more cooperative one, as more and more movement organizations, encouraged by a new generation of comprehensive urban revitalization programs, moved "from protest to program" (Mayer 1987). What initially looked like a good opportunity to put their precarious alternative practices onto more stable foot-ing created, over time, a split between the more and more professionalized, more or less alternative (development and service delivery) organizations on the one hand, and groups, whose needs were not addressed by these arrange-ments and who, in turn, radicalized. In addition, the movement terrain became even more complex in the 1980s due to the entry of a panoply of middle-class-based movements embracing a variety of concerns and demands, mostly focused on defending or preserving the quality of life of their neighborhood. These were frequently ecological or progressive in orientation, but in other cases the demands were reactionary or xenophobic, so that the urban move-ment milieus became increasingly fragmented into distinct components, and there were hardly any overarching battle cries or convergence in joint action any more.

Roll-out neoliberalization – fragmented movement milieus (1990s)

Since the 1990s, a regime of flanking mechanisms (roll-out neoliberalism) responded to the contradictions and problems, which the previous phase of retrenchment had generated. While the basic neoliberal imperative of mobi-lizing city space as an arena for growth and market discipline remained the dominant municipal project, it now emphasized flanking mechanisms such as local economic development policies and community-based programs to alleviate the problems previously generated. That is, these mechanisms now addressed social infrastructures, political cultures, and ecological foundations of the city – however, in a way that was to transform these into locational assets. New discourses of reform became fashionable – instead of poverty, what is now combated is "social exclusion," "welfare dependency" is to be ended, and the "activating state," programs of community regeneration, and the mobi-lization of "social capital" are supposed to play important roles in this new regime (Mayer 2003). Also, new institutions and modes of delivery for social services were fashioned – such as integrated area development, public–pri-vate partnerships in urban regeneration and social welfare, all with a heavy reliance on civic engagement. These discourses and policies in many ways integrated earlier movement critiques of bureaucratic Keynesianism, and have been quite successful in seizing formerly progressive goals and mottos such as "self-reliance" and "autonomy," while redefining them in a politically regres-sive, individualized, and competitive direction. Through this hijacking of the language of (earlier and contemporary) progressive movements, these measures and discourses harnessed the critical thrust of earlier movements towards the development of a revitalized urban (or regional) growth machine, becoming part of neoliberal governing techniques.

The consequences of these new urban development policies and of the *de facto* erosion of social rights they implied have further fragmented the movement terrain. On the one hand, they triggered the emergence of new defensive movements that would seek to protect themselves and whatever privileges they still enjoyed; but on the other, they politicized the conflicts towards the question whose city it is supposed to be. Again and again, in the course of this decade, waves of anti-gentrification struggles swept across New York, Paris, Amsterdam, Berlin, and later Istanbul or Zagreb, and slogans such as "Die, yuppie scum!" became literally global. *Reclaim the Streets* and similar local mobilizations of the anti-globalization movement popularized the slogan "Another world is possible," as well as "Another city is possible!" Simultaneously, the increasingly professionalized, formerly alternative community-based organizations became inserted into the new strategies of neighborhood revitalization and activation.

Climax and beginning of the crisis of neoliberalization – movements against the neoliberal city (2000s)

With the dot com crash of 2001, at the height of and simultaneously the start of the crisis of neoliberalism, a new (fourth) phase was initiated. Urbanization has gone global through the integration of financial markets that have used their flexibility and deregulation in order to debt-finance urban development around the world (Harvey 2008: 30). While economic growth rates began to stagnate during this phase (or, where growth has still occurred, it is increasingly jobless, as has been the case in the Euro–North American core), the sharper social divides have become expressed in intensifying sociospatial polarization. At the same time, social reforms have everywhere replaced welfare with workfare systems. The new urban, social, and labor market policies have "activated" large parts of the urban underclass into (downgraded) labor markets; but their impacts also affect many (former) social movement organizations, which increasingly reproduce themselves by implementing local social and employment programs or community development – and they probably do a better job "combating social exclusion" than any competing (private or state) agency ever could.

These developments have restricted and narrowed the space for social contestation in many ways. Movements no longer operate within the "Keynesian city," which provided openings for struggles around improved collective infrastructures. Instead, they are confronting the "neoliberal city," which offers primarily two fault lines along which movements have been mobilizing (Mayer 2007).

The *first fault line* is created by the strong prioritization that the neoliberal city ascribes to growth politics – investments in glitzy new city centers, megaprojects for sports and entertainment, the commercialization of public space, and the concomitant intensification of surveillance and policing are all integral parts of the dominant pattern of corporate urban development. This in turn triggers protests by movements that challenge the forms, goals, and effects of this type of development, the entrepreneurial ways in which cities market themselves in the global competition, as well as the concomitant neglect of neighborhoods falling by the wayside of these forms of growth politics.[8]

A *second fault line*, created by the neoliberalization of social and labor market policies, sparks mobilizations against the dismantling of the welfare state and for social and environmental justice, which increasingly come together in community/labor coalitions that fight for the rights of precarious and immigrant workers. In Germany it is the local Anti-Hartz mobilizations,[9] in Italy the Social Centers,[10] in the US the workers centers,[11] which bring worksite and community organizing together in new coalitions of social rights organizations and unions, and unite the demands of the precariously employed as well as the unemployed.[12]

The mobilizations around both of these fault lines have become intensified and taken on a global dimension when transnational anti-globalization movements[13] discovered "the local," their city, as the place where globalization "touches down" and materializes, where global issues become localized. Hence, these movements demand not only the democratization of international institutions such as the IMF, WTO, World Bank, EU, and the G8, but are also mobilizing in defense of public services and institutions in their cities, discovering that issues such as privatization or the infringement of social rights are actually connecting them with movements across the globe. Organizations such as the Social Forums or Attac[14] have taken the message of "global justice" to the local level, where they campaign against welfare cuts, rights for migrants as well as workfare workers and build alliances with local unions, social service organizations, and churches.[15]

While the neoliberalization of the city has thus in many ways created a more hostile and more difficult environment for progressive urban movements, it has also allowed for a more global articulation of urban protest. It has, for the first time since the 1960s, spawned a renewed convergence of different strands under the umbrella of the "right to the city" slogan.

The multiple meanings of the "right to the city"

The effects of the 2008 crisis and the ways in which national governments responded to the crisis have, if in uneven ways, further contributed to the politicization of urban movements. "We won't pay for your crisis!" has been the rallying cry at protests across Europe, from Athens to Copenhagen, from Reykjavik to Rome, from Paris to London, from Riga to Kiev. While many European countries erupted in demonstrations, strikes, and massive protests, which intensified in the peripheral countries as these were subjected to unheard of austerity measures, US cities initially saw more pragmatic and more needs-oriented movement activities in reaction to the accelerating crisis: tent cities sprang up across the US (National Coalition for the Homeless 2010), activist and support organizations decry the foreclosure and vacancy rates, stage rallies in front of vacant buildings as well as in front of banks, mobilize to get anti-warehousing ordinances passed and to make vacant houses available for the homeless, including many member groups of the Right to the City Alliance. ACORN chapters are putting local teams of "Home Defenders" between homeowners and those who want them out, while other organizations are calling for limited-equity co-ops (instead of foreclosures) and cooperatively owned financial institutions to provide customers with low-cost services and communities with economic development funds (Henwood 2009). After merely sporadic demonstrations in scattered cities and few nationally coordinated efforts in the years following the financial meltdown, protests have erupted forcefully in many state capitals as, since late 2010, the crisis has been used to not only cut back on services and public sector wages and benefits, but also to attack collective bargaining rights of public sector unions (Nichols 2011).

Across western nations, governments have spent massive amounts for bank bailouts and stimulus packages, while instrumentalizing the crisis for pushing through deep cuts in social and public sector programs. This has intensified the breaking points around which urban social movements have been rallying, suddenly validating their claims and arguments about the lack of sustainability and the destructiveness of the neoliberal growth model. As more and more civil, political, social as well as economic rights for more and more groups (but especially for low-income people and recipients of cash transfers) have become threatened or lost, the demand for the "right to the city" resonates with more and broader groups and has become a live wire issue. More and more conflicts erupt that spark more and more struggles, in which different groups come together in new campaigns and coalitions. This situation might enlarge the window of opportunity for the Lefebvrian "right to the city" demand, which is not about inclusion in a structurally unequal and exploitative system, but about democratizing cities and their decision making processes (Schmid, this volume).

As cities are increasingly experienced in transforming into gated communities and privatized public spaces where wealthy and poor districts are becoming separated if by invisible barriers, and access of the poor to urban amenities and infrastructures that once were accessible to all, have become more and more restricted, they now provoke the resistance of broad coalitions contesting these various forms of dispossession and exclusion – from the US Right to the City Alliance and local coalitions bringing together public sector workers, the new homeless, and precarious groups of all kinds against the cuts in social programs and public services, to the coalitions against Hamburg's downtown development policies or the campaign against "Mega Media Spree!" (against the displacement caused by a huge media complex near the Spree river in Berlin). All around, new types of coalitions have sprung up that join diverse groups together – in Germany more often small shop owners with artists and professionals from creative industries, long-time tenants, and various leftist and alternative groups and organizations; in the US usually tenant organizations with homeless activists, youth groups, domestic and other precarious workers, (often ethnically based) community organizations, and anti-foreclosure movements. Their reasons for coming together may differ: while the artists and creative types fear the loss of their work spaces, the tenants are threatened by displacement through luxury condo developments, the homeless organizations mobilize for better housing policies and look for allies to take over vacant housing, and the leftists use the various conflicts for anti-capitalist campaigns. More often than in the past, these local mobilizations succeed in bringing together deprived and excluded groups with the comparatively privileged ones that make up the anti-neoliberal or global justice movements (that are not necessarily materially disadvantaged, but rather culturally alienated and politically discontented) – a fusion that was often attempted during the rebellious 1960s and 1970s but rarely achieved.

On the global scale, where transnational networks and NGOs are active, efforts to legally peg down the "right to the city" have also gained momentum as municipal and other state actors have joined the fray with manifestos and guidelines designed to protect and guarantee the "right to the city" (Unger 2009; Sugranyes and Mathivet 2010).

The "right to the city" (another city) – as appropriation

The different movements and initiatives invoke the notion of the "right to the city" in diverse ways. In the Lefebvrian conception urbanization stands for a transformation of society and everyday life through capital. Against this transformation Lefebvre sought to *create* rights through social and political action: the street, and claims to it, are *establishing* such rights (Schmid, this volume). In this sense, the "right to the city" is less a juridical right, but rather an oppositional demand, which challenges the claims of the rich and powerful.[16] It is a right to redistribution, not for all humans, but for those deprived of it and in need of it. And it is a right that *exists only as people appropriate it*, and the city itself (Marcuse, Chapter 3 in this volume). It is this revolutionary form of appropriation, which Lefebvre meant to discover in 1968 Paris and which contemporary movements are referring to. They include the occupations and campaigns that in late 2009 forced the city of Hamburg to buy back, at a hefty loss, the blocks of old trade buildings in the so-called Gängeviertel, which had already been handed over to investors for development (see the Manifesto "Not in Our Name"[17]); similarly, a broad coalition against the Media Spree complex in Berlin (called Mega-Spree Coalition) comprising a host of different citizens initiatives, was able to mobilize for huge street protests in the summer of 2010 against the selling-off of the city to corporate investors (Schwarzbeck 2010; Scharenberg and Bader 2009); or the "Right to the City" group in Zagreb which for three years prevented – with petitions, blockades, and broad support from the public – the implementation of an investor plan to develop the central Flower Square into an upscale, exclusive, traffic-rich plaza with underground parking, to jumpstart gentrification of the surrounding area (Caldarovic and Sarinic 2008).[18] In the US, the "right to the city" was even turned into a platform, when neighborhood, tenant, and labor–community organizations based in New York, Los Angeles, Boston, and more than a dozen other cities not only networked with each other, but joined together in a nationwide Right to the City Alliance. These groups, while organized in regional networks, cooperate on supralocal and supraregional scales on the issues which have become so pressing to all of them of late – foreclosures and evictions, tenants' rights, discrimination of minorities, gentrification, and displacement (Goldberg 2008; Liss, this volume).

In all these various struggles, activists have been using the motto "right to the city" in order to build coalitions within, and in the US case also amongst, cities – coalitions between housing activists and artists, leftist groups and cultural workers, small shop owners and various precarious groups, all of whom feel threatened by investor-driven upgrading of their environment, by megaprojects and their displacement effects. In spite of their shared critique of the respective urban development policies, the coalitions do involve tensions, for example between classic movement activists on the one hand and cultural producers on the other. The latter often find their presence instrumentalized by neoliberal urban politicians seeking to exploit their "creative potential." Subcultural milieus, music scenes, hip neighborhoods filled with clubs and beach bars increasingly turn into key factors of official urban marketing discourses (Scharenberg and Bader 2009: 331). The signatories of the Hamburg Manifesto "Not in Our Name!" and the activists of the initiative "Sink Media Spree!" (one of the driving groups within the Mega-Spree coalition) are aware of and defiant of precisely such instrumentalization (Colomb and Novy 2011), but not all the participants of these alliances are concerned about the risks of such co-optation potentials that would come with concessions to and benefits for some of the alliance members while alienating and excluding others.

Occasionally, these "right to the city" campaigns of first world metropoles connect to struggles in cities of the global South, where the fight against privatization, dispossession, evictions, and displacement is even more existential. Also, transnational get-togethers such as Social Forum meetings on various scales as well as other gatherings of local movements that are increasingly networked across national boundaries have made the commonalities between the struggles in the global South and North quite tangible and real. Frequently, it is even the same real estate developers and the same global corporations that are responsible for the displacement, eviction, or the privatization of public goods. The past ten years of dialogue, information sharing, and collective mobilization via the Social Forum process and the get-togethers of the antiglobalization movement at counter summits have been used to explore the shared experiences and commonalities in the various struggles against privatization and dispossession. Such processes of exchange and cooperation are likely to become even more important in the future, because the differences between the urban struggles as well as the problems and deprivations confronting each are immense (see below).

Right(s) to the city (as it exists) – as formal recognition

At the same time, efforts by international NGOs and advocacy organizations to ensure a more legalistic guarantee to the "right to the city" have also gained significant traction. On local as well as global scales, organizations and policy networks with an urban agenda have been working to create a more stable institutional footing for the implementation of this right. The Polish right to the city organization *My Poznanciacy*, founded in 2007, declared on its website: "The only possibility to claim our right to the city consisted in establishing a legal entity, which would be officially recognized by state and administrative institutions."[19] Other, particularly transnational networks and international NGOs have been drafting authoritative guidelines spelling out what the "right to the city" is to imply.

This process started already in the beginning of the 1990s when Habitat International Coalition (HIC), together with other international as well as national organizations (such as the Brazilian National Forum for Urban Reform, FNRU) drafted transnational covenants "for just, democratic, and sustainable cities and villages" and had them adopted at various UN sponsored meetings of international and transnational NGOs and networks. From 1995 on, UNESCO also participated in such meetings for the development of urban agendas, and Brazilian organizations began pushing a "Charter for Human Rights in the City." These efforts accelerated when, in 2001, the World Social Forum (WSF) also joined the effort of drafting a World Charter for the Right to the City. In 2003 some international human rights groups put forward, together with UNESCO, a *World Charter for the Human Right to the City*; in 2004 the HIC together with other organizations presented a draft of a *World Charter on the Right to the City* at the Social Forum of the Americas in Quito and at the 2nd World Urban Forum in Barcelona; during the WSF in Porto Alegre in 2005 a *World Charter on the Right to the City* was adopted (Ortiz 2010).[20]

Adoption of (part of) such charters has also occurred on various state scales: in 2001 a City Statute was inserted into the Brazilian Constitution to recognize the collective right to the city (Fernandes 2007). On the local scale, Montreal in 2006 passed an urban "*Charter of Rights and Duties*." Also, a "*European Charter to Secure Human Rights in the City*" has been adopted (Ortiz 2010: 114). And the Fifth *World Urban Forum* chose the "right to the city" as its overarching topic with the view to nudge the UN towards official recognition of this right.

While the public recognition through governmental and UN institutions obviously helps to enhance the relevance and influence of these demands, these charters as well as the coalitions devising and promoting them, in the process modify the political content and meaning of the contested "right to the city."

For what is at stake in these documents is not *"the"* right to the city; instead, they list a series of specific rights, the protection of which they recommend to the municipalities and NGOs that are interested in *"good urban governance."* For example, it is the goal of the *World Charter to the Right of the City* to establish effective mechanisms and instruments for safeguarding the enforcement of the general human, civil, and social rights. To that end, UNESCO and UN-Habitat together with international NGOs seek, through regular annual conferences (organized by the *Standing Working Group on "Urban Policies and the Right to the City"*), to create a consensus among central actors about policies that are to guarantee sustainable, just, and democratic cities. These actors involve, importantly to the organizers, municipalities.

In their effort to put "our most vulnerable urban residents" rather than investors and developers at the center of public policy, they enumerate specific rights which progressive urban politics should particularly protect. Thus, for example, paragraph 11 of the World Charter indicates that the right to the city "encompasses the internationally recognized human rights to housing, social security, work, an adequate standard of living, leisure, information, organization and free association, food and water, freedom from dispossession, participation and self-expression, health, education, culture, privacy and security, a safe and healthy environment"; and paragraph 12 specifies yet a further list, according to which the right to the city "embodies claims to the human rights to land, sanitation, public transportation, basic infrastructure, capacity and capacity-building, and access to public goods and services – including natural resources and finance." In some places of the charter it says that these rights are supposed to hold for all "urban inhabitants," both as individuals and as collective, but in others particular groups are highlighted as deserving particular protection, such as the poor, ill, handicapped, and migrants.

What on first sight looks rather positive, implies, however, a problem. Not only because every list invariably excludes those that do not get listed, but also and particularly because the generic category of "urban inhabitants" reflects a view of civil society as basically homogenous and, *as a whole*, worthy of protection from (destructive) neoliberal forces – as if it itself did not encompass economic and political actors who participate in and profit from the production of poverty and discrimination. It thus obfuscates the fact that this entity is itself deeply divided by class and power, harboring both poor and precariously employed people as well as groups that reap benefits from neoliberal strategies or racist and anti-migrant policies.

Still, one might argue that, fully realized, these enumerated rights to access all that the existing city has to offer would spell significant improvements for urban residents. But unlike the Lefebvrian notion of the right to the city, the claims formulated here boil down to claims for inclusion in the current city as it exists. They do not aim at transforming the existing city – and in that process ourselves. The demands for rights as enumerated merely target particular aspects of neoliberal policy – for instance, in combating poverty, but not the underlying economic policies, which systematically produce poverty and exclusion.

In practice, these charters are to serve as blueprints for municipalities. UN-Habitat campaigns such as the "Global Campaign on Urban Governance" advertise and demonstrate how these principles can be implemented locally with toolkits on participatory decision making, transparency in local governance, or participatory budgeting. While these may, in some cases, offer helpful guidance, they systematically mask that a fundamental democratization of the city is always mediated by a struggle over power, which cannot be left to (local) governments, not even social-democratic or "left" ones.

Even though this form of depoliticization of the "right to the city" is particularly visible on the scale where global NGOs operate, its cause is hardly to be found in the up-scaling of a formerly grassroots, locally-based claim to the "higher" realms of global political arenas and institutions. The global scale, as for example manifest in counter summits organized to protest G8 meetings in Rostock 2007 or Toronto 2010, has been used by activists in highly politicizing ways. Camps and workshops have been organized at these counter summits, where activists identify the underlying connections between struggles around housing and displacement in the Global South with those against gentrification in the North, and where activists jointly develop radical demands. Hence, no causal relationship between scale-jumping of the "right to the city" activism and its political substance and orientation can be established.

Instead, it seems to be the type of civil society coalition "from below" as pushed by many (international) NGOs and advocacy organizations (which are in turn supported by UN organizations or also by the World Bank and the WTO) that is responsible for the dilution of the radical claim to the right to the city. These NGOs have massively expanded since the 1980s and are widely perceived as an increasingly important site of oppositional politics. In their encounters with states and corporations, NGOs tend to frame their struggle as one for rights, and it is the proliferation of this rights discourse which implies certain traps – on all scales, but in peculiar forms in the realm where transnational NGOs supported by UN organizations or the World Bank are prevalent. These forms are characterized by a dilution of the substance and political force of the radical claim to the "right to the city," implying a world view where strengthening civil society networks is regarded as positive because it enhances efficiency, and where collaboration of urban residents and municipalities is good because it furthers endogenous potentials and local growth; in this perspective local autonomy may be reconciled with international competitiveness, and sustainability with economic growth: neoliberalism with a human touch here seems possible.

This world view is vividly illustrated in the comparison Marcuse (2010) made of the UN-sponsored World Urban Forum (WUF) with the Social Urban Forum (SUF), which simultaneously took place in Rio de Janeiro in

March 2010. While both Forums addressed issues of poverty, homelessness, and insecurity, at the WUF these were "documented, measured, graphed and displayed in power point slides and the difficulties of measurement and the quality of indicators were often discussed" (Marcuse 2010: 30). Whereas at the SUF, the poor and their movements were recognized as subjects and actors, whose ideas and struggles were the central topics, at the WUF the poor were seen as objects and beneficiaries of the policies there debated. Discussions at the SUF revolved around real utopias, at the WUF around best practices (Marcuse 2010: 32).

The notion that economic growth, just distribution, and sustainability might be compatible and realizable by improved participation is, however, not restricted to the networks seeking to institutionalize the "right to the city" in global contexts. Such mystifications are also widespread within local movement milieus, and there have been quite a few local struggles in which the original radical claim to the "right to the city" has quickly faded. The recent history of urban struggles that succeeded, thanks to broad coalitions, in impeding or at least influencing neoliberal urban or community development, is filled with cases that sooner or later turned out to be have been merely defensive, achieving hardly more than saving a piece of urbanity or protecting their alternative life styles (Blechschmidt 1998). The risk for movement organizations to become co-opted or partially integrated into a neoliberal urban model has only become more acute in the most recent phase of urban development. Quite a few movement groups, among former squatters as well as among the cultural activists that have recently taken on such a visible role, increasingly foreground in the course of their campaigns their own interest in secured "free spaces" for engaging in their self-determined, autonomous, and other "politically correct" activities – and are no longer concerned with the exclusion or repression experienced by other, less favorably placed groups. Securing such "liberated spaces" and thereby securing the conditions for the survival of the respective alternative practice has actually become easier since urban policy makers have become very interested in marketing and instrumentalizing dynamic local culture scenes. The new "creative city" policies make use of (sub)cultural milieus in their branding strategies and harness them as location-specific assets in the intensifying interurban competition. Clubs, buildings, open spaces, and other "biotopes" that have been furbished and spiffed up by squatting anarchists or temporarily used and made interesting by precarious artists[21] are sought after in urban branding strategies, frequently yielding good bargains and advantages for activists who initially were struggling in the name and for the rights of marginalized groups beyond themselves (Novak 2010).

At the same time, alternative youth and cultural centers, affordable housing, local exchanges, and self-managed projects have also come under pressure and in many places given way to chic new designer stores, trendy bars, and expensive condos. "Saving" vibrant neighborhoods for upgrading and gentrifying strategies or for the tourism industry, and (re)absorbing "liberated" spaces and oppositional practices into dominant strategies are ever present possibilities; neoliberal urban policies have proven particularly successful in hijacking rebellious claims and action repertoires, and in integrating those into market-based creative concepts designed to enhance the competitive value of locational assets. This structural risk for movements in first world cities needs to be accounted for; it also points to the need for movements in the global North to pay more attention to the "right to the city" in a global perspective.

A global right to the city?

In the current period, the struggle for the "right to the city" is definitely on the agenda. The demand zeroes in on the widespread asocial impacts of the neoliberalization of cities and resonates with growing numbers of groups that are affected by these macro trends. Potential constituencies to engage in this struggle have become visible all around, and increasingly good chances for them to come together and coalesce have opened up. Next to these fertile conditions, however, novel pitfalls and mystifications lurk that tend to dilute the movement claims and which therefore need to be exposed and unmasked. Such a critical analysis presupposes an understanding of the real trends underlying these mystifications, and that involves an understanding of the new forms of uneven development and of the comparatively privileged position of cities of the global North within the globalized circulation of capital. The functions of first world cities in the contemporary international division of labor, which has turned them into global finance and service centers, bestow on them, on the one hand, intensifying social fragmentation, erosion of public space, and exacerbated exclusion of disadvantaged places, milieus, and social groups, but on the other also concessions and offerings to those groups that may be usefully absorbed into city marketing and locational politics for attracting investors, creative professionals, and tourists. The presence and interplay of both of these tendencies hampers contemporary progressive movements in developing a serious challenge to the structures of power and exploitation of *global* capitalism, as I will briefly show in this last section.

Urban movements in the so-called first world

Whereas in cities of the nineteenth and early twentieth centuries the factory and the proletarian public sphere provided a material basis for effective movement mobilization, and in the post-war era the Keynesian city presented conditions for system-threatening struggles around collective consumption, contemporary urban movements in the global North confront less conducive conditions for fulfilling the hopes and expectations placed on them to bring about fundamental social change. The actors in contemporary urban contestations are neither revolutionary factory workers nor social movements politicizing urban space along collective consumption demands (Harvey with

Wachsmuth, this volume). Instead, the political activism around producing the city today is carried out by disparate groups that share a precarious existence (whether in the informal sector, in the creative industries, or among college students), by middle class urbanites who seek to defend their quality of life, by radical autonomous, anarchist and alternative groups and various leftist organizations. These social groupings, though all are affected by contemporary forms of dispossession and alienation, occupy very different strategic positions within the postindustrial neoliberal city. With the bulk of manufacturing outsourced to the global South (at wages and working conditions below the "first world" standards of a century ago[22]), "post-industrial" cities have become playgrounds for the upper classes, serviced by armies of downgraded and precarious laborers.

With their ever-expanding gentrification strategies and hosts of policies and programs designed to attract tourists as well as "creative classes," these cities offer rich soil for alternative milieus and critical creatives to flourish – but also for their co-optation. To the extent these milieus organize and contest the neoliberal restructuring of urban space, struggle to protect liberated spaces and alternative life styles, or set up social economy projects, these activities, while crucial for emancipatory transformation, are not fundamentally threatening to the structures of power and exploitation of the *global* neoliberal system, not even if they succeed with particular demands or projects as described above.

However, the global antagonism is present within first world cities as well: the conflict between privileged city users on the one side and the growing "advanced marginality" on the other has, in fact, become increasingly characteristic of cities of the global North, as expanding low-wage and informal sectors employ more and more migrants and women, and their struggles against the discrimination and dispossession they experience have been turning these cities into arenas of anti-colonial as well as anti-racist and anti-sexist struggles.

These struggles face, just like the movements of their more comfortably positioned (potential) allies in the alternative, anarchist, and cultural scenes, a growing set of structural restrictions that impede broad mobilization towards social change – accelerating trends of privatization of public goods and services, proliferation of surveillance and policing measures, the spread of segregated zones, and the dismantling of municipal infrastructures have all contributed to the erosion of public spaces and the vanishing of spaces for collectivization, which are essential prerequisites for the emergence and politicization of (class) subjects and for building alliances.

Urban movements in the global South

At the same time, in many cities of the global South over the last years visible and invisible movements have emerged, which have – often in struggles with local governments and local elites that act as stooges for global corporations and global institutions – developed organizational structures and forms of protest of their own and do not always find the support of western NGOs and leftist movements helpful. The struggles of the pavement dwellers in India, the favela residents of Latin American cities (Lanz 2009), the slum residents of the rapidly urbanizing Asian "tiger" countries (Menon 2010; Roy and AlSayyad 2004), or of the shack dwellers of the urban peripheries of Capetown, Durban, and Johannesburg (Pithouse 2009a; Patel 2010) all demonstrate that the urban poor, in resisting dispossession, eviction, police violence, and repression, have organized themselves in independent structures, developed their own local protest cultures, and have achieved – through mass mobilization, occupations, and political protest – improvements in their living conditions. Their protest campaigns and their daily, unspectacular survival struggles challenge the connection between urbanization and civilization as claimed in neoliberal "development" concepts. For them, the western politics of development spell "a combination of crises (food, environmental, energy, financial, and climate)" (McMichael and Morarji 2010: 238). The new collective actors emerging in these movements on the basis of indigenous, marginalized, and (post)colonial experiences thus constitute a break with traditional notions of social movements – and have barely been acknowledged in the research on (urban) social movements.

Perspectives of the "right to the city" movements

Northern theories which imply that urban movements today must organize on a global scale – as, for example, David Harvey claims[23] – are frequently rejected by movement representatives from the global South. Talking about South Africa, Richard Pithouse (2009b) emphasizes that the shack dwellers have to organize their struggles on the basis of *their* realities, their resources, and their networks – which prevent them from directly participating in global organizing processes. He reproaches the activists and movement intellectuals from the North with not taking seriously the conditions in the South. Otherwise they would realize the enormous material and political difficulties confronted by those urban movements. These movements frequently find the support offered by transnational NGO networks less effective than that provided by local churches or by volunteers from the global North who spend some months with them, sharing their daily lives and struggles. Such forms of intense engagement require courage and commitment, but are immeasurably more helpful to the local movements than transnational networks, which are more oriented to the needs of the North than the specific local requirements (Pithouse 2009b).

It is also striking that concepts that do not loom large in the "advanced" western movement milieus, such as the dignity of the individual, here are an essential part of the movement vocabulary. As Pithouse (2009a: 246–7) wrote of the Abahlali Basemjondolo activists in Durban, "it was the traditional language of the dignity of each person, reworked into a cosmopolitan form appropriate for urban life, that was … given primary consideration ahead of any of the more explicitly political languages."

While this emphasis on the role of human dignity as part of the political struggle of the movements of the landless and poor in the global South distinguishes them from traditional progressive movements in the West, it does play a role in poor people's movements of the US, which in turn play a leading role in the practice and coalitions of the American social forum process. Similarly, the continuities between everyday life and protest action are not only characteristic of resistance movements in the global South (Bayat 2004), but also of the political mobilization of migrant informal workers in the "first world" (Boudreau et al. 2009).

While we increasingly find the orientations and protest forms of the movements of the urban poor of the South also in the disenfranchised and marginalized areas of northern metropoles, the mediation and connection between their struggle for the "right to the city" and that of the leftist, alternative, and creative challengers of neoliberal urban politics is not always simple. For De Sousa Santos, the symbolic and linguistic worlds of the different movement cultures are diametrically opposed: "On the one side, the language is about class struggle, power relations, society, state, reform and revolution, on the other it is about love, dignity, solidarity, community, rebellion or emotion" (2010: 130–1; my translation). These vast differences in both practice and theory, he concludes, cannot be synthesized; the goal can only be to take note of these differences and make this appraisal "into a factor of convergence and inclusion" (De Sousa Santos 2010: 131; my translation).

As was shown, the neoliberal city does present progressive movements with new opportunities for building broad alliances and translocal networks, but it also hampers the struggles of movements in western metropoles in peculiar new ways. Some of their demands appear as unrealizable, others are easily accomplished – if in co-opted or watered-down fashion. The various types of mobilizations under the "right to the city" banner appear to have strikingly different potentials for contributing to transformative change towards a just city for all. Particularly since the struggle for the "right to the city" today can only be conceived of globally, neither critical urban theory nor urban movements can rest satisfied with merely appropriating selected zones of Northern metropoles and remaking them "to their heart's desire" – as just, democratic, and sustainable havens in a heartless world. While the potential to help bring about fundamental change is clearly linked to contesting the global reach of capitalist accumulation, there are worlds of distance lying between the struggles in the global North and South, which need to be recognized by both theory and practice of urban movements. But they also need to identify the commonalities and connectivities generated in the realities of globalization. Both migrant struggles and poor people's movements within first world metropoles might offer increasingly direct opportunities and linkages: to support the everyday practices, forms of resistance and protest activities powered by (post)colonial migrants within the western metropoles might be more immediately obvious to progressive movements in Western metropoles than showing solidarity with shack and pavement dwellers' struggles in the global South – though in both growing distances in terms of cultural and everyday experience have to be actively surmounted.

Notes

1 Habitat International Coalition has played a leading role in this process, but also a variety of (especially Latin American) NGOs that are engaged in the World Social Forum (Ortiz 2010).

2 See, in Chapter 3 of this volume, Marcuse's distinction between the "right to the city" and "rights in the city."

3 Alexander Mitscherlich's important book *Die Unwirtlichkeit unserer Städte* (*The Inhospitality of Our Cities*) was first published in 1965 and recently (2008) republished.

4 Other, more overarching mottos such as "*Vogliamo tutto! Wir wollen alles!*" (We want it all!) reflected the stance of radical rejection of the Fordist model politically, socially, and culturally.

5 Thus, the first theoretician of urban social movements, Manuel Castells (1983: 319–20), developed his conception of urban social movements on the basis of this practice, claiming that only if they managed to combine activism around collective consumption with struggles for community culture and political self-management, could they be classified as urban social movements, i.e. capable of transforming urban meanings, and to produce a city organized on the basis of use values, autonomous local cultures, and decentralized participatory democracy.

6 Marcuse contrasts these groups as the "discontented" versus the "dispossessed."

7 On the periodization of the various phases of neoliberalization, see Brenner and Theodore 2002.

8 See, for example, Birke 2010; Porter and Shaw 2009; Maskovsky 2003; Uitermark, this volume and 2004.

9 The Hartz reforms (named after the head of the "Commission on the Modernization of Labor Market Services," CEO and personnel manager of Volkswagen, Peter Hartz) were implemented during 2003–5 and represent the turning point in German social and labor market policy, affecting about four million people, many of whom have since fallen under the poverty line. Coalitions of local social protest groups, unions, and community organizations have been organizing demonstrations and rallies as well as civil disobedience type actions against the more punitive criteria applied to benefit recipients.

10 Over 250 social centers have set up, usually in squatted properties in Italian cities that became the venue for social, political, and cultural events. They try to practice direct democracy in non-hierarchical structures while challenging the exclusionary effects of neoliberal governance (Mudu 2004).

11 These primarily serve immigrants working as low-wage restaurant workers, janitors, day laborers, garment workers, etc., i.e. groups that have so far rarely been organized by unions. About 140 worker centers exist nationwide. Most approach their goal of helping workers help themselves by drawing on broader communities of interest such as ethnicity and/or by linking workplace specific issues such as wages, benefits, working conditions, and respect on the job, with some form of direct service such as legal aid, English classes, computer or other job training, workers rights education, and leadership development (Fine 2006; Liss, in this volume).

12 See Eick et al. 2004; Küpper et al. 2005; Lahusen and Baumgarten 2010.

13 The mobilizations labeled by Europeans as "alter-" or "anti-globalization movements" and by North Americans as "global justice movements" are most manifest in the protests against supranational organizations such as the WTO and IMF and against summit

meetings (for example, of the G8), as they seize on the political opportunities and public attention which these meetings create. They are also manifest in the "open space" of the World Social Forum and in the national, regional, and local Social Forums, which have created novel transnational spaces of activism. Held simultaneously to the annual World Economic Forum in Davos, Switzerland, the WSF provides an "open space" where activists from around the planet discuss and share alternatives to neoliberal, free market globalization. The Forums have been held in different parts of the world such as India, Venezuela, Mali, Pakistan, and Kenya, but primarily in the home of its founding movements, Brazil.

14 Attac (*Association pour la Taxation des Transactions pour l'aide aux Citoyens*), founded in 1998 in order to implement the Tobin tax worldwide, today constitutes a network of professionalized NGOs that is particularly well grounded in France, Germany, and Switzerland with hundreds of local affiliate groups (see http://www.attac.org; Escola and Kolb 2002).

15 See, for example, Köhler and Wissen 2003; Della Porta 2005; McNevin 2006; Mayer 2011.

16 "... the right to the city is like a cry and a demand ... [it] cannot be conceived of as a simple visiting right or as a return to traditional cities. It can only be formulated as a transformed and renewed right to urban life ... as long as the 'urban,' place of encounter, priority of use value, inscription in space of a time promoted to the rank of a supreme resource among all resources, finds its morphological base and its practico-material realization" (Lefebvre 1996: 158).

17 The manifesto "Not in Our Name – Challenging the 'Brand Hamburg'" was signed by hundreds of people within just a couple of months. It can be found on the website of the initiative "Not in Our Name" http://nionhh.wordpress.com/about. See also Oehmke 2010; Birke 2010; Twickel 2010 for the Hamburg struggle.

18 Even when construction work for the underground garage began in spite of huge protests, activists – along with members of the city council – continued their blockades with civil disobedience actions (see http://oneworldsee.org/Blockade-of-Varsavska-street-suspended-temporarily, http://daily.tportal.hr/77508/Police-arrest-activists-at-Vasavska-construction-site.html).

19 http://www.my-poznaniacy.org/index.php/english (accessed June 27, 2011).

20 Details on this world charter are to be found on the website unesco.org.

21 Many cities have launched programs providing artists and creative workers with inter-mediate use of vacant space until investors are found to develop them, benefitting both empty city coffers and creative types that are in desperate need for space.

22 For example, garment workers at the outskirts of Dhaka, Bangladesh, who are sewing for Gap and Walmart, are making 28 cents an hour at the top wage. This amounts to one tenth of what garment workers in New York earned 100 years ago – who were also locked in a fire at the Triangle Shirtwaist Factory. At that factory, the women workers in 1911 worked 14 hours a day and had Saturdays off; at the Hameem factory, they work 12–14 hours seven days a week. While the Triangle fire unleashed public outrage and led to comprehensive workplace safety laws, paving the way for labor legislation reform of the New Deal era, the fire at the Hameem factory in Dhaka was not even investigated, and the workers demanding a wage increase to 35 cents an hour are bru-tally attacked by police forces (Kernaghan 2011). The wages and working conditions of many (especially undocumented) domestic and other low-wage service workers are approximating the standards prevalent in the global South.

23 "At this point in history, this has to be a global struggle, predominantly with finance capi-tal, for that is the scale at which urbanization processes now work" (Harvey 2008: 39).

References

Bayat, A. (2004) "Globalization and the Politics of the Informals in the Global South," in A. Roy and N. AlSayyad (eds), *Urban Informality: Transnational Perspectives from the Middle East, Latin America, and South Asia*, Lanham: Lexington Books, pp. 79–102.

Birke, P. (2010) "Herrscht hier Banko? Die aktuellen Proteste gegen das Unternehmen Hamburg," *Sozial.Geschichte 3*, [online] http://www.stiftung-sozialgeschichte.de (accessed March 18, 2011), pp. 148–91.

Blechschmidt, A. (1998) "Vom 'Gleichgewicht des Schreckens': Autonomer Kampf gegen Umstrukturierung im Hamburger Schanzenviertel," in StadtRat (ed.), *Umkämpfte Räume*, Hamburg: Verlag Libertäre Aktion, pp. 83–101.

Boudreau, J., Boucher, N., and Liguori, M. (2009) "Taking the Bus Daily and Demonstrating on Sunday", *City*, vol. 13, no. 2–3, pp. 336–46.

Brenner, N. and Theodore, N. (2002) "Cities and the Geographies of 'Actually Existing Neoliberalism'," *Antipode*, vol. 34, no. 3, pp. 349–79.

Caldarovic, O. and Sarinic, J. (2008) "Inevitability of Gentrification," paper presented at the ISA meeting in Barcelona, September.

Castells, M. (1983) *The City and the Grassroots*, London: Edward Arnold.

Colomb, C. and Novy, J. (2011) "Struggling for the Right to the (Creative) City in Berlin and Hamburg," *International Journal of Urban and Regional Research*, forthcoming.

Della Porta, D. (2005) "Multiple Belongings, Tolerant Identities, and the Construction of 'Another Politics': Between the European Social Forum and the Local Social Fora," in D. Della Porta and S. Tarrow (eds), *Transnational Protest and Global Activism*, Lanham: Rowman & Littlefield, pp. 175–202.

De Sousa Santos, B. (2010) "Entpolarisierte Pluralitäten," *Luxemburg: Gesellschaftsanalyse und linke Praxis*, vol. 2, no. 1, pp. 128–35.

Eick, V., Grell, B., Mayer, M., and Sambale, J. (2004) *Nonprofits und die Transformation lokaler Beschäftigungspolitik*, Münster: Westfälisches Dampfboot.

Eskola, K. and Kolb, F. (2002) "Attac: Entstehung und Profil einer globalisierungskritischen Bewegungsorganisation," in H. Walk and N. Boehme (eds), *Globaler Widerstand: Internationale Netzwerke auf der Suche nach Alternativen im globalen Kapitalismus*, Münster: Westfälisches Dampfboot, pp. 157–67.

Fainstein, N.I. and Fainstein, S. (1974) *Urban Political Movements*, Englewood Cliffs, NJ: Prentice-Hall Inc.

Fernandes, E. (2007) "Constructing the 'Right to the city' in Brazil," *Social and Legal Studies*, vol. 16, no. 2, June, pp. 201–19.

Fine, J. (2006) *Worker Centers: Organizing Communities at the Edge of the Dream*, Ithaca, NY: ILR Press.

Goldberg, H. (2008) "Building Power in the City: Reflections on the Emergence of the Right to the City Alliance and the National Domestic Workers Alliance," [online] http://inthemiddleofthewhirlwind.wordpress.com/building-power-in-the-city.

Harvey, D. (2008) "The Right to the City," *New Left Review*, vol. 53, pp. 23–40.

Henwood, D. (2009) "A Post-Capitalist Future is Possible," *The Nation*, [online] http://www.thenation.com/doc/20090330/henwood (accessed March 13, 2009).

Kernaghan, C. (2011) *Triangle Returns: Young Women Continue to Die in Locked Sweatshops. Report by Institute for Global Labour and Human Rights*, March, [online] http://videocafe.crooksandliars.com/heather/triangle-returns-young-women-continue-die (accessed March 30, 2011).

Köhler, B. and Wissen, M. (2003) "Globalizing Protest: Urban Conflicts and Global Social Movements," *International Journal of Urban and Regional Research*, vol. 24, no. 4, pp. 942–51.

Küpper, B., Andreas, Z., and Kühn, A. (2005) "Sozialer Protest zwischen Deprivation und Populismus: Eine Untersuchung zu den Hartz IV-Demonstrationen," *Journal für Konflikt- und Gewaltforschung*, vol. 7, no. 2, pp. 105–40.

Lahusen, C. and Baumgarten, B. (2010) *Das Ende des sozialen Friedens? Politik und Protest in Zeiten der Hartz IV-Reformen*, Frankfurt/M.: Campus.

Lanz, S. (2009) "Der Kampf um das Recht auf die Stadt: Städtische soziale Bewegungen in Lateinamerika," in J. Mittag and G. Ismar (eds), *"El pueblo unido?" Soziale Bewegungen und politischer Protest in der Geschichte Lateinamerikas*, Münster: Westfälisches Dampfboot.

Lefebvre, H. (1996 [1968]) "The Right to the City," in H. Lefebvre, *Writings on Cities*, E. Kofman and E. Lebas (eds), Cambridge, Mass.: Blackwell, pp. 63–184.

Lotta, C. (1972) *Nehmen wir uns die Stadt: Klassenanalyse, Organisationspapier, Kampfprogramm. Beiträge der Lotta Continua zur Totalisierung der Kämpfe*, München: Trikont Verlag.

Marcuse, P. (2010) "Two World Urban Forums, Two Worlds Apart," *Progressive Planning*, no. 183, pp. 30–2.

Maskovsky, J. (2003) "Global Justice in the Postindustrial City: Urban Activism Beyond the Global-Local Split," in J. Schneider and I. Susser (eds), *Wounded Cities: Destruction and Reconstruction in a Globalized World*, Oxford: Berg, pp. 149–72.

Mayer, M. (1987) "Städtische Bewegungen in USA: Gegenmacht und Inkorporierung," *Prokla*, vol. 68, no. 3, pp. 73–89.

Mayer, M. (2003) "The Onward Sweep of Social Capital," *International Journal of Urban and Regional Research*, vol. 27, no. 1, pp. 110–32.

Mayer, M. (2007) "Contesting the Neoliberalization of Urban Governance," in H. Leitner, J. Peck, and E. Sheppard (eds), *Contesting Neoliberalism*, New York: Guilford, pp. 90–115.

Mayer, M. (2011) "Multiscalar Mobilization for the Just City: New Spatial Politics of Urban Movements," in J. Beaumont, B. Miller, and W. Nicholls (eds), *Spaces of Contention*, Farnham: Ashgate.

McMichael, P. and Morarji, K. (2010) "Development and its Discontents," in P. McMichael (ed.), *Contesting Development: Critical Struggles for Social Change*, New York: Routledge, pp. 233–41.

McNevin, A. (2006) "Political Belonging in a Neoliberal Era: The Struggle of the Sans-Papiers," *Citizenship Studies*, vol. 10, no. 2, pp. 135–51.

Menon, G. (2010) "Recoveries of Space and Subjectivity in the Shadow of Violence: The Clandestine Politics of Pavement Dwellers in Mumbai," in P. McMichael (ed.), *Contesting Development*, New York: Routledge, pp. 151–64.

Mudu, P. (2004) "Resisting and challenging Neoliberalism: The Development of Italian Social Centers," *Antipode*, vol. 36, no. 5, pp. 917–41.

National Coalition for the Homeless (2010) "Tent Cities in America: A Pacific Coast Report," [online] http://www.nationalhomeless.org/publications/tent_cities_pr.html (accessed March 4, 2010).

Nichols, J. (2011). "Showdown in Wisconsin," *The Nation*, [online] http://www.thenation.com/article/159167/showdown-wisconsin (accessed March 10, 2011).

Novak, C. (2010) "Berlin's Last Squat Ends as Legit Housing | Projects Flourish," *Deutsche Welle*, [online] http://www.dw-world.de/dw/article/0,,5707925,00.html (accessed June 21, 2010).

Oehmke, P. (2010) "Squatters Take on the Creative Class: Who has the Right to Shape the City?" *Spiegel*, [online] http://www.spiegel.de/international/germany/0,1518,670600,00.html (accessed January 7, 2010).

Ortiz, E. (2010) "The Construction Process towards the Right to the City: Progress Made and Challenges Pending," in A. Sugranyes and C. Mathivet (eds), *Cities for All: Proposals and Experiences towards the Right of the City*, Santiago, Chile: Habitat International Coalition.

Patel, R. (2010) "Cities without Citizens," in P. McMichael (ed.), *Contesting Development*, New York: Routledge, pp. 33–49.

Pithouse, R. (2009a) "Abahlali Basemjondolo and the Struggle for the City in Durban, South Africa," *CIDADES*, vol. 6, no. 9, pp. 241–70.

Pithouse, R. (2009b) "Let's Keep it Real: The Anti-Politics of Most Attempts at Global Solidarity," presentation at the First International Conference of the Graduate Program "Transnational Spaces," the "Transnationality of Cities," Viadrina University, Frankfurt/O. (December).

Porter, L. and Shaw, K. (eds) (2009) *Whose Urban Renaissance?* London/New York: Routledge.

Roy, A. and AlSayyad, N. (eds) (2004) *Urban Informality: Transnational Perspectives from the Middle East, Latin America, and South Asia*, Lanham: Lexington Books.

Scharenberg, A. and Bader, I. (2009) "Berlin's Waterfront Site Struggle," *CITY*, vol. 13, no. 2–3, pp. 325–35.

Schwarzbeck, M. (2010) "Die neue APO. Wo einst jeder für sich kämpfte, geht es jetzt um das große Ganze: die Rückeroberung der Stadt," *Zitty*, no. 16 (July 29).

Sugranyes, A. and Mathivet, C. (eds) (2010) *Cities for All: Proposals and Experiences Towards the Right of the City*, Santiago, Chile: Habitat International Coalition.

Twickel, C. (2010) *Gentrifizierungsdingsums oder eine Stadt für alle*, Hamburg: Edition Nautilus.

Uitermark, J. (2004) "Looking Forward by Looking Back: Mayday Protests in London and the Strategic Significance of the Urban," *Antipode*, no. 36, pp. 706–27.

Unger, K. (2009) "'Right to the City' as a Response to the Crisis: 'Convergence' or Divergence of Urban Social Movements?" *Reclaiming Spaces*, [online] http://www.reclaiming-spaces.org/crisis/archives/266 (accessed February 14, 2009).

6

SPACE AND REVOLUTION IN THEORY AND PRACTICE

Eight theses

Kanishka Goonewardena

Thesis 1: space = politics

> Is it conceivable that the exercise of hegemony might leave space untouched?
>
> (Henri Lefebvre 1991 [1974/1958]: 11)

How can space be political? Evidently, a few good answers to this question have been obvious to the rulers of the world in the age of cities, and to their architects and urban planners, who knew well what Henri Lefebvre called the "production of space" had to do with what Antonio Gramsci named political hegemony – in both objective and subjective terms. We can see this most clearly with the benefit of some historical distance, as does Kevin Lynch at the outset of *Good City Form* (1981), by observing not only the material embodiment of political authority in urban space, but also the dialectical unity of urban forms and cosmologies projected by them in the ancient cities of various civilizations. But it was Friedrich Engels who first offered a truly critical perspective on the politics of space at the dawn of industrial capitalism, in *The Condition of the Working Class in England* in 1844:

> Owing to the curious lay-out of the town it is quite possible for someone to live for years in Manchester and to travel daily to and from his work without ever seeing a working-class quarter or coming into contact with an artisan. He who visits Manchester simply on business or for pleasure need never see the slums, mainly because the working-class districts and the middle-class districts are quite distinct ... To such an extent has the convenience of the rich been considered in the planning of Manchester that these plutocrats can travel from their houses to their places of business

in the centre of the town by the shortest routes, which run entirely through working-class districts, without even realizing how close they are to the misery and filth which lie on both sides of the road.

(1968 [1845]: 54–5)

Engels does not mince too many words on the understated purpose of such "hypocritical" urban planning: "hiding from the wealthy ladies and gentlemen with strong stomachs and weak nerves the misery and squalor which are part and parcel of their own riches and luxury" (Engels 1968 [1845]: 54–5). It is much in the same spirit that Walter Benjamin, nearly a century later, reflects on urbanism in his famous essay on Paris (1935/1939) with reference to the most symptomatic moment of modern urbanism: Georges-Eugène Haussmann's legendary reconstruction of the "capital of the nineteenth century," with an expertise informed by his reading of *Le Guerre des Rues et des Maisons* (1847) by Marshall Thomas Robert Bugeaud, the military man in charge of the French invasion of Algeria in the 1840s, who was the first to pen the principles of modern urban warfare, having himself rehearsed them with legendary brutality in Algiers while the twenty-two-year-old Engels was rushing his manuscript on the predicament of the English proletariat to press (Misselwitz and Weizman 2003). "Haussmann's ideal in city planning consisted of long straight streets opening onto broad perspectives," within which "the temples of the bourgeoisie's spiritual and secular power were to find their apotheosis" (Benjamin 1999: 24). Contemporaries called it "strategic embellishment," but Benjamin is quick to point out that "the true goal of Haussmann's projects was to secure the city against civil war" by "widening the streets" in order to "make the erection of barricades in the streets of Paris impossible for all time" (23). Here, the new grand boulevard perspectives – which, "prior to their inauguration, were screened with canvas draperies and unveiled like monuments" (24) – were also meant to "connect the barracks in straight lines with the workers' districts" (23), to facilitate rapid troop movement in the event of revolution. Converging on Haussmann's megalomaniac monumentalism were not only aesthetics and politics, but also economics. The enabling condition for the reformatting of Paris, Benjamin notes proleptically, "is … Napoleonic imperialism, which favors investment capital" (23) as "Haussmann's expropriations give rise to speculation that borders on fraud" (23). What about the expropriated? "In 1864, in a speech before the National Assembly," reports Benjamin, Haussmann

vents his hatred of the rootless urban population, which keeps increasing as a result of his projects. Rising rents drive the proletariat into the suburbs. The *quartiers* of Paris in this way lose their distinctive physiognomy. The 'red belt' forms. Haussmann gave himself the title of "demolition artist," *artiste démolisseur*. He viewed his work as a calling.

(12)

So witnessed Benjamin the primal scene of capitalist-imperial-colonial urbanism – the durably violent form of which continues to haunt the best exposés of radical urban thought even after modernity was discursively displaced by postmodernism, and capitalism by globalization, as readers of Mike Davis on Los Angeles or Neil Smith on the "revanchist city" can attest. But in the dismal state of affairs reported in *The Planet of Slums* (2006) by Davis, we forget too easily that architecture and urban planning – now resigned to covering up social antagonisms rather than eliminating them, if not condemned to pimping for city governments lusting for "public–private" affairs with corporate capital – once entertained a revolutionary vocation: to radically change both space *and* society.

Thesis 2: modernism = Breton + Corbusier + Lenin

To encompass both [André] Breton and Le Corbusier – that would mean drawing the spirit of contemporary France like a bow, with which knowledge shoots the moment in the heart.

(Walter Benjamin 1999: 459)

Today, as capital roams the globe behind the sanctimonious veil of human rights and democracy, it is fashionable to dismiss those efforts to change the world as the ruse of reason gone mad, as so many pervasions of the *laissez-faire* spirit by control freaks. Better to understand what happened – as Susan Buck-Morss urges us to do in *Dreamworld and Catastrophe: The Passing of Mass Utopia in East and West* (2000). An adequate consideration of why revolution failed, so to speak, involves of course the close study of those world-historical forces that triangulated radical thought, revolutionary politics and metropolitan life in the twentieth century. Their transatlantic trajectories – from the revolutionary conjunctures between the two World Wars through military-Keynesian and state–socialist restorations of capital to the uneven globalization of neoliberal imperialisms – now provide us with the essential politico-historical vectors to make sense of radical conceptions and politics of the city. The most misunderstood moment in this train of historical events, especially in the time of postmodern amnesia, is the overdetermined conjuncture framed by the two World Wars: modernism. As Perry Anderson (1984: 96–113) noted in a memorable debate with Marshall Berman (*All That Is Solid Melts Into Air*, 1982) on the meaning of modernity, it consisted of three basic coordinates: the formal novelty of radical aesthetic practices variously opposed to the academicism of the status-quo as much as bourgeois society at large (expressionism, constructivism, surrealism, cubism); the new forces of production ushered in by the second industrial revolution (automobile, airplane, telephone); and, above all, the actuality of revolution (Bolshevik, Spartacist, anarchist). It is this explosive fusion of aesthetics, technology, and politics – especially in Germany, Italy, France, and during the instructive early years of the Soviet Union – that still animates Walter Benjamin's famous "artwork essay" as much as his "theses on the philosophy of history." The constructivist optimism of these texts stands as a valuable corrective to perceptions acquired by the critical theory of his Frankfurt School colleagues as "negative" or "pessimistic." If the early Frankfurt School is better understood as a dialectical mediation of critique and utopia with recourse to the imaginaries and technologies of revolutionary art, then it is to this art that properly modernist architecture and urban planning surely belong – as ably recounted in Anatole Kopp's *Town and Revolution* (1970 [1967]) and *Changer la vie, changer la ville* (1975), works that strongly influenced Henri Lefebvre's pioneering work on space, but which are rarely read nowadays by architecture, planning, or geography students. Radical urban theory begins at this extraordinary moment of modernism energized by the vanguard as much as the avant-garde, by experimenting with the roles of architecture and urban planning in revolutionizing the totality of society. In the immediate aftermath of the Bolshevik revolution, before its avant-garde projec*ts* were brought in line with the imperatives of modern*ization* under Stalin, a variety of approaches to politicized art were very much in evidence in the Soviet Union: "democratic control (proposed by the Workers' Opposition), popular participation (proposed by the Kronstadt rebels), cultural creativity (proposed by [Aleksandr] Bogdanov as head of Proletkult), [and] human self-realization (proposed by [Anatolii] Lunacharskii as Commissar of Enlightenment)" (Buck-Morss 2000: 58). As such, it should be well worth the effort to reconstruct the revolutionary constructivism of modernism with some critical detail and nuance, which is barely registered in the reductive repudiations of it found in celebrated texts of postmodern urbanism – ranging from iconoclastic classics such as *Learning from Las Vegas* (1972) by Robert Venturi and his co-authors to the more hum-drum successes of Richard Florida's *The Rise of the Creative Class* (2002) and Leonie Sandercock's *Towards Cosmopolis* (1998). For such liberal-populist blockbusters on creativity and diversity offer little hope for radical urban theory, beyond small fortunes to be made by rebranding Bohemia or the occasional amendment of North American planning by-laws to accommodate a mosque here and a temple there in the "mongrel" suburb. Radically different ideals were worshipped to be sure by the architects and planners surveyed by Kopp; and their profound appreciation of the fundamental relationship between society and space belonged to what we may call a sequence of *urban* "events" (*à la* Alain Badiou 2010) – the Paris Commune, the battles of Stalingrad and Algiers, the "events" of Paris 1968 – that led the Situationists as much as Lefebvre to insist on a different space for a different life. Insofar as no theory is possible without practice, there exists therefore no such thing as the legacy of radical urban theory without the real or imaginary proximity of revolution and its urban praxis.

Thesis 3: modernization = modernism – revolution

> History consists, for the greater part, of the miseries brought upon the world by pride, ambition, avarice, revenge, lust, sedition, hypocrisy, ungoverned zeal, and all the train of disorderly appetites, which shake the pubic with the same.
>
> (Edmund Burke 1968 [1790]: 247)

Whatever happened to the *revolution* of modernism? Radical urban theory could do worse than to approach this question through architecture and urban planning, by returning to an even more famous question posed by Le Corbusier: "Architecture or Revolution?" He responded polemically to his own rhetorical question in the famous last words of *Towards a New Architecture* published in 1923: "Revolution can be avoided" (Corbusier 1986 [1923]: 289). The message, of course, was that architecture and urban planning could resolve the crisis of Europe, without having to go through revolution. It is important to recall that this question arose in the very heat of the moment of modernism in Europe, at a time when objective as well as subjective conditions seemed ripe for a radical transformation of both space and society in the Old World. Indeed, on this historic occasion more than a handful of artists, architects, and planners – under the auspices of its unique conjunction of art, technology, and politics – aligned their vocation with that of the revolution. Their thinking was condensed not into a question but a slogan: "Architecture and Revolution!" As we know, however, the attempt to revolutionize both space *and* society miscarried; but not because modernism was led by some Occidental affliction called "reason," unaware of the virtues of *laissez-faire* (Friedrich von Hayek) or *Gelassenheit* (Heidegger) in the "building, dwelling, thinking" of commodity form. On the contrary, it is precisely the transatlantic triumph of military-Keynesian capitalism after the Second World War and the consolidation of state socialism in the Comintern era after Lenin that exhausted and extinguished the revolutionary energies of modern*ism*, ushering in modern*ization*, in a triumphant union of what Lefebvre identified in *The Urban Revolution* (1970) as neo-*dirigisme* (state) and neo-*liberalism* (market). Yet, our run-of-the-mill textbook on urban planning essentially misrecognizes this counterrevolutionary turn of events. The first sentence in the Le Corbusier chapter (City of Towers) of Peter Hall's "intellectual" history of urban planning and design entitled *Cities of Tomorrow* attributes the error of modernism to the form-giver's "evil" (Hall 1996 [1988]: 204). If only Corbu was a "good" man! To the extent that a concept of modernism may be found at all in *Cosmopolis*, its central tendency appears to Sandercock as nothing but totalitarian: a brutal dictatorship of reason's will to power, indistinct in form from the unreason of fascism. James Scott's *Seeing Like a State* (1998), though more firmly grounded in history and theory than is *Cities* or *Cosmopolis*, ultimately passes a similar verdict on modernism. His telling subtitle, *How Certain Schemes to Improve the Human Condition Have Failed*, locates its critique in a venerable tradition stretching from Edmund Burke through Hayek to Jane Jacobs – as noted in perceptive reviews by conservative political philosopher John Gray (1998) and radical anthropologist Fernando Coronil (2001). The role assigned to modernist architects and urban planners in the worldviews propounded by these liberal-postmodern texts remains structurally identical to the one ascribed to Al-Qaeda and Taliban terrorists by the liberal-democratic cosmology of the White House. An Axis of Evil runs here, too, not from Pyongyang through Damascus to Caracas, but from Hegel's Absolute Spirit via modernist architects and planners to Hitler's Auschwitz and Stalin's Gulags, effectively equating modernism with madness. Such sweeping denunciations of something called "reason" as found in *Las Vegas* or *Cosmopolis*, characteristic of *fin-de-siècle* postmodernism, drew easy inspiration from the charisma of Michel Foucault, but apparently without having read him too attentively: in his famous "governmentality" lectures at the Collège de France in 1978–9 entitled *The Birth of Biopolitics*, the master of madness makes no mistake in stating explicitly that his "critique of knowledge … does not in fact consist in denouncing what is continually – … monotonously – oppressive under reason, for after all, … insanity (*déraison*) is just as oppressive" (Foucault 2008 [2004]: 36). Foucault in fact faulted socialism here for not differing radically from liberalism:

> I would say that what socialism lacks is not so much a theory of the state as governmental reason, the definition of what a governmental rationality would be in socialism … I do not think that for the moment there is an autonomous governmentality of socialism … What would really be the governmentality appropriate to socialism? Is there a governmentality appropriate to socialism? … We know only that if there is a really socialist govenmentality, then … it must be invented.
>
> (91–4)

In any case, the trouble with the category of evil conjured by avowedly anti-modernist critics here is clear: just as it could not deal with the "Why do they hate us?" question tossed up by President George W. Bush's speechwriters, so it fails to offer students of the city a useful account of what went wrong with modernism. More historical and materialist concepts can do better than proposing the tautology: "evil people – architects, planners, terrorists – do evil things." They do render the fate of modernism differently from received postmodern opinion, indeed in a more dialectical and redemptive light. For in full postmodernity, nothing dominates the dominant discourses of urbanism more than the ideology of modernization, especially if postmodernism, as Fredric Jameson (1991: 1) theorized it on the first page of his path-breaking work on the subject, "is what you have when the modernization process is complete." So, the difference between modernism and modernization assumes an immense import for us, and the essence of it can be represented, with reference to Anderson's (1984) periodization, in a formula: modernization = modernism – revolution.

Thesis 4: Americanism + Fordism = counterrevolution

> Dialectical reason is, when set against the dominant mode of reason, unreason.
>
> (Theodor Adorno 1978/1974 [1951]: 72)

The passage of architecture, urban planning, and much else from modernism to modernization in the age of what Antonio Gramsci called "Americanism and Fordism," in other words, cannot be understood without reference to the waning of the prospects of revolution in the West. The latter cannot be adequately explained by the lack of common sense on the part of modernists, in spite of Scott's (1998: 309–41) attempt to do precisely that, with a spirited rendition of the Greek concept of *metis*, as if such good sense is a privilege accorded by history solely to the victims of modernism – and to scholars like himself. Nor can it be attributed to a congenital defect of the Enlightenment, as Sandercock's (1998) passing references to the evils of "reason" embodied by planners and architects seem to suggest. The Enlightenment, which Jacques Derrida (2004) has defended with passion against populist postmodernism, surely deserves a more nuanced critical treatment, as the modernist Adorno for one demonstrated by dialectical example, notwithstanding the superficial readings of *Dialectic of Enlightenment* (1944) in urban studies and planning. So does history, as any reader of Sankar Muthu's *Enlightenment Against Empire* (2003) must appreciate. If the highly influential publication in New York of Henry Russell Hitchcock and Philip Johnson's *The International Style* cataloguing MOMA's (Museum of Modern Art, New York) watershed architectural exhibition a year before CIAM's Charter of Athens in 1933 dates the death of modernism and the birth of modernization in the realm of urbanism, rather than the misleading timing suggested in *The Language of Postmodern Architecture* (1977) by Charles Jencks struck by the spectacle of Pruitt-Igoe's demolition at 3:32pm on July 15, in 1972 in St Louis, then a few factors suggest themselves for consideration in relation to the question: How did the revolution go astray? Foremost here is class struggle, among other struggles, already operating at urban, national, and global scales, which assumed the dominant form of inter-imperialist rivalry between the two World Wars contemporaneous with modernism, ushering in powerful forms of nationalism, which consolidated corresponding structures of the capitalist state – fascist and Keynesian, above all. These forces arrayed against "the withering away of the state" (*à la* Marx and Lenin), without which the ideals of revolutionary modernism could not be actualized, were veritably inter-national and lay beyond the sole control of avant-garde architects or planners. Some of them remained true to their purpose in practice better than others, no doubt about it; yet we have to look beyond the good and evil of their own characters at the more decisive logics of capital and state to account for the transition from modernism to modernization. I submit therefore that the politics of this fateful historical mutation of space is best seen not from the seemingly diverse perspectives of those who sought to demonstrate that a "revolution could be avoided," ranging from the functional-ism of the Charter of Athens to the populism of *Learning from Las Vegas*, but from a standpoint located in the revolutionary *future* that was promised but nowhere produced by modernism. This is the least that urban theory can still learn from the utopian methods of the Frankfurt School. From that perspective, the crucial line to be drawn in the sand of architecture and urban planning through the last century runs *not* between what are often casually referred to as "modernism" and "postmodernism"; it runs between those who found out how a "revolution could be avoided" and those who fought for "architecture *and* revolution." For it is the former who embraced so readily the ideology of modernization – the episteme of development – and ushered in the reifications of technology and efficiency that have since been regnant in the production of space, not only in the overdeveloped West, but also in the former socialist and still underdeveloped countries long compelled to follow the advanced capitalist world very much on its own economistic and imperialist terms of combined and uneven devel-opment. While it remains to be seen if the subaltern classes of China or India will offer a break from their rule, the political-economic nature of what appears here to be a deplorable but inevitable triumph of instrumental reason is in fact better theorized in classical Marxist terms: i.e. as an outcome of the conceit of liberating humanity by the development of only the *forces* of production, while safeguarding or indeed spreading on a planetary scale the actually existing *relations* of production – instead of freeing them from their capitalist forms (Fordist or post-Fordist), and with them, the totality of social relations.

Thesis 5: postmodernism = revolutionary reaction

> Revolutions revolutionize counterrevolutionaries.
> (Régis Debray 1967)

Both Benjamin and Lefebvre – two of the most insightful Marxist students of the city – certainly saw bourgeois urbanism in this light, as a mismatch between the deployments of new technology and those utopian yearnings active in the social imaginary. Benjamin scholar Buck-Morss identifies capitalist "'urban renewal' projects" in *The Dialectics of Seeing* (1989: 89) "as a classic example of reification," because they "attempted to create social utopia by changing the arrangement of buildings and streets – objects in space – while leaving social relationships intact." In the first volume of *Critique of Everyday Life* (1991 [1947/1958]), Lefebvre noted how similar reifications of "progress" also affected state socialism:

> It is ludicrous to define socialism solely by the development of productive forces. Economic statistics cannot answer the question: "What is social-ism?" Men do not fight and die for tons of steel, or for tanks or atomic bombs. They aspire to be happy, not to produce.
> (Lefebvre 1991 [1947/1958]: 48)

Their critiques of the ideology of modernization stand worlds apart, however, from those offered by a whole series of anti-modernist manifestos of more or less postmodern urbanism, beginning famously with Jane Jacobs' devastating attack on urban planners, soon followed by libertarian celebrations of Los Angeles by Reyner Banham and Las Vegas by Robert Venturi as the new postmodern ideal of *laissez-faire* metropolitan form. The postmodern contribution to urban planning rests largely on elaborations of difference, but only occasionally with reliable reference to the concept of *différence* proposed by Derrida and his poststructuralist students harboring a considerable diversity of theoretical and political sensibilities. In the latter cases the critical emphasis usually falls on the socially constructed if not historically contingent nature of our social and cultural identities, and therefore the political possibility of also questioning them, in order to deconstruct in particular those categories such as race, gender, and sexuality that demarcate lines of domination in the realm of social relations. Debates on the relationship of such politics to struggles against capitalism – between Nancy Fraser, Iris Marion Young, Judith Butler, Slavoj Žižek, Ernesto Laclau, Chantal Mouffe, and others – have, in fact, contributed some of the most original insights into radical urban theory in the past two decades. Yet for the bulk of what passes for postmodern thought in the planning field, the agenda of difference has little to do with deconstruction as such; the inspiration for it, if it can be called that, comes rather from liberal-populist valorizations of ethno-cultural identity, more often than not aligned with state-sponsored ideologies of "multiculturalism." The "celebration" of actually existing identities becomes the norm here, if not "toleration"; but rarely "critique." The insidious inadequacies of such postmodern multiculturalisms have been demonstrated on both sides of the Atlantic by Himani Bannerji in *The Dark Side of the Nation* (2000); Ambalavanar Sivanandan in *Communities of Resistance* (1990) and the journal *Race and Class*; Vijay Prashad in *The Karma of Brown Folk* (2000); and Alain Badiou in *Ethics* (2001 [1998]), *Metapolitics* (2005 [1998]), and *Polemics* (2006 [2005/2004/2003]). Yet they flood the left-liberal discursive space of our mongrel cosmopolis, currently in blissful union with the "creative class," some three decades after the decidedly more "unhappy marriage" between feminism and Marxism.[1] These celebrations of postmodern difference are at peace with the reifications of capital and state; as such they are a far cry from what Lefebvre called forth by the concept of "differential space" in *The Production of Space* (1991 [1974]: 352–400). Needless to add, such advocates of difference are oblivious to the difference between forces and relations of production in identifying modernism with totalitarianism, under the spell of Cold War ideology no doubt, while celebrating some version of market populism (mom-and-pop or corporate) as the way to go. Recall how Venturi summed up the distinction between the dull modernist city and the joyous Las Vegas Strip: "Building for Man" versus "Building for men (markets)." The implication of this Hayekian equation of "men" with "markets," in case we miss it, is spelled out clearly in

Learning from Las Vegas: the concern of the architect "ought not to be with what ought to be but with what is" (Venturi et al. 1972: 21). Connoisseurs of such counter-revolutionary counsel are to be found not only in the casino circuits of contemporary capital, but also in the halls of academia – wherein the discourses of postmodern urbanism, and a lot of their critiques too, can be counted on studiously to avoid the revolution.

Thesis 6: Marxist urban theory = excrescence of capital

> How much time is it going to take to recognize that the subtitle of *Capital*
> (*Critique of Political Economy*) had to be taken literally?
>
> (Henri Lefebvre 1972: 70)[2]

What happened to radical urbanism after the revolution was derailed by state socialism and taken off the political agenda in the West by military-Keynesianism mirrors the fate suffered by Marxism under the same circumstances. Both registered a debilitating split between practice and theory; or a death of practice compensated by a new life in theory, itself conducted largely in academia rather than the realm of politics. In *Considerations on Western Marxism* (1976), Perry Anderson underlined that the "hidden hallmark" of this tradition was one of "*defeat,*" noting that "its major works were, without exception, produced in situations of political isolation and despair." Whereas Marx's own thought moved from philosophy to politics to economics, the trajectory of Western Marxism under these conditions ran in the opposite direction, "to concentrate overwhelmingly on . . . *superstructures.*" Here, "it was culture that held the central focus of attention"; and "within the realm of culture itself, it was *Art* that engaged the major intellectual energies and gifts of Western Marxism" (Anderson 1976: 42, 75–6). The distinctly postmodern phenomenon of "cultural studies" – or what is simply called *theory* – illustrates but a logical extension of this tendency after the disappointment of the radical political aspirations of the more or less left intelligentsia in the West after 1968. The city as such did not figure prominently in the canon of Western Marxism, it should be noted – Benjamin, Lefebvre, and the Situationists stand as the signal exceptions that prove this rule. When Marxist urban studies came into its own in the Anglo-American academy in the 1970s, however, none of them played any role to speak of in it: Benjamin was barely mentioned; Guy Debord was as good as a dead dog; only Lefebvre featured here as an intriguing but errant inspiration, no sooner abandoned than invoked. It was the distinction of Marxist urban studies in its formative moment to bypass the entire output of Western Marxism, and return to Marx himself and to his mature work *Capital*. In so doing, the pioneering work of David Harvey and his students reversed the path Western Marxism had travelled from economics to philosophy and art with ever more sophisticated applications of the Hegelian concept of *mediation* or the Althusserian alternative of *overdetermination*; their contribution to Marxism and valuable counterpoint to the substantive trend of the Frankfurt School lay precisely in anchoring "production of space" *à la* Lefebvre (1991 [1974]) firmly in capital's "laws of motion" *à la* Marx (1976 [1867]). In *The Urban Revolution* (1970: 160), Lefebvre noted in passing that "as the principal circuit ... industrial production ... begins to slow down, capital shifts to the second sector, real estate," pointing out how "it can even happen that real-estate speculation becomes the principle source for the formation of capital, that is, the realization of surplus value." Yet, his aim in that and other contemporaneous texts was not to develop a political economy of the city, but to explore more fundamentally the urbanization of the world and the attendant politicization of space. The intricate explication of the role played by the production of urban space in the accumulation of capital and vice-versa – especially in overcoming crises of overproduction or underconsumption – may yet qualify as the major theoretical contribution of critical urban theory to Marxism, as canonically presented in Harvey's *Limits to Capital* (1982). Closely tied to this is the vital development by Neil Smith (2008/1990/1984) of a theory of *uneven development*, originally espoused of course by Lenin and Trotsky in the context of classical imperialism, but now focused on the urban and regional scales as well as questions concerning nature–society–history relations. While critical urban theory helped in this way to bring Marxism back to economics by means of space, paralleling Ernest Mandel's *Late Capitalism* (1978/1975 [1972]) more than Theodor Adorno's *Aesthetic Theory* (1997 [1970]), it shared with Western Marxism however a soft spot on politics.

Thesis 7: urban political economy = capital + city – politics

I think what is Marxist, and also Leninist – and in any case *true* – is the idea that any viable campaign against capitalism can only be political. There can be no economic battle against the economy.

(Alain Badiou 2001 [1998]: 105)

"Of all the arts, architecture is the closest constitutively to the economic, with which, in the form of commissions and land values, it has a virtually unmediated relationship" – so begins *Postmodernism, or, The Cultural Logic of Late Capitalism* by Jameson (1991: 5). Urbanization, in other words, bears a more direct relationship than does political struggle or cultural production to the dynamics of capital, which, in the case of space, makes that much dreaded determination in the last instance by the economy more real than imagined. Proximity to capital in this sense renders space eminently amenable to rigorous political–economic conceptions that are more economic than political. But there is a price to be paid for that kind of precision on the economics of space, not affordable when it comes to the politics of space. For while such political–economic approaches clearly excel at explaining how the city came to be what it is, they are less adept at saying what a good city may look like, and how we might go from the city we have to the city we love. The structural–functional

cast of Marxist urban theory of the 1970s onwards only accentuates both ret-
rospectively and prospectively the value of some key Western Marxists either
missing or marginalized within it: Benjamin, Lefebvre, and Debord. Benjamin
– not mentioned at all in *The Urban Question* (1977 [1972]) by Manuel Castells
or *Social Justice and the City* (1973) by Harvey – found material evidence of
dreams for a liberated life as well as their non-actualization by the logic of
capital in the everyday life of the city – especially in his major unfinished work,
Passagenwerk. Few addressed the persistence of utopia with such originality as
he did in the tradition of historical materialism, as something to be actualized by means of a dialectical articulation of unrealized dreams of the past and
unconscious ones of the present for a better world with the new technologies
("new nature") of modernism. Here, he was, on the one hand, following a
famous letter written by Marx to Arnold Ruge in 1843:

> Our motto must ... be: reform of consciousness not by means of dogmas,
> but by analyzing the mystical consciousness unclear to itself, whether it
> appears religiously or politically. It will then become clear that the world
> has long possessed in the form of a dream something of which it only has
> to become conscious in order to possess it in reality.[3]

And on the other hand, Benjamin was responding to the real challenges of
building actually existing communism that he knew from his visits to Moscow
in the mid 1920s. In Buck-Morss' words, his radical contribution to the
"superstructural" encounter between new technologies and the oneiric desire
for a better world consisted in asking how to bring forth

> both technology and imagination out of their mythic dream states, through
> making conscious the collective's desire for social utopia, and the potential
> of the new nature to achieve it by translating that desire into the "new
> language" of its material forms.
>
> (Buck-Morss 1989: 124–5)

In their own ways, Lefebvre and Debord also understood the city as the arena
for the revolutionary fusion of aesthetics, politics, and technology, especially
by proposing the concept of everyday life, which even today seems quite alien
to political–economic renditions of Marxism. One of their original contributions to Marxism consisted in developing an historical materialist concept of
everyday life, a notion hitherto resident most influentially in Heidegger's philosophy of being, in spite of having been understood politically as the testing
ground of the October Revolution by Lenin and Trotsky. The fascinating
political–philosophical history of this concept sketched by John Roberts in
Philosophizing the Everyday (2006) and Peter Osborne in *The Politics of Time*
(1995) offers for us an indispensible lesson: the category of everyday life is as
urban and political as it is philosophical. It lies at the heart of radical politics,

the locus of which is increasingly the city. As such, everyday life also ought to be the central concern of any radical urban theory not simply content with offering us vivid descriptions of cities and capital, but also intent on producing a new *concept* of politics – beyond the exhausted attachments to party, state, and parliament, not to mention "social capital," "civil society," or "citizenship," none of which are adequate to the struggle for the right to the city.

Thesis 8: socialist revolution = urban revolution

> Lefebvre was right to insist that the revolution has to be urban, in the broadest sense of that term, or nothing at all.
>
> (David Harvey 2008: 204)

"Let everyday life become a work of art! Let every technical means be employed for the transformation of everyday life!" (Lefebvre 1984 [1968]: 204). These are Lefebvre's words, uttered in unison with Benjamin's. Together with Debord, Lefebvre defined Marxism above all as a critique of everyday life, and understood by means of this concept a level of social reality that is dialectically articulated with two other fundamental ones: the urban and the "global," i.e. the level of the most general economic and political logics of the social totality (neo-liberalism and neo-dirigisme). In Lefebvre's work taken as a whole, we thus find a new conception of *totality* presented in terms of *levels* of the *social*, each of which possesses their own dynamic scales, and among which the urban level now plays the most decisive mediating role. The radical implication of this contribution by Lefebvre to Marxism is spelled out in both *Critique of Everyday Life* and *The Urban Revolution*: there can be no social(ist) revolution without an urban revolution, no urban revolution without a social(ist) revolution, and neither without a revolution in everyday life. This is the backdrop against which Lefebvre's concept of *the* right to the city must be understood – not as another addition to the self-contradictory liberal-democratic list of "human rights," but rather the right to a radically different *world*. Lefebvre's insights on the urban therefore offer an invaluable *starting* point for radical urban theory to focus its theoretical horizons and sharpen its political vision, as shown for example by Kristin Ross' engagement with the problematics of gender and colonization in her penetrating study of French postwar modernization: *Fast Cars, Clean Bodies* (1995). The extension of urban theory in such directions assumes paramount import in the current imperial conjuncture, as the far-flung order of our global social totality appears to be at a moment of geo-political–economic reformatting, if not crisis, to enquire into the possible roles assumed by cities and their subjects in a new world system. Such efforts, however, must not merely be descriptive, if we are to grasp the increasingly intimate relationship between the urban form of global space and the value form of global capital, as George Simmel did for his own time in "Metropolis and Mental Life" (1903) and as David Cunningham argues in his suggestive essay "The Concept of Metropolis" (2005). Neither can they afford to abandon today the question of *politics*, the symptomatic silence on which in Western Marxism is all the more conspicuous by the absence of one communist in Jameson's magisterial consummation of this tradition: Gramsci. But can our thought of politics be rescued from the grip of capital and state, while being vigilant of them? Adorno (1978/1974 [1951]: 132) once said: "economics is no joke, and merely to understand it one has to 'think eco-nomically.'" The utopian moments of Benjamin and Lefebvre provide us with an orientation to escape the state-capital circuits imprinted in our minds; but we also need a new concept and practice of politics liberated from a transitive relation to capital, as Badiou has pointed out. Not accidentally, he has noted himself in this context the urgency of the "fundamental problem" posed for radical politics today by the global urban condition (Badiou 2008: 657). Badiou's one-time student Slavoj Žižek (2006: 268) recently asked: "What if the new proletarian position is that of the inhabitants of the slums of the new megalapolises?" His Mike Davis-inspired answer: "While we should of course resist the easy temptation to elevate and idealize the slum-dwellers into a new revolutionary class, we should nonetheless, in Badiou's terms, perceive slums as one of the few authentic 'evental sites' in today's society" (Žižek 2006: 268). Likewise, Tony Negri (2009 [2002]) has underlined the centrality of urban struggles to revolutionary politics today, arguing that "the metropolis is to the multitude what the factory used to be to the working class."[4] More proper names may be added to this list of leading thinkers of *politics* in the world today who have turned on the paramount import of the metropolis for radical praxis, vindicating in no uncertain terms the fundamental thesis of Lefebvre's *The Urban Revolution*. It remains for radical urban theory to return the compliment. For its future now rests on delivering a "politics of prescription" (Hallward 2005: 769–89) capable of doing justice to the emancipatory possibilities alive in our Age of Empire and Planet of Slums.

Notes

1 The expression is Heidi Hartmann's; see also Sargent 1981: 1–41.
2 I am using Stefan Kipfer et al.'s (2008) translation here.
3 Benjamin quotes these words of Marx in the famous Konvolut N (section of method) of his *Passagenwerk*; this translation is from Buck-Morss 1989: 281.
4 This text was originally published in Italian in the journal *Posse* and then circulated on multitudes-infos@samizdat.net on January 20, 2002.

References

Adorno, T. (1997 [1970]) *Aesthetic Theory*, trans. by R. Hullot-Kentor, London and New York: Continuum.
Adorno, T. (1978/1974 [1951]) *Minima Moralia*, trans. E.F. Jephcott, London and New York: Verso.

Anderson, P. (1984) "Modernity and Revolution," *New Left Review*, I/144, pp. 96–113.

Anderson, P. (1976) *Considerations on Western Marxism*, London: New Left Books.

Badiou, A. (2010) *The Communist Hypothesis*, trans. S. Corcoran and D. Macey, London: Verso.

Badiou, A. (2008) "'We Need a Popular Discipline': Contemporary Politics and the Crisis of the Negative," *Critical Inquiry*, 34, pp. 645–59.

Badiou, A. (2006 [2005/2004/2003]) *Polemics*, trans. S. Corcoran, New York: Verso.

Badiou, A. (2005 [1998]) *Metapolitics*, trans. J. Barker, London and New York: Verso.

Badiou, A. (2001 [1998]) *Ethics: An Essay on the Understanding of Evil*, trans. P. Hallward, New York: Verso.

Bannerji, H. (2000) *The Dark Side of the Nation*, Toronto: Canadian Scholars' Press.

Benjamin, W. (1999) *The Arcades Project*, trans. H. Eiland and K. McLaughlin, Cambridge, Mass.: Harvard.

Berman, M. (1982) *All That is Solid Melts into Air*, London: Verso.

Buck-Morss, S. (2000) *Dreamworld and Catastrophe*, Cambridge, Mass.: MIT Press.

Buck-Morss, S. (1989) *The Dialectics of Seeing*, Cambridge, Mass.: MIT Press.

Bugeaud, T.R. (1997 [1847]) *La Guerre des Rues et des Maisons*, Paris: Jean-Paul Rocher.

Burke, E. (1968 [1790]) *Reflections on the Revolution in France*, C.C. O'Brien (ed.) London: Penguin.

Castells, M. (1977 [1972]) *The Urban Question: A Marxist Approach*, trans. A. Sheridan, Cambridge, Mass.: MIT Press.

Corbusier, L. (1986 [1923]) *Towards a New Architecture*, trans. F. Etchells, New York: Dover.

Coronil, F. (2001) "Smelling Like a Market," *American Historical Review*, 106, 1, [online]. Available at: http://www.historycooperative.org/journals/ahr/106.1/ah000119.html (accessed September 28, 2010).

Cunningham, D. (2005) "The Concept of Metropolis: Philosophy and Urban Form," *Radical Philosophy*, 133, 13–25.

Davis, M. (2006) *Planet of Slums*, London and New York: Verso.

Debray, R. (1967) *Revolution in the Revolution*, trans. B. Ortiz, New York: Grove Press.

Derrida, J. (2004) "Enlightenment Past and to Come," *Le Monde diplomatique*, [online]. Available at: http://mondediplo.com/2004/11/06derrida (accessed September 28, 2010).

Engels, F. (1968 [1845]) *The Condition of the Working Class in England*, trans. W.O. Henderson and W.H. Chaloner, Stanford: Stanford University Press.

Florida, R. (2002) *The Rise of the Creative Class*, New York: Basic Books.

Foucault, M. (2008 [2004]) *The Birth of Biopolitics, 1978–79*, trans. G. Burchell, ed. M. Senellart, New York: Palgrave.

Gray, J. (1998) "The Best Laid Plans", *The New York Times* (Books), 19 April, [online]. Available at: http://query.nytimes.com/gst/fullpage.html?res=9802E5DD143DF93AA 25757C0A96E958260&sec=&spon=&pagewanted=all (accessed September 28, 2010).

Hall, P. (1996 [1988]) *Cities of Tomorrow*, updated edition, Oxford and Cambridge, Mass.: Blackwell.

Hallward, P. (2005) "The Politics of Prescription," *South Atlantic Quarterly*, 104, 4, pp. 769–89.

Harvey, D. (2008) "The Right to the City," *New Left Review*, 53, pp. 23–40.

Harvey, D. (1982) *The Limits to Capital*, Oxford: Blackwell.

Harvey, D. (1973) *Social Justice and the City*, Baltimore: Johns Hopkins University Press.

Hitchcock, H.R. and Johnson, P. (1932) *The International Style: Architecture since 1922*, New York: W. W. Norton.

Jameson, F. (1991) *Postmodernism, or, The Cultural Logic of Late Capitalism*, Durham, NC: Duke University Press.

Jencks, C. (1977) *The Language of Postmodern Architecture*, New York: Rizzoli.

Kipfer, S., Goonewardena, K., Schmid, C., and Milgrom, R. (2008) "On the Production of Henri Lefebvre," in K. Goonewardena, S. Kipfer, R. Milgrom, and C. Schmid (eds) *Space, Difference, Everyday Life: Reading Henri Lefebvre*, New York: Routledge, pp. 1–23.

Kopp, A. (1975) *Changer la vie, changer la ville: de la vie nouvelle aux problèmes urbains, URSS 1917–1932*, Paris: Union Générale d'Éditions.

Kopp, A. (1970 [1967]) *Town and Revolution: Soviet Architecture and City Planning, 1917–1935*, trans. T.E. Burton, New York: George Braziller.

Lefebvre, H. (2003 [1970]) *The Urban Revolution*, foreword N. Smith, trans. R. Bononno, Minneapolis: University of Minnesota Press.

Lefebvre, H. (1991 [1974]) *The Production of Space*, trans. D. Nicholson-Smith, Oxford: Blackwell.

Lefebvre, H. (1991 [1947/1958]) *Critique of Everyday Life*, 1, trans. J. Moore, New York: Verso.

Lefebvre. H. (1984 [1968]) *Everyday Life in the Modern World*, trans. S. Rabinovitch, New Brunswick: Transaction Publishers.

Lefebvre, H. (1972) *Le pensée marxiste et la ville*, Paris: Casterman.

Lynch, K. (1981) *Good City Form*, Cambridge, Mass.: MIT Press.

Mandel, E. (1978/1975 [1972]) *Late Capitalism*, trans. J. De Bres, London: Verso.

Marx, K. (1976 [1867]) *Capital: A Critique of Political Economy*, 1, trans. B. Fowkes, London: Penguin.

Misselwitz, P. and E. Weizman (2003) "Military Operations as Urban Planning," in A. Franke (ed.) *Territories: Islands, Camps and other States of Utopia*, Berlin and Köln: KW Berlin and Walther König.

Muthu, S. (2003) *Enlightenment Against Empire*, Princeton: Princeton University Press.

Negri, A. (2009 [2002]) "The Multitude and the Metropolis," *Generation online*, trans. A. Bove, [online]. Available at: http://www.generation-online.org/t/metropolis.htm (accessed September 28, 2010).

Osborne, P. (1995) *The Politics of Time*, New York: Verso.

Prashad, V. (2000) *The Karma of Brown Folk*, Minneapolis: University of Minnesota Press.

Roberts, J. (2006) *Philosophizing the Everyday: Revolutionary Praxis and the Fate of Cultural Theory*, London: Pluto.

Ross, K. (1995) *Fast Cars, Clean Bodies*, Cambridge, Mass.: MIT Press.

Sandercock, L. (1998) *Towards Cosmopolis*, Chichester: John Wiley.

Sargent, L. (ed.) (1981) *Women and Revolution*, Boston, Mass.: South End Press.

Scott, J. (1998) *Seeing Like a State*, New Haven, Conn.: Yale University Press.

Simmel, G. (1903) "The Metropolis and Mental Life," [online]. Available at: http://www.altruists.org/static/files/The%20Metropolis%20and%20Mental%20Life%20%28Georg%20Simmel%29.htm (accessed November 1, 2010).

Sivanandan, A. (1990) "RAT and the Degradation of the Black Struggle," in *Communities of Resistance*, New York: Verso, pp. 77–122.

Smith, N. (2008/1990/1984) *Uneven Development*, 3rd edition, Athens, Ga.: Georgia University Press.

Venturi, R., Scott-Brown, D., and Izenour, S. (1972) *Learning from Las Vegas*, Cambridge, Mass.: MIT Press.

Žižek, S. (2006) *The Parallax View*, Cambridge, Mass.: MIT Press.

7

THE PRAXIS OF PLANNING AND THE CONTRIBUTIONS OF CRITICAL DEVELOPMENT STUDIES[1]

Katharine N. Rankin

Planning theory shares with critical urban theory an orientation toward normative political questions and a "politics of the possible" (Lefebvre, 2003) – insofar as it does not just analyze and predict, but also develops criteria for judgment and advocates change. Beyond those broad contours, however, it is fair to say that only a thin slice of planning theory takes up the normative commitments of critical urban theory: to challenge the violence of capitalism, to seek out the agents of revolutionary social change, and to interrogate the ends in relation to the means of practice.

In this normative terrain, Peter Marcuse furnishes an "ethical conscience" for the discipline (Goonewardena, this volume); he stands apart as a pioneer of critical praxis geared toward exposing injustice and extending the right to access and participate in urban life. His contributions not only articulate a reflexive and critical theory of urban planning and everyday life (see Slater, this volume, for example, on a politically potent conceptualization of displacement), but also consistently bring such formulations to bear on engaged public analysis of contemporary political events. After the 9/11 attacks, the New Orleans travesty, the financial crisis of 2008, and countless other occasions of immediate political urgency, Marcuse has put forward pragmatic steps for planning action rooted in principles of social justice; he has issued these through public statements, professional mailing lists, and publications geared toward both academics and practitioners. For those of us caught up in the audit cultures infecting academia in the age of neoliberalism, these ethical interventions are a steady reminder of the privilege and responsibility we have to engage academia as "a profound edge of struggle at the heart of empire" – for justice, democracy, equity, and the right to the city (Roy, 2006: 9).

In this chapter I aim to build on these normative commitments by drawing on the theoretical resources available in critical development studies – an approach within the formally institutionalized discipline of development studies that views actually existing development practices in relation to processes of imperialism, racialization, male domination, and the expansion of capital.[2] The meaning of "critical" in critical development studies is analogous to that in "critical urban studies" as it has been elaborated by Neil Brenner, Peter Marcuse, and Margit Mayer in this volume – a questioning stance toward the world that exposes both the negative and the positive; takes a fundamentally antagonistic stance in relation to the logic of capital accumulation and other modes of domination; and identifies possibilities for more just and sustainable social formations. I argue that such perspectives have been notoriously absent from planning theory as it has been formulated with reference to planning praxis in cities of the global North.

There are three reasons why I think a planning theory committed to defending the right to the city might benefit from encompassing a perspective on critique derived specifically from studies of "big D" Development (Hart, 2001) transpiring largely in the global South (though see Silvey and Rankin (2010) for a review of work that challenges this geographic imaginary within critical development studies, and the neocolonial binaries it perpetuates). First, the professional practices which both critical development studies and planning theory take as their object of study share a duplicitous relationship to processes of capitalist accumulation and liberal notions of benevolent trusteeship. Yet, critical development studies has clearly committed itself more consistently to tracing the entanglements of projects of improvement with projects of empire. When such theorizations about development are brought to bear on the more subtle object of planning, here too the flagrancies of liberal benevolence – the ethical perils of telling other people what to do in the name of progress, sustainability, empowerment, or participation – can be exposed and challenged. Second, critical perspectives within planning and development studies have evolved as parallel, yet largely disconnected, domains; little attention has been devoted to exploring the potential for mutual enrichment.[3] My third reason relates to the opportunities arising in planning from a relatively stronger commitment to praxis. In critical development studies, the reflexivity in relation to post-colonial geopolitics would seem to have produced a reticence toward praxis, and an understanding of critique as taking place at a necessary distance from the work of "programming" (Li, 2007). Planning theory refuses this distinction and is thus well positioned to put the critical resources of critical development studies to good practical use. Doing so might go a long way toward developing an "ethics of postcoloniality" in planning aimed, as Ananya Roy (2006) has suggested, at uncovering points of the profession's complicity with neoliberal globalization and at building practice around a core principle of accountability to marginalized people and groups.

The chapter is organized into three sections that take up key domains in which I believe planning theory can draw (or has drawn) productively from critical development studies to strengthen its capacity to envision and defend the right to the city. These are: (a) the relationship of planning to imperialism and globalization; (b) resistance and the cultural politics of agency; and (c) the contributions of transnational feminism to a praxis of solidarity and collaboration. In elaborating these domains this chapter will review the shared terrain of planning theory and critical development studies – putting them into dialogue with one another to uncover some promising new directions and themes for articulating an ethics of postcoloniality in planning theory.

Planning, imperialism, globalization

With the institutionalization of development as a professional practice in the post-War period, critical development studies was concerned primarily to expose how underdevelopment is produced by the penetration of capitalist social relations into the non-capitalist periphery, and the complicity of institutionalized "big D" Development practice in deepening these relations (Baran, 1957; Frank, 1967). Critical development studies also drew on the work of Fanon (1967) to reveal the psychic deprivations endured by the subjects of development through subjection to universalized "white," Western norms. Within planning theory, of course, these fundamentally Marxist perspectives are well represented in the *oeuvre* of geographer David Harvey, who makes two interrelated arguments about the mutually enforcing relationship between the production of urban space and the accumulation of capital, and the implication of urban planning in both. First, planning is instrumental to the logic of capital accumulation insofar as it furnishes the technologies for investments in the secondary and tertiary circuits of capital (Harvey, 2007 [1982]). In so doing, it plays a crucial role in mitigating class struggle and crises of overproduction and underconsumption, and thus securing a spatio-temporal fix for the reproduction of the capitalist social order at the urban scale (others have likewise contributed specifically urban perspectives on Marxism, as in Neil Smith's canonical theory of uneven development, recently updated through Loic Waquant's (2009) stunningly provocative assessment of urban neoliberal governance in the US and France). Second, shifts in the ideology of planning – from rational comprehensive to advocacy, and so on – can be tied to the cyclical fixing of capitalist urbanization in particular constructed landscapes. For example, periods of territorial instability (housing crises, devaluation of existing transport facilities, and so on) require planning to intervene with disciplined collective action for urban reform (Roweis and Scott, 1981). It is the logic of capitalist accumulation that "plan[s] the ideology of planning" (Harvey, 1996 [1985]).

A second wave of work in critical development studies attends more specifically to the discursive production of ideology. It maintains a critical orientation toward core periphery-relations but focuses on the ways in which neocolonial representations of the periphery contribute to, and in fact furnish the political conditions of possibility for, material processes of underdevelopment. Edward Said's *Orientalism* (1978) inspired a flourishing of discourse analysis examining how development discourse worked to politically constitute both the First World (as the referent for modernity, progress, and reason) and the Third World (as the undeveloped, dependent other; see also Ferguson, 1990; Crush, 1995; Escobar, 1995). Peter Marcuse has perhaps done the most to translate the contributions of Said for planning and critical urban theory. In a 2004 article for *Antipode*, Marcuse likens the contemporary manifestation of imperialism which he calls "globalism" to orientalism. Globalism represents actually existing globalization in a manner that legitimates global capitalism over all other forms of social organization found within actually existing globalization or that could be imagined for its alternative trajectories. In so doing, globalism rests upon a particular theoretical genealogy, assembling the anti-planning treatises of Friedrich von Hayek with Rostow's modernization theory and the market triumphalism of Francis Fukuyama. It is a representation that depicts a world of markets unencumbered by "tradition" or intrusive states as natural, inevitable, and true.

We can thus think about planning's role in reproducing the popular legitimacy of globalism, for example in its current enthrall with "creative city" ideologies that constitute the latest version of supply-side inducements to global capital (Peck, 2005). Or in its pandering to corporate capital in the name of "green capitalism" (Prudham, 2009). Or in its silences with regard to the original violences that constitute city space and the ongoing processes of "accumulation by dispossession" through which the poor and marginal are routinely displaced from urban spaces deemed desirable for capital accumulation (Blomley, 2004; Harvey, 2003; Roy, 2006). For Marcuse, the political imperative for theory is to reveal the difference between the ideology of globalism and actually-existing-globalization, for the sake of dismantling the former (with its discourses of freedom, diversity, and growth) and developing the political strategy and constituency to confront inequality and suffering resulting from the latter.

Deferring for a moment the matter of constituency, we may turn to the work of Jennifer Robinson, which ventures more explicitly into the domain of practice – derived not so much from critique of dominant ideology, but from critique precisely of the false separation between development studies and urban studies identified at the outset of this chapter. In *Ordinary Cities* (2006), Robinson contends that such distinctions perpetuate neocolonial binaries – North/South, modern/developing, colonizer/colonized – that obscure the "diverse cosmopolitanisms" of everyday urban experience. Robinson advocates instead a postcolonial understanding of cities wherein the diversity and complexity of urban experience could be engaged for both theory making and city building everywhere. On this basis she sees a role for planning in fostering agglomeration economies that build linkages among diverse economic activities in neighborhoods and communities, while also embedding such support for local capacities within city-wide development strategies aimed at providing universal access to infrastructure, financial services, logistics management, skilled labor, and so on. The challenge, as the work of Tania Li on *The Will to Improve* (2007) in Indonesia so powerfully (and skeptically) suggests, is to undertake this kind of praxis in a manner that does not become complicit in mainstream governmental agendas (competitive capitalism, neoliberalism, neocolonialism), but instead transforms them.

An orientation toward relationality is one key contribution of critical development studies that offers some interesting possibilities in this regard, and here the work of geographer Gillian Hart is particularly instructive. Developing a Gramscian interpretation of the post-colonial condition, Hart (2002, 2004, 2006) offers the notion of "relational comparison" to emphasize the political–economic and cultural–political processes through which the center and the periphery continually make and remake one another. Critical analysis begins here with a notion of place as "nodal points of connection within wider networks of socially produced space" (2006: 995; referencing Massey, 1994); the specificity of any place thus arises from the particular mix of interconnections to the forces and relations that lie beyond it. The task becomes one of charting material processes of interconnection to explore how multiple forces come together in practice to produce particular dynamics or trajectories within cities – as illustrated through her research on Taiwanese industrialists in the South African countryside (Hart, 2002). The widespread Taiwanese presence, she argues, must be linked analytically and politically to the land reforms in Taiwan, which provided the social wage to underwrite such a massive mobilization of Taiwanese peasant labor into the industrial sector of a postcolonial transitioning economy. The displacements she observes of South African peasants are not just a "natural" process of accumulation by dispossession endemic to the logic of capital accumulation; rather they are socially produced and rooted in a specific space–time conjuncture linking rural Taiwan and South Africa.

For planning theory there is an important political implication here. Unexpected similarities in experience across connected historical geographies could become the foundation for critical practices, common responses, and alternative trajectories, for – as geographer Cindi Katz (2001, 2004) puts it – a countertopography of global capitalism. An orientation toward comparative relationality is especially imperative in the context of the so-called financial crisis (which, as Marcuse points out in this volume, is not only a financial crisis, but more importantly a visible symptom of deep-seated contradictions in a fundamentally flawed economic system), when cities and social movements in the global North may be tempted to turn increasingly inwards and respond to the problems facing their core constituencies with forms of economic nationalism and racism (Hanieh, 2008). The challenge for planning theory is to expose the common causes of peoples' day-to-day struggles everywhere as a basis for building a constituency for the collaboration and solidarity that will be necessary to push for a better economic system in which the demands of all can be met. Developing *analytical* capacities for tracing conjunctural formations would alone go a long way toward supporting this function. It would also help to dismantle the occidentalist view of the world that prevails in the planning profession and the institutions of planning education – a view that disaggregates relational histories and turns difference into hierarchy (Hart, 2006: 997).

So, while what occurs by way of progressive responses to financial crisis in Argentina or Bolivia may not seem to matter too much in the metropolitan centers of the global North, we might turn this around to think about possibilities for building strategic translocal alliances within the profession that might respond progressively to the conjunctural relationalities among cities (Chatterton, 2005; Faulk, 2008; North and Huber, 2004). This is not meant in a naïve "best practices" sense, but in a perspective that asks: where do opportunities for solidarity lie? And how can the diversity of practices elsewhere help inform a theory about what can be done within conjuncturally specific structures of opportunity and constraint (Robinson, 2006)? The experience in Vietnam with a nationalized banking system disbursing subsidized credit to poor producers in the context of long-term investments in human development and physical infrastructure, for example, might provide some inspiration in the current conjuncture for thinking ambitiously about alternative models of banking rooted in a principle of social rights (Rankin, 2009). The aborted initiative of the Non-Aligned Movement of peripheral states to collectively negotiate the resolution of the so-called "Third World debt crisis" with the IMF likewise presents some insights into the opportunities and challenges for developing – at a municipal scale – collective bargaining vis-à-vis footloose corporate capital (Morphet, 2004). A progressive response to today's "more-than-financial "crisis (Marcuse, this volume) depends on the capacity of people to recognize their material struggles and their emotional discontent in collective rather than individual terms, and here, too, we can think about insights from critical development studies in articulating a role for planning theory.

Resistance and the cultural politics of agency

In the article on globalism, Marcuse (2004: 640) predicts that as the internal contradictions to actually-existing-globalization periodically burst out, organized opposition and noteworthy political shifts (such as that witnessed in the 2008 US electorate) are likely to grow. This is an orientation toward the key question of how the constituency for socialist futures will be built that of course reflects strong continuities with the Frankfurt School. As Brenner notes in this volume, critical theory within the Frankfurt School was unified in a common search for a revolutionary subject. In the context of twentieth-century capitalism, Frankfurt School theorists abandoned Marx's faith in the proletariat as a class for itself but struggled with the challenge of identifying a clear agent of social change. At the same time, as many contributions to this volume suggest, critical urban theory maintains a fundamental orientation toward capitalism as a system marked by fractures and contradictions that furnish the conditions for critical, antagonistic forms of social knowledge. Critical development studies shares this preoccupation with transformative agency, made possible through the contradictions of capitalism, and related hegemonic projects and governmental programs of big "D" development (Li, 2007) that unintentionally produce social groups sharing a common experience – for example, of eviction from a state forest; of being "technically assisted" to grow cash crops instead of subsistence foods; or of forced Israelization, as Yiftachel described for the case of Bedouin Arabs in this volume. The shared experience of dispossession of land and livelihood creates possibilities for those whose conduct is being conducted to recognize common interests and mobilize for change (Scott, 1998; Li, 2007).

Planning theory and critical urban theory have a lot to say about organized resistance by already-constituted, marginalized social groups, and, in the case of planning theory, about the need for advocacy on their behalf or inclusionary, participatory processes that interject their demands and interests into planning processes. But they do not have as much to say about other forms that resistance might take or the cultural politics of agency. What about the places and times in which the contradictions of hegemonic projects are not readily apparent to people who occupy marginal social locations within them? Or the reality that people routinely make bargains with hegemony even as they may recognize their own subjection to it or the contradictions within it (Kandiyoti, 1991, 1994)? Or that when they do resist, they may do so covertly and individually, so as not to jeopardize what standing they do have in the rubrics of hegemonic power (Shakya and Rankin, 2008). Under what conditions, moreover, might overt critique and resistance arise and pose a challenge to the stability of hegemonic projects?

I think there is an important role for critical urban theory to play in broaching these questions – and the imperative is doubly strong for planning theory given its orientation to praxis and potential role in supporting and promoting mobilizations for urban justice. Anthropologist Lila Abu-Lughod (1990) poses the question of subaltern agency particularly poignantly in an essay on the "romance of resistance" addressing Bedouin women's resistance to male domination in Egypt:

> First, how might we develop theories that give women credit for resisting in a variety of ways the power of those who control so much of their lives, without either misattributing to them forms of consciousness or politics that are not part of their experience – something like a feminist consciousness or a feminist politics – or devaluing their practices as pre-political, primitive, or even misguided? Second, how might we account for the fact

that Bedouin women both resist and support the existing system of power, without resorting to analytical concepts like false consciousness, which dismiss their own understanding of their situation, or impression management, which makes of them cynical manipulators?

(1990: 47)

Several recent contributions engage the literatures on resistance and subaltern agency in development studies and urban studies (Boudreau et al., 2009; Marcuse, this volume; Yiftachel, this volume), and it is worth juxtaposing these approaches more systematically for the sake of articulating a perspective appropriate to a radical planning praxis committed to pursuing the right to the city.

In critical development studies, the extensive writings of political scientist James Scott offer the canonical theory of subaltern resistance under conditions of socioeconomic domination (see especially Scott, 1990). Through ethnographic and archival research in peasant societies of Southeast Asia, Scott identifies the "hidden transcripts," or offstage discourses, through which subordinate groups express a critique of the powerful, as well as their "infrapolitics" – the footdragging, gossip, and other subversive actions that take place beyond the visible spectrum of political practice (see Scott, 1987, 1990). Urban theorist Michel de Certeau, develops a comparable approach to considering how outward public accommodation can mask subversion in the context of everyday urban life (1984 [1980]). For de Certeau the operative concept is "tactics," guileful manoeuvres and tricks performed in the cracks of elite power, by which the weak temporarily stretch the limits imposed by dominant systems.

But the differences between the two approaches are important for our purposes of developing normative planning theory. Working in the Gramscian tradition of cultural politics, Scott (1987) sees infrapolitics and hidden transcripts – "weapons of the weak" – as the foundational form of politics, the roots of more overt, collective social mobilizations. De Certeau's contribution to resistance studies formed part of the post-modernist, post-Marxist turn in urban and cultural studies; as such it refrains from positing an idealized propensity for collective critical consciousness and romantic portrayals of subalterns as essentially morally good political subjects. The focus on consumption in de Certeau's work offers nuanced insights into the ways people occupy positions of marginality – fractured, divisive, certainly not inherently benign, often not harbouring a strong collective identity, and not even necessarily intentionally subversive. But the approach lacks any structural engagement with problems of social justice or any consideration of how tactics interpolate strategy (Ruddick, 1996). Thus, complex and ambiguous questions of political agency arise.

The challenge for planning, I suggest, is to develop a theory of resistance that retains Scott's commitment to political engagement and social transformation, while also acknowledging the significance of de Certeau's and Abu-Lughod's insights about the contradictory nature and political ambiguity of subaltern practices. To this end we may distinguish between "subversion" and "resistance" as overlapping zones of practice (Shakya and Rankin, 2008). "Resistance" itself may be specified as collective, overt actions that are intended to challenge prevailing systems of power. "Subversion," by contrast, denotes more ambiguous political agency – individual, covert instances of nonconformity that engage tactics to get as much as possible out of a constraining situation. Crucially, subversion may be unintentional, just the outcome of people trying to get by – support families, repay debts, meet social obligations, and so on (much as Boudreau et al. (2009) and Yiftachel (this volume) describe for participation by marginalized groups in political action – domestic workers in Los Angeles and Bedouin Arabs in Beersheba, Israel/Palestine, respectively). The subversive agency lies in the ways in which people put dominant cultural productions into their own moral and social frame of reference. At the same time it would seem reasonable to suggest that marginalized people may not possess the concepts with which to transpose this mode of agency into a fully formed critique of neoliberal urbanism (Hall, 1996). Nor are subversions inherently progressive; they may reinforce existing social hierarchies. On the other hand, subversions reveal fissures and weak points in the dominant apparatus, exposing the fragility of hegemony. And in some cases they can have long-term, destabilizing effects.

How might these distinctions help to inform a postcolonial ethics of planning that is accountable to marginalized groups and aims to engage people's agency in progressive ways? A first order of accountability might be to learn to read the "hidden transcripts," "infrapolitics" and tactics that convey nonconformity and contradictory consciousness in *both* its covert and overt forms – a mode of "listening" that rests not on other people's capacity to participate in liberal democratic venues but on the skills and the will of the planner as organic intellectual (cf. Forester, 1989). It then becomes possible to recognize subversion as "a diagnostic of power" (Abu-Lughod, 1990) – as conveying important information about the political rationalities of specific planning regimes as well as the conditions of peoples' lives. The small-scale initiatives of ordinary citizens to build a composting toilet out of cob construction in a Toronto public park, for example, can expose the rigidity of planning protocols designed fundamentally to appease the owners of private property. Non-participation by new-immigrant entrepreneurs in the opportunities afforded by Business Improvement Districts, again in Toronto, one of the most so-called "multicultural" cities in the world, reveals the fragmenting effects of devolving responsibility for local economic development onto populations that are differentially capable and endowed (Rankin, 2008). For radical planning praxis, such diagnostics uncover points of the profession's complicity with neoliberal urbanism in everyday professional practice. They also provide an imperative to respond not by judging or punishing deviance or non-participation, but by viewing subversive behavior as a window on the conditions people face and re-evaluating planning action accordingly.

Transnational feminism, critical reflexivity, solidarity

A second order of accountability to marginalized groups must broach the challenge of catalyzing collective critical consciousness among those engaged in individual subversive practice. Under what conditions might those in marginalized social locations come to recognize the arbitrary foundations of prevailing systems of exclusion as well as interests in common with those who are differently marginalized? This is the question Peter Marcuse poses with respect to groups experiencing material deprivation and emotional discontent in the current political–economic conjuncture: how could these groups find common cause *against* a profit-oriented capitalist world order and *for* a generalized right to the city? To consider what role planners might play in facilitating such circumstances it is necessary to consider two key contributions that transnational feminism has made to critical development studies. First, the orientation in transnational feminism toward critical reflexivity can go a long way toward bringing a principle of relational comparison (Hart, 2004, 2006) into planning praxis in a more reflexive way than is commonly found in Gramscian cultural politics (for a discussion of reflexivity from a critical theory perspective, see also Brenner, this volume). Second, feminist perspectives introduce procedural questions in a way that does not bracket out difference (as can be found in so much of the literature on communicative action in planning theory, see Goonewardena and Rankin, 2004), but engages it politically.

Planning theory shares with social science and humanistic disciplines a "turn" toward cultural concerns and explanations in the post-socialist age, and in this the question of difference figures prominently. In planning a plethora of publications emerged in the 1990s celebrating cultural diversity and hybridity as resources for critique and transformation (Sandercock, 1998a, 1998b, 2003; Healey, 1992, 1997). In response to these developments, I would like to suggest that planning theory would do well to heed the cautions offered by feminist philosopher Nancy Fraser who develops a theory of justice that engages a politics of recognition in conjunction with a politics of redistribution (see Fraser, 1997). Her argument goes like this: socioeconomic difference demands practices of redistribution which aim to eliminate difference; cultural difference demands practices of recognition which aim to valorize difference; injustices arise from both forms of difference – as maldistribution and misrecognition – and the challenge is to find remedies that support both redistribution and recognition; many remedies on the contrary exacerbate one form of injustice while trying to alleviate another – as with redistributive programs that stigmatize the poor or multi-culturalist policies that balkanize them (Fraser, 1997; Bannerji, 2000). The latter dynamic is particularly pertinent for postmodernist planning theory, which has increasingly turned away from state-based modes of redistributive planning in favor of civil society as the appropriate terrain on which to build a "postmodern utopia" (Sandercock, 2003) rooted in a politics of "making sense together while living differently" (Healey, 1992). What emerges in practice is little more than mainstream multiculturalism within which difference is aestheticized – voided of its political–economic determinants, depoliticized and presented as a palatable spectacle for consumption and commodification (Goonewardena and Kipfer, 2006).[4] The problem with most formulations of cultural diversity in planning theory, then, is that they ignore the socioeconomic base of so much cultural difference (Goonewardena and Rankin, 2004; Goonewardena and Kipfer, 2006).[5]

Clearly, planning needs strategies which confront both cultural and socio-economic in/justice simultaneously, as indeed Marcuse's formulation of the separate registers of deprivation and discontent also suggests. Fraser (1997) offers a further insight that can also be useful in this regard: actually-existing remedies for injustice can operate either in an affirmative register – leaving undisturbed the underlying structural frameworks that generate inequitable outcomes – or in a transformative one – correcting inequitable outcomes precisely by restructuring the underlying generative framework. A theory of justice (and thus a normative planning theory) must advocate transformative rather than merely affirmative strategies for redistribution, recognition, and encounter. Transformative redistribution may seem increasingly elusive in an era of neoliberal urbanism but it is easy enough to imagine – as socialism or other governmental forms that would resocialize the economy and create alternative (to capitalist) modes of surplus appropriation. Transformative recognition, which Fraser conceptualizes as "deconstruction" or changing the structures of valuation that underlie prevailing understandings of cultural difference, has been relatively poorly elaborated in planning theory.

In this regard I want to mention an extraordinary book called *Playing with Fire* written as a collaboration involving women development workers in India and geographer Richa Nagar (2006). As the Sangtin Writers (*sangtin* being Hindi for "solidarity"), they recount a process of their collective political conscientization where, in relating to one another their experiences, they come to recognize how they have each had to "drag the institutions" of patriarchy, capitalism, and castism with them differently – in some cases resisting them, in some cases reproducing them, in some cases strategically inhabiting them. The stories here are poignant – about the day-to-day joys and sorrows experienced by the women of the collective, as children, young daughters-in-law, mothers, and NGO workers. But the transformative moment arises only when the women collectively come to recognize how their modes of collaboration in development practice have overlooked their different relationships to oppression and in so doing have deepened those oppressions and compromised their shared mission of women's development and empowerment. Recognition of their mutual implication in the intersectionality of caste, class, and gender oppressions then forges a solidarity among the Sangtin Writers that enables them to collectively challenge class-based injustices within their own development organization, and ultimately to catalyze an entire social movement rethinking of the nature of expertise within the women and development sector in India.

How might this account inform a practice of "cultural deconstruction" in conjunction with a transformative politics of redistribution? Three key domains of practice emerge rooted in the fundamental feminist principle that change begins "at home" with everyday practice and experience (Martin and Mohanty, 1986). The first has to do with historicizing experience and reflexively querying positionality in order to educate oneself about one's own experiences in relation to the histories of others who are the beneficiaries of planning action, as well as one's implication in those relational histories (Abu-Lughod, 1998; Razack, 2007; Mohanty, 2003; Roy, 2006). It is here that Hart's principle of relational comparison can infuse planning praxis in a more reflexive way – demanding that we understand difference in terms of historical relationality and accountability rather than as static, embodied categories, and experience as constructed and relational, rather than as purely personal or visceral. Historicizing difference in this way creates possibilities for the second domain of practice, building solidarities across difference out of which can emerge stronger theorizations of universal concerns. Finally, new modes of political agency might be forged. The solidarities arising from a reflexive, interpersonal "relational comparison" themselves constitute a social change process, insofar as they involve the formation of new political subjects able to engage in critical activism.

How can this engagement with feminist theory inform the initial query: Under what conditions do those who are oppressed in particular socio-spatial arenas develop a critical consciousness of hegemonic processes and mobilize together to change their situation? Confronting the complex question of subaltern agency offered some analytical resources for distinguishing among different modes of consciousness. It was necessary, however, to broach issues of cultural difference – and specifically the articulation of a politics of recognition with a politics of redistribution – in order to conceive a role for planning in catalyzing the conditions for collective action. The insights of transnational feminism suggest that a planning action rooted in reflexively querying positionality might play such a catalytic role and help build the political constituencies needed for claiming the right to the city.

The challenge of reflexivity and the praxis of collaboration across seemingly intractable differences may seem to pose an onerous responsibility upon planners. But the challenge is imperative for the sake of harnessing "diversity" to the critique of actually-existing-globalization. A praxis of collaboration produces critiques that are potentially more potent than those that might be formulated exclusively within planning institutions or planning academia – substantively because they encompass knowledge situated in experience, and procedurally because they build a political base for social change. It also holds out the possibility that reflexive practice might produce an immanent critique of those planning institutions themselves, exposing the gaps between the principles of justice and empowerment they promote and the work practices and modes of relationality that they exhibit in practice. At the very least, a praxis of collaboration requires a shift in the criteria for judgment. Good planning theory must not just accurately and authentically represent the exclusions of the neoliberal city or strategically articulate the rights people must have to access and participate in urban life. What is equally significant politically is the possibility for theory-making to constitute individual and collective agency in the service of critical activism.

Notes

1 For comments on earlier drafts of this paper, heartfelt thanks go to Neil Brenner, Martin Danyluk, Stephanie Gris, Peter Marcuse, and Margit Mayer. Thanks also go to Kathryn White and Rachel Silvey for support and inspiration on the themes of this chapter.
2 Gillian Hart (2001) offers the useful distinction here between "big D" Development as intentional practice (e.g. poverty alleviation programs) and "little d" development as immanent process (capitalism and the uneven development).
3 Some exceptions in this regard include the work of Peter Marcuse, as well as that of Ananya Roy, Oren Yiftachel, Kanishka Goonewardena, Faranak Miraftab, Jennifer Robinson, Vanessa Watson, and others who have explicitly confronted the politics of postcoloniality in relation to radical planning theory.
4 See Roy and AlSayyad's 2004 book on informality and the "aestheticization of poverty" from which this argument is formulated.
5 Anthropologist Jim Ferguson argues similarly in his book *Global Shadows: Africa in the Neoliberal World Order* (2007) that however much the "alternative modernities" cele-brated by anthropologists might aim to treat diverse cultural traditions as "equal," real and lived cultural differences typically index membership in unequal social groups.

References

Abu-Lughod, L. (1990) "The romance of resistance: tracing transformations of power through Bedouin women," *American Ethnologist*, 17(1), pp. 41–55.

Abu-Lughod, L. (1998) "Feminist longings and postcolonial conditions," in L. Abu-Lughod (ed.), *Remaking Women: Feminism and Modernity in the Middle East*, Princeton: Princeton University Press, pp. 1–31.

Bannerji, H. (2000) *The Dark Side of the Nation*, Toronto: Canadian Scholars' Press.

Baran, P. (1957) *The Political Economy of Growth*, New York: Monthly Review Press.

Blomley, N. (2004) *Unsettling the City*, New York: Routledge.

Boudreau, J., Boucher, N., and Liguori, M. (2009) "Taking the bus daily and demonstrating on Sunday: reflections on the formation of political subjectivity in an urban world," *City*, 13(2–3), pp. 336–46.

Chatterton, P. (2005) "Making autonomous geographies: Argentina's popular uprising and the Movimiento de Trabajadores Descocupados (Unemployed Workers Movement)," *Geoforum*, 36(5), pp. 545–61.

Crush, J.S. (1995) *Power of Development*, London and New York: Routledge.

De Certeau, M. (1984 [1980]) *The Practice of Everyday Life*, Berkeley: University of California Press.

Escobar, A. (1995) *Encountering Development*, Princeton: Princeton University Press.

Fanon, F. (1967) *Black Skin, White Masks*, trans. by C.L. Markmann, New York: Grove Press.

Faulk, K.A. (2008) "If they touch one of us, they touch all of us: cooperativism as a counterlogic to neoliberal capitalism," *Anthropological Quarterly*, 81(3), pp. 579–614.

Ferguson, J. (1990) *The Anti-Politics Machine*, Cambridge: Cambridge University Press Archive.

Ferguson, J. (2007) *Global Shadows: Africa in the Neoliberal World Order*, Durham, DC: Duke University Press.

Forester, J. (1989) *Planning in the Face of Power*, Berkeley: University of California Press.

Frank, A.G. (1967) *Capitalism and Underdevelopment in Latin America*, New York: Monthly Review Press.

Fraser, N. (1997) *Justice Interruptus: Critical Reflections on the "Postsocialist" Condition*, New York: Routledge.

Goonewardena, K. and Kipfer, S. (2006) "Spaces of difference: reflections from Toronto on multiculturalism, bourgeois urbanism and the possibility of radical urban politics," *International Journal of Urban and Regional Research*, 29(3), pp. 670–8.

Goonewardena, K. and Rankin, K.N. (2004) "The desire called civil society: a contribution to the critique of a bourgeois category," *Planning Theory*, 3(2), pp. 117–49.

Hall, S. (1996) "When was 'the post-colonial'? Thinking at the limit," in C. Chambers and L. Curti (eds), *The Post Colonial Question*, New York: Routledge, pp. 242–60.

Hanieh, A. (2008) "Making the world's poor pay: the economic crisis and the global south," *The Socialist Project E-Bulletin*, 155, [online]. Available at http://www.socialistproject.ca/bullet/bullet155.html (accessed March 2, 2009).

Hart, G. (2001) "Development Critiques in the 1990s: *Culs de Sac* and Promising Paths," *Progress in Human Geography*, 25(4), pp. 649–58.

Hart, G. (2002) *Disabling Globalisation*, Berkeley: University of California Press.

Hart, G. (2004) "Geography and development: critical ethnographies," *Progress in Human Geography*, 28(1), pp. 91–100.

Hart, G. (2006) "Denaturalizing dispossession: critical ethnography in the age of resurgent imperialism," *Antipode*, 38(5), pp. 977–1004.

Harvey, D. (1996 [1985]) "On planning the ideology of planning," in S. Campbell and S. Fainstein (eds), *Readings in Planning Theory*, Boston, Mass.: Blackwell, pp. 176–97.

Harvey, D. (2003) *The New Imperialism*, Oxford: Oxford University Press.

Harvey, D. (2007 [1982]) *The Limits to Capital*, 2nd edition, New York: Verso.

Healey, P. (1997) "Traditions of planning thought," Chapter 1 in *Collaborative Planning: Shaping Places in Fragmented Societies*, Vancouver: UBC Press, pp. 7–30.

Healey, P. (1992) "Planning through debate: the communicative turn in planning theory," *Town Planning Review*, 63(2), pp. 143–62.

Kandiyoti, D. (1991) "Islam and patriarchy: a comparative perspective," in N.R. Keddie and B. Baron (eds), *Women in Middle Eastern History*, New Haven, Conn.: Yale University Press, pp. 23–42.

Kandiyoti, D. (1994) "Identity and its discontents: women and the nation," in P. Williams and L. Chrisman (eds), *Colonial Discourse and Post-colonial Theory: A Reader*, New York: Columbia University Press, pp. 363–91.

Katz, C. (2001) "On the grounds of globalization: a topography for feminist political engagement," *Signs*, 26(4), pp. 1213–34.

Katz, C. (2004) *Growing Up Global*, Minneapolis: University of Minnesota Press.

Lefebvre, H. (2003) *The Urban Revolution*, trans. R. Bononno, Minneapolis: University of Minnesota Press.

Li, T. (2007) *The Will to Improve: Governmentality, Development and the Politics of Development*, Durham, DC: Duke University Press.

Marcuse, P. (2004) "Said's orientalism: a vital contribution today," *Antipode*, 36(5), pp. 809–17.

Martin, B. and Mohanty, C.T. (1986) "Feminist politics: what's home got to do with it?" in T. de Lauretis (ed.) *Feminist Studies, Critical Studies*, Indianapolis: Indiana University Press, pp. 191–212.

Massey, D. (1994) *Space, Place, and Gender*, Minneapolis: University of Minnesota Press.

Mohanty, C.T. (2003) *Feminism without Borders: Decolonizing Theory, Practicing Solidarity*, Durham, DC: Duke University Press.

Morphet, S. (2004) "Multilateralism and the non-aligned movement: what is the global south doing and where is it going?" *Global Governance*, 10(3), pp. 517–37.

North, P. and Huber, U. (2004) "Alternative spaces of the Argentinazo," *Antipode*, 36(5), pp. 964–84.

Peck, J. (2005) "Struggling with the creative class," *International Journal of Urban and Regional Research*, 29(4), pp. 740–70.

Prudham, S. (2009) "Pimping climate change: Richard Branson, global warming, and the performance of green capitalism," *Environment and Planning A*, 41(7), pp 1594–613.

Rankin, K.R. (2009) "Microfinance and the financial crisis," paper delivered at a conference titled "*Understanding the Financial Crisis: Critical Approaches, Alternative Policies*," University of Toronto, January 30, 2009.

——— (2008) "Commercial change in Toronto's Downtown West neighborhoods," research paper 214, Toronto: Cities Centre, University of Toronto.

Razack, S. (2007) "Stealing the pain of others: reflections on Canadian humanitarian responses," *The Review of Education, Pedagogy and Critical Analysis*, 29, pp. 375–94.

Robinson, J. (2006) *Ordinary Cities*, London: Routledge.

Roweis, S.T. and Scott, A.J. (1981) "The urban land question," in M. Dear A.J. Scott (eds), *Urbanization and Urban Planning in Capitalist Society*, New York: Methuen, pp. 123–57.

Roy, A. and AlSayyad, N. (2004) *Urban Informality: Transnational Perspectives from the Middle East, South Asia and Latin America*, Lanham, Md.: Lexington Books.

Roy, A. (2006) "Praxis in the time of empire," *Planning Theory*, 5(1), pp. 7–29.

Ruddick, S. (1996) *Young and Homeless in Hollywood*, New York: Routledge.

Said, E. (1978) *Orientalism*, London: Vintage Books.

Sandercock, L. (1998a) "Framing insurgent historiographies for planning," in L. Sandercock (ed.) *Making the Invisible Visible*, Berkeley: University of California Press, pp. 1–33.

Sandercock, L. (1998b) *Towards Cosmopolis*, New York: Wiley.

Sandercock, L. (2003) *Cosmopolis II: Mongrel Cities of the Twenty-first Century*, New York: Continuum.

Sangtin Writers and Nagar, R. (2006) *Playing with Fire: Feminist Thought and Activism through Seven Lives in India*, Minneapolis: University of Minnesota Press.

Scott, J.C. (1987) *Weapons of the Weak*, New Haven, Conn.: Yale University Press.

Scott, J.C. (1990) *Domination and the Arts of Resistance*, New Haven, Conn.: Yale University Press.

Scott, J.C. (1998) *Seeing Like a State*, New Haven, Conn.: Yale University Press.

Shakya, Y.B. and Rankin, K.N. (2008) "The politics of subversion in development practice: an exploration of microfinance in Nepal and Vietnam," *Journal of Development Studies*, 44(8), pp. 1181–202.

Silvey, R. and Rankin, K. (2011) "Development Geography: Critical Development Studies and Political Geographic Imaginaries," *Progress in Human Geography*, 35(2), pp. 1–9.

Wacquant, L. (2009) *Punishing the Poor*, Durham, NC: Duke University Press.

Writers, S. and Nagar, R. (2006) *Playing with Fire: Feminist Thought and Activism through Seven Lives in India*, Minneapolis: University of Minnesota Press.

8

ASSEMBLAGES, ACTOR–NETWORKS, AND THE CHALLENGES OF CRITICAL URBAN THEORY[1]

*Neil Brenner, David J. Madden,
and David Wachsmuth*

The field of urban studies is today confronted with significant theoretical, conceptual, epistemological, and methodological challenges. As was arguably also the case in the late 1960s and early 1970s, when debates on the "urban question" (Castells 1979 [1972]; Harvey 1973; Lefebvre 2003 [1970]) destabilized inherited Chicago School ontologies, established paradigms of urban research now appear increasingly limited in their ability to illuminate contemporary urban changes and struggles. As in previous rounds of debate on the urban question, the source of the contemporary "urban impasse" (Thrift 1993) is the restless periodicity and extraordinary slipperiness of the urban phenomenon itself. Even more so than in the 1970s, urbanization today "astonishes us by its scale; its complexity surpasses the tools of our understanding and the instruments of practical capacity" (Lefebvre 2003 [1970]: 45). A decade ago, Soja (2000: xii) aptly captured this state of affairs:

> It may indeed be both the best of times and the worst of times to be studying cities, for while there is so much that is new and challenging to respond to, there is much less agreement than ever before as to how best to make sense, practically and theoretically, of the new urban worlds being created.

Some strands of urban studies, particularly those rooted in the professionalized routines of academic disciplines, remain mired in outdated research agendas that only partially grasp the contours and consequences of emergent urban transformations. Fortunately, however, there is elsewhere considerable intellectual adventurousness on display, as urbanists across the social sciences and humanities, as well as in the cognate fields of planning, architecture, and design, grapple creatively with the tasks of deciphering the rapidly transforming world-wide landscapes of urbanization (Roy 2009; Sassen 2000; Soja 2000; Taylor 2004). Among the key agendas for such researchers is to investigate the evolving positionalities of cities – and urban landscapes more generally – within such large-scale, long-term trends as geoeconomic restructuring, market-driven regulatory change (including both privatization and liberalization), the world-wide flexibilization/informalization of labor, mass migration, environmental degradation, global warming, the creative destruction of large-scale territorial landscapes, and the intensification of polarization, inequality, marginalization, dispossession, and social conflict at all spatial scales.

In the face of these developmental dynamics, we believe there is an increasingly urgent need to rethink our most basic assumptions regarding the site, object, and agenda of "urban" research. The "urban question" famously posed four decades ago by Lefebvre, Harvey, and Castells remains as essential as ever, but it arguably needs to be *reposed*, in the most fundamental way, in light of early twenty-first-century conditions. In other words: do we *really* know, today, where the "urban" begins and ends, or what its most essential features are, socially, spatially, or otherwise? At minimum, the town/country divide that once appeared to offer a stable, even self-evident, basis for delineating the specificity of city settlements, today appears increasingly as an ideological remnant of early industrial capitalism that maps only problematically onto contemporary urban processes (Wachsmuth 2010). More radically still, a case can be made that Lefebvre's (2003 [1970]) postulate of an incipient process of "complete" or "planetary" urbanization is today being actualized in practice (see also Schmid, this volume; Brenner, this volume). Despite pervasive sociospatial unevenness and persistent territorial inequality, the entire fabric of planetary settlement space is now being both extensively and intensively urbanized (Madden 2011; Schmid 2005; Soja and Kanai 2005). In the face of this prospect, and especially given the unprecedented pace, scale, and volatility of contemporary worldwide urbanization, it seems essential to consider whether inherited concepts and methods for understanding and transforming cities remain at all adequate to contemporary conditions. Quite simply, the oft-repeated mantra that a global "urban transition" has recently occurred due to the apparent fact that over half of the world's population now lives within cities does not even begin to capture the intellectual, representational, and political complexities associated with the contemporary global urban condition.

It is, we would argue, certainly not a moment for intellectual modesty or a retreat from grand metanarratives, as advocated by some poststructuralists a few decades ago. On the contrary, from our point of view, there is today a need for ambitious, wide-reaching engagements – theoretical, concrete, *and* practical – with the planetary dimensions of contemporary urbanization across diverse places, territories, and scales. Yet, it would be highly problematic to suggest that any single theory, paradigm, or metanarrative could, in itself, completely illuminate the processes in question.[2] Theoretical ambition need not be pursued through the construction of reductionist, simplifying frameworks; the task, rather, is to create concepts and methods that *open up* new questions and horizons – for both thought and action. Accordingly, in contrast to some of the more closed models of urbanism that prevailed during the highpoints of Chicago School urban research in the 1930s through the 1960s and, in a different way, within the structuralist Marxisms of the 1970s, urban theory today must embrace, and even celebrate, a certain degree of eclecticism. Today, more than ever, there is a need for a collaborative, open-minded spirit to prevail in urban studies, particularly among those scholars who are most committed to confronting the daunting challenges of reconceptualizing the parameters and purposes of this research field. When such scholars make divergent or opposed theoretical, conceptual, and methodological choices, useful opportunities may emerge for all those involved to clarify the stakes of such choices, and their possible implications.

In that spirit, our goal in this chapter is to evaluate critically an influential new tendency in urban studies associated with actor–network theory (invariably referred to by its initials, ANT), an approach to social science developed by Bruno Latour, Michel Callon, John Law, and their followers (Latour 2005; Law and Hassard 1999; for a critical overview see Castree 2002). Although ANT has influenced several important strands of contemporary urban thinking (see, for example, Amin 2007; Amin and Thrift 2002; Graham and Marvin 2001), its most dedicated proponents in urban studies have presented the concept of "assemblage" as its analytical centerpiece and as the basis for a new ontology of the urban (Farías 2010; Farías and Bender 2010; Latour and Hermant 2006 [1998]; McFarlane 2011a, b). Accordingly, throughout this chapter we refer to this newly emergent ANT-based strand of urban studies generically as "assemblage urbanism."[3]

Given our remarks above regarding the situation of contemporary urban studies, we welcome the efforts of assemblage urbanists to transcend certain inherited, intellectually constraining assumptions regarding the urban question, and on this basis, to open up new methodological windows into the various forms in which that question is being posed and fought out today. However, as we detail below, our own orientations for such an endeavor diverge considerably from those that have to date been proposed by the major authors advancing an ANT-based framework. While *empirical* and *methodological* applications of the assemblage concept have generated productive insights in various strands of urban studies by building on political economy, we suggest that the *ontological* application favored by several contemporary ANT urbanists contains significant drawbacks. In explicitly rejecting concepts of structure in favor of a "naïve objectivism" (Sayer 1992), this approach deprives itself of key explanatory tools for understanding the sociospatial "context of contexts" (Brenner et al. 2010) in which urban spaces and locally embedded social forces are positioned. Relatedly, such approaches do not adequately grasp the ways in which contemporary urbanization continues to be shaped and contested through the contradictory, hierarchical social relations and institutional forms of capitalism. Finally, the normative foundations of such approaches are based upon a decontextualized standpoint rather than an immanent, reflexive critique of actually existing social relations and institutional arrangements. These considerations suggest that assemblage-based approaches can most effectively contribute to critical urban theory when they are linked to theories, concepts, methods, and research agendas derived from a reinvigorated geopolitical economy.

In outlining these arguments, our intention is not to attempt to patrol the boundaries of theoretical innovation in urban studies. Rather, we hope to contribute to a broader dialogue regarding the challenges of contemporary critical urban theory, and the most appropriate strategies for confronting them. Because we do not believe there is any single correct "solution" to such challenges, our questions are intentionally open-ended. The goal, we repeat, is to open up horizons for thought and action, and through collective dialogue, investigation, and debate, to begin to explore these horizons.

Actor–networks, assemblages, and the urban question

During the last decade, ANT has become an increasingly prominent stand of poststructuralist social theory and social science (Castree 2002). Known as the "sociology of associations" or "sociology of translation," ANT grew out of science studies, and sees all things, as its name implies, as networks of actors. Networks are understood to be working alliances of multifarious composition. Actors, or actants, are simply things that act – anything that resists or impacts other things. Actants in ANT, famously, are human as well as non-human, animate as well as inanimate, material as well as ideational, large and small, those things called "natural," "cultural," and "social." As Latour (1993: 163) puts it in an early programmatic statement, ANT starts from the ideas of irreducibility and infinite combinability: "Nothing can be reduced to anything else, nothing can be deduced from anything else, everything may be allied to everything else." Despite the word "theory" in its name, ANT actually contains several intertwined layers of argumentation. It is a method for framing field sites and research objects, and more generally, it is an argument for what sociology should and should not be. Perhaps most generally, it entails both an ontology and an epistemology – an account of what exists and a linked set of claims about how to generate valid knowledge about the latter.

Ostensibly opposed to essentialism of any sort, ANT sees the world as immanent, contingent, heterogeneous, and ontologically flat, disclosing no other levels, final explanations, or hidden core. ANT is thoroughly constructivist, although it has a number of criticisms to make of the standard language of social construction (Latour 2003). Whereas mainstream social constructionism asserts the social character of what appears "natural," ANT calls into question the society/nature division itself, rejecting the analytical coherence of both the "social" and the "natural" as categories. The prime ANT injunction that flows from this position is "to follow the actors themselves" (Latour 2005: 12). This should be done, actor–network theorists argue, while staying true to the "principle of generalized symmetry" (Callon 1986), which holds that human and nonhuman actors should be described using common concepts.

It is impossible to point to a specific set of empirical findings or conclusions to be drawn from actor–network studies, although diverse aspects of human/ nonhuman networks have been investigated. For example, studies in this tradition often seek to uncover the heterogeneity and multiplicity of ostensibly well-integrated networks. Actants often attempt to make themselves "obligatory passage points" which are necessary for the continued success of the network. When all is running correctly, networks often manage to "black box" themselves, hiding their artificiality under the illusion of integrality. This black boxing only becomes apparent when networks fall apart due to quasi-entropic decay, strategic missteps, or intentional refusal on the part of one or another actant.

While ANT has influenced diverse urban thinkers during the past decade (see Amin 2007; Amin and Thrift 2002; Bender 2010; Graham and Marvin 2001), its core arguments have been most systematically imported into urban studies via the concept of assemblage, which has recently been presented as the conceptual lynchpin and ontological foundation for a radically new approach to the urban question (Farías 2010; Farías and Bender 2010; McFarlane 2011a, b). Although the word "assemblage" is sometimes used in a descriptive sense, to describe the coming together of heterogeneous elements within an institution, place, built structure, or art form (Madden 2010a; Sassen 2006), its philosophical usage in English derives principally from the work of Deleuze and Guattari (1987 [1980]). Their concept of *agencement* was translated as assemblage by Brian Massumi in the English version of *A Thousand Plateaus* published in the late 1980s, and this convention was generally preserved through a "loose consensus" among subsequent translators and commentators (Phillips 2006: 108). But, as Marcus and Saka (2006) demonstrate, the concept of assemblage has subsequently been mobilized in multifarious ways, only some of which are explicitly Deleuzoguattarian (as in, for instance, the influential work of De Landa 2006). Aside from the heterodox, broadly Deleuzoguattarian strand of architectural theory and criticism developed as of the late 1980s in the now-defunct journal *Assemblages*, the dominant inflection of assemblage thinking in contemporary urban studies is most tightly associated with the tradition of ANT, as summarized above.

On a descriptive level, an assemblage-theoretical approach to the urban question entails viewing the city as a bundle of networks. As Bender (2010: 316) explains:

> The metropolis … is made up of networks – human networks, infrastructural networks, architectural networks, security networks; the list could be almost infinite, and they are not confined by a circumferential boundary

> … Networks agglomerate into assemblages, perhaps a neighborhood, or a crowd at a street festival, or a financial center like Wall Street in New York City. The metropolis, then, is an assemblage of assemblages.

In itself, however, the emphasis on the networked character of contemporary urbanism is relatively uncontroversial, and resonates with any number of approaches to urban studies that have not been influenced by ANT (see, for example, Castells 1993; Cronon 1991; Taylor 2004). However, beyond this general emphasis on urban networks, the major advocates for an ANT-based approach to urbanism have larger ambitions, proposing an extremely wide array of ontological, analytical and/or normative purposes to which the concept of assemblage may be applied, and attributing to it some rather impressive explanatory capabilities (Farías 2010; McFarlane 2011a, b).

The recent work of McFarlane (2011a, b) illustrates this tendency. Rather than disavowing the idea's mercurial nature, McFarlane affirms it, noting that the term assemblage is "increasingly used in social science research, generally to connote indeterminacy, emergence, becoming, processuality, turbulence, and the sociomateriality of phenomena" (McFarlane 2011a: 206). According to McFarlane (2011a), as a motif within urban studies, the notion of assemblage is primarily focused upon "sociomaterial transformation" (206), "grammars of gathering, networking and composition" (207), and "interactions between human and nonhuman components" that as "co-functioning" can be "stabilised" or "destabilised" through "mutual imbrication" (208). Assemblages are processual relationships that "cannot be reduced to individual properties alone" (208). Assemblage thinking highlights processes of composition and recognizes diverse forms of human and nonhuman agencies – while striving to avoid reification, reductionism, and essentialism. In this sense, McFarlane contends, assemblage thinking has an "inherently empirical focus" (209). As urban theory, assemblage thought asks how urban "things" – including, quite appropriately, the urban itself – are assembled, and how they might be disassembled or reassembled.

McFarlane (2011a) outlines three specific contributions that he sees the assemblage approach making to critical urban theory. First, he sees assemblage thought as an empirical tool for engaging in thick description of "urban inequalities as produced through relations of history and potential" (2011a: 208). He suggests that by paying detailed, ethnographic attention to processes of assemblage, urbanists may better understand how actually existing urban situations are constituted and, on this basis, may be better equipped to imagine alternatives to those situations. Second, McFarlane notes, assemblage thought can help attune researchers to the problematic of materiality – that is, to the significance and purported agency of materials themselves, "whether [they] be glossy policy documents, housing and infrastructure materials, placards, banners and picket lines, new and old technologies, software codes, credit instruments, money, commodities, or of course the material conditions of urban poverty, dispossession and inequality" (215). By "distributing agency across social and material" entities, such that both human and non-human forms of agency may be considered coevally, "assemblage thinking diversifies the range of agents and causes of urban inequality, while potentially multiplying the spaces of critical intervention" (219). Third, McFarlane sees the assemblage idea as activating a more general critical "imaginary" (219) and political sensibility containing a distinctive image of the desirable city-to-come. While noting the risk of the idea's co-optation by various elitist or oppressive projects, McFarlane offers "cosmopolitanism" as a "normative political project of urban assemblage" (219).

For McFarlane (2011a), then, the concept of assemblage is said to open up a variety of new urban questions – or at least new orientations towards inherited urban questions – as well as new sites of analysis, methodological tools, targets of critique, and political visions (see also Farías 2010). As an illustration of the potential of this discourse, McFarlane briefly discusses his own work on urban informality in Mumbai, where he observed "the crucial role that various materialities play in the constitution and experience of inequality, and in the possibilities of a more equal urbanism" (McFarlane 2011a: 216). Here, marginalized city dwellers "recycle" the city by gathering "materials … from local construction debris, riverbeds, manufacturing waste, or patches of tree cover" (216). Unequal access to infrastructure and other resources is shaped by the state and various other powerful actors. For some activists, the material networks of the city can be used as objects of resistance and tools of protest, generating a subaltern form of urban cosmopolitanism or "one-worldism" (220) that militates for a new urban commons. McFarlane suggests that an assemblage-based urban imaginary can produce "new urban knowledges, collectives and ontologies" (221) that invoke and pursue new rights to the city among the most marginalized city-dwellers.

Insofar as they enable urban scholars to question outdated categories and epistemologies, to demarcate new objects and terrains of urban research, and to highlight the political stakes and consequences of previously taken-for-granted dimensions of urban life, the perspectives advanced by proponents of assemblage urbanism open up some important new prospects onto the urban question. The question, however, is how much and what type(s) of intellectual and political work the concept of assemblage, and the mode of analysis associated with it, can plausibly be expected to accomplish. For, despite their contributions, we believe that assemblage-theoretical approaches to the urban question remain too broadly framed, at times even indeterminate, to realize their proper analytical potential. And this very indeterminacy, we argue below, amounts to a retreat from precisely those political positions and analytic vantage points that enable urban theory to engage in the project of critique.

In our view, the power of assemblage-theoretical approaches to urban studies may be most productively explored when their ontological dimensions are eschewed entirely, and when, correspondingly, their conceptual, methodological, empirical, and normative parameters are circumscribed rather precisely. Against interpretations of this concept as the basis for "transforming the very ground of urban studies" and as "an alternative ontology for the city" (Farías 2010: 8, 13), we argue here for a narrower, primarily methodological application. The concept of assemblage is most useful, we contend, when it is mobilized in the context of a broader repertoire of theories, categories, methods, and research agendas that are not derived internally from ANT. In elaborating these concerns, we are particularly interested in addressing what we view as the highly ambiguous status of political economy, and the concept of capitalism itself, within assemblage-theoretical approaches to urban studies. This issue is closely intertwined with the still larger question of the goals, tools, and techniques of critical urban theory.

The spectre of political economy

At the outset, it might appear that radical urban political economy and the new theoretical idioms associated with assemblage urbanism could coexist and even mutually transform each other's methodological orientations, descriptive categories and objects of analysis (Castree 2002; Farías and Graham 2010; McFarlane 2011a). However, an often unstated but nonetheless pervasive agenda of assemblage urbanism seems to be a redescription of urban processes, transformations, and inequalities with almost no reference to the key concepts and concerns of radical urban political economy – for instance, capital accumulation, class, property relations, land rent, exploitation, commodification, state power, territorial alliances, growth coalitions, structured coherence, uneven spatial development, spatial divisions of labor, and crisis formation, among others. Most frequently, this displacement is often simply *enacted*, accompanied by neither an explicit critique of political–economic concepts nor a clear argument for how assemblage-based approaches might better illuminate the dimensions of contemporary urbanization to which such concepts have generally been applied. Yet the social relations, institutions, structural constraints, spatio-temporal dynamics, conflicts, contradictions, and crisis tendencies of capitalism do not vanish simply because we stop referring to them explicitly – especially under conditions in which their forms are undergoing deep metamorphoses, they arguably still require explicit theorization and analysis in any critical account of the contemporary global urban condition.

At the same time, however, among many of the major practitioners of assemblage-based approaches, there appears to be considerable confusion as to whether such categories should be mobilized to deepen, extend, transform, or supersede the analysis of capitalist structurations of urbanization. Does the term "assemblage" describe a type of hitherto-neglected *research object* to be studied in a broadly political–economic framework – thus generating a political economy of urban assemblages? Is assemblage analysis meant to extend the *methodology* of urban political economy in new directions, thus opening up new interpretive perspectives on dimensions of capitalist urbanization that have been previously neglected or only partially grasped? Or, does the assemblage approach offer a new *ontological* starting point that displaces or supersedes the intellectual project of urban political economy?

Following from these questions, Table 8.1 identifies what we view as the three major articulations between assemblage thinking and political economy that have been developed in the recent urban studies literature. The rows in the table represent both the core logical positions in terms of how this articulation may be understood and the major analytical strategies that have

TABLE 8.1 Articulations of assemblage analysis and urban political economy

	Relation to urban political economy	*Exemplary research foci*	*Representative authors*
Level 1: empirical Political economy of urban assemblages.	Assemblage is understood as a specific type of research object that can be analyzed through a political–economic framework and/or contextualized in relation to historically and geographically specific political–economic trends.	Technological networks within and among cities (e.g. electrical grids); intercity networks; assemblages of territory, authority, and rights.	Ali and Keil (2010); Graham (2010); Graham and Marvin (2001); Sassen (2006).
Level 2: methodological Assemblage as a methodological extension of urban political economy.	Assemblage (often in conjunction with the closely related concept of as "metabolism") is presented as a methodological orientation through which to investigate previously neglected dimensions of capitalist urbanization. The core concerns of critical urban political economy remain central, but are now extended into new realms of inquiry.	The production of socionatures; infrastructural disruption or collapse; flows of energy, value, substances, microbes, people, ideas.	Bender (2010); Graham (2010); Heynen et al. (2006); Kaika (2005).
Level 3: ontological Assemblage as an "alternative ontology for the city" (Farías 2010: 13).	Assemblage analysis displaces the investigation of capitalist urban development and the core concerns of urban political economy (e.g. the commodification of urban space, inequality and power relations, state intervention, polarization, uneven spatial development).	Urban materialities and infrastructures, including buildings, highways, artifacts, informal settlements, communications systems, traffic flows, inter-urban networks.	Farías (2010); Latham and McCormack (2010); Latour and Hermant (2006 [1998]); McFarlane (2011a, b); Smith (2010); Tironi (2010).

been adopted in practice by researchers who have been influenced, in varying degrees, by ANT.

The first row demarcates the use of assemblage as a distinctive type of research object within urban political economy. Sassen (2006), for example, uses assemblage to refer to a particular historical interrelation of territory, authority, and rights, while Graham and Marvin's *Splintering Urbanism* conceives of infrastructure networks as "sociotechnical *assemblies* or 'machinic complexes' rather than as individual causal agents with identifiable 'impacts' on cities and urban life" (Graham and Marvin 2001: 31, original emphasis). These authors do not draw on assemblage thinking as an ontological foundation, but instead mobilize certain propositions from such approaches in order to reframe concrete urban analysis on an *ad hoc* basis. Consequently, authors working in this tradition tend to analyze the assemblages they have identified along more or less political–economic lines – in effect, they are engaged in a political economy of urban assemblages.

In the second row, assemblage thinking generates a predominantly methodological approach that builds upon urban political economy while extending and reformulating some of its core elements and concerns, in part through selective appropriations from ANT. This procedure parallels the ways in which the cognate field of urban political ecology has used the idea of "metabolism" to capture the interconnected yet fluid dynamics that characterize the production of urban socionatures (Gandy 2004; Heynen et al. 2006; Kaika 2005; Swyngedouw 2006). As these authors note, the metabolism concept has a long heritage in political economy (Foster 2000) as well as obvious affinities with some strands of contemporary assemblage analysis. Urban political ecology explicitly connects these two positions, using the concept of metabolism and selected methodological tools from ANT to build upon and reformulate the treatment of socionatures within critical urban political economy. For these authors, the concept of metabolism serves simultaneously as a way to characterize objects of inquiry (particularly urban socionatural networks) and also as an explanatory and theoretical device. On the one hand, the metabolic circulation of matter causes it to become "'enrolled' in associational networks that produce qualitative changes and qualitatively new assemblages" (Swyngedouw 2006: 26). On the other, urbanization itself is retheorized as "a metabolic circulatory process that materializes as an implosion of socio-natural relations, a process which is organized through socially articulated networks and conduits" (Swyngedouw 2006: 35). Such arguments amount to a substantial rethinking of urban theory, but it is one that retains the central concerns, concepts and analytical orientations of political economy within a methodologically expanded framework.

Finally, in the third row, ANT subsumes the entire conceptual apparatus and explanatory agenda of urban studies. Authors working in this manner look to ANT as a way to reconceptualize the fundamental character of the (urban and non-urban) social world. The urban process is now conceived as a huge collection of human and nonhuman actants within a flat ontology devoid of scalar or territorial differentiations. Ways of understanding the city based on concepts from political economy or spatial sociology are considered illegitimate or at least bracketed; categories of sociospatial structuration such as scale and territory are understood primarily as data to be interpreted rather than as theoretical, explanatory, or interpretive tools (Smith 2010). In this way, the *problematique* of assemblage formation comes to function as a radical ontological alternative to political economy: assemblage is no longer merely a conceptual motif, an empirical tool or a methodological orientation, but the ontological basis for an alternative mapping of the urban social universe. Representative examples of this position include Latour and Hermant's (2006) study of Paris, Farías' (2010) programmatic statement on ANT and urban studies, several contributions to Farías and Bender's (2010) edited volume on assemblage urbanism (Latham and McCormack 2010; Smith 2010; Tironi 2010), and recent articles by McFarlane (2011a, b).

Distinguishing between these three broad ways of articulating assemblage thought and political economy should clarify that there is no single "assemblage urbanism," and therefore no coherence to arguing for or against the concept of assemblage in general terms. At the same time, as the preceding discussion indicates, we believe that some of its specific manifestations are more defensible than others. Specifically, we would argue that the merits of levels 1 and 2 – the empirical and methodological levels – have been convincingly demonstrated in the urban studies literature, and certainly warrant further elaboration in future theoretical and substantive research. These strands of assemblage thinking, through selective appropriation of insights from ANT and other sources, have productively amended and continue to transform the research focus and theoretical orientation of urban political economy. However, for reasons we now elaborate, we are much more skeptical regarding the possible contributions of analyses conducted on level 3 of Table 8.1 – assemblage as an ontology – particularly with regard to their relevance to the project of *critical* urban studies around which the present book is framed.

An ontology of naïve objectivism

A notable strength of ANT is its attention to the multiple materialities of socionatural relations. Additionally, approaches derived from ANT have pioneered the analysis of how and when nonhuman actants, from buildings and building materials to infrastructural grids, forms of energy, and even weather systems, may generate significant forms of "reactive power" or agency.[4] But without recourse to political economy or to another theoretical framework attuned to the structuration of urban processes (whether by capital, states, territorial alliances, or social movements), an ontologically inflected appropriation of assemblage analysis confronts serious difficulties as a basis for illuminating the contemporary global urban condition.

In particular, the descriptive focus associated with ontological variants of ANT and assemblage urbanism leaves unaddressed important explanatory questions regarding the broader (global, national, and regional) structural contexts within which actants are situated and operate – including formations of capital accumulation and investment/disinvestment; historically entrenched, large-scale configurations of uneven spatial development, territorial polarization, and geopolitical hegemony; multiscalar frameworks of state power, territorial alliance formation, and urban governance; and the politico-institutional legacies of sociopolitical contestation around diverse forms of dispossession, deprivation, and discontent. In explicitly rejecting concepts of structure as remnants of an outdated model of social science explanation, or in simply ignoring the questions raised by such concepts, ontological approaches to assemblage analysis deprive themselves of a key explanatory tool for understanding the sociospatial, political–economic, and institutional contexts in which urban spaces and locally embedded social forces are positioned. Within such a framework, moreover, there is no immanent principle for distinguishing relevant and irrelevant actants, whether of a human or nonhuman nature. As Bender (2010: 305) suggests, such approaches risk engaging in an "indiscriminate absorption of elements into the actor–network" with the "effect of levelling the significance of all actors." The result of this procedure is a metaphysics of association based on what Sayer (1992: 45) has elsewhere aptly termed a "naïve objectivism." This mode of analysis presupposes that the "facts" – in this case, those of interconnection among human and nonhuman actants – speak for themselves rather than requiring mediation or at least animation through theoretical assumptions and interpretive schemata.

The intellectually problematic and politically neutralizing consequences of such positions are very much in evidence within recent applications of ANT to the investigation of contemporary urban development. Consider, for example, McFarlane's (2011a) account of informal housing in Mumbai, which offers a broad description of housing arrangements in a marginalized neighborhood of that city. The experience of poverty and inequality, he shows, is crucially mediated through the building materials and infrastructural elements that comprise the built environment. On this basis, McFarlane appropriately suggests that the materiality of informal housing in Mumbai deserves more analytical attention due to its important role in mediating the everyday experience of poverty. As he indicates, housing is "both *made* and *edited*, in contexts of deeply unequal resources and precarious lives" (McFarlane 2011a: 216; original emphasis). But does the thick description of assemblages offered in his analysis suffice to illuminate the specific forms of inequality and deprivation under investigation? To what degree does an assemblage–theoretical analysis help explain the underlying contexts and causes of urban sociospatial polarization, marginalization, and deprivation, whether in Mumbai or elsewhere?

While McFarlane's rendering of assemblage may shed valuable light on the dynamics of making and editing, and on the broad spectrum of socionatural processes involved in the latter, it is precisely the "contexts of deeply unequal resources and precarious lives" (McFarlane 2011a: 216) that are bracketed in his analysis. This bracketing is problematic insofar as it leaves underspecified the question of what historical geographies of land ownership, dispossession, deprivation, and struggle generated and entrenched the unequal distribution of resources and the precarious life-conditions in the areas under discussion. After all, many of the details McFarlane gives of informal housing materiality – found construction materials, vertical modular construction, accreted rather than planned built forms, and the like – would equally well describe socio-material conditions within other zones of informality and marginalization in mega-cities across Latin America, the Middle East, and South Asia (Roy and AlSayyad 2004). Yet the shantytowns and squatting settlements within each of these global regions are positioned in quite different ways within any number of broader historical geographies of power – for instance, global divisions of labor and circuits of capital investment/disinvestment; legacies of colonial and postcolonial statecraft; modes of geopolitical control, subordination, and inter-vention by imperial powers and global institutions such as the World Bank and the International Monetary Fund; differential patterns of agro-industrial transformation and associated rural–urban migration; state strategies to shape urbanization through speculative real estate development, infrastructural production, housing policy, and slum clearance; and diverse forms of social movement mobilization at various spatial scales. In an analytical maneuver that is characteristic of this strand of assemblage analysis, contexts such as these are scarcely mentioned, much less theorized or systematically analyzed. However, without a sustained account of this *context of context*, the analysis remains radi-cally incomplete.[5]

While the assemblage ontology focuses on the materials themselves, it is essen-tial to consider the political–economic structures and institutions in which they are embedded. In McFarlane's account of informal housing in Mumbai, the build-ing materials are highly polysemic and promiscuous. Graffiti paint, unadorned brick, dirt in backyard gardens, corrugated metal – each can be an expression of precarious impoverishment or of dominating, aestheticized prosperity, depend-ing upon its context. In a telling illustration of his conception of sociomaterial assemblages, McFarlane (2011a: 218–19) asks, "what [is] the particular agency of Richard Florida's sleek powerpoint presentations of the 'creative city' […] when set against existing local urban plans?" But is the real issue here the sociomaterial-ity of PowerPoint, or the structural contexts and institutional locations in which this technique is deployed? It is quite possibly the case that policy entrepreneurs who are aligned with real estate developers will use sleek PowerPoint presenta-tions while, say, working-class housing activists will not. But what matters about the PowerPoint presentations are the projects of ideological legitimation towards which they are mobilized; the words, phrases, and narratives they contain have a non-arbitrary relationship to historically and geographically situated, differen-tially empowered social movements, forces, alliances, and institutions. Substitute a PowerPoint presentation focused on the purported benefits of the creative class or a state-subsidized office tower for one focused on residential displacement, political disempowerment, or labor rights, and it is an assemblage with a very different form and function, even though it may appear identical in purely material terms. An empirical focus on such assemblages could be helpful in unraveling certain aspects of such dynamics, but this would entail exploring their contested instrumentalities within the political–economic and institutional forcefields mentioned above. By contrast, an ontological conception of assemblage substitutes for such considerations a naïve objectivism that is difficult to reconcile with the basic questions about power, inequality, injustice, politicization, struggle, and mobilization that lie at the heart of critical urban theory (Marcuse, Chapter 3 this volume; Soja 2010).

Actuality, possibility, and critique

The major theoretical proponents of ANT have been explicitly hostile to what they see as "critical sociology" (Latour 2004, 2005; Madden 2010b); this generalization applies to significant strands of assemblage analysis as well. Perhaps for this reason, those branches of critical urban studies that have incorporated assemblage thinking into their intellectual apparatus have tended to marry it to more explicitly political–economic approaches which supply a strong dose of critical energies. The authors whose work is positioned on the empirical and methodological levels of Table 8.1 thus rely extensively upon urban political economy to ground the critical elements of their respective analyses. By contrast, advocates of ANT argue explicitly against critical social science – as in Latour's (2005: 12) account of his own position as "harsh and … truly obnoxious" towards critical sociology, seeing in the "infatuation with emancipation politics" (2005: 52) a renunciation of a properly scientific attitude.[6]

At the same time, other urbanists, including several authors discussed or mentioned above, have sought explicitly to link assemblage analysis to critical urban theory. Thus Farías (2010: 3) extols ANT's "radicality," while McFarlane (2011a: 210) argues that assemblage urbanism is concerned with the relationship between the actual and the possible, and specifically, with the question of how formations of the urban might "be assembled differently." The issue, however, is not *whether* the actual and the possible are related, but *how*. Here, we believe, there is a fundamental distinction worth making between the dialectical approaches to critique that often motivate political–economic analyses and those derived internally from assemblage analysis. In McFarlane's account, which formulates a position that is common to much assemblage thinking, potentiality is exteriority: any assemblage may, in principle, be decomposed and a new one formed by incorporating new sociomaterialities; these new elements, which lie outside the extant assemblage, supply the possibility for different arrangements of human and nonhuman relations. This possibility is ontologically presupposed rather than being understood as historically specific or immanent to the sociomaterial relations under investigation. Although McFarlane (2011a) introduces fruitful normative categories such as the right to the city, the commons, and cosmopolitanism, the assemblage approach appears to operate primarily by describing alternatives unreflexively, as abstract possibilities that might be pursued. In our view, however, this approach offers no clear basis on which to understand how, when, and why particular critical alternatives may be pursued under specific historical–geographical conditions or, more generally, why some possibilities for reassemblage are actualized over and against others that are suppressed or excluded.

Critical theory, by contrast, holds that capitalism and its associated forms contain the possible as an immanent, constitutive moment of the real – as contradiction and negation (Lefebvre 2009; Marcuse 1990 [1960]; Ollman 2003; Brenner, this volume). Specific historical structures produce determinate constraints on the possibility for social transformation, as well as determinate, if often hidden or suppressed, openings for the latter. Within such a framework, the impulse towards critique is not an external, normative orientation or a mental abstraction, but is embedded within, and enabled by, the same structures, contradictions, and conflicts that constrain the realization of what might be possible. From this point of view, a key challenge for any critical theory is to explicate reflexively its own conditions of emergence – not simply as a matter of individual opposition or normative commitment, but in substantively historical terms, as an essential moment within the same contradictory, dynamically evolving social totality it is concerned to decipher and ultimately to transcend (Marcuse 1990 [1960]; Postone 1993).

When we compare this immanent, dialectical conception of negation with the externalist normative orientation of assemblage theory, we also find a difference in political outlook. Despite its stated goal of expanding our understanding of agency into nonhuman realms (as argued forcefully by Bennett 2010), ontological forms of assemblage thinking are not well equipped to identify the specific human agents and social forces that might engage in the process of social transformation. Instead, a passive-voice politics prevails in which assemblages and actor–networks are anonymously, almost mysteriously destabilized or dismantled. McFarlane argues, for example, that "urban assemblages are structured through various forms of power relation and resource and information control" (2011a: 210). But if this is the case, it is essential to explore *who* (or *what*, as the case may be) is doing the structuring to whom. In a world animated by passive interactions among actants, the forcefield of struggle among diverse sociopolitical agents battling to appropriate and reappropriate urban space (Marcuse, this volume; Mayer, this volume; Harvey with Wachsmuth, this volume) is relegated to the background. While there are strands of assemblage theory that have successfully articulated powerful, even radical, visions of alternative futures (see Bennett 2010), it seems impossible to pursue the latter without engaging with the fundamentally *political* dimensions of human agency. In short, perhaps because of the inert way that they interpret the world, ontological variants of assemblage thought do not offer much guidance for how to change it.

Reassembling assemblage urbanism?

In a recent assessment of contemporary urban theory, Roy (2009: 2) argues that "it is time to blast open [the] theoretical geographies" associated with late twentieth-century urban studies and thus to produce new "geographies of theory" that can come to terms with the contemporary global urban moment in both North and South. Our goal in this chapter has been to assess the degree to which various emergent strands of assemblage–theoretical urban studies can contribute to this wide-ranging intellectual and political task. While we are broadly sympathetic to the empirical research agendas and methodological orientations that have been opened up through such discussions, we have expressed a range of reservations regarding the more ontologically grounded applications of assemblage urbanism, which offer no more than a partial, if not misleading, basis for critical urban studies.

By way of conclusion, we want to reiterate the need for intellectual adventurousness and experimentation in this research field, and to underscore the useful ways in which, despite its blind spots, the debate on urban assemblages is productively contributing to such impulses. It is certainly not the case that critical urban theory, as it currently exists, has ready-made analytical tools for deciphering the rapidly transforming condition of worldwide urbanization. Without a doubt, the questions posed by assemblage urbanists – for instance, regarding human/nonhuman interfaces, networked interdependencies, and the production of sociomaterial infrastructures – are essential ones, and they certainly deserve serious, sustained exploration in future forays into the urban question.

Today, new forms of urbanization and world making (Lefebvre 2009; Roy 2009; Schmid, this volume) co-constitute each other in a volatile context of geoeconomic, geopolitical, and environmental crisis, ongoing market-driven regulatory experimentation, and intense sociopolitical contestation at all spatial scales. As the urban condition becomes worldwide, it does so not through the absolute territorial expansion of an inherited urban object, but rather through the emergence of qualitatively new, genuinely planetary forms of urbanization in which a densely if unevenly urbanized fabric of sociospatial and political–economic interconnectivity is at once stretched, thickened, and continually redifferentiated across places, territories, and scales, throughout the space of the entire globe. This becoming worldwide (in Lefebvre's (2009) terms, *mondialisation*) of the urban is not simply a quantitative expansion of city populations or an outwards extension of inherited metropolitan jurisdictional boundaries, but has entailed a qualitative *reconstitution* of the urban itself in which a host of inherited spatial oppositions – for instance, city/suburb; urban/rural; core/periphery; North/South; society/nature – are being fundamentally rearticulated, if not superseded entirely.

In light of these unprecedented trends and transformations, a key challenge for any critical approach to urban theory is to generate a new lexicon of spatial difference through which to grasp emergent forms of uneven geographical development in ways that capture their tendential, planet-wide systematicity as well as their equally pervasive volatility, precariousness, and mutability. Could it be precisely here, faced with the extraordinary challenge of mapping a worldwide yet internally hierarchized and differentiated urban ensemble (Lefebvre 2003 [1970]), that the conceptual and methodological gesture facilitated through assemblage approaches becomes most productive? Whereas the concept of "structured coherence" presented by Harvey (1989) confronted this problem at the scale of an individual urban region, there is today a need to decipher the variegated articulations among the disparate spatial, political-institutional, and environmental elements of the emergent planetary urban configuration.[7] This task is especially urgent given the continued circulation of ideological projections of world capitalism as a heterarchical, cosmopolitan, flexible, borderless, and creative "world order" that mask an entrenched repressive agenda of (reconstituted) market fundamentalism, accumulation by dispossession, and deepening environmental catastrophe. Because assemblage thinking opens up the prospect for thinking space as a relationally overdetermined plenitude (Bender 2010; see also Massey 2005), it may offer useful insights for exploring and mapping these emergent geographies of dispossession, catastrophe, and possibility – but, as we have suggested, such an exercise will be most effective when it is linked systematically to the intellectual tools and political orientations of critical geopolitical economy.

Even though the urban process has taken on new forms in its planetary mode, we have suggested that it remains a fundamentally capitalist urban process. In our view, this dimension of urbanization – mediated, of course, through state institutions, diverse social forces, and systemic crisis tendencies at all spatial scales – figures crucially in producing and reproducing contemporary geographies of deprivation, dispossession, and marginalization, both within and among urban regions throughout the world. Consequently, for urban theory to remain intellectually and politically relevant, it must continue to explore the prospects for the critique of capitalism that are immanent within contemporary sociospatial relations across places, territories, and scales.

The approach to critical urban theory proposed here is not grounded upon a transhistorical metaphysics of labor, a structuralist framing of the urban, or a class-theoretical reductionism. Instead, through a spiral movement involving a combination of theoretical reflection, methodological experimentation, and concrete research forays (Sayer 1992), it reflexively subjects its own explanatory apparatus to continual re-evaluation and reconstitution in light of the ongoing trends, contradictions, and struggles associated with contemporary forms of sociospatial restructuring. Against this background, a key challenge is to link the analytical and methodological orientations of assemblage urbanism to the tools of geopolitical economy in ways that contribute to a genuinely critical approach to ongoing planetary urban transformations – one that is attuned not only to local specificities and contingencies, but also to broader, intercontextual dynamics, trajectories, and struggles (Roy 2009). In short, the present age demands neither the inert categories of traditional urban theory nor the conceptual quietude to which some strands of assemblage thought are unfortunately susceptible. Instead, we must continue to seek out the ingredients – intellectual *and* political – for a critical imagination that is oriented towards the possibility of a radically different type of worldwide space (Lefebvre 2009). This, in turn, requires forging a critical urban theory that is capable of grasping our global urban world "by the root" (Marx 1963: 52).

Notes

1 This chapter builds upon Brenner et al. (2011) and Madden (2010b). We are grateful to Colin McFarlane for stimulating our work on this topic and for comradely dialogue on the issues at stake. We also thank Hillary Angelo for helpful discussions of critical urban theory.
2 This claim applies not only to the contemporary conjuncture. urbanization has always been an "open system" insofar as its basic patterns and consequences cannot be derived from any single theoretical framework or causal mechanism (Sayer 1992).
3 We argue below, however, that it is both possible and desirable to mobilize the assemblage concept in a manner that does not entail an embrace of ANT and its associated ontologies.
4 Although she does not link it specifically to the field of urban studies, Bennett (2005, 2010) offers an impressively clear philosophical and sociological explication of this position. Latour (2005) offers the more standard reference point on these matters in the context of a rather sweeping critique of twentieth-century social science.
5 For a discussion of the need for consideration of the "context of context" in relation to neo-Foucauldian analyses of neoliberalization see Brenner et al. (2011). Our critique of the ontological strand of assemblage urbanism here closely parallels this argument.
6 See Madden (2010b) on ANT's contradictory merger of a neo-positivist insistence on the separation of science from politics with its anti-positivist recognition that the knowing subject interacts with the known object.
7 On this problem in general, see Ong and Collier (2004); with reference to Harvey's work, see Brenner (1998); see also Sassen (2006) on the nature of the "global."

References

Ali, S. H. and Keil, R. (2010) "Securitizing network flows: infectious disease and airports," in S. Graham (ed.), *Disrupted Cities*, New York: Routledge, pp. 111–30.
Amin, A. (2007) "Re-thinking the urban social," *CITY*, 11, 1, pp. 100–14.
Amin, A. and Thrift, N. (2002) *Cities*, London: Polity.
Bender, T. (2010) "Reassembling the city: networks and urban imaginarie," in I. Farías and T. Bender (eds), *Urban Assemblages: How Actor–Network Theory Changes Urban Research*, New York: Routledge, pp. 303–23.
Bennett, J. (2010) *Vibrant Matter*, Durham, NC: Duke University Press.
Bennett, J. (2005) "The agency of assemblages and the North American blackout," *Public Culture*, 17, 3, pp. 445–65.

Brenner, N. (1998) "Between fixity and motion: accumulation, territorial organization and the historical geography of spatial scales," *Environment and Planning D: Society and Space*, 16, 5, pp. 459–81.

Brenner, N., Madden D. J., and Wachsmuth, D. (2011) "Assemblage urbanism and the challenges of critical urban theory," *CITY*, 15, 2, pp. 225–40.

Brenner, N., Peck, J., and Theodore, N. (2010) "Variegated neoliberalization: geographies, modalities, pathways," *Global Networks*, 10, 2, pp. 182–222.

Callon, M. (1986) "Some elements of a sociology of translation: domestication of the scallops and the fishermen of St. Brieuc Bay," in J. Law (ed.) *Power, Action and Belief: A New Sociology of Knowledge?* London: Routledge, pp. 196–223.

Castells, M. (1993) *The Rise of the Network Society*, Cambridge, MA: Blackwell.

Castells, M. (1979 [1972]) *The Urban Question: A Marxist Approach*, trans. by A. Sheridan, Cambridge, MA: MIT Press.

Castree, N. (2002) "False antitheses? Marxism, nature and actor–networks," *Antipode*, 34, 1, pp. 111–46.

Cronon, W. (1991) *Nature's Metropolis*, New York: Norton.

De Landa, M. (2006) *A New Philosophy of Society: Assemblage Theory and Social Complexity*, New York: Continuum.

Deleuze, G. and Guattari, F. (1987 [1980]) *A Thousand Plateaus*, trans. by B. Massumi, Minneapolis, MN: University of Minnesota Press.

Farías, I. (2010) "Introduction: decentering the object of urban studies," in I. Farías and T. Bender (eds), *Urban Assemblages: How Actor–Network Theory Changes Urban Research*, New York: Routledge, pp. 1–24.

Farías, I. and Bender, T. (eds) (2010) *Urban Assemblages: How Actor–Network Theory Changes Urban Research*, New York: Routledge.

Farías, I. and Graham, S. (2010) "Interview with Stephen Graham," in I. Farías and T. Bender (eds) *Urban Assemblages: How Actor–Network Theory Changes Urban Research*, New York: Routledge, pp. 197–203.

Foster, J. B. (2000) *Marx's Ecology*, New York: Monthly Review Press.

Gandy, M. (2004) "Rethinking urban metabolism: water, space and the modern city," *CITY*, 8, 3, pp. 363–79.

Graham, S. (2010) "When infrastructures fail," in S. Graham (ed.), *Disrupted Cities*, New York: Routledge, pp. 1–26.

Graham, S. and Marvin, S. (2001) *Splintering Urbanism*, New York: Routledge.

Harvey, D. (1989) *The Urban Experience*, Baltimore: Johns Hopkins University Press.

Harvey, D. (1973) *Social Justice and the City*, Baltimore: Johns Hopkins University Press.

Heynen, N., Kaika, M., and Swyngedouw, E. (eds) (2006) *In the Nature of Cities*, New York: Routledge.

Kaika, M. (2005) *City of Flows*, New York: Routledge.

Latham, A. and McCormack, D. (2010) "Globalizations big and small: notes on urban studies, actor–network theory, and geographical scale," in I. Farías and T. Bender (eds) *Urban Assemblages: How Actor–Network Theory Changes Urban Research*, New York: Routledge, pp. 53–72.

Latour, B. (2005) *Reassembling the Social*, New York: Oxford University Press.

Latour, B. (2004) "Why has critique run out of steam? From matters of fact to matters of concern," *Critical Inquiry*, 30, pp. 225–48.

Latour, B. (2003) "The promises of constructivism," in D. Idhe and E. Selinger (eds), *Chasing Technoscience: Matrix for Materiality*, Bloomington: Indiana University Press, pp. 27–46.

Latour, B. (1993) *We Have Never Been Modern*, Cambridge, MA: Harvard University Press.

Latour, B. and Hermant, E. (2006 [1998]) *Paris: Invisible City*, trans. by L. Carey-Libbrecht. Available online at http://www.bruno-latour.fr/livres/viii_paris-city-gb.pdf (accessed July 6, 2011).

Law, J. and Hassard, J. (eds) (1999) *Actor Network Theory and After*, Cambridge, MA: Blackwell.

Lefebvre, H. (2009) *State, Space, World*, trans. by S. Elden, N. Brenner and G. Moore, Minneapolis, MN: University of Minnesota Press.

Lefebvre, H. (2003 [1970]) *The Urban Revolution*, trans. by R. Bononno, Minneapolis, MN: University of Minnesota Press.

Madden, D. (2011) *City Becoming World: Nancy and Lefebvre on Global Urbanization*, unpublished manuscript.

Madden, D. (2010a) "Revisiting the end of public space: assembling the public in an urban park," *City & Community*, 9, 2, pp. 187–207.

Madden, D. (2010b) "Urban ANTs: a review essay," *Qualitative Sociology*, 33, 4, pp. 583–90.

Marcus, G. and Saka, E. (2006) "Assemblage," *Theory, Culture & Society*, 2–3, pp. 101–6.

Marcuse, H. (1990 [1960]) "A note on dialectic," in A. Arato and E. Gebhardt (eds), *The Frankfurt School Reader*, New York: Continuum, pp. 444–51.

Marx, K. (1963) *Early Writings*, ed. and trans. by T. B. Bottomore, New York: McGraw-Hill.

Massey, D. (2005) *For Space*, London: Sage.

McFarlane, C. (2011a) "Assemblage and critical urbanism," *CITY*, 15, pp. 2204–224.

McFarlane, C. (2011b) "The city as assemblage: dwelling and urban space," *Environment and Planning D: Society and Space*, forthcoming.

Ollman, B. (2003) *Dance of the Dialectic*, Chicago: University of Illinois Press.

Ong, A. and Collier, S. (eds) (2004) *Global Assemblages*, Cambridge, MA: Blackwell.

Phillips, J. (2006) "Agencement/Assemblage," *Theory, Culture & Society*, 2–3, pp. 108–9.

Postone, M. (1993) *Time, labor and social domination*, New York: Cambridge University Press.

Roy, A. (2009) "The 21st century metropolis: new geographies of theory," *Regional Studies*, 43, 6, pp. 819–30.

Roy, A. and AlSayyad, N. (eds) (2004) *Urban Informality: Transnational Perspectives from the Middle East, Latin America and South Asia*, Lanham, MD: Lexington Books.

Sassen, S. (2006) *Territory, Authority, Rights: From Medieval to Global Assemblages*, Princeton: Princeton University Press.

Sassen, S. (2000) "New frontiers facing urban sociology at the millennium," *British Journal of Sociology*, 51, 1, pp. 143–59.

Sayer, A. (1992) *Method in Social Science*, 2nd edition, London and New York: Routledge.

Schmid, C. (2005) "Theory," in R. Diener, J. Herzog, M. Meili, P. de Meuron, and C. Schmid (eds), *Switzerland: An Urban Portrait*, 1, Zurich: Birkhaeuser, pp. 163–224.

Smith, R.G. (2010) "Urban studies without 'scale': localizing the global through Singapore," in I. Farías and T. Bender (eds), *Urban Assemblages: How Actor–Network Theory Changes Urban Research*, New York: Routledge, pp. 73–90.

Soja, E. (2010) *Seeking Spatial Justice*, Minneapolis, MN: University of Minnesota Press.

Soja, E. (2000) *Postmetropolis*, Cambridge, MA: Blackwell.

Soja, E. and Kanai, M. (2005) "The urbanization of the world," in R. Burdett and D. Sudjic (eds), *The Endless City*, London: Phaidon, pp. 54–89.

Swyngedouw, E. (2006) "Metabolic urbanization: the making of cyborg cities," in N. Heynen, M. Kaika, and E. Swyngedouw (eds) *In the Nature of Cities*. New York: Routledge, pp. 21–40.

Taylor, P. J. (2004) *Global Urban Network*, New York: Routledge.

Tironi, M. (2010) "Gelleable spaces, eventful geographies: the case of Santiago's experimental music scene," in I. Farías and T. Bender (eds), *Urban Assemblages: How Actor–Network Theory Changes Urban Research*, New York: Routledge, pp. 27–52.

Thrift, N. (1993) "An urban impasse?" *Theory, Culture & Society*, 10, 2, pp. 229–38.

Wachsmuth, D. (2010) "City as ideology," paper presented at the Association of American Geographers annual conference, April 14, Washington DC.

9

THE NEW URBAN GROWTH IDEOLOGY OF "CREATIVE CITIES"

Stefan Krätke

Not all urban theory is useful in promoting "cities for people." Some such theories in fact serve as an ideological justification for cities for "profit" and reinforce the right to the city of those that already have it. Richard Florida's (2004, 2005) influential theory of the creative class is an example of the latter that, despite its conceptual and methodological weaknesses, has received an affirmative reception among regional scientists and politicians in North America and Europe.

Florida's theory is perceived as containing very clear theoretical statements: it is perceived as giving appropriate empirical evidence on these theoretical statements; and it is thought to deliver a practical recipe for policy intervention. Particularly on the urban level, Florida's concept is viewed as a "message of hope" and as guidance for future successful economic development. Basically, Florida has presented a new urban growth theory claiming that we can expect successful economic development in those cities or regions where the members of the "creative class" like to live and where they are concentrating; thus we should make cities and regions attractive particularly for this stratum of people. Florida deals with the specific attraction factors of cities for the members of the creative class and recommends that political decision makers supply a high standard of living and leisure amenities for the creative class, since this group is said to attract further creative activities and is thus of great importance to future regional development (Fritsch and Stützer, 2007: 15).

This theory has been popularized among politicians and social scientists in Germany (Berlin-Institut, 2007) as well as in other European countries, across North America, and beyond. Based on a more comprehensive investigation (Krätke, 2011), this chapter presents a critique of Florida's theory of the "creative class," extending the critique offered by Peck (2005). In his earlier analysis,

Peck (2005: 740) focused on the urban policy dimension of the new-found cult of urban creativity, emphasizing that the contemporary spread of creativity strategies perfectly works with "the grain of extant neoliberal development agendas, framed around interurban competition, gentrification, middle-class consumption, and place-marketing" (see also Keil, this volume). In this chapter, I extend Peck's critique by considering the problems within Florida's concept of class and capitalist development and his correspondingly inadequate recognition of various essential factors of urban economic development. Additionally, I question Florida's view of cities as "cauldrons of creativity" by suggesting that many cities (particularly global cities) today are better characterized as cauldrons of neoliberal gangs' actions to ruin the world economy. The rise of what I term the "dealer class" in contemporary capitalism has led to the invention of diverse new weapons of financial mass destruction, which have been deployed quite effectively at the expense of people all over the world. Against this background, the catchy thesis of a "creative age" (Florida and Tinagli, 2004) acquires a highly ambiguous, if not blatantly ideological, meaning.

The chapter is organized in two parts. First, I criticize Florida's theory due to its affirmative concept of the creative class and of the current regime of capitalist development. Second, I consider the impact of the so-called "creative industries" on urban economic growth, emphasizing in particular the proliferation of flexibilized labour relations and the extension of gentrification within major cities (on the latter, see also Slater, this volume).

Towards a deconstruction of the "creative class"

Florida's theory presents a concept of social classes which is predominantly based on arbitrary assignments and which supports a self-glorification of the "leading" occupational groups of contemporary capitalism. Among the traditional classes, Florida differentiates the working class, the service class (said to be composed of people with less skilled service sector occupations), and the agricultural class. According to Florida, a new class, which he labels the "creative class," has today become decisive for economic development.

In introducing this notion, Florida does not consider the difficulties of accurately delimiting different types of creative activity (Howkins, 2001), a problem that is seriously exacerbated in contemporary industrial societies by the fact that today nearly all occupational groups are subject to a certain mix of creative and primarily executive tasks. If a large share of the workers in industrial manufacturing occupations did not possess highly developed tacit knowledge and creative problem-solving capacities in dealing with complex technological systems and organizational procedures, contemporary capitalism would sooner or later run into severe disturbances. Additionally, as Wilson and Keil (2008) have recently pointed out, creativity is also a major survival resource for the working poor in the diverse urban worlds of contemporary capitalism.

According to Florida (2004), the creative class is composed of three different occupational groups. A first group comprises the "supercreative core," which contains natural scientists and engineers, information scientists, economists and social scientists, the medical profession (physicians), architects, academic staff, and related occupations. A second group is called the "bohemians," which comprises the diverse occupational groups in the sphere of arts (writers, visual and performing artists, musicians, designers, etc.) as well as those in a wider sense artistically creative occupations that are active in the sphere of media and entertainment. A third group is branded by Florida as the "creative professionals" and is said to be composed of employees in mostly high skilled occupational groups such as managers, organizational experts, mediators, and brokers. This latter grouping includes the occupations of legal and business consulting, as the management of firms and other organizations, and the professionals of the finance and real-estate business; additionally, it also includes the members of legislative bodies, political functionaries, and skilled professionals and managers of public administration. Florida assigns to the group of creative professionals the function of "supporting" economic development, while the occupations of the supercreative core are said to function as the innovators. The latter group is thus characterized as the driving force behind economic and technological development.

Florida's delimitations of the creative class are highly questionable. It is problematic to classify under the same rubric occupational groups that are engaged in technological research and development activities and the artistically creative occupations of the cultural economy alongside the group of "creative professionals." It is here that Florida transforms his approach into a strongly affirmative or uncritical conception of the contemporary class structure.

In contemporary capitalism, the professionals of the finance and real-estate business do not at all serve to promote knowledge-based economic development. Rather, this occupational group represents what I term a "dealer class" which attempts to profit from a finance-dominated, increasingly speculation driven regime of capitalist development (Harvey with Wachsmuth, this volume). The financial sector no longer has a merely "supporting" function within the capitalist economy; rather it has become the dominating, driving force of a new capitalist model of development, whose influence is spreading to all spheres and subsectors of the economy. The social agents of the contemporary finance-dominated regime of accumulation are indeed continuously creating financial "innovations" and new financial "products," but the latter have served mainly to destabilize economic development in the Western industrialized countries and beyond, and to damage the development potential and innovation capacity of the "real economy" sectors (such as manufacturing industries). Given the extreme destructiveness of contemporary financial markets (Huffschmid et al., 2007), as recently illustrated in the world economic recession that erupted in 2007 and continues to this day (Marcuse, this volume), Florida's classification of financial and real-estate professionals as members of a new "creative class" appears highly ideological. In a nutshell, the dealer economy associated with the neoliberal model of capitalist development is not creative in any meaningful sense of the word; it actually constitutes a serious threat to economic development.

The rise of the dealer class, however, also includes other occupational groups that fall within Florida's category of creative professionals. In a finance-dominated model of capitalist development, the occupational groups of legal and business consulting/management serve decisive functions associated with bringing private sector firms into line with the principles of "shareholder value" and the logic of financial investment deals. Under the pressure of financial investors, the management practices of a dealer economy have spread to the basic manufacturing and service sectors at the expense of far-sighted and innovation-oriented models of business development. With regard to the consulting branch, the creative performance gains envisioned by Florida appear quite dubious if we compare the highly standardized products generated by the prominent market leaders in this field (such as McKinsey) to the creative initiative that is associated with the development of new technologies. Additionally, as Schumpeter (1952) emphasized long ago, only a minority of entrepreneurs and firm managers actually serve as "creative innovators"; the large majority of this social group consists of brave imitators of familiar routines, business models, and product configurations.

Considerable doubt can also be expressed regarding Florida's view of members of the "political class" – legislators, political functionaries, and skilled professionals and leading managers of public administration – as part of the "creative class." This rather fanciful classificatory move fosters an extraordinary depoliticization of the activities, assumptions, and ideologies of political office holders and functionaries within a broader context of neoliberalized class struggle. In the contemporary German context, the purportedly "creative" activities of the political class consist mainly in actively participating in the speculative financial operations of the neoliberal dealer economy. The involvement of various large public financial corporations (*Landesbanken*) of Germany in the contemporary global financial crisis (due to their investment in bundles of sub-prime mortgages in the United States) generated a disastrous financial loss of more than €21 billion. These losses, along with a €480 billion package for preventing the collapse of the entire banking sector, have now been transferred onto the German taxpayers.

The preceding considerations point towards an obvious conclusion: the questionable concept of the "creative class" needs to be disaggregated (Markusen, 2006). The group of "high ranking" professionals in finance, real estate, management, and consulting does not contribute more significantly to regional economic development than the technologically and artistically creative occupations or, for that matter, the economic activities of the working class as a whole. This proposition can be tested empirically by analyzing the impact of diverse occupational groups on various dimensions of regional economic success (Krätke, 2011).

As empirical proof of his theory, Florida (2005) claims to have demonstrated a significant correlation between regional concentrations of his "creative class" aggregate and regional growth in high technology sectors. Yet a statistical correlation does not necessarily entail a causal relationship. In fact, Florida's "creative class" aggregate represents nothing more than a co-presence of quite heterogeneous social and functional groups – but the latter is, by definition, a defining property of nearly all large cities. In such contexts, many statistical correlations between diverse "populations" of the respective territory are detectable – for instance, between the stock of hot-dog stands, high technology firms, drug dealers, financial products dealers, and so forth – but the latter often have no sociological significance of any kind.

For Florida, the high technology sectors are thought to represent a key indicator for successful regional economic development. He does not consider the possibility – which has been investigated in detail by economic geographers (Krätke, 2011) – that cities and regions might also achieve a successful economic development on the basis of quite different sectoral profiles. Indeed, the wealth of regions stems from different economic profiles and development paths. In headquarter cities and financial centres, economic development hinges to a large extent upon the appropriation of wealth that was created through productive activities in other regions. For the populations of cities and regions, the most important indicator of regional economic success is the overall growth of regional employment figures; income distribution and development in different strata of the regions' workforce represent further relevant indicators of economic success. It is only within the framework of neoliberal market ideology that income polarization is not considered harmful to urban and regional economies. More generally, in the long run, regional economic success is dependent on a region's capacity to upgrade its sectoral structure and innovative capabilities (Cooke, 2002).

Creative cities: "poor but sexy"?

The notion of the "creative city" based on flourishing "creative industries" has become attractive to urban political decision makers due to the expectation that a local agglomeration of artistically creative workers and the growth of urban culture industries will have a positive impact on urban economic development and regeneration. This is the reason why Florida's theory of the creative class has been taken up as a "message of hope" in many cities, including established urban centres of the culture industry, as well as cities that are confronted with economic decline in traditional manufacturing and service sectors and associated labor market pressures. Indeed, the culture industry (which represents by far the largest part of so-called creative industries) might be characterized as one of the "leading sectors" of the twenty-first century (Scott, 2000) as changing consumption patterns are fostering a growing demand for cultural products and the culture industry has become the central supplier of "content" for the new media business, the capitalist economy's expanding marketing activities, and the accelerated proliferation of commercial entertainment through the commodification of cultural forms.

However, the concentration of the artistically creative workforce within the urban system is highly selective in spatial terms: only a limited number of specific cities and metropoles can make use of the cultural economy sector as a relevant focus for their development strategy. In recent years, many cities of Europe's old industrial regions (such as Bilbao, Glasgow, and Manchester) have drawn on "cultural strategies" for economic regeneration, including support for the cultural economy sector as well as the extension of cultural facilities and selective "upgrading" of urban built environments. Comparative research does show that cultural strategies can play a supportive role in regenerating cities of old industrial regions, but mainly as an image booster rather than as a job creation machine (Benneworth and Hospers, 2009). The potential capacity of the cultural economy to compensate for shrinking employment opportunities in various "old" industries is limited in quantitative terms; thus no city can rely solely upon the culture industries' growth to sustain its economy. This state of affairs directly contradicts many of the salvational promises made by the "creative city" urban growth ideology.

Let us consider the example of Berlin, which represents a prime centre of creative industries in the German urban system. According to Berlin's government report on the cultural economy (Senatsverwaltung für Wirtschaft, 2008), the city's cultural economy workforce (including employees, entrepreneurs, and self-employed freelancers) amounted to 160,000 persons in 2006 and contained a share of 10 percent of the city's total workforce. In Berlin, then, the cultural economy sector has a comparatively strong share of the urban economy in terms of firm numbers and employment. Yet, with regard to the entire urban economy of the metropolis, it actually represents a rather small "island of growth" alongside various other knowledge-intensive sectors such as biotechnology, medical engineering, and advanced producer services. These islands of growth are situated in a sea of job decline in other sectors, including traditional manufacturing industries and low skilled services. An analysis of data maintained by the Federal Institute for Employment reveals that in Berlin between 1995 and 2005, the total number of employees decreased by 18 percent, which amounts to a loss of 229,000 jobs. This results primarily from a loss of 136,000 jobs in manufacturing occupations and 59,000 jobs in less skilled service occupations. In the same period, the city's cultural economy sector recorded an increase of 5,200 employees (plus 20 percent) – a figure that does not include the increasing number of self-employed freelancers and artists, which comprise approximately 50 percent of the cultural economy's workforce. If the latter group is taken into account, the cultural economy's job growth might be estimated to reach a total of approximately 10,000. Other sectors of employment growth in Berlin were the knowledge-intensive services, which experienced an increase of 48,000 jobs. In quantitative terms, these islands of growth could compensate for just 25 percent of Berlin's total job losses. With regard to the cultural economy sector, the potential for fixing Berlin's overall labour market problem is even more restricted. Notwithstanding the fact that Berlin is a well-established center of the cultural economy, there is no way to expect that the city's economic regeneration could rely primarily on this sector. In comparative perspective, the most important feature of the Berlin case is the mismatch between flourishing creative industries and regional economic growth. The Berlin economy as a whole is comparatively weak even while the creative industries are expanding – in the words of the city's mayor, Berlin is "poor but sexy." Hence, the Berlin case provides a powerful counterargument against Florida's causal claims regarding the relationship between creative industries and urban economic growth.

In contrast to affirmative conceptions of the creative industries' contribution to job growth and urban economic regeneration, it is essential to recognize the widespread prevalence of precarious, "low quality" jobs lacking social safeguards and benefits throughout the so-called creative economy. The creative industries have long assumed a leading role in introducing neoliberalized labor market conditions freed from social protections. Labour relations in these industries are dominated by permanent freelance work, temporary contract work, and one-person companies (Howkins, 2001). The private sector, which accounts for the vast majority of job growth in the "creative economy," prefers these short-term and part-time employment relations. With a view to the flexibilization of labour and the expanding ranks of the self-employed, the culture and media industries can be regarded as forerunners of a quite problematic trend of restructuring. The culture and media industries are characterized by a pronounced polarization between flexible employees with a "privileged status" and flexible workers situated in extremely precarious employment situations. The privileged group of flexible employees contains the high-powered members of the entertainment branch and the highly-skilled Internet and multimedia experts. This fraction of flexible employees might enjoy chances for "individual self-determination" in their professional lives. However, the majority of workers in the media and culture industries have to accept multiple jobs in short-term contracts, excessive working hours and low wages. The majority of artistically creative workers now constitute the "middle-class working poor" of the skilled service sector.

In Berlin, many high skilled creative workers, particularly freelancers, can scarcely survive on the payments received from contract work in the cultural economy and thus apply for supplementary social support through the "Hartz IV" legislation (*Tagesspiegel*, November 22, 2009). Precarious contract work, low earnings, and excessive working hours underscore the ambivalence of chances for "individual self-determination" in the creative sector's labor relations; such conditions stand in stark contrast to uncritical accounts by Florida and others that tend to highlight the purportedly positive aspects of flexible "self-determination" of working hours and multi-tasking (Oßenbrügge et al., 2009).

According to the recent report on Berlin's cultural economy (Senatsverwaltung für Wirtschaft, 2008), in 2006 the workforce in this sector consisted of 77,000 "regular" employees, 12,000 workers with a "minor" employment relation (that is, short-term work and minimum wage levels), and 70,000 self-employed freelancers and (mostly micro-) entrepreneurs. Hence the majority (52 percent) of workers in this sector are self-employed freelancers or "minor" job holders. The percentage of freelance workers in the cultural economy has doubled since 1998 (Senatsverwaltung für Wirtschaft, 2008: 97–8).

In Berlin, the particularly strong growth of this sector may be best interpreted as an expression of the city's overall shortage of employment opportunities, that is, as a crisis symptom rather than as a unique "strength" of Berlin's economic development. This growth dynamic is further enhanced due to a situation of comparatively easy market access for micro-firm start-ups, particularly in the cultural economy sector. Additionally, the sustained migration of artists and young creative workers to Berlin (due in part to the city's sociocultural attractiveness for artistically creative people and the availability of low rent flats) leads to the formation of a "culture-industrial reserve army" providing a flexible reservoir of cheap labour among skilled creative workers; this is welcomed and exploited by the capitalist corporations of the culture and media industries. These conditions are experienced by the majority of creative freelancers in the form of increasing competition for temporary jobs and contracts, which in turn contributes to shrinking individual earnings in the freelance workforce. In this way, coupled with neoliberal policy prescriptions, the "creative industries" are spearheading a larger trend towards more deregulated, flexibilized, and precarious forms of employment. These arguments challenge Florida's ideological contention that the "creative industries" will play a key role in shaping a successful and sustainable urban economic development path.

Aside from its implications for urban economic development and labor relations, the culture industry and its creative workforce are playing a specific role in urban sociospatial restructuring. A flourishing cultural economy sector regularly triggers local spatial "upgrading" and restructuring processes that contribute to increasing sociospatial inequality and polarization within cities. The local agglomeration of cultural producers and artistically creative workers in inner-city areas can be interpreted as a precarious reindustrialization within the metropolitan core (Hutton, 2008), in which the weaker firms and the low income strata of creative workers are constantly confronted with instability and displacement. This instability is particularly acute for artists due to their subsistence-level incomes and their precarious tenure "in the steeply inflating property markets of the inner city" (Hutton, 2008: 32). The local displacement of "creative industry" firms and workers can result both from industrial "upgrading" within the sector – that is, newly established, upscale media firms edging out less affluent artists – and from processes of residential gentrification. Displacement may also occur in the framework of large-scale inner-city redevelopment projects.

At the intra-metropolitan scale, the local agglomeration of artists and cultural economy activities functions as a "seedbed" for gentrification (Lees et al., 2008; Slater, this volume). Specific inner-city districts containing older buildings, lower prices, and a large element of mixed uses are usually the milieus of artistically creative people and the less well-established cultural economy firms. Such local cultural clusters contribute to gentrification processes in those districts. In effect, the artists become the "pioneers" of gentrification – the explorers and regenerators that bring life into run-down areas and foster the development of support structures such as "cool" pubs and clubs, cafés, and restaurants. They then attract a more middle-class clientele which prefers to live in such trendy, culturally attractive urban quarters. On the supply side of gentrification, capitalist real-estate developers and investors invest in the upgrading of such urban districts' housing stock and built environment. The real-estate business frequently involves the creative scene actors as temporary users of old factory buildings which are destined for upgrading, a practice which often enhances the projects' "marketability" in terms of symbolic value.

The phenomenon of gentrification also highlights the competitive struggle for urban spaces among the different strata of the cultural economy's creative workforce. The classical pioneers of gentrification consist to a large extent of artistically creative people, low income bohemians and highly skilled young people at the bottom of the labour market. As gentrification proceeds, these pioneers are subsequently dislocated by the more affluent subgroups of the creative workforce and other sectors – high-income urban professionals who prefer to live in trendy inner-city districts in order to pursue yuppie or bobo (bourgeois bohemian) lifestyles. However, the outmigration of the original explorers and regenerators of formerly neglected districts impairs the "creative atmosphere" of the district, reduces the potential for local cross-sectoral impulses, and threatens its "subcultural capital." With time, the original creative scene is forced to relocate to another "low value" location, and a new cycle of settlement and gentrification is set into motion.

In Berlin, the relocation of creative milieus across the city has been clearly recognizable over the last two decades. The most prominent "trendy district" before 1990 was Kreuzberg. In the next decade, which was shaped above all by the city's reunification, this function was taken over by the districts of Prenzlauer Berg and Mitte. These districts have experienced the spread of gentrification processes with a far-reaching displacement of the original population (Krätke and Borst, 2000; Holm, 2006; Bernt and Holm, 2009) and the subsequent outmigration of artists and creative workers with low income and precarious job opportunities. Nonetheless, both districts are still characterized by an agglomeration of artistically creative workers and cultural economy firms. Gentrification has changed the social composition of the creative workforce residing in the area. Over the past decade, the "creative scene" of explorers and regenerators has again relocated, now moving on to the districts of

Friedrichshain and (back) to Kreuzberg, from which it has recently also spread to the adjoining district of (northern) Neukölln.

As the example of the "Media Spree" development project in the district Kreuzberg-Friedrichshain demonstrates, the local agglomeration of "creative industries" in formerly neglected inner-city areas of Berlin has also been utilized by real-estate developers for large-scale projects aimed at the conversion of old industrial waterfront sites into prime real estate (Scharenberg and Bader, 2009). The Media Spree project covers an area situated at the eastern edge of the city centre on both sides of the river Spree. Prominent large firms such as MTV Europe and Universal Music Germany are located in this area, side by side with many small- and medium-size firms of the music, fashion, and media industries. At the same time, the area is home to various related creative milieus, a vibrant club culture and subcultural scene. As Scharenberg and Bader (2009: 331) emphasize, "the creative and alternative image of the neighborhood played a crucial role in attracting enterprises to the area, and comprised a major aspect of the presentation of Media Spree in public discourse." It seems quite obvious that the area's creative scene and cultural economy firms are utilized by the real-estate dominated Media Spree business association for a large-scale development of office space and apartments at the edge of the city-centre – a development that would lead to the future displacement of the cultural economy's "creative periphery" firms and the currently present creative scene of explorers and regenerators (that is, the low-income strata of creative workers and artists).

This case can be regarded as a specific manifestation of how gentrification has increasingly come to function as a *global* urban development strategy (Smith, 2002). This strategy today includes a broad range of "upgrading" projects in the built environment of cities beyond the well-known processes of residential gentrification – particularly, large-scale projects for the conversion of old industrial sites in inner-city areas. The extended forms of contemporary gentrification such as the Media Spree project function "as a vehicle for transforming whole areas into new landscape complexes that pioneer a comprehensive class-inflected urban remake" (Smith 2002: 96).

Returning to Florida's comprehensive "creative class" aggregate, we might conclude that there is class struggle *within* the "creative class": the creative professionals of the real-estate business are organizing the dislocation of the original population of low-income artists and "creative periphery" firms by the upper strata of the "supercreative core" (yuppies, bobos, and upscale firms of the "creative industries"). With regard to its urban policy implications, Florida's theory has been appropriated as an ideological justification for neoliberal urban policies, particularly for approaches to urban restructuring – for instance, gentrification and real-estate development projects – that privilege the functional elites within the neoliberal model of society (Peck, 2005; Brenner and Theodore, 2002). Across Europe and beyond, in response to Florida's claim that cities have to compete in the new "race for talent," creative city policies have been mobilized to shape the city according to the purported needs of the "creative class." When such strategies entail public subsidies for the local arts scene, street-level spectacles and improved urban façades, they generally entail a new legitimation for all-too-familiar approaches to urban regeneration (Peck, 2005).

Conclusion

Critical urban theory must confront the intellectual and political challenges posed by the new urban growth ideologies. Currently, the notion of creative cities has acquired a leading position among such ideologies of urban booster-ism. The preceding discussion has deconstructed Florida's concept of a creative class: it underscores the need to disaggregate this questionable grouping of occupations among quite diverse economic functions within the framework of contemporary capitalist development; and it demonstrates that the dealer class (in Florida's terms, the creative professionals) does not at all have a significant (positive) impact on regional economic development. Furthermore, this chapter has offered a much gloomier depiction of contemporary "creative industry" labor markets than that promulgated by Florida: the growth of a freelance or informalized workforce with low wages, excessive working hours, and dis-continuous job flow in such sectors can be interpreted as a "crisis symptom" articulating the post-Fordist restructuring of major urban economies. Finally, I have shown that the cultural economy and its creative workforce are also contributing to sociospatial restructuring processes by which inner-city locali-ties are gradually gentrified. In this context, the local agglomeration of cultural economy firms and "creative scenes" in formerly neglected inner-city areas is utilized by real-estate developers for large-scale projects aimed at the conver-sion of old industrial sites into prime real estate (see Slater, this volume).

In light of the foregoing analysis, it is evident that there is no justifica-tion for urban policies that favor the interests of the functional elites within neoliberalizing capitalism. Contrary to the claims of Florida and his follow-ers, the development of sustainable regional economic structures, supported by networked regional innovation systems and associated human resources, is not at all dependent upon gentrification and large-scale real-estate develop-ment projects. The ideological construct of a "creative class" draws upon the generally positive connotation of "creativity" while masking the economically, politically, and socially destructive actions of the dealer class. For this reason, the theory serves to reinforce the right to the city of those that already have it.

References

Benneworth, P. and Hospers, G.-J. (eds) (2009) *The Role of Culture in the Economic Development of Old Industrial Regions*, Münster, Hamburg: LIT.

Berlin-Institut für Bevölkerung und Entwicklung (2007) *Talente, Technologie und Toleranz – wo Deutschland Zukunft hat*, Berlin.

Bernt, M. and Holm, A. (2009) "Is it, or is not? The Conceptualization of Gentrification and Displacement and its Political Implications in the Case of Berlin-Prenzlauer Berg," *City*, 13, 2–3, pp. 312–24.

Brenner, N. and Theodore, N. (eds) (2002) *Spaces of Neoliberalism*, Oxford: Blackwell.

Cooke, P. (2002) *Knowledge Economies*, London: Routledge.

Florida, R. (2004) *The Rise of the Creative Class*, New York: Basic Books.

Florida, R. (2005) *Cities and the Creative Class*, New York: Routledge.

Florida, R. and Tinagli, J. (2004) *Europe in the Creative Age*, Milan: Demos.

Fritsch, M. and Stützer, M. (2007) "Die Geographie der kreativen Klasse in Deutschland," *Raumforschung und Raumordnung*, 65, pp. 15–29.

Holm, A. (2006) *Die Restrukturierung des Raumes*, Bielefeld: Transcript.

Howkins, J. (2001) *The Creative Economy*. London, New York: Penguin Press.

Huffschmid, J., Köppen, M., and Rhode, W. (eds) (2007) *Finanzinvestoren: Retter oder Raubritter?* Hamburg: VSA.

Hutton, T. (2008) *The New Economy of the Inner City*, New York, London: Routledge.

Krätke, S. (2011) *The Creative Capital of Cities*, Oxford: Wiley-Blackwell.

Krätke, S. and Borst, R. (2000) *Berlin – Metropole zwischen Boom und Krise*, Opladen: Leske & Budrich.

Lees, L., Slater, T., and Wyly, E. (2008) *Gentrification*, New York, London: Routledge.

Markusen, A. (2006) "Urban Development and the Politics of a Creative Class," *Environment and Planning A*, 38, 10, pp. 1921–40.

Oßenbrügge, J., Pohl, T., and Vogelpohl, A. (2009) "Entgrenzte Zeitregime und wirtschaftsräumliche Konzentrationen," *Zeitschrift für Wirtschaftsgeographie*, 53, 4, pp. 249–63.

Peck, J. (2005) "Struggling With the Creative Class," *International Journal of Urban and Regional Research*, 24, pp. 740–70.

Scharenberg, A. and Bader, I. (2009) "Berlin's Waterfront Site Struggle," *City*, 13, 2–3, pp. 325–35.

Schumpeter, J.A. (1952) *Theorie der wirtschaftlichen Entwicklung*, 5th edition, Berlin: Duncker & Humblot.

Scott, A.J. (2000) *The Cultural Economy of Cities*, New York, London: Sage.

Senatsverwaltung für Wirtschaft, Technologie und Frauen (ed.) (2008) *Kulturwirtschaft in Berlin*, Berlin.

Smith, N. (2002) "New Globalism, New Urbanism: Gentrification as Global Urban Strategy," in N. Brenner and N. Theodore (eds) *Spaces of Neoliberalism*, Oxford: Blackwell, pp. 80–103.

Wilson, D. and Keil, R. (2008) "The Real Creative Class," *Social and Cultural Geography*, 9, pp. 841–7.

10

CRITICAL THEORY AND "GRAY SPACE"

Mobilization of the colonized

Oren Yiftachel

Let us begin with a public speech delivered by Hussein al-Rifa'iya, Chair of the Council of the Unrecognized Bedouin Villages in the Naqab (Negev) region around Beersheba. On January 2, 2009, al-Rifa'iya was inaugurating a self-rebuilt mosque in the locality of Wadi al-Na'am, demolished a few days earlier by the Israeli authorities. al-Rifa'iya stated:

> We will help rebuild every demolished house. Yes, it is officially "illegal" but our people have been here for generations and have nowhere to go. We built this mosque to show the state and the community that the Arabs of the south will not succumb … Israel may use force and destruction, both in the Naqab and in Gaza, but we will always rebuild.

This statement, one of several speeches delivered in the inauguration rally of the modest mosque (see Figures 10.1 and 10.2), can be brushed aside as another hype of a local leader preparing for nearing elections. But it also signals the incipient emergence of a new political strategy and with it a new subjectivity developing among the Bedouin Arabs living in dozens of "unrecognized" small towns and villages around Beersheba. It illustrates the new politics of "gray spacing" – emergence from the struggle for informal development – at the "periphery of peripheries," by the Bedouins vis-à-vis the ethnocratic Jewish state, but also in relation to surrounding Jewish communities and other Palestinian communities known in the Naqab region as "Northerners."[1]

FIGURE 10.1 Hussein al-Rafi'yah, Head of the RGUV, speaking to local community, Wadi al-Na'am, January 2009

FIGURE 10.2 Rebuilding the mosque, Wadi al-Na'am, January 2009

The episode described above links to the two main theoretical arguments I wish to advance here. First, that most critical urban theories (CUT), while providing vital foundations for the understanding of cities and regions, have not sufficiently accounted for the implications of a new political geography, characterized by the proliferation of "gray spaces" of informalities and the emergence of new urban colonial relations. The new geography thrusts the politics of identity as a central foundation of urban regimes, intertwined with, but far from subsumed under, class or civil engines of change typically highlighted by CUT. Second, that this new geography is recreating subjectivities, which no longer solely orbit the state's central power. This is illustrated below by tracing the impact of "gray spacing" on the articulation of Bedouin Arab struggle, and on the process of radicalization and disengagement in three main practices: sumood (hanging on to the land against state eviction plans), memory building, and autonomous politics.

The new politics often distance identities and mobilizations from the state, signaling the fragmentation of the apparatus of power "from below." They often begin with struggles for "insurgent citizenship," as identified by Holston (2008), but may go further and transform into struggles for multiple sovereignties. Such a transformation is rarely clear-cut or fully articulated, and is inevitably riddled with contradictions and tensions. Yet, there is a point in the struggle when citizenship, integration, and equality – emphasized by key scholars in the field (see Harvey, 2008; Holston, 1998, 2008; Marcuse, 2002) are no longer the dominant goals, but are intertwined with efforts to create autonomous ethnic spaces of development and identity.

This constellation illustrates a paradox – the central power which initiates "gray spacing" as a method of control, is now being undermined by this very process. Not only do political processes and identities move away from the state, they also breed political radicalism among those occupying or creating "gray space" which is channeled into alternative identity projects. In other words, the political stability sought by state oppression, in an attempt to prolong existing power relations, is now disrupted by destabilizing processes deriving from its own oppressive policies. Though still weak, the subaltern are shifting their strategies by partially (it not completely) disengaging their behavior, identity, and resource-seeking from the state, and by developing an alternative vision to civil integration as citizens in an inclusive state.

These arguments, however, must also be qualified. First, the state remains a powerful actor, as it attempts to deal with this development either by active cooptation or aggressive marginalization and oppression. Hence, the making of gray space is forever contentious, illustrating a site of political conflict and societal transformation. Second, the struggle rarely entails heroic confrontations with the authorities, nor does it produce comprehensive strategies or finely defined agendas. Most commonly, as Bayat (2007) and Perera (2009) show, gray spacing entails a "slow encroachment of the ordinary" through "familiarization" of the "cracks" in the working of oppressive power. This struggle is made of thousands of small movements in spaces of survival and stealth, neither fully coordinated, nor fully articulated, but cumulatively significant to upset the prevailing urban order.

My analysis draws on a recent comparative research project focusing on the new political geography of ethnocratic cities (Yiftachel, 2007; Yiftachel and Yacobi, 2004), and from long-term direct personal involvement in several Palestinian struggles, most notably with the indigenous Bedouins of the Beersheba region.[2] Hence, the chapter attempts to use both structural and "enmeshed" epistemologies to portray the manner in which space, power, and development create new urban citizenship, classes, and identities. In this vein, it does not treat Israel/Palestine as an exception, but rather a hyper example of structural relations unfolding in thousands of cities around the changing globe.[3]

"Gray space"

The concept of "gray space" refers to developments, enclaves, populations, and transactions positioned between the "lightness" of legality/approval/safety, and the "darkness" of eviction/destruction/death. Gray spaces are neither integrated nor eliminated, forming pseudo-permanent margins of today's urban regions, which exist partially outside the gaze of state authorities and city plans (see Yiftachel, 2009). The identification of "gray spacing" as a ceaseless process of "producing" social relations, by-passes the false modernist dichotomy between "legal" and "criminal," "oppressed" and "subordinated," "fixed" and "temporary." As such, it can provide a more accurate and critical lens with which to analyze the making of urban space in today's globalizing environment, marked by growing mobility, ethnic mixing, and political uncertainty.

Gray spaces have become a dominant feature of contemporary urbanism, mainly, but far from solely, in the less developed world. While the concept also covers the creation of informal spaces "from above" by powerful groups linked to the centers of power (Yiftachel, 2009), this chapter focuses on the most common expression of this phenomenon – the creation of peripheral, weakened, and marginalized spaces. Yet, communities subject to "gray spacing" are far from powerless recipients of urban policies, as they generate new mobilizations and insurgent identities, employ innovative tactics of survival, and use gray spaces as bases for self organization, negotiation, and empowerment. To be sure, power relations are heavily skewed in favor of the state, developers, or middle classes. Yet the "invisible" population of informal settlement is indeed an important actor in shaping cities and regions.

In the urban policy sphere, gray spaces are usually quietly tolerated, while subject to derogatory discourses about their putative "contamination," "criminality," and "danger" to the desired "order of things." The disjuncture between actual tolerated reality and its "intolerable" legal, planning, and discursive framing, puts in train a process of "gray spacing," during which the boundaries between "accepted" and "rejected" constantly shift, trapping whole populations in a range of unplanned urban zones, lacking certainty, stability, and hence development. The consequences are clear in many cities – whole neighborhoods and quarters lack basic services to realize their urban citizenship, forming new urban colonial relations, as detailed later (for earlier accounts, see Davis, 2006; Fernandes and Varley, 1998).

Gray spacing is a power-laden process. Therefore, the concrete emergence of "stubborn" informalities is typically handled not through corrective or equalizing policy, but by employing a range of delegitimizing and criminal-izing discourses, regulations, and violence. This creates boundaries that divide urban groups according to their status; a process of "separating urban incor-poration" and "creeping apartheid" whereby the meaning of urban citizenship depends on arbitrary features such as ethnicity, place of birth, or class. The double-edged move of "separating incorporation" preserves gray spaces in a state of "permanent temporariness"; concurrently tolerated and condemned, perpetually waiting "to be corrected" (see Davis, 2006; Neuwrith, 2006; Roy, 2005, 2009b; Roy and AlSayyad 2004). I return to these theoretical aspects below.

The "gray spacing" of Bedouin Arabs

The Bedouin Arab population now residing in the Naqab/Negev desert, at the southern regions of Israel/Palestine, is the most marginalized and impoverished group in historic Palestine. It is an indigenous group, with its own history, tra-ditions, and identity, made of the fragments of communities remaining in Israel after the 1948 Nakbah (disaster in Arabic), during which around 70 percent of Palestinians (including the Bedouins of course) were driven out of what is now Israel, mainly to Gaza, West Bank, and Jordan. The on-going sufferings, dislo-cations, and violence experienced by the Bedouins since 1948 have prompted a local poet, Saleh al-Ziadnah to write, "in the Naqab we breathe/the Nakbah everyday/… in the thick air of our sand/in our dust/in the violent shattering of our walls/… in our endless search to re-find/our home…" (Nakbah cer-emony, al-Qrein village, May 14, 2008).

The 180,000 Naqab Bedouins of the Beersheba region are composed of three main sub-groups: (a) those living on their ancestors land (mostly in unrec-ognized localities); (b) those evicted from their original villages and transferred to new unrecognized towns and villages; and (c) those urbanized into modern planned towns. The first two reside in "gray spaces" and number in late 2008 around 90,000 people (see Figures 10.3 and 10.4 and Goldberg, 2008).

Since gaining sovereignty in 1948, Israel has used internal colonial policies to Judaize most areas inhabited, owned, or claimed by Arabs. A major tool in the Judaization policy has been the declaration of all unregistered lands as belonging to the state, and the parallel establishment of an exclusively Jewish Israel Land Authority to manage state lands. Most Naqab Bedouins did not register their land during the periods of Ottoman and British rule. This is due

FIGURE 10.3 Chashem Zaneh, an unrecognized Bedouin locality with the city of Beersheba in the background, August 2008

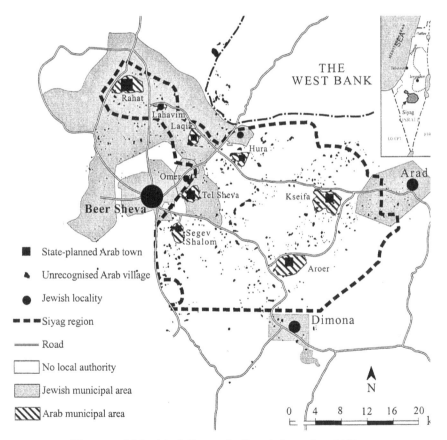

FIGURE 10.4 Human and Municipal Geography Beersheba region, 2005
Source: adapted from maps of Israel's Ministry of the Interior.
Note: most Arab localities lack recognition and municipal status.

to a variety of reasons, but chiefly due to the existence of a well-functioning customary land system and a historical view of most foreign rulers as temporary. The lack of formal registration in the pre-1948 period did not affect the manner in which Bedouins used and developed their lands (see Ben-David, 2004; Falah, 1989; Kedar, 2004; Meir, 2005).

Following Israel's independence, and the attempt to forcefully urbanize Bedouins, a bitter land conflict developed. The Israeli state denied the Bedouins indigenous land rights, and subsequently declared them legally as "trespassers" and "invaders" in their own historic localities. In an effort to force them to relocate, the state prevented the supply of most services, including roads, water, electricity, clinics, and planning. House demolition campaigns are launched on a regular basis (see abu-Saad, 2008; Meir, 2005; Swirski, 2008).

As a consequence, levels of poverty, child mortality, and crime have become one of the worst in Israel/Palestine, creating a metropolitan geography of stark ethno-class contrast with the well-serviced adjacent Jewish localities. The Beersheba metropolis has come to resemble many Third World cities that comprise a well-developed modern urban core, and a range of peripheral informal localities, suffering severe deprivation. It is here that the process of "creeping apartheid" and the emergence of new colonial relations are most evident.

Bedouin Arab representation in urban and regional planning affairs has ranged between non-existent and negligible. Despite being the indigenous inhabitants of the region, and constituting nearly a third of its current population, Bedouin presence in planning bodies has been meager and random. During the past decade, for example, only two Bedouins have sat on the district planning council (each in turn being one among 13 Jews in the council), and not even one Bedouin is represented on the Beersheba city council. Other relevant planning bodies such as the Israel Land Authority, Ministry of Housing, Welfare and Education have occasionally included a single Arab member, but always in a position of distinct and ineffectual minority.

The conflict has material and symbolic dimensions. A central flashpoint has revolved around the renowned and architecturally significant Beersheba mosque, which was built by the Ottomans to serve the region's population. Despite constant Arab demands, the city refuses to open it for Muslim worship. In this vein, the deputy mayor at the time, Eli Bokker claimed in 2003: "the mosque will never be reopened … the region has dozens of mosques in Bedouin villages and towns … why do they want to come here? Everybody must remember: Beersheba is a Jewish city, with the right to protect its urban character" (*Sheva* [local newspaper]), May 16, 2005).

Following a recent appeal by several NGOs, the Israeli high court ruled in favor of opening the mosque for "Arab cultural uses." Despite the latest ruling, however, the city is steadfast in its refusal, and has now condemned the building as too dangerous for human use. Several attempts by Arabs to stage public prayers were met with police violence followed by the fencing off of the building. As a result, the Mosque has been lying idle for decades, and is now in an advanced state of deterioration. This urban conflict adds an explosive dimension to planning and development tensions and to the growing sense of on-going colonization by the ethnocratic Jewish state (abu-Saad, 2008).

Urban colonialism and the "new CUT"

A central point of this paper is the development of new subjectivities among excluded groups, particularly in urban colonial situations where such groups are out of the reach of hegemonic projects, yet within the economy and "ground" politics of their cities. This dynamic is linked to the need, identified above, for new critical urban theories – the call for a new, expanded CUT. In the current age, the new CUT would not simply replace, but rather expand the critical urban analysis to the multitude of connections between urban struggles and identity transformations, and to the manner in which these are embedded within the material, discursive, and political aspects of "gray spacing." To be sure, several important works have begun to address this issue (Bayat, 2007; Mbembe and Nuttal, 2004; Roy, 2009b; Simone, 2006), and my suggestions here are aimed to add further weight to this type of work, while making explicit its engagement with the main discourses of critical urban theory.

To interpret the dynamic of oppressive "gray spacing" and identity transformation, I draw on a wide body of critical theories, with particular reference to Gramscian-inspired approaches, as well as theories of neo-colonial urban relations (Kipfer and Goonewardena, 2007; Legg, 2008; Mbembe and Nuttal, 2004). Gramscian-inspired approaches perceive the making of identities as part of a ceaseless political process. They differ from most Marxian or liberal theories which regard most collective identities as pre-political. The continuous remaking of identities through contentious politics, is attributed both to the bourgeoisie classes, which formulate the backbone of what Gramsci termed the "passive revolution," as they daily reproduce the pillars of hegemony; and to subaltern groups, which respond to their persisting oppression by *articulating* anti- and counter-hegemonic struggles and identities.

Articulation is a key concept in Gramscian-inspired approaches, alluding to the process through which class position and cultural forms are combined in the making of collective identities, during the ongoing struggles and negotiations over power and resources. Articulation is a particularly apt trope to the study of peripheral and insurgent identities, due to the rise of these through resistance to subordination and oppression. Scholars such as Holston (1998, 2008), Laclau and Mouffe (2001), Miraftab (2009), and Roy (2009a) link this process to the emergence of insurgent and radicalizing identities.

Based on the Gramscian-inspired work of Laclau and Mouffe (2001), we may conceptualize the process of radicalizing identities as oscillating between *agonism* (the articulation of difference within the leading value system) to *antagonism* (the articulation of difference outside the main value system). Radical articulation is based on the development of collective antagonism against a hegemonic order which attempts to impose a specific set of values, interests, cultural orientations, while subordinating the subaltern to the desired order. Drawing further inspiration from thinkers such as Brenner (2006), Holston (2008), Jacobs (1998), Marcuse (2002), Mayer (2008), Roy (2009a), and Samaddar (2007), we can trace the link between oppression and antagonistic articulation, through various media of urban mobilizations. When marginalized groups become politically aware of the impregnable barriers to their equality and inclusion, and when they can marshal enough resources to act, their agonistic opposition is likely to shift to antagonistic radicalism, and the horizon of equal integration may be challenged by an agenda of autonomous disengagement from the societal mainstream (see also Laclau, 1994; Mouffe, 1995).

This process is particularly active as a response to urban colonial relations associated with the proliferation of gray spaces, as shown by recent critical writing on African and Asian cities, where such conditions pervasively develop (Mbembe and Nuttal, 2004; Miraftab, 2009; Roy, 2009a). This is also the case in the Beersheba metropolis, where – as shown above – Israel has persistently sought to Judaize and de-Arabize land and development, creating a process of urban colonialism under the monopolistic Zionist development order. Significantly, "colonial" in the current analysis does not relate necessarily to European (capital "C") Colonialism, or to the subsequent "postcolonial" relations. Rather, I draw here on earlier scholarship on "internal colonialism" (Hechter, 1975; Zureik 1979) and on a deeper historical understanding of the term, as elaborated by the likes of Anderson and O'Dowd (1999), Agamben (2006), and Kipfer (2007). These scholars relate to colonial processes as denoting multi-faceted formations of power which facilitate appropriation and domination. A colonizing urban political economy is thus characterized by several key dimensions:

- expansion of dominant interests (spatially or otherwise);
- exploitation of marginalized groups;
- essentialization of identities;
- hierarchical and coerced segregation.

Notably, colonial relations are strangely absent from the main corpus of critical urban theories, which often take the basic condition of formally equal citizenship and political membership as a point of departure. But given the growing prevalence of colonial-type relations in a vast number of cities, and the amplification of gray spaces, it clearly appears that a "new CUT" is now needed, expanding its pervious foundation to include the forces shaping the new colonial order. This is because critical theorists, whether associated with the Frankfurt School, French and Continental philosophy, neo-Gramscian scholars, or the recent Anglo neo-Marxian and neo-Weberian scholarship, have generally overlooked the centrality of colonial relations in the formation of urban social relations. Under such settings the very notions of membership and citizenship are deeply ruptured. Rather than inclusive, they become the very tool of exclusion and denial.

Gramsci's discussion on the "Southern Question," which portrays a process of involuntary incorporation and exploitation of an outlying region, comes close to describing a process of internal colonialism. However, the concept of hegemony itself, with its fundamental assumption regarding the willingness and ability of dominant strata to incorporate the peripheries, has notable limitations when dealing with colonial settings, in which the working of power is premised on structural, impregnable, exclusion. This weakness also pervades through other leading critical theories, be they Frankfurt-inspired, Foucauldian, Lefebvrian, or neo-Marxian, which brilliantly, but only partially, explain the ability of upper strata to discipline, subordinate, and manage social relations "within society."

Colonial settings are characterized by the permanent presence of groups existing outside the limits of "society," and hence beyond the nets of imagined incorporation and control cast by hegemonic or governmentality projects. This is a structural element in most ethnocratic states (Yiftachel, 2006; Yiftachel and Ghanem, 2004), as well as the growing metropolitan regions mainly, but not only, in the global South-East (Roy, 2008; Simone, 2006; Yiftachel, 2007). There, the mechanisms of co-optation and governmentality often lack the intention, will, or capacity to incorporate colonized groups.

The critical literature includes an abundance of insightful critical concepts accounting for the power of elites to assimilate, co-opt, and tame the subaltern. These include the Gramscian concept of "transformismo"; Foucauldian "discipline" and "governmentality" or neo-Marxian "neoliberalization of Empire" (Hardt and Negri, 2000; AlSayyad and Roy, 2006). Yet, these concepts fall short of explaining the development of group relations and collective subjectivities, in colonial settings, where subaltern groups are often cast as too different, too hostile or too geographically distinct, to be included within the limits of societal hegemonic projects.

A new articulation may find inspiration in the much talked about concept of the right to the city (Brenner and Elden, 2008; Harvey, 2008; Kipfer, 2007; Lefebvre, 1996; Mitchell, 2003; Yacobi, 2006). Despite its wide appeal, the notion is rather vague, noting a legitimate claim to appropriate urban space and participate in the shaping of its future. Lefebvre (1996) further argues that the right to the city entails a just claim to "centrality and difference." Although he never developed his theory academically or practically, the concept he coined does create an opening to mobilize against urban oppression which entails of course the denial of the right to the city.

But as recognized by a group of critical scholars, much more work is needed to put "flesh" on the bones of Lefebvre's concept, academically and – more importantly – materially and politically. Substantiation of the concept must also steer away from the common, liberalized, and mainly legal or moral notion of "rights," extracted out of its historical and material context. Instead, as argued elsewhere (Yiftachel, 2009), the right to the city should be buttressed by more materialized and politicized notions such as "planning citizenship," urban sovereignty, and group's self-determination, in order to respond to the very material deprivations and exclusions experienced in gray space, against which a rights-based approach may not suffice (Kipfer and Goonewardena, 2007; Mbembe and Nuttal, 2004; Tzfadia, 2008; Watson, 2002).

Space, identity, class, and power must therefore combine to sketch the limits of hegemony, and such limits invoke dominant powers to impose ghettoizing, often violent, forms of colonial control, rather than legitimizing types of power. The need for a new and expanded CUT begins by recognizing the limits of groundbreaking, yet bounded critical approaches which have unproblematically assumed the prior existence of a "society," whose membership, at least in a formal sense, is not questioned sufficiently. Groundbreaking in this line was Marcuse's work on the black ghetto (Marcuse, 1997, 2002), in which he engaged with economic, identity, and spatial regimes to provide a landmark account of the transformation of the ghetto from "classical" to an "outcast" urban space and community, later to be "softly" encroached and weakened by neoliberal gentrification. Other examples, such as Kipfer's work on colonialism and the city (Kipfer, 2007), Watson's critical analysis of planning theory (Watson, 2002), Roy's reflections on planning and subjectivities in the age of neoliberalism (Roy, 2005, 2008), Robinson's sensitive yet critical analysis of the development of Southern cities (Robinson, 2006), and Simone's work on the new spaces of informality in African cities (Simone, 2006), illustrate clearly that such an approach is not only possible but highly worthy.

Radicalization and the Bedouins

How does the processes of articulation actually take place "on the ground"? How do indigenous Arabs change their struggle and subjectivity in the face of their long-term existence in gray space? Here, the central conceptual elements of the dynamic I described above are weaved together – the consequences of colonial relations, the new articulation of class and collective identity, and the critical role of informal spatialities, all lead to a gradual, yet conspicuous, process of radicalization (abu-Saad and Yonah, 2000; Meir, 2005; Yonah et al., 2004).

Notably, Bedouin radicalization appears more as *anti*, than *counter*-hegemonic, principally because this peripheral community has no ability to imagine challenging, let alone replacing, state hegemony. It is hence mainly radical in the sense of drawing agendas which radically departs from state goals, as well as "searching for the roots" (root = radic), as a foundation for setting new communal agendas. It is thus a "non-heroic" struggle, aimed at survival in the personal and collective sense. The Bedouins are constructing a new collective identity through the discourses and materiality of physical development. This identity is formed despite inevitable tensions and divisions, not only vis-à-vis the oppressive Israeli regime, but also with the multitude of coterminous belongings – the tribe, the region, Israel, the Palestinians in Israel, the wider Palestinian people, and the Arab and Islamic worlds.

This complex process of articulation and radicalization is composed of dozens of practices, movements, discourses, and mobilizations. I chose to highlight three here – "sumood," memory building, and autonomous politics. Obviously this list is not exhaustive, and can be supplemented by other important practices and initiatives in the spheres of economics, criminality, gender relations, and cultural production, to name but a few. Yet, these three practices can sketch the main dynamics of identity construction, and the ways in which it is related to place, materiality, history, and power. Let me briefly attend to each.

Sumood

Sumood is an Arabic term denoting perseverance, patience, and quiet determination. The term has come to symbolize the Palestinian attempt to mentally overcome the consequences of the 1948 Nakbah, during which large numbers of Palestinians were driven out or fled in fear of war, and have subsequently lost their lands and villages. Sumood is widely practiced by the Naqab Bedouins, who have remained on their land, refused forced urbanization, and have preserved many of their traditions.

Sumood is closely linked to the "gray spacing" phenomenon. Most unrecognized Bedouin localities existed before 1948, but the state's denial of their land rights placed them in a legal category of "trespassers" on their own land (Amara, 2008; Human Rights Watch, 2008). The disputed land status has also been used by the state as a "reason" to deny recognition of dozens of villages and towns. Hence, over the past six decades, the state's legal and planning decisions deliberately created a process of "gray spacing," in which all developments, even for the most mundane reasons such as family expansion, are deemed "illegal." At the same time, there is no realistic exit option because movement to planned towns is often impossible due to chronic lack of available building blocks, but it is also threatening in terms of losing land possession and collective identity (abu-Saad, 2008).

Sumood, therefore, has been translated from a general national ideal to the art of surviving in the criminalized zone of planning illegality, and to a set of tactics for developing the villages, bit by bit, to meet basic needs such as water, electricity, mobility, education, and health. Nowhere is this strategy more evident than in the collective efforts to rebuild demolished homes. The magnitude of this phenomenon are revealing: during 2007, for example, Israel demolished some 197 homes, and by the end of 2008, nearly all of them were replaced by new structures (see http://www.dukium.org).

The failure of the state to convince or coerce people to leave their land, and the subsequent discrimination, criminalization, and suffering is at the heart of the process of radical articulation. During this process both deprivation and identity have combined in the struggle to construct a new orientation. In this context, note the testimony of Atiya al-Athamin, committee head in the locality Chashem Zaneh, in a public hearing staged in June, 2008, about future plans for Beersheba:

> in our rightful "*sumood*," we have no choice but to break the law … because the law and its plans came to this place and tried to erase it many years after we were here … our community belongs to this place, and the place belongs to our community … even if our houses are demolished again, we shall remain on our land … we cannot ever accept the plan that destroys our only community.
>
> (protocols of special committee to hear planning objections, Southern District, 28 June 2008)

Memory building

In parallel to the practice of *sumood*, Bedouin Arabs have begun to cultivate their collective memory as a foundation of rebuilding their identity. This process followed decades of erasure of Beersheba's and Naqab's Arab past, expressed in both popular and state discourses, as well as a myriad of physical practices. Most conspicuously, the names of all 45 Bedouin Arab villages around Beersheba (many of which existed before the state of Israel) have never been included in any official document or map, making this population invisible. In addition, Arab names of the topography and historical sites have almost entirely been renamed in Hebrew (Benvenisti, 2001). Beersheba's Arab city is widely called "Turkish" by the Israeli public, as are all City and District documents. Various histories written for the city tend to minimize its Arab past by emphasizing the "Ottoman" or "British" regime (while ignoring the region's population), and generally leap over the 1948 war and the eviction of the city's Arab population (for typical examples see Cohen, 2006; Gradus, 1993, 2008). In planning terms, the city offers no Arab cultural or communal facilities, and no mosques, as highlighted earlier, despite being the center for the entire regional Bedouin population, and the direct place of residence for around 4,000 Arabs (abu-Rass, 2006).

The official erasure, as well as a tide of Palestinian mobilization to reconstruct national memory during the last decade, spurred Bedouin cultural agents to begin to cultivate their own historical memories. These appear in three main forms: traditional, Islamic, and Palestinian. It is not easy to gauge the relative strength of these coterminous practices, but they are all very present in Bedouin discourse, though not mutually exclusive. It appears as if memory building in general has increased markedly during the last decade, and that the Islamic and most recently Palestinian varieties are gaining popularity, thereby creating the foundation for a new subjectivity which gradually draws away from any normative attachment to Israeli citizenship, let alone emotional solidarity with the Zionist state.

Traditional agents attempt to cultivate the Bedouin tribal and "desert" culture. They have commonly worked in co-operation with state or regional authorities in the establishment of museums, tourist centers, and some educational facilities. The state sees this as an outlet for the minority which may be compatible with the distorted and Orientalist perceptions of most Jews and Westerners who view the Bedouins as exotic and nomadic people. This also supports popular "truths" about Bedouin modern tribalism and the putative rule of "tribal elders," which further splits and weakens the Bedouin community, and enhances traditional, often chauvinist, and reactionary elements (abu-Rabia-Queder, 2008). Nevertheless, even with this partially co-opted memory generation, Bedouins have been developing an alternative consciousness, identity, and subjectivity that is gradually moving away from the notion of equal and assimilated Israeli identity.

The Islamization of memory and identity has been popular among local political leaders and their followers, and facilitated by the well-established Islamic Movement in the Naqab. Local leaders have sought a path to mark their distinction from the Zionist state, without openly building a Palestinian counter identity. They hope to increase their popularity while avoiding criminalization by the often racist and anti-Palestinian authorities. This has been a powerful strategy, during which new discursive and institutional links have been built between Bedouin communities and the newly-constructed Islamic past. Its expressions are everywhere – in textbooks, street names, the rapid development of mosques around the Naqab, and the increasingly religious dress and family codes, including pervasive polygamy. Subsequently, in recent years the mosque has become an important focus for shaping Bedouin identity and a sense of historical Islamist consciousness (Ben-Yisrael and Meir, 2008; Luz, 2008).

Most politically controversial is the Palestinization of Bedouin memory. Yet, it is historically and geographically natural since the Naqab Bedouins have been present on the land from the early twentieth century as part of the budding Palestinian nation. The lines distinguishing Bedouins from other Palestinian ethnicities are blurred and constantly shifting (Parizot, 2004, 2005). Here, the most notable memory practice is the growing use of the Palestinian Nakbah. The Bedouins have "discovered" the Nakbah in recent years, devoting growing space in public speeches, media discourse, and local commemorations to the traumatic past (abu-Rabia, 2008; abu-Mahfouz, 2008). As noted from the outset, for many Bedouins the Nakbah is not just a distant memory, but a living reality, given the state's persisting policies of dispossession and forced removal.

The Nakbah increasingly appears as a repeated trope on a variety of issues, such as the plight of the distressed villages; the status of the "internally displaced" (Kedar, 2004); the loss of lands and houses; and the prevention of Bedouins returning to their original pre-1948 locations. With the Nakbah also appears the *'awdah* (the return) which signals for most Palestinians the hope of historical correction. In this context, note the following words from 'Ali abu-Shcheita, committee head of the village of al-Qrein, during the first ever public

FIGURE 10.5 Day of Nakbah commemoration, al-Krein, May 2008

Nakbah commemoration held in the Naqab in May 2008. The ceremony was held adjacent to the ruins of a recently demolished home, and featured a march of 45 children carrying large signs of all the 45 unrecognized communities around which the Bedouin struggle is waged (see Figure 10.5). The event was opened by abu-Shcheita:

> As you can see, we are standing near one of our homes, demolished by the authorities. Thirteen more homes, including our mosque, are under demolition orders. We never moved from here, but were suddenly declared "illegal" six years ago. For us, the Nakbah is well and truly alive … but look at these kids and the way they return our villages to the public eye, to the plans and maps … this is the beginning of our *'awdah* (return).

Autonomous politics

The third aspect of changing Bedouin subjectivity appears clearly in the realm of political organization and mobilization. A conspicuous trend is the development of autonomous institutions which develop their agendas in close connection with the communities. Several active NGOs, as well as organizations related to political parties and Arab local governments have been established during recent times. Most notable was the 1997 establishment of the Regional Council of the Unrecognized Villages (RCUV). The Council was formed as a response to constant claims by the authorities, typified by the previous powerful head of the ministry of the Interior Southern District, Shalom Danino, who noted in 1994: "it is well known that the Bedouins have no leadership … one can never tell what they want … they speak in 100 voices" (*Sheva*, May 24, 1994, p. 7).

This common Israeli approach simultaneously reflects and recreates the age-old colonial practice of "divide and rule." Accordingly, Israel has attempted to deepen tribal, class, and locational divisions among the Bedouins, and then exploited these divisions to weaken opposition to its control policies. The establishment of the RCUV attempted to combat this practice, by setting a representative body not only to represent the Bedouins vis-à-vis the authorities, but to initiate a democratic process for self-managing Bedouin space. The council consists of elected representatives of the 45 unrecognized villages, who in turn elect the council Head. This was reduced to 36 members, as nine localities have been recognized since 1997. So far three elections have been held (1997, 2001, 2005), each producing a different leadership, ensuing a relatively (though not entirely) smooth transition of power.

Importantly, the RCUV carves out an autonomous zone not only against what they perceive as a hostile state, but also vis-à-vis "Northern" Arab and Palestinian influences which have tended to dominate, and at times appropriate, the Bedouin's campaign. This reflects long-standing tensions among Palestinian communities, but also a sense among southern Arabs that they exist under double colonization, Jewish and "Northern." The RCUV general manager, 'Atwa abu-Freich, recently claimed, "the RCUV is the authentic voice of southern Arabs, and it is theirs only" (Rebuilding Ceremony, Wadi al-Na'am, January 2, 2009).

The reception of RCUV by Israeli authorities was initially hostile. The state refused to recognize the representative council, and instead strengthened a bureaucratic body known as "The Managing Authority for the Advancement of the Bedouins" (MAAB) – an Orwellian term for a body renowned for its persistent attempts to remove and resettle Bedouins. In 2003, for example, the government launched the Sharon-Livni plan for "finally managing the Bedouin problem," in which it trebled the budgets for "law enforcement" through the MAAB, but offered no new hope for recognition of villages or towns. Neither did it allow the Bedouin communities participation in the determination of their own future. Later new state projects, such as the "Daroma" (southward) plan, the Metropolitan Plan for Beersheba and the Goldberg Commission Report,[4] all stressed law enforcement, with only scant official attention to the claims articulated by the RCUV.

Yet, despite official non-recognition of the RCUV, the government began to include the new leadership in unofficial consultations, and even began to compromise on the long-standing hard-line denial of village recognition. This followed a persistent campaign by the RCUV (aided by other key organizations, such as the Association for Human Rights, Coexistence Forum, Adalah, and Doctors for Human Rights) for recognition of villages and towns, and for the establishment of Arab local governments in the Bedouin region. In 1999 the RCUV published a "blueprint" document demanding the recognition of the 45 villages and towns it had identified and named in their original Arabic names.

Over the years, the RCUV published maps and reports about the 45 communities seeking recognition, and showed that all of them were viable, each accommodating at least 500 people – well beyond the minimal limit of 40 families determined by the Israeli planning authorities for recognizing (Jewish) localities. The RCUV plan was widely dismissed as "unprofessional," "wild," and "ridiculous,"[5] but the public pressure bore some results: by 2008, the government recognized nine of the 45 localities, and began to draw plans for legalizing homes and providing some infrastructure. The government also established a new regional local government named "abu-Bassma" to provide municipal services for the newly recognized villages. Although the new municipality is still headed and managed by Jews, it forms a possible foundation for a future Arab local government in the area.

The place of the RCUV as leading the indigenous struggle for recognition, and the intense internal and external conflicts that surround its existence, naturally warrant a far more detailed analysis. The main point here is to demonstrate the rise of informal and autonomous leadership "from below" against an ethnocratic hard-line policy of denial and forced removal. The RCUV involvement in the recognition struggle has given the dispersed communities a political and professional framework to continue their *sumood*. It has thereby gradually institutionalized their long-term future in gray space, while setting the foundations for incipient forms of indigenous sovereignty.

Conclusion

In closing, let me return to the site of the mosque rebuilding in Wadi al-Na'am quoting the address made by 'Atwa abu-Freich of the RCUV.

> We know this is a long haul, and that this new mosque will probably be followed by further demolitions and legal penalties … but we also know that the attempts to remove us will never fully succeed, like the failure in burning and resisting Gaza. This is because we are sons of this soil, and we know how to survive on it, and we will … the state calls us "criminals" just for living in our localities … this does not matter, as we'll always remain the people of this place, not for the state, but for our own communal future.

Abu Freich's words echo the colonial settings, the enduring deprivation typical to gray space, the subsequent rise of antagonism, and the radicalization now evident among the suffering peripheries. All the above, as argued throughout this chapter, must be incorporated into new versions of CUT, to credibly account for urban struggles, their materialities, politics, and articulations, and for the remaking of urban societies in the current neo-colonial age.

Notes

1 The term "Bedouin" is used here with caution, mainly because the local population widely uses it. It must be remembered from the outset that this term denotes a sub-identity within the larger Palestinian and Arab nations, and that the boundaries between those entities are fluid and porous.
2 Since 2005 the author has worked as a planner for the (unrecognized) Regional Council of the Unrecognized Bedouin Villages (RCUV).
3 While most readers would associate Israel/Palestine with exceptionalism, ceaseless conflict, and political drama, I argue that these are the surface expressions of the pervasive forces of ethno-nationalism, capitalism, governmentality, old and new colonialism with its ensuing class, identity, and gender politics; Israel/Palestine is constructed in the world media and politics as an exception, although the above forces are evident in most non-Western cities and states, quite often with similar ferocity, and increasingly so in the Western world.
4 "Daroma" is a development plan adopted by the Israeli government in 2005 to hasten investment in the Negev/Naqab region; the District and Metropolitan plans are statutory land use documents, which steer future development into planned zones; the Goldberg Commission was appointed by the government to submit a plan to "resolve the Bedouin planning, settlement and land problems"; its report was tabled at the Government meeting in January 2009, and a new committee was set-up to draw a plan for its implementation.
5 Protocols of District Planning Committee, where the plan was debated during 2000 and 2001 reveal a range of derogatory comments, disqualifying the plan on professional, legal, and substantive grounds. Apart from occasional RCUV intervention, no even one of the 14 Committee members supported the plan, fully, or partially.

References

abu-Mahfouz, M. (2008) "The odyssey of the abu-Mahfouz tribe: from al-Naqab to exile," *Hagar – Studies in Culture, Polity and Identities*, 8(2), pp. 65–92.
abu-Rabia, S. (2008) "Between memory and resistance: an identity shaped by space: the case of the Naqab Arab Bedouins," *Hagar – Studies in Culture, Polity and Identities*, 8(2), pp. 93–120.
abu-Rabia-Queder, S. (2008) *Excluded and Loved: Educated Arab Women in the Naqa*, Jerusalem: Eshkolot (Hebrew).
abu-Rass, T. (2006) "Land dispute in Israel: the Bedouin case," *Adalah notebooks* [online]. [Accessed June 15, 2011]. Available at: http://www.adalah.org/newsletter/heb/apr06/ar2.pdf.
abu-Saad, I. (2008) "Introduction: state rule and indigenous resistance among al-Naqab Bedouin Arabs," *Hagar – Studies in Culture, Polity and Identities*, 8(2), pp. 3–24.
abu-Saad, I. and Y. Yonah (2000) "Identity and political stability in an ethnically diverse state: a study of Bedouin Arab youth in Israel," *Social Identities*, 6(1), pp. 49–61.
Agamben, G. (2006) "Metropolis," *Generation online* [online]. [Accessed June 1, 2011]. Available at: http://www.generation-online.org/p/fpagamben4.htm.
AlSayyad, N. and A. Roy (2006) "Medieval modernity: on citizenship and urbanism in a global era," *Space and Polity*, 10(1), pp. 1–20.
Amara, A. (2008) "The Goldberg Committee: legal and extra-legal means to solving the Naqab Bedouin case," *Hagar – Studies in Culture, Polity and Identities*, 8(2), pp. 227–40.
Anderson, L. and O'Dowd, J. (1999) "Borders, border regions and territoriality: contradictory meanings, changing significance," *Regional Studies*, 33(7), pp. 593–604.
Bayat, A. (2007) "The quiet encroachment of the ordinary," *Chimmrenga*, pp. 8–15.

Ben-David, J. (2004) *The Bedouins in Israel – land conflicts and social issues*, Jerusalem: Jerusalem Institute for Israel Studies (Hebrew).

Benvenisti, M. (2001) *Sacred Landscapes*, Los Angeles: University of California Press.

Ben-Yisrael, A. and A. Meir (2008) "Renaming space and reshaping identities: the case of the Bedouin town of Hura in Israel," *Hagar – Studies in Culture, Polity and Identities*, 8(2), pp. 65–92.

Brenner, N. (2006*) New State Spaces: Urban Governance and the Rescaling of Statehood*, Oxford: Oxford University Press.

Brenner, N. and S. Elden (eds) (2008) *Henri Lefebvre: State, Space, World*, Minneapolis: University of Minnesota Press.

Cohen, E. (2006) *Beer Sheva: the Fourth City*, Tel-Aviv: Carmel (Hebrew).

Davis, M. (2006) *Planet of Slums*, London: Verso.

Falah, G. (1989) "Israel state policy towards Bedouin sedentarization in the Negev," *Journal of Palestine Studies*, 18, pp. 71–90.

Fernandes, E. and A. Varley (eds) (1998) *Illegal Cities*, London: Zed.

Goldberg, E. C. (2008) *Report of the Committee for the Regulation of Bedouin Settlement in the Negev*, Jerusalem: Ministry of Construction and Housing (Arabic, Hebrew).

Gradus, Y. (1993) "Beer-Sheva: capital of the Negev Desert," in Y. Golani, S. Eldor, and M. Garon (eds), *Planning and Housing in Israel in the Wake of Rapid Changes*, Jerusalem: The Ministry of the Interior, pp. 251–65.

Gradus, Y. (2008) *Introduction. Beer Sheva: Metropolis in the Making*, Y. Gradus and E. Meir (eds), Beer Sheva: BGU Press, pp. 1–12.

Hardt, M. and A. Negri (2000) *Empire*, Boston: Harvard.

Harvey, D. (2008) "The right to the city," *New Left Review*, 53, pp. 23–40.

Hechter, M. (1975) *Internal Colonialism*, Berkeley: University of California Press.

Holston, J. (1998) "Spaces of insurgent citizenship," in. L. Sandercock (ed.) *Making the Invisible Visible*, Berkeley: University of California Press, pp. 37–56.

Holston, J. (2008) *Insurgent Citizenship*, Princeton: Princeton University Press.

Human Rights Watch (2008) *Off the Map: Land and Housing Rights Violations in Israel's Unrecognized Bedouin Villages*, New York: Human Rights Watch.

Jacobs, J. (1998) *Edge of Empire*, London: Routledge.

Kedar, S. (2004) "Land settlement in the Negev in international law perspective," *Adalah Newsletter*, 8(1).

Kipfer, S. (2007) "Fanon and space: colonization, urbanization and liberation from the colonial to the global city," *Environment and Planning D: Society and Space*, 25(4), pp. 654–63.

Kipfer, S. and K. Goonewardena (2007) "Colonization and the new imperialism: on the meaning of urbicide today," *Theory and Event*, 10(2), pp. 1–39.

Laclau, E. (ed.) (1994) *The Making of Political Identities*, London: Verso.

Laclau, E. and C. Mouffe (2001) *Hegemony and Socialist Strategy*, London: Verso.

Lefebvre, H. (1996) "Philosophy of the city and planning ideology," *Writings on Cities*, London: Blackwell, pp. 97–101.

Legg, S. L. B. (2008) *Spaces of Colonialism*, London: Blackwell.

Luz, N. (2008) "The making of modern Beer Sheva: an imperialistic Ottoman project," in Y. Gradus and E. Meir (eds), *Beer Sheva: Metropolis in the Making*, Beer Sheva: BGU Press, pp. 163–78 (Hebrew).

Marcuse, P. (1997) "The enclave, the citadel and the ghetto," *Urban Affairs Review*, 33(2), pp. 228–64.

Marcuse, P. (2002) "The partitioned city in history," in P. Marcuse and R. Van Kempen (eds), *Of States and Cities*, Oxford: Oxford University Press, pp. 11–35.

Mayer, M. (2008) *The Terrain of Urban Social Movements in the Age of Neoliberalism* [online]. [Accessed May 15, 2011]. Available at: http://www.policing-crowds.org/speaker/2006/margit-mayer.html.

Mbembe, A. and S. Nuttal (2004) "Writing the world from an African metropolis," *Public Culture*, 16(3), pp. 47–372.

Meir, A. (2005) "Bedouins, the Israeli state and insurgent planning: globalization, localization or glocalization?" *Cities*, 22(3), pp. 201–35.

Miraftab, F. (2009) "Insurgent planning: situating radical planning in the global South," *Planning Theory*, 8(1), pp. 32–50.

Mitchell, D. (2003) *The Right to the City*, New York: Guilford.

Mouffe, C. (1995) "Post-Marxism: democracy and identity," *Environment and Planning D: Society and Space*, 13, pp. 259–65.

Neuwrith, R. (2006) *Shadow Cities*, London: Routledge.

Parizot, C. (2004) *Crossing and Constructing Borders within Daily Contact*, Aix-en-Provence: Institute de recherches et d'études sur le monde arabe et musulman (IREMAM) [online]. [Accessed May 15, 2011]. Available at: http://halshs.archives-ouvertes.fr/halshs-00080661/en.

Parizot, C. (2005) *Entrepreneurs without Borders: Bedouins between Negev and Dahariyya*, Aix-en-Provence: Institute de recherches et d'études sur le monde arabe et musulman (IREMAM) [online]. [Accessed May 15, 2011]. Available at: http://halshs.archives-ouvertes.fr/halshs-00094746/en.

Perera, N. (2009) "People's spaces: familiarization, subject formation and emergent spaces in Colombo," *Planning Theory*, 8(1), pp. 51–75.

Robinson, J. (2006) *Ordinary Cities*, London: Routledge.

Roy, A. (2005) "Urban informality: toward an epistemology of planning," *Journal of the American Planning Association*, 71(2), pp. 147–58.

Roy, A. (2008) "The 21st-century metropolis: new geographies of theory," *Regional Studies*, 42(4), pp. 69–86.

Roy, A. (2009a) "Civic governmentality: the politics of inclusion in Beirut and Mumbai," *Antipode*, 41(1), pp. 159–79.

Roy, A. (2009b) "Strangely familiar: planning and the worlds of insurgence and informality," *Planning Theory*, 8(1), pp. 7–12.

Roy, A. and AlSayyad, N. (2004) *Urban Informality: Transnational Perspectives from the Middle East, South Asia and Latin America*, Lanham, Md.: Lexington Books.

Samaddar, R. (2007) *The Materiality of Politics*, London: Anthem Press.

Simone, A. (2006) "Pirate towns: reworking social and symbolic infrastructures in Johannesburg and Douala," *Urban Studies*, 43(2), pp. 357–70.

Swirski, S. (2008) "Transparent citizens: Israeli policy towards the Negev Bedouins," *Hagar – Studies in Culture, Polity and Identities*, 8(2), pp. 25–46.

Tzfadia, E. (2008) "Abusing multiculturalism: the politics of recognition and land allocation in Israel," *Environment and Planning D: Society and Space*, 26(6), pp. 1115–30.

Watson, V. (2002) "The usefulness of normative planning theories in the context of Sub-Saharan Africa," *Planning Theory*, 1, pp. 27–52.

Yacobi, H. (2006) "From Rakevet to neighborhood of Neve-Shalom: planning, difference and the right to the city," *Makan*, 1(1), pp. 21–32.

Yiftachel, O. (2006) *Ethnocracy: Land and Identity Politics in Israel/Palestine*, Philadelphia:

University of Pennsylvania Press.

Yiftachel, O. (2007) "Re-engaging planning theory," *Planning Theory*, 5(3), pp. 211–22.

Yiftachel, O. (2009) "Theoretical notes on 'gray space': the coming of urban apartheid?" *Planning Theory*, 8(1), pp. 88–101.

Yiftachel, O. and A. Ghanem (2004) "Understanding ethnocratic regimes: the politics of seizing contested territory," *Political Geography*, 22(4), pp. 538–68.

Yiftachel, O. and H. Yacobi (2004) "Control, resistance and informality: Jews and Bedouin-Arabs in the Beer-Sheva region," in N. AlSayyad and A. Roy, *Urban Informality in the Era of Globalization: A Transnational Perspective*, Boulder: Lexington Books, pp. 118–36.

Yonah, Y., I. abu-Saad, and I. Kaplan (2004) "De-Arabization of the Bedouin: a study of an inevitable failure," in O. Yiftachel, D. Newman, A. Kemp, and U. Ram (eds), *Hegemonies, Identities and Challenges: Israelis in Conflict*, Eastbourne: Sussex Academic Press, pp. 65–80.

Zureik, E. T. (1979) *Palestinians in Israel: a Study of Internal Colonialism*, London: Routledge and Kegan Paul.

11

MISSING MARCUSE

On gentrification and displacement[1]

Tom Slater

> In 1999 my landlord doubled the rent in the apartment but we didn't
> understand why ... My rent went from $750 to $1200. So he almost dou-
> bled it. There were five other families in the building, one from Ecuador,
> one from Columbia ... worked in factories all of their lives, lived there
> for about 28 years; we were there for 8 years ... My apartment was taken
> over by a couple and their cat. So that's what he wanted. He always said
> he wanted to put trees on the block ... He put trees on it, fixed the gates
> and then sends everybody a letter saying the rent doubled. It wasn't that he
> wanted to make it nice for us. That's where gentrification affects people.
> He was making it look better and fixing it up but he was doing it with a
> mission to put in luxury condos for other people.
> (A displaced New York tenant quoted in Newman and Wyly, 2006: 44)

> In particular, gentrification needs to decouple itself from its original asso-
> ciation with the deindustrialisation of metropolitan centres ... and from its
> associations with working-class displacement.
>
> (Butler, 2007: 162)

How many writers on gentrification have quoted the passage where Ruth Glass
first coined the term 'gentrification' (Glass, 1964), but not read the rest of the
beautifully written essay in which it appears? Glass was not only a wonderful
troublemaker; she was a politically committed scholar whose writings always
displayed a powerful sense of urban social justice. Her 1964 classic contains an
astonishingly prescient prediction about the fate of the city where she lived:

Since the fifties, town and country planning legislation has, in essence, been anti-planning legislation … [D]evelopment rights have been de-nationalized, development values have been unfrozen; real estate speculation has thus been 'liberated'. These measures, together with the relaxation of rent control, have given the green light to the continuing inflation of property prices with which London, even more than other large cities, is afflicted. In such circumstances, any district in or near London, however dingy or unfashionable before, is likely to become expensive; and London may quite soon be a city which illustrates the principle of the survival of the fittest – the financially fittest, who can still afford to work and live there. Thus London, always a 'unique city', may acquire a rare complaint … [It] may soon be faced with an *embarrass de richesse* in her central area – and this will prove to be a problem, too.

(Glass, 1964: xix–xx)

Forty-five years later, reading this is both illuminating and depressing; not just because Glass' predictions have proved correct,[2] but because the principles of social justice that animated Glass' concerns about gentrification are not so apparent in much of the writing on the subject today (Slater, 2006). 'Gentrification' as a concept and a political rallying cry has in many places been swept away by an alliterative garble of revitalization, renaissance, regeneration, renewal, redevelopment, rejuvenation, restructuring, resurgence, reurbanisation and residentialisation – terms that bolster a neoliberal narrative of competitive progress (Peck and Tickell, 2002) that carves the path for ever more stealth forms of gentrification (Wyly and Hammel, 2001). In the past decade we have witnessed a dramatic expansion of this process all over the world, to the extent that many activists – and therefore anti-gentrification struggles – have been displaced from the central city (Hackworth and Smith, 2001; Hartman, 2002; Roschelle and Wright, 2003). These have been lean times for those fighting for affordable housing, protecting against displacement and insisting on viewing housing not as a commodity but as a source of basic need satisfaction, upon which people depend absolutely. Urban scholars, in a far more comfortable position than those standing up to successive waves of gentrification, have a key role to play in finding strategies to reclaim 'gentrification' from its sugarcoated present (Smith, 2002).

This chapter charts and challenges the politics of knowledge production on this pivotal urban process by critically engaging with some recent arguments that celebrate gentrification and/or deny displacement. I draw on Peter Marcuse's contributions to this topic to refute several claims that gentrification can be a positive thing even for those most likely to be affected by the process. Such claims not only strip gentrification of its historical meaning and gut it of its conceptual content; they are also analytically defective when considered alongside Marcuse's conceptual clarity on the various forms of displacement in gentrifying neighbourhoods. In recent literature, scholars have not only been focusing powerful analytical lenses on the life and times of gentrifiers; they have been changing their minds about gentrification, calling it something else, or even disputing its negative effects from the outset. Resuscitating and understanding Marcuse's crucial arguments on displacement helps to foreground once more the question of social justice in gentrification debate, and offers much political ammunition for scholars and activists engaged in the Right to the City movement.

Some definitional clarity before proceeding – I define gentrification as the transformation of a working-class or vacant area of a city into middle-class residential and/or commercial use (see Lees *et al.*, 2008). 'Vacant' may trouble some readers, but I include it because of the many instances of exclusive 'new build' gentrification, which often occurs on formerly working-class industrial spaces.[3] To define displacement I borrow an earlier definition from Chester Hartman *et al.*'s (1982) classic volume *Displacement: How to Fight It*: 'The term describes what happens when forces outside the household make living there impossible, hazardous, or unaffordable' (p.3). Far too much ink has been consumed arguing about definitions; what is important is that definitions have both *analytical* and *political* usage, and that class inequality is at the forefront of any consideration of gentrification.

Comment is expensive

Every day the online version of *The Guardian* newspaper features several provocative commentaries by invited contributors on attention-grabbing topics, in a section entitled *Comment is Free*.[4] The list of contributors over the past few years is impressive for its diverse cast of politicians, journalists, scholars and activists, and with few exceptions each commentary generates substantial public feedback in the form of online postings. A recent recruit is the renowned urban geographer Chris Hamnett. Some of his commentaries on the current global financial implosion have proved astute and informative, but one commentary in particular, a muse on gentrification tellingly entitled 'The regeneration game' (Hamnett, 2008) is memorable for its miserable amalgam of factual inaccuracy and analytical confusion. Before explaining further, it is necessary to provide some brief background on Hamnett's contributions to the study of gentrification, for his political metamorphosis offers a telling illustration of just how far the debate on gentrification has shifted, especially in the UK.

Hamnett produced the first academic study of gentrification following Ruth Glass' 1964 coinage (Hamnett, 1973). It focused on Inner London and the impact of the 1969 Housing Act, which set out 'to supplement the moribund level of new housing construction by raising the standard of the existing housing stock' (p.252). One of the Act's key provisions was discretionary 'improvement grants' for owners, developers and landlords to upgrade the quality of their housing – substantial sums which proved 'extremely lucrative' (p.253) for grant holders seeking to maximise returns on property investment.

Thousands of dwellings across London were 'improved' under this scheme, but Hamnett was critical of what was going on:

> Where it [the 1969 Housing Act] has been far less successful has been in the improvement of conditions for the original residents who are often displaced in the process of improvement … Owners can sell immediately after the improvement, without any obligation to pay back the grant in part or whole, and developers or landlords are at liberty to give notice to existing tenants and either sell or rent at triple or quadruple the rent after the improvement. Though this 'no strings' policy has without doubt led to a marked improvement in the standard of part of London's housing stock, it is precisely that part which has traditionally provided accommodation to the lower income groups.
>
> (p.252–3)

In the 1980s, Hamnett turned his attention towards tenurial transformation in London, and produced some fascinating co-authored studies of what was known as the 'flat break-up market' (the sale for individual occupation of what were previously purpose-built blocks of privately rented flats) (Hamnett and Randolph, 1984, 1986). Their analysis focused on capital investment flows lubricated by building society mortgage finance; their conclusion was that this type of gentrification led to the erosion of affordable private renting and, crucially, displacement, '[A]ffordable private renting in central London today is no longer a possible option for many. Those who cannot rent here have in effect been displaced to alternative locations beyond the central area' (Hamnett and Randolph, 1986, p.150).

In 1991 we saw a less critical and more argumentative Hamnett emerging in a highly cited essay (Hamnett, 1991) that chiselled away at Neil Smith's rent-gap theory before arguing that it is the professionalization of London's labour force and the pressures that consumer demand places on the housing market which explains gentrification in that city (and more generally).[5] In 2003, thirty years on from his first contribution, Hamnett appeared in a special issue of *Urban Studies* (appropriately entitled 'The Gentry and the City'[6]) with a paper examining the 'middle-class remaking of Inner London, 1961–2001' (Hamnett, 2003a). As well as unnecessarily repeating desperately tired criticisms of production-side explanations,[7] Hamnett denied that large-scale displacement has ever occurred in London:

> There is a consistent assumption in the literature that gentrification is a direct cause of working-class displacement. While this is undoubtedly true in some cases, it is argued here that the slow reduction of the working-class population in many inner-city areas is, in part, a result of a long-term reduction in the size of the working-class population of London as a whole (by a combination of retirement, death, out-migration or upward social

mobility) and its replacement by a larger middle-class population. In other words, *the key process may be one of replacement rather than displacement per se.*
(p.2419)

The argument emerged from his longitudinal study of Inner London's occupational class structure and its links to the housing market – a study that appears to have no room for his earlier arguments that displacement on a significant scale had occurred in London. Not only is it interesting how Hamnett now views working-class displacement in the gentrification literature as a consistent *assumption* (even his 1991 paper treated displacement as a *fact*, and a key reason that gentrification research is so important), he now comments on how well London's 'out-migrating' working-class might have done out of gentrification, '[S]ome working-class owners, including ethnic minorities, may have taken the opportunity of rapidly rising prices to sell up and move out' (p.2422).

Perhaps more troubling is that the last sentence of the paper contradicts everything he says before: 'working-class residents have been priced out of most of the private housing market' (p.2424). For Hamnett, the 'pricing out' is due to the inflationary housing prices caused by the expansion of professional middle-classes in London – yet throughout his paper we are told that gentrification-induced displacement has not occurred. Some time ago Smith (1992) noted that Hamnett had abandoned an earlier concern for social justice in favour of a pro-gentry philosophical individualism. In his 2003 paper, we can see that Hamnett has gone further and now denies significant displacement during the wholesale gentrification of London that Ruth Glass predicted, because the occupational class structure 'shows' that Londoners are mostly middle class now.

Hamnett's *Comment is Free* piece is sad to read. Accusations of collective amnesia are made from the outset:

> Some critics of gentrification have selective or limited memories. They forget that 30 years ago Britain's inner cities seemed to be in a long term spiral of economic and social decline and the middle classes were leaving in droves. The question the gentrification critics have to address is what would they do? Would they like to turn back the clock, to the urban dereliction and decay of 40 years ago, or would they accept that gentrification may have some positive benefits? Would they prefer the middle classes to abandon the inner cities and flee to the suburbs as they did in the 1970s and are still doing in the US, or return to the inner cities? They can't have it both ways.

This argument, rooted in an empiricist concern for the middle classes as an expanding group who 'have to live somewhere', is hardly new, but can be thoroughly refuted in at least three ways:

1   It erroneously treats the middle classes as the exclusive agents of urban restructuring, with the fate of cities entirely dependent on their hallowed, sacred presence.
2   It ignores a body of scholarship confirming that it is *not* from the suburbs where most gentrifiers originate.[8] Hamnett thus has a selective or limited memory of the very literature on which he is an acknowledged expert.
3   Gentrification is treated as *the only conceivable remedy* for pathological 'urban dereliction and decay'. Those in the path of urban transformation are presented with a false choice: they can either have decay or gentrification. There is no alternative. This aligns Hamnett with established neoliberal urban policy discourses.

Here is how he portrays and reacts to the downside of gentrification:

> So, let's look at the downside. There is little doubt that urban regeneration success has helped to push up property prices in inner city areas, making some areas unaffordable to local residents. At £250,000 and upward for a small new apartment, local working class residents will not be buying in Clerkenwell, docklands or other, similar, regenerated areas. And the gastropubs and wine bars are likely to be too expensive for the local population who will also have lost some of the cheaper local shops and cafes. But is this a convincing argument against gentrification? The class structure of many British cities is changing with a growing middle class and a shrinking working class.

This passage exhibits two hallmarks of Hamnett's recent writing: first, reducing neighbourhoods to an 'urban regeneration success' of gastropubs and wine bars *trivialises* the loss of the right to housing suffered by working class people in gentrifying contexts; second, the insistence on a changing class structure to refute critics of gentrification *exaggerates* the expansion of the middle classes beyond all sensible limits. As one of his former students (Watt, 2008) has pointed out, Hamnett's analyses of class change in London are based upon occupational categories drawn from the census that focus on the economically active only – meaning that the economically *inactive* (the long-term unemployed, the sick, disabled and the elderly, many of whom are likely to be working class) disappear off the analytical radar. Furthermore, as Watt explains, 23.2 per cent of London's 16- to 74-year-old population were officially categorized as 'not classified' in the class schema on the basis of 2001 census data, as indeed were all those Londoners aged 75 years and over. Does this massive absence of evidence provide, as Hamnett is trying to, a convincing argument *for* gentrification?

Social class simply cannot be reduced to measurement. It is grounded in sets of power relations (domination and exploitation) which are etched onto urban space in the form of inequality – of which gentrification is a neighbourhood expression. Measurement is too often divorced from a broader theoretical view of the urban question and, in Hamnett's case, a *political* view that recognises that changing patterns of social class and housing in London reflect profound injustice.[9] But perhaps such an apolitical interpretation is to be expected in the city where Hamnett is based: just recently, a house in Highgate Cemetery sold for £6 million (see Davis and Alexander, 2008). The most famous occupant of that cemetery is doubtless turning in his grave.

'Gentrification is a pretty good thing'

'[T]he way to ensure that one's research has an impact is to tell policymakers and practitioners what they are already thinking, so that they can then claim that what they are proposing is research-based' (Hammersley, 2005, p.328). When Chris Hamnett reprimands critics of gentrification, he is not alone. Three contributions in the 'positive gentrification' mould have recently informed media interpretations and policy/planning circles in the United States, and have even attracted attention beyond their national context. Each contribution maintains that critics of gentrification have got it all wrong, and contains broadly similar conclusions: that gentrification doesn't displace many people, and has a good side that should be encouraged.

In 2002 the neoclassical economist Jacob Vigdor, funded by the Brookings Institution, authored a paper entitled 'Does Gentrification Harm the Poor?' (Vigdor, 2002) – the most stunning example of an economist asking a rhetorical question since Cutler and Glaeser's (1997) 'Are Ghettos Good or Bad?'. To his credit, Vigdor does acknowledge the literature beyond urban economics, particularly work by scholars who have tackled the displacement question, and does marshal a great deal of statistical evidence from the American Housing Survey to assess longitudinal changes in Boston's housing market (sensibly divided into 'core' and 'fringe' gentrifying census tracts, following Wyly and Hammel, 1999). Unfortunately, Vigdor's explanation of gentrification is not so wide-ranging, and rooted in conventional neoclassical land theory (each household's willingness to pay for land in a given neighbourhood based on its valuation of local amenities), 'What is the underlying cause of gentrification? Gentrification can occur when the preferences of high-status households change, or when the income disparity between high- and low-status households increases' (p.171).

Not surprisingly, Vigdor is unwilling to acknowledge the many critical reactions to this sort of reasoning (which is actually more *description* than explanation), and dives headfirst into a tortured modelling exercise of 'preference-driven gentrification' that assumes consumer sovereignty. This approach also guts the concept of its inherent class character, for the section of his essay attempting to answer the question 'What is gentrification?' *does not even mention the word 'class'*; indeed, that word appears only twice (preceded by middle- and upper-) in an essay stretching to forty pages. Class inequality is further jettisoned by a section entitled 'Gentrification in General Equilibrium' which smoothes over dislocation and smooches policy with the following:

> Gentrification might create job opportunities for low-status households, or relocate existing opportunities for low-status households, or relocate existing opportunities into areas more accessible to them. Second, increases in land values present property tax-dependent local governments with additional resources, which might translate into improved services or lower effective tax burdens for poor residents. Finally, the process of gentrification might improve neighbourhood quality for poor residents, offsetting the hypothesized negative effects of middle-class and upper-class abandonment of the central city.
>
> (p.144–5)

On displacement in Boston, Vigdor sifts and sorts through a numbing array of independent variables and finds that for low-income households, 'the importance of a high-quality neighbourhood appears to outweigh that of a high-quality housing unit' and that 'less-educated households are actually significantly more likely to remain in their housing unit than they are elsewhere in the metropolitan area' (p.161). This leads to a conclusion that Vigdor, in his concern for finding spatial equilibrium, appears desperate to reach throughout his article:

> Does gentrification displace low-status households? Whilst anecdotal evidence suggests that displacement does indeed occur, these results place the magnitude of the phenomenon in context. The exit of less educated households from units in gentrifying areas occurs no more frequently – and may indeed occur less frequently – than in other areas.
>
> (p.161)

The obligatory dismissal of non-statistical evidence as 'anecdotal' leads Vigdor to advance further conclusions that are entirely speculative and not at all supported by his own evidence:

> Gentrification might make central city neighborhoods more attractive to low-status households … The upgrading and socioeconomic integration of revitalizing neighborhoods might make them better places to live … Neighborhood revitalization is not a market failure; as modeled here, it is an efficient outcome of changes in preferences or the income distribution in a local economy.
>
> (p.172)

Vigdor ends with a consideration of 'proper policy responses', and offers the shocking suggestion that older individuals living alone should be offered state and/or regional government assistance in 'finding and moving into a new, less expensive residence' (p.173). No suggestions are offered as to how such individuals might be offered assistance to remain where they are at a more affordable rate. In effect, Vigdor is advocating displacement where he finds none. Qualitative studies across America from Marc Fried to Chester Hartman to John Betancur to Winifred Curran have found the sense of bereavement that comes with being displaced to be particularly acute among the elderly. Yet bereavement cannot be part of Vigdor's calculations, for it is not an independent variable: upset displacees would upset a search for logical, natural, inevitable gentrification within a broader spatial equilibrium framework. It is also worth remembering that Vigdor is writing about the city in which one of the first studies of urban displacement was undertaken. Its title needs no elaboration: 'Grieving for a Lost Home' (Fried, 1963).

Vigdor was soon joined in his sharp challenge to critics of gentrification by Lance Freeman. Three publications in particular have placed Freeman at centre-stage in policy and media attempts to recast gentrification as a collective urban good; a co-authored study using mobility data drawn from the triennial New York City Housing and Vacancy Survey (NYCHVS) (Freeman and Braconi, 2004); a national study also using mobility data, but drawn from the Panel Study of Income Dynamics (Freeman, 2005); and a book that takes a more mixed-methods approach in two New York City neighbourhoods, entitled (misleadingly) *There Goes the 'Hood: Views of Gentrification from the Ground Up* (Freeman, 2006). Freeman's point of departure was that previous studies have 'failed to quantify displacement due to gentrification in a convincing fashion … [and] failed to shed much light on what happened to the putative displacees' (2005, p.466). In some respects he is correct, but he refuses to accept the principle reason why: there are no statistical data available for such a task. Freeman believes that his data sources provide helpful indicators of the rate and extent of entry and exit from gentrifying neighbourhoods, but two immediate problems call this into question. First, using government housing databases to measure displacement precludes the propitious role of the government in the phenomenon being measured, as García-Herrera *et al.* (2007) explain:

> Insofar as the state at various scales adopts gentrification as a housing policy … it has little self-interest in collecting the kind of data that documents the level of displacement and the fate of displacees, data that would be tantamount to exposing the failure of these policies.
>
> (p.280)

Second, and taking the NYCHVS as an example, housing databases cannot capture the struggles low-income and working-class people endure *to remain where they are* in the face of neoliberal urban restructuring. Newman and Wyly (2006) are right on the case:

The NYCHVS ... is ill-suited for an analysis of the full social complexity of individual and family circumstances. Renters who cannot compete in the city's red hot real estate market and who leave for New Jersey (or elsewhere) disappear from view. Displaced individuals and families who are forced to double-up cannot be identified. And the structure of the survey (allowing only one choice on the question for the householder's reason for moving) terribly simplifies the circumstances of renters who were pushed out of their homes in the midst of other crises, such as unexpected bills that made it more difficult to meet the rent, job loss, or a divorce.

(p.42)

Nevertheless, Freeman and Braconi (2004) concluded with considerable fanfare that between 1996–9, in seven gentrifying neighbourhoods in New York City, lower-income and lesser-educated households were 19 per cent less likely to move than those in other neighbourhoods. They hypothesised that such households appreciate the improvements in services and amenities brought about by gentrification, and went public soon afterwards with pre-dictable media reaction. Freeman's (2005) national study did not find lower mobility rates, but concluded that 'the relationship between gentrification and displacement is not especially robust' (p.483) and that gentrification is 'a gradual process that, although displacing some, leaves its imprint by changing who moves into a neighbourhood' (p.488). This is not news to anyone who researches gentrification, even if Freeman insists that 'for students of neigh-bourhood change, this is an important lesson to understand' (p.488). Students of neighbourhood change, however, need to treat with utmost caution the sentences that immediately follow:

From a policy perspective, the implications are perhaps subtler. Gentrification brings with it increased investment and middle-class house-holds to formerly forlorn neighbourhoods. This could potentially enhance the tax base of many central cities and perhaps increase socio-economic integration as well. After decades of disinvestments and middle-class flight, these benefits from the gentrification should not be overlooked.

(p.488)

Here we reach the perils of a 'nuanced' analysis. Freeman is aware of prob-lems that gentrification can bring to disinvested neighbourhoods (he follows the above sentences with a brief discussion of them), but he does not *fore-ground* those problems from a policy perspective – one which is introduced alongside the supposed benefits of gentrification. Perhaps this is why *USA Today* seized upon Freeman's work and massaged it into the headline: 'Studies: Gentrification a Boost for Everyone'.

There Goes the 'Hood is admirable for its awareness in the limitations of sta-tistical analysis. Two gentrifying neighbourhoods of New York City constitute the geographical focus – Harlem in Manhattan and Clinton Hill in Brooklyn, both of which experienced racialised disinvestment (severely in the former). Freeman's strategy was to interview 43 'indigenous residents'[10] in Harlem and 22 in Clinton Hill,

> to elicit from respondents their perceptions about how the neighbourhood was changing and how those changes were affecting them. Particular focus was given to changes in amenities, services, demographics, and neighbourhood social interaction. The interviews also sought information about respondents' housing situations and their future mobility plans.
>
> (p.10)

Freeman concludes from these interviews that: (1) gentrification can bring improvements to neighbourhood services and amenities that long-term residents appreciate; (2) a great deal of 'cynicism' has greeted the arrival of gentrification; (3) residents are worried about displacement even if 'widespread displacement is unlikely' (p.79); and (4) that gentrifiers can be both good and bad neighbours.

The most pervasive argument of his book is that long-term residents appreciate an improving neighbourhood, and that it has to be better than its recent past. Freeman and his respondents see gentrification as better than the 'alternative' of severe disinvestment and its symptoms, and that while gentrification raises the 'specter' of displacement, it has a good side to be encouraged because it makes places look better than they did before, and provides them with better services. (The crucial question never considered by Freeman is: why does it have to be gentrification that brings better services?) However, ethnographic analyses of gentrification in black ghettos, such as Michelle Boyd's work in Bronzeville, Chicago (Boyd, 2005), rejects as an *illusion* the contention that gentrification is happening in the interests of – and with the approval of – the poor black residents it threatens to displace. Class – the essence of gentrification – is something experienced *through* race in Boyd's analysis; in Freeman's, race *trumps* class, thwarting an investigation of gentrification that is sensitive to its conceptual content and its historical meaning.

Vigdor and Freeman both position themselves as lonely voices of reason, and appear rather unaffected by how their research findings can get away from them and be amplified and aggravated to suit certain agendas. Newman and Wyly's (2006) reaction implicitly raises the question of ethical responsibility once research findings are available:

> The new evidence on gentrification and displacement … has rapidly jumped out of the obscure scholarly cloister to influence policy debates that have been ripped out of context … [and] used to dismiss concerns about a wide range of market-oriented urban policies of privatisation, home-ownership, 'social mix' and dispersal strategies designed to break up

the concentrated poverty that has been taken as the shorthand explanation for all that ails the disinvested inner city. If displacement is not a problem, many are saying, then regeneration (or whatever else the process is called) is fine too. Perhaps it will even give some poor people the benefits of a middle-class neighbourhood without requiring them to move to a middle-class community.

(p.25)

The last two sentences accurately capture the tenor of the most recent national study to trumpet the low mobility rates of the poor in gentrifying neighbourhoods, and to exhibit little restraint when journalists come knocking. Urban economists McKinnish *et al.* (2010) begin with a clear statement of intent:

> We analyze the characteristics of the households moving into, moving out of and staying in these [low-income] neighborhoods. These basic demographic facts of neighborhood gentrification are largely unknown due to a lack of suitable data, and it is difficult to discuss policy issues related to gentrification without establishing such facts.
>
> (p.180)

Unfortunately this is where clarity ends. Their literature review is woefully skeletal, and the section of their paper entitled 'Definition of Gentrification' is desperately confused; in fact, it contains no definition at all. Instead, they simply look at which poor census tracts experienced an increase in average family income between 1990 and 2000 of at least $10,000. Boasting somewhat about their privileged access to statistics usually under lock and key, they claim that their narrowing of geographical scale and provision of more detailed demographic information on 'movers and stayers' allows them to validate beyond all doubt Vigdor and Freeman's suspicions regarding why low-income minorities do not appear to exit gentrifying contexts:

> Overall, we find that rather than dislocating non-white households, gentrification creates neighbourhoods that are attractive to middle-class minority households, particularly those with children or with elderly householders … [T]he neighborhoods we define as gentrified have already experienced massive income growth … yet still have very sizeable fractions of non-white and non-college-educated households, and sizeable in-migration of these same demographic groups. These facts alone suggest that the stark gentrification-displacement story was not the norm during the 1990s.
>
> (p.191–2)

Aside from the embarrassment of presenting as a novel research finding the established fact that gentrification creates neighbourhoods attractive to the middle-classes and increases their incomes, of most concern should be what happened once an earlier draft of this paper was produced. The National Bureau of Economic Research circulated the draft widely and soon afterwards *Time* magazine produced an article entitled 'Gentrification: Not Ousting the Poor?' Particularly bothersome was the comment by one of the authors of the study (Walsh), 'We're not saying that there aren't communities where displacement isn't happening. But in general, across all neighbourhoods in the urbanized parts of the US, it looks like gentrification is a pretty good thing.'

The *Time* article concluded that 'the study paints a more nuanced picture of gentrification than exists in the popular imagination' – precisely the same language (forming the bedrock of the current *academic doxa* on the topic) which Jacob Vigdor and Lance Freeman have used in their efforts to maximise the visibility and impact of their research.

The studies under scrutiny here are, in fact, not that 'nuanced' at all. Indeed, what appears to have motivated them was deep suspicion of radical perspectives on gentrification which present this process as one which causes low-income and working-class communities anything from serious anxiety to serious upheaval. There is little sense of moral outrage at moving people from their homes, denying them the right to housing via the erosion of affordability, and the commodification of a basic human need. One only has to read the first few pages of *Displacement: How to Fight It* (Hartman *et al.*, 1982), as much a challenge to neoclassical land theory as a guidebook for community activists, to see the importance of what has been silenced by those who have been insisting on gentrification's positives:

> *Moving people involuntarily from their homes or neighbourhoods is wrong.* Regardless of whether it results from government or private market action, forced displacement is characteristically a case of people without the economic and political power to resist being pushed out by people with greater resources and power, people who think they have a 'better' use for a certain building, piece of land, or neighborhood. The pushers benefit. The pushees do not. [It is also] *fundamentally wrong to allow removal of housing units from the low-moderate income stock, for any purpose, without requiring at least a one-for-one replacement.* Demolition, conversion, or 'upgrade' rehab of vacant private or publicly owned lower-rent housing should be just as vigorously opposed as when those units are occupied.
>
> (p.4–5, emphasis in the original)

The ongoing search for 'robust evidence' – the same foraging which allows Chris Hamnett to refute his own earlier findings – has also shut out any chance of conceptual development and analytical sophistication with regard to urban displacement and its links to gentrification. The communicators of low mobility rates among the poor need an analytical corrective to land in their epistemological pumpkin patch, and this can be found in the writings of Peter Marcuse.

Missing Marcuse: gentrification and displacement explained

> What makes a subject hard to understand – if it's something significant
> and important – is not that before you can understand it you need to be
> specially trained in abstruse matters, but the contrast between understand-
> ing the subject and what most people *want* to see. Because of this the very
> things which are most obvious may become the hardest of all to under-
> stand. What has to be overcome is a difficulty having to do with the will,
> rather than with the intellect.
>
> (Ludwig Wittgenstein, 1977 [1931])

New York City in the early 1980s exhibited a landscape where two processes
that appeared to be polar opposites were happening simultaneously – abandonment and gentrification. To policymakers, the former was painful, and nothing
could be done to stop it short of triage. Gentrification, on the other hand, was
highly desirable to policymakers – a cure for abandonment, financed mostly
by the private sector, and any displacement it causes would be trivial. For low-
income communities, however, urban policy didn't exactly offer much hope;
the message was that you can either have abandonment, or gentrification. Peter
Marcuse took a knife to the soft underbelly of this false choice with a series
of papers[11] showing how abandonment and gentrification are neither opposites nor alternatives, but tightly connected (Marcuse, 1985a, 1985b, 1986).
With typical conceptual precision, here is Marcuse (1985a) summarising his
argument:

> Abandonment drives some higher-income households out of the city, while
> it drives others to gentrifying areas close to downtown. Abandonment
> drives some lower-income households to adjacent areas, where pressures
> on housing and rents are increased. Gentrification attracts higher-income
> households from other areas in the city, reducing demand elsewhere, and
> increasing tendencies to abandonment. In addition, gentrification displaces
> lower-income people – increasing pressures on housing and rents. Both
> abandonment and gentrification are linked directly to changes in the eco-
> nomic polarization of the population. A vicious circle is created in which
> the poor are continuously under pressure of displacement and the wealthy
> continuously seek to wall themselves within gentrified neighbourhoods.
> Far from a cure for abandonment, gentrification worsens the process.
>
> (p.196)

In its commendable simplicity, this account offers a devastating indictment
of consumer sovereignty interpretations of gentrification and abandonment,
which hold that the former is explained by rising demand for housing, the
latter by falling demand. As Marcuse showed, 'dual market' housing demand
arguments (gentrification in one market, abandonment in the other) are

immediately derailed by the geographical fact that 'the two phenomena often occur around the corner from each other' (p.197). Crucially, gentrification and abandonment were not explained as the result of individual household preferences, but rather as disturbing outcomes of the private and public institutional factors *behind* any preferences; quite simply, the state of the housing market and of public policy.

But what of the extremely difficult displacement question? Marcuse built upon and extended the earlier work of Grier and Grier (1978), and LeGates and Hartman (1981), to conceptualise four types of displacement:[12]

1 *Direct last-resident displacement*: this can be physical (e.g. when landlords cut off the heat in a building, forcing the occupants to move out) or economic (e.g. a rent increase).
2 *Direct chain displacement*: this looks beyond standard 'last resident' counting to include previous households that 'may have been forced to move at an earlier stage in the physical decline of the building or an earlier rent increase'.
3 *Exclusionary displacement*: this refers to those residents who cannot access housing as it has been gentrified/abandoned:

> When one household vacates a housing unit voluntarily and that unit is then gentrified or abandoned so that another similar household is prevented from moving in, the number of units available to the second household in that housing market is reduced. The second household, therefore, is excluded from living where it would otherwise have lived.
>
> (p.206)

4 *Displacement pressure*: this refers to the dispossession suffered by poor and working-class families during the transformation of the neighbourhoods where they live:

> When a family sees the neighbourhood around it changing dramatically, when their friends are leaving the neighbourhood, when the stores they patronise are liquidating and new stores for other clientele are taking their places, and when changes in public facilities, in transportation patterns, and in support services all clearly are making the area less and less livable, then the pressure of displacement already is severe. Its actuality is only a matter of time. Families living under these circumstances may move as soon as they can, rather than wait for the inevitable; nonetheless they are displaced.
>
> (p.207)

Whilst anchored in an analysis of New York City's housing market in the 1980s, the huge literature on gentrification since the 1980s provides nothing obvious to suggest that these insights are not applicable elsewhere. Marcuse was arguing for a panoramic view of displacement where there is abandonment and gentrification, 'The full impact of displacement must include consideration of all four forms … It must include displacement from economic changes, physical changes, neighbourhood changes, and individual unit changes' (p.208).

He was acutely sensitive to the difficulties in measuring gentrification-induced displacement precisely, yet he was pointing out that it is essential to have *conceptual clarity before research on displacement begins, and before any conclusions can be drawn*. This is a masterclass for all gentrification researchers, but sadly it has been skipped by those whose work has made the headlines.

Let us take exclusionary displacement as an example. The studies reported in the last section all maintained that lower household mobility rates among the poor in gentrifying neighbourhoods suggested that concerns about displacement are overblown and, in turn, suggests that poor people must appreciate the 'improvements' taking place in those neighbourhoods, and find ways to stay. Here is Marcuse's (2005) response:

> Do they have a 'lower propensity to move' because they are finally getting decent neighborhood services (an odd phrase, incidentally, quantitatively considered: judging just by statistics, prison inmates have a 'low propensity to move'); or are they not moving because the very process of gentrification reduces their possibilities of finding affordable housing, in a tight and tightening market?

Freeman's (2008) counter-charge is as follows:

> It is unlikely that this [exclusionary displacement] would explain Freeman and Braconi's results for it does not explain why mobility rates would be *lower* in gentrifying neighborhoods and those experiencing the most rapid rental inflation. Presumably, poor households in non-gentrifying neighborhoods would also be trapped [because so much of the city's housing has gentrified] as well.
>
> (p.187)

The 'poor households in non-gentrifying neighbourhoods' to which Freeman refers represent the control group from the Freeman and Braconi (2004) study, and this group includes residents from some of the poorest parts of New York City (parts of Brooklyn and Queens with high poverty rates, plus all of the Bronx). Refuting exclusionary displacement by saying that this group would be unable to access gentrified housing too is an interesting defence, but not one sensitive to a litany of studies which document high levels of *forced* mobility for poor renter households (via evictions):

> [R]enters, who have far less security of tenure than homeowners, are disproportionately represented among involuntary movers. And since, compared with homeowners, renters tend to be disproportionately minority and to have lower incomes, the problem of involuntary moves disproportionately affects the more vulnerable households in our society.
>
> (Hartman and Robinson, 2003, p.467)

So, as Newman and Wyly (2006) explain with respect to Freeman and Braconi's control group, 'We might expect that these residents move more frequently than those in other areas of the city, producing an artificially high standard to use as a comparison for displacement rates from gentrifying neighbourhoods' (p.28).

In addition, if gentrification theory teaches us anything, we should know by now that *rent gaps are widest in non-gentrifying neighbourhoods* (when the gap between the actual ground rent in the area and the ground rent that could be extracted were the area to undergo reinvestment becomes wide enough to allow that reinvestment to take place). Higher levels of mobility – especially evictions – are to be expected as landlords and developers realise that systematic disinvestment has reached a point where neighbourhoods can be redeveloped at substantial profit (see also Clark, 1987; Hammel, 1999). To put all this in clearer conceptual terms, direct displacement (last-resident and probably chain forms) is suffered by poor households in non-gentrifying neighbourhoods, and exclusionary displacement is suffered by poor households in gentrifying neighbourhoods, where low mobility is also to be expected.

To claim that displacement concerns are overblown, and to replace those concerns with the hypothesis that poor people must appreciate the 'improvements' taking place in gentrifying neighbourhoods, is greatly to disregard the ongoing struggles non-gentrifiers endure in order to make rent as 'improvements' around them make everything more expensive; not to mention the constant fear of displacement among vulnerable renters in particular. Freeman (2006) discusses this fear, but throughout his book unfortunately characterises it as 'cynicism'[13] that can and should be 'dampened' by community organizations (p.186). In addition, he wonders if displacees will be fine in the long run:

> There is a strand of research in social psychology that suggests people routinely underestimate their reslience in the face of adverse life events like the loss of a limb or a loved one. Displacement could possibly be similar in this way.
>
> (p.164)

Another example of how scholars conveniently miss Marcuse can be found in a recent paper by Hamnett (again!) and Whitelegg (2007) on loft conversions in Clerkenwell, London:

> Commercial gentrification … [has] significantly and probably irrevocably changed the social mix and ethos of the area which was dominated by social rented housing tenants. This has not, however, been accompanied by significant residential displacement as almost all the new housing units were in what were previously warehouses, industrial, or office buildings. As such, it is a clear example of gentrification without displacement although it may well be accompanied by growing feelings of relative deprivation on the part of existing residents who have seen traditional working men's cafes and pubs replaced by swish restaurants, wine bars, kitchen shops, and florists.
>
> (p.122)

Gentrification without displacement … yet the social mix has changed, the area *was* (it no longer is) dominated by social rented housing tenants, and working men's cafés and pubs have disappeared in favour of swish establishments? What Hamnett and Whitelegg are describing is Marcuse's *displacement pressure* – so they have actually uncovered a clear example of gentrification *with* displacement. It is also a pity that they did not consult the recent scholarship on 'indirect displacement' in surrounding neighbourhoods as warehouse, industrial and office building conversions elevate rental and sales prices in 'up and coming' areas adjacent to those conversions (Davidson, 2007); furthermore, the work of Curran (2004, 2007) on *industrial displacement* in Williamsburg, Brooklyn, reveals the futility of seeing gentrification-induced displacement as something that just affects occupied housing units.

A final note regarding the wider applicability of Marcuse's conceptual logic – his writings have much to offer anti-gentrification struggles. Exclusionary displacement is a potentially devastating *political* reaction to all those who have been pressing the view that low mobility among the poor in cities of the Global North is tantamount to the poor appreciating gentrification. When New Urbanist blowhard Andres Duany (2001) asks 'So what's all the fuss about over gentrification?' ridiculing neighbourhood activism in the process, the Marcuse-inspired reply is that gentrification has removed so much affordable housing that poor people in gentrifying neighbourhoods are trapped. They do not in fact 'appreciate' gentrification, as it has severely limited their residential mobility. In cities in the Global South, slum clearances for mega-events (such as the Beijing Olympics) mean that 'direct last resident displacement' and 'direct chain displacement' could not be more relevant to understanding the magnitude of dislocation,[14] and the dynamics behind it. It is only by grasping the mechanisms that create different forms of displacement can any attempt to legitimise upheaval be effectively refuted.

Conclusion: on alternatives

> Eviction from the neighbourhood in which one was at home can be almost as disruptive of the meaning of life as the loss of a crucial relationship.

> Dispossession threatens the whole structure of attachments through which purposes are embodied, because these attachments cannot readily be re-established in an alien setting.
>
> (Marris, 1986, p.57)

The debate over both gentrification and displacement is currently dominated by mainstream perspectives which rob the former of its historical meaning as the neighbourhood expression of class inequality, and gut the latter of its conceptual content by viewing low mobility among poor residents in gentrifying neighbourhoods as robust evidence that the displacement concerns of anti-gentrification activists are overblown. These perspectives, anchored in neoclassical urban economics and dressed up in methodological sophistication and nuanced reasoning, have proved highly seductive to journalists seeking soundbytes and neat statistics, and to urban policymakers searching for a 'reliable evidence base' free from 'anecdotes'.

The task for critical urban studies is to reject the celebration of gentrification and the denial of displacement by reorienting the debate away from the positivist humdrum of independent variables drawn from survey categories (legitimised by appeals to 'policy relevance'), and towards a sturdier analytical, political and moral framework which is rooted in *housing as a question of social justice*, and in particular, adequate and affordable housing as a human right and a basic human need. Housing is a fictitious financial asset (Harvey, 1985); its non-fictional status as shelter and as *home* is beyond question. 'Home' tends to evoke some of the most elevated human reactions:

> A home exists where sentiment and space converge to afford attachment, stability, and a secure sense of personal control. It is an abiding place and a web of trustworthy connections, an anchor of identity and social life, the seat of intimacy and trust from which we pursue our emotional and material needs.
>
> (Segal and Baumohl, 1988, p.249)

Dispossessing or depriving someone of their home is therefore 'a heinous act of injustice' (Smith, 1994, p.152), and one that makes the decade-long preoccupation with researching the consumer preferences of middle-class gentrifiers even more baffling. As grim as the current global financial implosion may seem (it was caused in large part by housing becoming the major vehicle of capital accumulation), there is a golden opportunity for critical urbanists among the detritus left in the wake of the mobilization of state power in the extension of market rule (Tickell and Peck, 2003). In the US, the widespread analogies with the Great Depression offer an unexpected opening, for in the 1930s the threat of massive unrest around issues of housing and unemployment led to moratoria on mortgage foreclosures, strong federal support for low-income homeownership (as opposed to private support), and the enactment of a nationwide public housing program (Squires, 1992). So, the large-scale displacement caused by epidemic foreclosures and repossessions should not only be analysed as symptomatic of the fundamental flaws of three decades of economic deregulation; it should be analysed as part of a wider intellectual project *to bring social justice back in* to research on the housing question (and, of course, the urban question).

This will not be straightforward. Careful scrutiny of recent issues of the journals *Housing Studies* and *Urban Studies* reveals them to have become instruments of the 'growing heteronomy of urban research' (Wacquant, 2008); that is, research guided by the priorities of policymakers and city rulers, and the worries of the mainstream media, sidelining autonomous intellectual projects carrying a 'higher theoretical payload' (p.203). There appears to be little room for perspectives which call into question the underlying structure of socio-political interests constituting capitalist urban and land economies and policies,[15] or what Neil Smith (1996) called 'all the economic and political exploitation which makes gentrification possible' (p.xx). Urban researchers – often funded by the state – seldom have the capacity to formulate their own questions and to seek answers with total freedom, no matter where their inquiries lead them. The function of 'policy relevant' research seems to be less about changing cities for the better, but rather to stand guard and protect the dominant class from the impertinent questioning of critical reason (Wacquant, 2004).

But what of alternatives to gentrification? This is hardly a topic bursting with ideas lately. In fact, one of the more striking trends in recent scholarship has been a proliferation of policy-oriented suggestions on how we might 'manage' gentrification, rather than stop it (for an exception, see Ley and Dobson, 2008). This research precludes the vital moral question of *what property ought to be* (Blomley, 2004). DeFilippis (2004) gets right to the heart of the problem to be tackled:

> The importance of gentrification … is that it clearly demonstrates that low-income people, and the neighbourhoods they live in, suffer not from a lack of capital but from a lack of power and control over even the most basic components of life – that is, the places called home.
>
> (p.89)

DeFilippis' insightful discussion of assorted efforts to gain power and control in communities across America[16] nudges us closer to a consideration of possibilities for the *decommodification of housing*. Particularly exciting in this regard is that Peter Marcuse co-authored a punchy essay in this very issue in the mid-1980s (Achtenberg and Marcuse, 1986). Policy researchers would probably dismiss this essay as some sort of radical idealism (or even socialist madness), but much of the content of this essay is highly relevant to today's housing meltdown:

Now that the political counterattack on housing is in full force and housing and economic conditions are worsening, there is an opportunity to
develop a broad-based progressive housing movement than can unite
low- and moderate-income tenants and homeowners around their common interest in decent, affordable housing and adequate neighbourhoods
… Needed is a program that can alter the terms of existing public debate
on housing, that challenges the commodity nature of housing and its role
in our economic and social system, and that demonstrates how people's
legitimate housing needs can be met through an alternative approach.

(p.475)

Achtenberg and Marcuse carefully outlined the goal of such a program:

To provide every person with housing that is affordable, adequate in size
and of decent quality, secure in tenure, and located in a supportive neighbourhood of choice, with recognition of the special housing problems
confronting oppressed groups.

(p.476)

A strategy for housing decommodification[17] would be an attempt 'to limit
the role of profit from decisions affecting housing, substituting instead the
basic principle of socially determined need' (p.476). They called for the social
ownership of housing, the social production of housing supply, public control
of housing finance capital, the social control of land, the resident control of
neighbourhoods, affirmative action and housing choice, and equitable resource
allocation.

Now, to advocate the decommodification of housing is neither to get carried away in some romantic haze that is divorced from empirical reality, nor
to cop out of practical solutions to the immediate problem of gentrification
and displacement. It is simply to argue that there is considerable mileage in
resuscitating these ideas at a time when they are so urgently needed.[18] The
eloquence with which they were written, their theoretical sophistication, their
scientific rigour and their deep-seated concern for the plight of those most
affected by urban sociospatial restructuring provide a compelling case for, at
the very least, serious discussion and debate. The task for scholars engaged in
the 'Right to the City' movement is not just ongoing inquiry into what leads
some to have more rights to the city than others, but the construction of a set
of morally defensible principles which might bring about the political will to
do something about the class inequalities so vividly written into the landscape
of the neoliberal metropolis. As Marcuse (1986) himself argued:

The large question is not *whether* abandonment can be avoided, gentrification controlled, displacement eliminated, or even *how* these things can be

done, but rather whether there is the desire to do them. That is a question that can only be answered in the political arena.

(p.175)

Notes

1 This title is a deliberate play on Peter Marcuse's memorable (1991) book *Missing Marx: A Personal and Political Journal of a Year in East Germany, 1989–90*, an absorbing personal and political account of the dissolution of the socialist state based on his observations of key events and experiences in the tumultuous year of 1989.

2 Global financial institutions liberated by economic deregulation have turned central London – and indeed much of south-east England – into an appallingly expensive place, especially in terms of housing.

3 Jason Hackworth (2002: 815) has defined gentrification as 'the production of space for progressively more affluent users', the justification being 'in light of several decades of research and debate that shows that the concept is usefully applied to non-residential urban change and that there is frequently a substantial time lag between when the subordinate class group gives way to more affluent users. That is, the displacement or replacement is often neither direct nor immediate, but the process remains 'gentrification' because the space is being transformed for more affluent users' (p.839).

4 http://www.guardian.co.uk/commentisfree. The title is a reference to a famous sentence in a 1921 essay written by a former *Guardian* editor C. P. Scott: 'Comment is free, but facts are sacred'.

5 For much of the 1990s, Hamnett lambasted Saskia Sassen for presenting a 'polarization' view of global cities that did not take into account changing occupational structures (in particular, an expanding professional middle class). He never considered, however, the wider political messages contained in her work (this presumably explains why Sassen never felt it necessary to respond in print).

6 The issue emerged from a conference in Glasgow in September 2002 entitled 'Upward Neighbourhood Trajectories', and was notable for its almost exclusive focus on gentrifiers (despite a wide-ranging call for papers), a striking lack of critical perspectives, its unearthing of old debates (Redfern, 2003) and assessments of 'positive gentrification' (Cameron, 2003).

7 Smith pointed out this problem after Hamnett delivered his conference paper in Glasgow, and several influential contributions in the 1990s and beyond have insisted gentrification researchers move on from this theoretical quagmire. But neither Hamnett, peer reviewers, the editor of the special issue or the editors of the journal took any notice.

8 This literature is so extensive that it's a challenge to single out a few examples, but see Marcuse (1985a) for a discussion of the 'back-to-the-city' myth, and Beauregard (1993) for a very detailed discussion of the 'discourse of decline' which led to erroneous assumptions of gentrification being a physical movement away from suburbia. To be sure, gentrifiers certainly rejected suburbia, but this was for what it symbolised – most never left the central city (see Ley, 1996).

9 Particularly galling is the fact that Hamnett (2003b) has recently accused contemporary human geographers of 'fiddling while Rome burns' – but on the basis of his arguments about gentrification, might they have borrowed his fiddle?

10 The 'indigenous residents' were all non-white, 37 per cent of them college educated (gentrifiers?), and the median length of tenure for both neighbourhoods was 17 years, even though a few residents interviewed were not indigenous at all but 'recent arrivals'.

11 He was not the first to point this out. Neil Smith (1979) had challenged hegemonic neoclassical economic thought with his rent-gap thesis, where abandonment represented the most extreme stage of capital devolarization in the built environment before opportunities for profitable redevelopment could be captured.

12 This discussion also serves as a corrective to Atkinson's (2000, p.150–1) summary of Marcuse's work, which gets confused and misses 'displacement pressure' altogether.

13 Re-casting any opposition to gentrification as 'cynicism' on the part of residents is a powerful political move, implying that such residents are falsely conscious, incapable of understanding that gentrification is good for them. I am grateful to Martine August for this point.

14 Shenjing He and Fulong Wu's (2005) study of the gentrification of the working-class Xintiandi neighbourhood in Shanghai revealed that 1950 households were evicted and displaced to poor suburbs within six months, and in neighbouring Taipingqiao Park, 3800 households and 156 work units were evicted and displaced in 43 days (the record for the fastest displacement ever in Shanghai) to make way for a public park connected to gentrification. The consequences of direct displacement were emotionally and economically devastating: 'Although these residents have been offered resettlement housing, many people have become chronically unemployed after a few years, due to excessive commuting costs and broken social networks' (He, 2007, p.194).

15 In their editorial introduction to a recent special issue of *Urban Studies* entitled 'Gentrification and Public Policy', Lees and Ley (2008) hope that the scholarship within the issue 'may aid a first step towards a more inclusive policy portfolio that addresses head-on the unequal life chances associated with the contemporary gentrification project' (p.2383). This erroneously assumes that (a) policymakers are going to read the issue, and (b) that policymakers are interested in resisting neoliberal urbanisation.

16 DeFilippis focuses on Limited Equity Housing Cooperatives, Community Land Trusts and Mutual Housing Associations; forms of collective ownership that hardly disrupt the wider political–economic status quo, but at least remove land and housing from the brutality of the market.

17 Smith and Williams (1986) concluded their edited volume as follows: 'In the long run, the only defence against gentrification is the decommodification of housing' (p.272). It is a sign of the times that Peter Williams ended up as the Deputy Director of the Council of Mortgage Lenders in the UK!

18 There can be little doubt that capitalized ground rent is now on a downward spiral, and that there is a great deal of devalorization taking place. Any talk of 'degentrification' should really be stalled by the likelihood that the neighbourhoods hit hardest by foreclosures will be the gentrifying neighbourhoods of five to eight years from now. It may be more fruitful to think about the decommodification of housing in the context of preventing widening rent gaps from being exploited by the owners of capital.

References

Achtenberg, E.P. and Marcuse, P. (1986) 'Toward the decommodification of housing', in R. Bratt, C. Hartman and A. Meyerson (eds), *Critical Perspectives on Housing*, Philadelphia: Temple University Press, pp.474–83.

Atkinson, R. (2000) 'Measuring gentrification and displacement in Greater London', *Urban Studies*, 37, pp.149–66.

Beauregard, R. (1993) *Voices of Decline*, Oxford: Blackwell.

Blomley, N. (2004) *Unsettling the City*, New York: Routledge.

Boyd, M. (2005) 'The downside of racial uplift: the meaning of gentrification in an African-American neighbourhood', *City & Society*, 17, pp.265–88.

Butler, T. (2007) 'For gentrification?' *Environment and Planning A*, 39, pp.162–81.

Cameron, S. (2003) 'Gentrification, housing redifferentiation and urban regeneration: "going for growth" in Newcastle upon Tyne', *Urban Studies*, 40, pp.2367–82.

Clark, E. (1987) *The Rent Gap and Urban Change*, Lund: Lund University Press.

Curran, W. (2004) 'Gentrification and the nature of work: exploring the links in Williamsburg, Brooklyn', *Environment and Planning A*, 36, pp.1243–58.

Curran, W. (2007) 'From the frying pan to the oven: gentrification and the experience of industrial displacement in Williamsburg, Brooklyn', *Urban Studies*, 44, pp.1427–40.

Cutler, D. and Glaeser, E. (1997) 'Are ghettos good or bad?' *Quarterly Journal of Economics*, 112, pp.827–72.

Davidson, M. (2007) 'Gentrification as global habitat: a process of class formation or corporate creation?' *Transactions of the Institute of British Geographers*, 32, pp.490–506.

Davis, H. and Alexander, L. (2008) 'Karl would not be amused', *The Times*, August 15.

DeFilippis, J. (2004) *Unmaking Goliath*, New York: Routledge.

Duany, A. (2001) 'Three cheers for gentrification', *American Enterprise Magazine*, April/May, pp.36–9.

Freeman, L. (2005) 'Displacement or succession? Residential mobility in gentrifying neighborhoods', *Urban Affairs Review*, 40, pp.463–91.

Freeman, L. (2006) *There Goes the 'hood: Views of Gentrification from the Ground Up*, Philadelphia: Temple University Press.

Freeman, L. (2008) 'Comment on "the eviction of critical perspectives from gentrification research"', *International Journal of Urban and Regional Research*, 32, pp.186–91.

Freeman, L. and Braconi, F. (2004) 'Gentrification and displacement: New York City in the 1990s', *Journal of the American Planning Association*, 70, pp.39–52.

Fried, M. (1963) 'Grieving for a lost home', in L. J. Duhl (ed.), *The Urban Condition: People and Policy in the Metropolis*, New York: Basic Books.

García-Herrera, L., Smith, N. and Mejías Vera, M. (2007) 'Gentrification, displacement and tourism in Santa Cruz de Tenerife', *Urban Geography*, 28, pp.276–98.

Glass, R. (1964) 'Introduction: aspects of change', in Centre for Urban Studies (ed.), *Aspects of Change*, London: MacGibbon and Kee, pp.xiii–xlii.

Grier, G. and Grier, E. (1978) *Urban Displacement: A Reconnaissance*, Washington DC: US Dept. of Housing and Urban Development.

Hackworth, J. (2002) 'Postrecession gentrification in New York City', *Urban Affairs Review*, 37, pp.815–43.

Hackworth, J. and Smith, N. (2001) 'The changing state of gentrification', *Tijdschrift voor Economische en Sociale Geografie*, 92, pp.464–77.

Hammel, D. J. (1999) 'Re-establishing the rent gap: an alternative view of capitalized land rent', *Urban Studies*, 36, pp.1283–93.

Hammersley, M. (2005) 'The myth of research-based practice: the critical case of educational inquiry', *International Journal of Social Research Methodology*, 8, pp.317–30.

Hamnett, C. (1973) 'Improvement grants as an indicator of gentrification in Inner London', *Area*, 5, pp.252–61.

Hamnett, C. (1991) 'The blind men and the elephant: the explanation of gentrification', *Transactions of the Institute of British Geographers*, 16, pp.173–89.

Hamnett, C. (2003a) 'Gentrification and the middle-class remaking of inner London, 1961–2001', *Urban Studies*, 40, pp.2401–26.

Hamnett, C. (2003b) 'Contemporary human geography: fiddling while Rome burns?' *Geoforum*, 34, pp.1–3.

Hamnett, C. (2008) 'The regeneration game', *The Guardian*, June 11. Retrieved from http://www.guardian.co.uk/commentisfree/2008/jun/11/housing (accessed 1 July 2011).

Hamnett, C. and Randolph, B. (1984) 'The role of landlord disinvestment in housing market transformation: an analysis of the flat break-up market in Central London', *Transactions of the Institute of British Geographers*, 9, pp.259–79.

Hamnett, C. and Randolph, B. (1986) 'Tenurial transformation and the flat break-up market in London: the British condo experience', in N. Smith and P. Williams (eds), *Gentrification of the City*, London: Allen and Unwin, pp.121–52.

Hamnett, C. and Whitelegg, D. (2007) 'Loft conversion and gentrification in London: from industrial to postindustrial land use', *Environment and Planning A*, 39, pp.106–24.

Hartman, C. (2002) *City for Sale: The Transformation of San Francisco*, Berkeley: University of California Press.

Hartman, C., Keating, D. and LeGates, R. with Turner, S. (1982) *Displacement: How to Fight It*, Berkeley: National Housing Law Project.

Hartman, C. and Robinson, D. (2003) 'Evictions: the hidden housing problem', *Housing Policy Debate*, 14, pp.461–501.

Harvey, D. (1985) *The Urbanization of Capital*. Baltimore: Johns Hopkins University Press.

He, S. (2007) 'State-sponsored gentrification under market transition: the case of Shanghai', *Urban Affairs Review*, 43, pp.171–98.

He, S. and Wu, F. (2005) 'Property-led redevelopment in post-reform China: a case study of Xintiandi redevelopment project in Shanghai', *Journal of Urban Affairs*, 27, pp.1–23.

Lees, L. and Ley, D. (2008) 'Introduction to special issue on gentrification and public policy', *Urban Studies*, 45, pp.2379–84.

Lees, L., Slater, T. and Wyly, E. (2008) *Gentrification*, New York: Routledge.

LeGates, R. and Hartman, C. (1981) 'Displacement', *Clearinghouse Review*, July 15, pp.207–49.

Ley, D. (1996) *The New Middle Class and the Remaking of the Central City*, Oxford: Oxford University Press.

Ley, D. and Dobson, C. (2008) 'Are there limits to gentrification? The contexts of impeded gentrification in Vancouver', *Urban Studies*, 45, pp.2471–98.

Marcuse, P. (1985a) 'Gentrification, abandonment and displacement: connections, causes and policy responses in New York City', *Journal of Urban and Contemporary Law*, 28, pp.195–240.

Marcuse, P. (1985b) 'To control gentrification: anti-displacement zoning and planning for stable residential districts', *Review of Law and Social Change*, 13, pp.931–45.

Marcuse, P. (1986) 'Abandonment, gentrification and displacement: the linkages in New York City', in N. Smith and P. Williams (eds), *Gentrification of the City*, London: Unwin Hyman, pp.153–77.

Marcuse, P. (1991) *Missing Marx*. New York: Monthly Review Press.

Marcuse, P. (2005) 'The politics of research about gentrification', unpublished manuscript, New York: Department of Urban Planning, Columbia University.

Marris, P. (1986) *Loss and Change* (revised edition), London: Routledge and Kegan Paul.

McKinnish, T., Walsh, R. and White, K. (2010) 'Who gentrifies low-income neighborhoods?' *Journal of Urban Economics*, 67, pp.180–93.

Newman, K. and Wyly, E. (2006) 'The right to stay put, revisited: gentrification and resistance to displacement in New York City', *Urban Studies*, 43, pp.23–57.

Peck, J. and Tickell, A. (2002) 'Neoliberalizing space', *Antipode*, 34, pp.380–404.

Redfern, P. (2003) 'What makes gentrification "gentrification"?' *Urban Studies*, 40, pp.2351–66.

Roschelle, A. and Wright, T. (2003) 'Gentrification and social exclusion: spatial policing and homeless activist responses in the San Francisco bay area', in M. Miles and T. Hall (eds), *Urban Futures: Critical Commentaries on Shaping the City*, London: Routledge, pp.149–66.

Segal, S. P. and Baumohl, J. (1988) 'No place like home: reflections on sheltering a diverse population', in C. J. Smith and J. A. Giggs (eds), *Location and Stigma: Contemporary Perspectives on Mental Health and Mental Health Care*, London: Unwin Hyman, pp.250–63.

Slater, T. (2006) 'The eviction of critical perspectives from gentrification research', *International Journal of Urban and Regional Research*, 30, pp.737–57.

Smith, D. M. (1994) *Geography and Social Justice*, Oxford: Blackwell.

Smith, N. (1979) 'Toward a theory of gentrification: a back to the city movement by capital, not people', *Journal of the American Planning Association*, 45, pp.538–48.

Smith, N. (1992) 'Blind man's buff, or Hamnett's philosophical individualism in search of gentrification?' *Transactions of the Institute of British Geographers*, 17, pp.110–15.

Smith, N. (1996) *The New Urban Frontier: Gentrification and the Revanchist City*, London: Routledge.

Smith, N. (2002) 'New globalism, new urbanism: gentrification as global urban strategy', *Antipode*, 34, pp.427–50.

Smith, N. and Williams, P. (eds) (1986) *Gentrification of the City*, London: Allen and Unwin.

Squires, G. (ed.) (1992) *From Redlining to Reinvestment: Community Responses to Urban Disinvestment*, Philadelphia: Temple University Press.

Tickell, A. and Peck, J. (2003) 'Making global rules: globalisation or neoliberalization?' in J. Peck and H. W.-C. Yeung (eds), *Remaking the Global Economy*, London: Sage, pp.163–81.

Vigdor, J. (2002) 'Does gentrification harm the poor?' *Brookings-Wharton Papers on Urban Affairs*, pp.133–73.

Wacquant, L. (2004) 'Critical thought as solvent of doxa', *Constellations*, 11, pp.97–101.

Wacquant, L. (2008) 'Relocating gentrification: the working class, science and the state in recent urban research', *International Journal of Urban and Regional Research*, 32, pp.198–205.

Watt, P. (2008) 'The only class in town? Gentrification and the middle-class colonization of the city and the urban imagination', *International Journal of Urban and Regional Research*, 32, pp.206–11.

Wittgenstein, L. (1977 [1931]) *Culture and Value*, Oxford: Blackwell.

Wyly, E. and Hammel, D. (1999) 'Islands of decay in seas of renewal: housing policy and the resurgence of gentrification', *Housing Policy Debate*, 10, pp.711–71.

Wyly, E. and Hammel, D. (2001) 'Gentrification, housing policy, and the new context of urban redevelopment', in K. Fox-Gotham (ed.), *Critical Perspectives on Urban Redevelopment*, 6, New York: Elsevier Science, pp.211–76.

12

AN ACTUALLY EXISTING JUST CITY?

The fight for the right to the city in Amsterdam

Justus Uitermark

The Nieuwmarkt subway station has a collage of monuments of resistance and reminders of oppression. One picture on the wall shows a sign "*Juden Viertel*" and a road block. The Nieuwmarkt neighborhood had been a predominantly Jewish neighborhood and the Nazi occupiers closed it off and turned it into a repository for Jews that were to be deported to concentration camps. On another picture we see a person blindfolded on a stage. Perhaps it was one of the dock workers who went on strike to protest against the deportations and had to pay with their life.

The walls also tell another story, namely that of the resistance against draconic urban renewal that hit the neighborhood two decades after the war. The authorities wanted to raze the entire neighborhood. The old buildings as well as the messy street plan had to be replaced by straight roads, a metro, and high rises that would allow people, traffic, and capital to circulate with unprecedented speed. On one of the pictures some of the houses are still standing amidst the rubble. On another picture the riot police are gearing up to sweep protesters out of the streets to make way for the next round of demolition. On one side of the platform, just before the tunnel, there is a small and fractured wooden wall with a slogan on it – "we will continue living *here*" (*wij blijven hier wonen*). On the upper platform, in a corner, the wall is made of red brick instead of the usual sterile light grey paint. There are beams and girders sticking out of the wall and, as if to remind us that this is not just a forgotten corner, a replica of a wrecking ball.[1]

It would be grotesque to draw a parallel between the atrocities of the Nazi occupier and the modernization agenda of an elected government – but I do not think that this is what the monument intends. The monument, in fact, seems to lack coherence. The pictures just hang there and I never found any sign to explain what is on display and why it is there.[2] The only printed text is below a giant, kitschy picture frame and says "Greetings from the Nieuwmarkt" (*groeten van de Nieuwmarkt*). There is a broken mirror in the frame but it is unclear whether this was the intention of the creator or the work of vandals. If this collage of pictures, props, and murals has any meaning, it does not lie in the parallels but in the differences between the two eras; differences that, I think, capture the essence of democracy and the essence of the right to the city. During the occupation, the Jewish residents of the Nieuwmarkt neighborhood were exterminated and the resisters were executed. Any outcry against injustice or solidarity with the Jewish residents only reinforced the atrocities. During the urban renewal operation, by contrast, the authorities not only allowed residents to voice their discontent but also – ultimately – gave in. Above ground, one can see where modernism was halted: at the border of the Nieuwmarkt neighborhood, at Waterlooplein, where the four-lane highway ends. Where hotels and banks were planned, there is now social housing (Figure 12.1).

The fact that the government memorialized the resistance against itself signals the difference between the darkest pages of Amsterdam's history and the heydays of democratization: whereas protest against inhumane authorities was considered a crime during the occupation, it was regarded as a duty after the Nieuwmarkt resistance. The official memorialization of resistance against state-mandated urban renewal projects graphically illustrates Amsterdam's importance as a source of inspiration for contemplating what the just city might actually look like. This chapter therefore identifies the qualities of a just city and investigates how the "actually existing just city" of Amsterdam came into being. However, it also makes the argument that Amsterdam today does not approximate the ideal of the just city. In fact, it appears that the achievements of the 1970s and 1980s – strong tenant rights, a large social housing

FIGURE 12.1 Social housing in the Nieuwmarkt neighborhood
Source: Goezde Tekdal

stock, formalized resident consultation – serve to ease the neoliberal turn in Amsterdam's development.

The just city and Amsterdam

The achievements of urban social movements in Amsterdam have been extensively documented and praised in the international literature. In the late 1960s, Amsterdam attracted the attention of Henri Lefebvre, who ventured to Amsterdam to explore the city with artists and activists who were experimenting intellectually and practically with new strategies for resisting modernization. Around ten years later, in 1977, Susan Fainstein arrived in Amsterdam for the first time and discovered in it an equitable alternative to the cities of the United States. In the 1990s, Ed Soja wrote of Amsterdam as a city that fosters a culture of tolerance and civic engagement (Soja, 1992). After several return visits in the late 1990s and early 2000s, Fainstein praised Amsterdam as a city that approached her ideal of a just city (Fainstein, 2005). In 2008 US urban sociologist John Gilderbloom organized a conference in Amsterdam on the "ideal city," praising the conference site as a place where people are "more tolerant, secure, happier, and healthier compared to citizens in the United States" because of a unique blend of progressive policies (with respect to drugs and prostitution) and a comprehensive welfare state (Gilderbloom, 2008, n.p.; see also Gilderbloom et al., 2007).

Gilderboom's assessment highlights that the city compares favorably to many other cities on several criteria. Fainstein's understanding of the just city is more specific. For instance, "growth" can help to promote justice but it might just as well exacerbate injustices. Likewise, it is very well possible to imagine a city that is sustainable, yet replete with inequalities. In order to clearly differentiate the just city from an ideal – or nice or prosperous or sustainable or safe – city (all of which have their specific contribution to make to the well-being of urbanites), I adopt and modify Fainstein's (2010) conception of the "just city."

For Fainstein, an equitable distribution, primarily of housing, is the first criterion for assessing whether a city is just. She identifies two secondary evaluative criteria: diversity and democracy. Diversity refers to the extent to which a city is open to difference and allows culturally and economically diverse neighborhoods. Democracy refers to the extent to which community demands find their way into government policy. Fainstein identifies a number of tensions between these different criteria. For instance, urban renewal policies which force poor minority households to relocate from neighborhoods where they are concentrated may increase diversity at the cost of equity and democracy (Fainstein, 2010, p. 73). In case of a tension or tradeoff between different criteria, according to Fainstein, equity should prevail. Fainstein's approach is valuable because it defines clear criteria for evaluating cities as well as plans. I also accept Fainstein's underlying principle of the just city – it would be the city that people choose from behind a Rawlsian "veil of ignorance." However,

I place somewhat different emphases to arrive at a (slightly) more radical interpretation of the just city and to differentiate it more sharply from the ideal city.

Equity

Fainstein prefers the concept of "equity" to "equality" for largely pragmatic
reasons. Equality, for Fainstein

> acts like a magnet for all the objections based on rewards to the most
> deserving, on questions of the obliteration of incentives, on the trade-off
> between growth and equality, and on the unfairness of penalizing every-
> one above the median in the name of the greater good.
>
> (2010, p. 36)

She therefore prefers the term "equity" which is commonly used in policy
analysis and implies "fairness" which is a "more broadly accepted value than
equality. It has the power to gain wider political support than terms that
explicitly target the better-off" (2010, p. 36). Equity, then, refers not to equal
treatment of every individual but to treatment that is "appropriate" or to "public policy that does not favor those who are already better off at the beginning"
(2010, p. 36). While it is clear that different sorts of cities would be built
if planners would adopt this notion of equity, the idea of "appropriateness"
takes the sting out of the concept of justice. For instance, policy makers in
Amsterdam feel it is "appropriate" that people with low incomes live in social
housing while people with high incomes live in owner-occupied housing.
Since owner-occupied housing is directly available through the market while
there is a waiting list for social housing, this conception of appropriateness
implies unequal treatment.

I would therefore argue that a first precondition for the just city is that the
distribution of scarce urban resources, in particular housing, be disconnected
from the distribution of income or capital. The commitment to make the city
accessible to each and every person irrespective of their purchasing power is
a cornerstone of any project that aims to fairly distribute scarcity.[3] This means
that the just city would either have an egalitarian income distribution or that it
would create institutions that prevent households and investors from translating their economically privileged position into a privileged position in land and
housing markets (which therefore would cease to be markets). Criteria to distribute the intrinsic scarcity could be waiting time, need, or a combination of
both. Distributing resources according to waiting time or need does not only
result in a more egalitarian distribution, it also has implications for diversity.
When purchasing power or other forms of power play no role in the distribution of housing, it is likely that class segregation will be low.

Democracy

Fainstein conceptualizes democracy as the extent to which the city meets popular demands. Fainstein is skeptical towards planning theorists who prioritize democratic values like communicative rationality and inclusiveness because people may use their democratic rights to buttress and reproduce relations of inequality. When residents in a particular neighborhood want to keep out lower income groups or minorities, then heeding those demands may be democratic but at the expense of both equity and diversity. However, residents should be able to engage directly and consequentially in the ongoing project of making their living environment (Harvey, this volume; Purcell, 2002). Since it is usually the state that enforces equality, there is a very real danger that power is concentrated in the hands of an authoritarian bureaucratic apparatus, as happened in actually existing socialism. I would therefore argue that a second precondition for the just city is that residents have control over their living environment, that is, they engage with the polity of which they form a part. Rather than passively receiving whatever provisions are allocated to them, residents should have the possibility to inform and shape the distribution of universal provisions in particular ways; they should have the right and ability to organize in such a way that they can effectively inform and shape the distribution of universal provisions according to their particular needs.

Demanding the impossible

While Fainstein starts from the radical assumption that justice should be defined according to a Rawlsian logic, in her actual definitions she adopts a more pragmatic approach. This is particularly the case for equity. She chooses this concept over equality in order not to evoke the negative connotations that the phrase "people above the median" may have. Equity in turn is defined in such a way (as "appropriateness" or "fairness") that it is easily brought in line with extant power structures. In this chapter, my starting point is the same as Fainstein's but whereas her conceptualization is formulated to convince planners to adopt policies leading towards a more just city, I favor a conception that can – and indeed did – inspire urban movements' radical claims. The two preconditions mentioned above are formulated so as to demand the impossible, namely the full implementation of the right to the city (Marcuse, this volume). Such a process would not come about without considerable resistance. Creating an equitable distribution of scarce resources implies that a very large number of urban inhabitants lose much of their privilege; the richer (or more connected, worthy, etc.) they are, the more they have to lose if they can no longer translate their purchasing power into a favorable position on the housing market. State administrators, too, would lose considerable power as they would no longer be in charge of making the city. In this understanding, the just city will not be built by planners or other power holders, it will be conquered from them.

There is, to my knowledge, no city in the world that can live up to the two standards of a just city mentioned above.[4] But, some come closer than others, and it is exactly for this reason that we should be interested in concrete approximations of abstract ideals, in actually existing just cities that can serve as inspiring counter examples to actually existing neoliberal cities (compare Brenner and Theodore, 2002). As I will explain in the following section, Amsterdam can serve this purpose. However, I argue that Amsterdam should not only be held up as an example of a just city, but should also be viewed as an illustration of how quickly and dramatically movements struggling for the just city can lose their momentum. Amsterdam, I suggest, has degenerated from a city that aspires to be just for all into a city that is nice for many.

The ascendancy of the just city

In the 1960s and 1970s, the state as well as capital discontinued investments into inner cities. Investors as well as governments felt that the city had to be drastically renewed and restructured according to the demands of the time. The demands of the time, in turn, were defined in modernist terms. Through modernist lenses the city looked like a hopelessly dysfunctional, chaotic, and ugly mess. But a growing number of people identified strongly with exactly those parts of the city that disgusted the modernist planners. And, equally important, those urban residents no longer perceived the government's wishes as divine law. Criticism and imagination democratized rapidly. The authorities that had previously appeared as skillful servants of the general interest were now recast as modernist fanatics.

In the course of the 1970s, resident resistance intensified in cities throughout Western Europe (Castells, 1983). In the case of Amsterdam, the emergence of the squatting movement contributed to an intensification and radicalization of resident protests. In the 1970s squatters gained significance as a movement against the demolition of affordable housing and the imposition of modernist fantasies on urban space. In the Nieuwmarkt and many other Amsterdam neighborhoods, vacancy rates accelerated in anticipation of demolition. Large numbers of squatters moved into the vacant housing and created a barrier against the modernistic renewal plans. Squatters have always been disliked by large parts of the Dutch population, but during this time they were a natural ally of residents who mobilized against the destruction of their living environments. Everywhere in the city residents – tenants and squatters – successfully opposed modernist renewal plans. In the space that had been left by capital and had not been colonized by the state, a resident movement grew that propagated an alternative view of the city. This movement advocated the construction of new houses, the maintenance of the existing stock, and the democratization of planning (Pruijt, 1985; Mamadouh, 1992).

The strength of this movement ultimately led to the overthrow of the modernistic technocrats within the ruling Labor Party. More than anyone else, Jan Schaeffer personified the new urban vision. He had actively resisted modernistic renewal in the Amsterdam neighborhood of De Pijp during the 1960s and early 1970s, and he had subsequently made his way into the higher ranks of the Labor Party on the wings of the resident movement. In 1973, he became Junior Minister of Public Housing in the national government, and in that position he would help to create the institutional preconditions for a further deepening and broadening of the residents' movement. In the most left-wing cabinet that the Netherlands had ever seen, he could break with the conception that urban renewal should serve to restructure the city to better meet the "demands of the time." Instead he helped to popularize and institutionalize the slogan "building for the neighborhood" and to work out the concept of the "compact city." Rather than razing entire neighborhoods, projects would be realized as much as possible within the existing urban structure and, wherever possible, renovation would be chosen over demolition. The central government made considerable budgets available to stimulate housing production.

When he moved back to Amsterdam in 1978 as a local party leader and alderman for urban renewal, he could demonstrate that his approach was not only more humane, but also more effective: housing construction exploded from 1,100 units in 1978 to 9,000 units in 1984 (Dienst Wonen, 2008, p. 7). The recession of that period did not at all hinder Schaeffer's plans. At the national level, the expenditures for housing were considered essential and beneficial for the economy. Because private owners were confronted with high interest rates, protesting residents, and low demand, they often preferred to sell their properties to the government. Around 35,000 houses (circa 15 percent of the stock) were taken out of the market and put under the control of housing associations and the state (Dienst Wonen, 2008, p. 12).

Decommodification and equity

Even though the mechanisms for allocating housing and determining rent levels are dynamic and intricate, we can nevertheless observe three general trends in the direction of a decommodified housing stock. These trends occurred nation-wide but they were especially pronounced in Amsterdam as a result of the strength of the residents' movement. First, the rights of owners to determine rent levels were gradually curtailed. Over time a comprehensive system was created to determine a fair rent, the so-called point system (*puntensysteem*). In the point system rents are based on the use value of a house. Use value is calculated according to objective criteria, like the size of a house and the quality of its amenities (Huisman and Kelk, 2008). These regulations apply to all houses regardless of ownership. The points system does not apply if the total number of points surpass a certain threshold. Currently that threshold corresponds to a rent of 650 euros but before 1991 it was substantially higher. This basically meant that the entire rental sector was subject to strong regulation. And since owner-occupied houses constitute a very low share of the stock (13 percent in 1997), it meant that, by the late 1980s, the Amsterdam housing market had in effect become decommodified (Huisman, 2009, p. 9). These measures decreased the inequalities between different tenure types in such a way that residence rather than ownership defined access to scarce resources. The opportunities for investors to profit from speculation were drastically reduced as the resident movement effectively argued that the city was for people, not for profit.

Second, the rights of owners to determine the use of their properties were gradually curtailed. Property owners in the 1960s still had major discretion to choose their tenants, but in the course of 1970s their discretion was circumscribed through the centralization and standardization of allocation. Standardization was achieved through the formulation of universal criteria of eligibility. Waiting time is by far the most important criterion, but under some conditions (urgent) need also plays a role. Centralization was achieved through the creation of a city-wide distribution system. Private landlords had to register their property and the municipality and the landlord alternately allocated the accommodation that would become available. Housing associations initially each had their own waiting lists but these were gradually fused together.

Third, access to the centrally allocated housing supply was gradually universalized. Initially only married couples qualified for housing that was distributed through the municipality but in the 1960s the growing group of single-person households and unmarried couples also qualified. The age limit was gradually reduced from 26 in the early 1960s to 18 in the early 1980s. The housing associations initially only catered to specific groups like members of unions or other professional associations but they gradually opened up access to the general public. Corporations thus never catered only to the needs of the poorest segments of the population but there was a conscious effort in the 1980s to develop a housing stock that provided appropriate and affordable housing to all income groups. Although definitions of what is appropriate varied over time, it meant roughly that a two-person household would have a two-room apartment, a three-person household would have a three-room apartment, and so on. In other words: household composition rather than income would determine what is appropriate and what is not.

Democratization and engagement

The growing power *of* the state was absolutely central to this project but so was the power of residents *over* the state. Many specific institutions were created in the 1970s and the 1980s to ensure that residents would be able to claim their right to the city. Official organizations to provide support to organized resident groups as well as the legal assistance to individual tenants were created, offering activists the chance to transform their movement careers into careers in state bureaucracy. Many young activists went to schools for social work (*sociale academie*) which – under pressure of the students – adopted an increasingly suspicious attitude towards authority in general and the state in particular. There was a paradoxical development: the state increasingly took social work out of the hands of private initiative and civil society, but social workers increasingly saw themselves as an ally to residents in their struggles against the state (Duyvendak and Uitermark, 2005). They could afford to take this position – another irony – because they were fully funded by the central state. Since they were not dependent on local governments or housing associations, they could choose the side of protesters and critics.

Community workers were just one actor in a larger network that provided logistical and professional support to residents who wanted to change plans to better meet their demands. With state subsidies and voluntary support of sympathizing professionals, residents could win the advice of architects, academics, and planners. With all these institutions and professions working increasingly as an extension of the residents' movement, abstract ideals could be translated into concrete policy suggestions. It is this power to translate intuitions and desires into formal representations that is crucial for shaping urban space in such a way that it meets the needs of residents both as individuals and as (diverse and overlapping) collectives.

The birth of a just city

The history of Amsterdam's housing politics after 1960 was a double development: grassroots mobilization brought the state under democratic control and the housing market was gradually brought under state control. The resident movement and emerging institutions helped to create a decommodified

FIGURE 12.2 Social housing of the 1980s in the Oosterparkbuurt in Amsterdam East. In the 1960s and 1970s, the quality of social housing was often poor according to contemporary standards. However, quality gradually improved and houses in these kinds of complexes can sell for anywhere between 150,000 and 300,000 euros. This block is still 100 percent social housing.
Source: Goezde Tekdal

housing stock that universalized accessibility and maximized affordability, while in the process promoting resident engagement and facilitating direct action and direct democracy (see Figure 12.2).[5] If we want to decide on a birth year for the just city of Amsterdam, it would have to be 1975 – the moment that residents and squatters united around the preservation of the Nieuwmarkt neighborhood. It reached maturity in 1982 when the city constructed no less than 9,000 housing units and had reduced the waiting time for a two-room apartment to an all-time low of two years.

These really were revolutionary developments: they gave the city to its people and they helped generate a vibrant creativity in spaces that had been freed from both the state and the market.[6]

Recommodification and disengagement

The emergence of a just city was the outcome of the interaction between a radical resident movement and a national housing policy that was designed to solve the housing shortage through massive investments in social housing (Fainstein, 2000). But in the late 1980s national policies were starting to change. Following political economic trends elsewhere, the government took a range of austerity measures. While the supply of housing had been a hallmark of the Keynesian–Fordist welfare state, in the course of the 1980s the large expenditures were increasingly regarded as costs rather than investments. The idea took hold that the government should only take responsibility for those who cannot take responsibility for themselves. Whereas first social housing was considered a universal provision, it was turned into a residual social provision for people who could not afford to buy (Malpass, 1990; Priemus, 1995). As neoliberal ideologies pervaded the government, subsidies for social housing and housing construction were increasingly questioned. Budget-cutters reasoned that there was plenty of scope to drastically reduce public expenditures on social housing while preserving tax incentives for owner-occupiers. For the first time, administrators said that the housing shortage was "qualitative" rather than "quantitative" – they claimed that everyone could find accommodation. The government therefore decided that no subsidies should be made available to promote housing construction and that the upgrading of the housing market should be promoted through privatization: the large-scale selling of social housing should generate funds for maintaining the stock while creating a stimulus for private investments into the more expensive segments of the market.

Segregating the housing stock

The ideological core of the new policy discourse on housing is that all income groups should have their own segment of the housing market. Only the lower classes, according to this discourse, should live in social housing. If their rents are high in proportion to their income, they can claim rent subsidies. The middle and higher classes should own their houses; the government supports them with subsidies for purchasing a house. Whereas in the old policy constellation, subsidies were used to make social housing available to all income groups, in the new policy constellation subsidies are used to segregate the housing stock; residualization of the social sector is not merely a side effect of policies but one of the key objectives (compare Malpass (1990) for the British case). Notice that this is drastically different from, for instance, education or health care. It would still be considered immoral to segregate students or patients according to their purchasing power. But it is common sense now to ensure that middle and high incomes should have the chance to buy their way into the most attractive segments of the housing stock.

The national policies of the 1990s were a direct assault on the universal provisions that had been created in the 1980s. The problem of the housing shortage was declared solved, which meant – in the case of Amsterdam – that the 50,000 people on the waiting list for social housing simply disappeared as a target group. The general trend of bringing the housing stock under state control, and of bringing the state under control of the resident movement, was thus reversed. Housing associations were formally privatized and transformed into housing corporations. The housing corporations were given some directives – the most important being to sell houses – but they escape control from both the state and tenants. Whereas tenants previously controlled housing associations, now they have been reduced to consumers (*woonconsumenten*) and not even the most important category of consumers. That privileged role has now been assumed by the middle classes. They are expected to purchase the newly privatized social housing and to invest the capital necessary to upgrade the properties. Apart from relegating each class to its own segment of the housing market, the government fragmented residents through the creation of new tenure types, such as so-called anti-squatters and temporary tenants.[7] Anti-squatters are residents without tenant contracts and (hence) without tenant rights. They can be ordered to leave their residences within a day or within a month, depending on the agreements between property owners and anti-squatters. Temporary tenants also do not enjoy the legal protection of regular tenants but they do have contracts which stipulate that the property owner needs to inform them at least one month before they have to move out. Anti-squatters and temporary tenants have a position on the housing market that is analogous to flex workers in the labor market: because their position is so precarious they are extremely unlikely to protest against property owners.

These general trends in Dutch housing policy – privatization of the housing stock and fragmentation of residents into different tenure groups – did not pass by Amsterdam. In the late 1980s, the Amsterdam government protested against the national policies to privatize the housing market, but during the course of the 1990s it began to adopt such policies. The government no longer considered the large stock of social housing as a universal provision for the general population but as an impediment to a well-functioning housing market. The former alderman for housing, Tjeerd Herema, recently summarized this new, market-based vision for local housing policy: "The housing policy aims at a much more diverse group than before. The focus is no longer exclusively on the lowest incomes. Amsterdam is a city for everyone" (press release December 7, 2007). This quote is interesting not least due to its flagrant misrepresentation of Amsterdam's recent history. Policies in the 1980s were based on the premise that no differentiation should be made between different income groups, because all households could apply for social housing. It is not the case that higher incomes were discriminated against. Like all others, they could live in social housing. This misrepresentation of history allows the government to present its focus on the higher income groups as an inclusive measure: they, not the lower classes, suffer. The number one target group for current policies are the so-called *scheefwoners*: tenants with high incomes who are, according to the policy discourse, trapped in a segment where they do not really belong. They should thus be seduced to leave their small and affordable social housing to purchase or rent larger houses on the market. A visualization of this discourse is depicted in Figure 12.3.

Figure 12.3 suggests quite forcefully what would previously have been considered absurd and what is still absurd from the perspective of the just city outlined earlier, namely that there is a large surplus of affordable housing in Amsterdam. It suggests, further, that the main challenge is to reduce the number of affordable dwellings so that the housing market becomes more "balanced" (Gemeente Amsterdam, 2008, p. 27). The municipality uses several tools to achieve this. One simple strategy is to allow owners – both housing associations and private real estate firms – to sell apartments that were previously in the regulated sector.

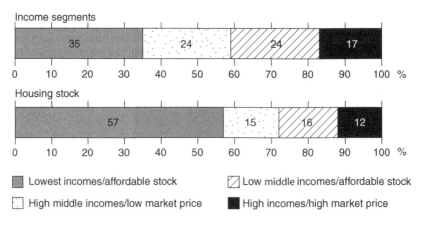

FIGURE 12.3 Income segments and housing market segments compared
Source: Gemeente Amsterdam (2008, p. 27)

Another strategy has been to use urban renewal policies to change tenure compositions. Instead of constructing housing for a broad cross-section of the population, the government and the housing associations now pursue a strategy of "social mixing" which refers – as usual – to attempts to replace a proportion of the low-income households with high-income households (see Uitermark et al., 2007). The goal of "building for the neighborhood" has been replaced by the goal of making neighborhoods "livable" through altering the neighborhood population (Aalbers, 2010).

Livability has been a central concept in Dutch urban policies since the late 1970s. Initially, it was used by resident groups who protested large-scale demolitions and who argued for more subtle interventions that do not force tenants to relocate. Now, 20 years later, housing associations and governments argue that their own policies are supposed to promote livability. But if we look at the operationalization that is used for calculating livability scores,[8] it is evident that the concept has been completely redefined (Uitermark, 2005). Residents' perceptions are still included in the operationalization, but the score is also said to be based on "objective" criteria. For example, if a neighborhood has a high share of ethnic minorities, the score goes down. If it has a high share of lower-income households, the score goes down. If it has a high share of affordable housing, the score goes down. In short, what is really being measured here is not the extent to which residents can live a pleasant and affordable life in the neighborhoods, but the extent to which *housing associations* and *governments* can govern these neighborhoods and extract profits out of them. Hence, in practice, the ideal of "undivided cities" means that policies try to disperse concentrations of migrants and lower-income groups. With this discursive shift, the focus of policies has shifted from empowering deprived communities to promoting gentrification and displacement.

The erosion of just urbanism

There are many possible criticisms against these policy discourses and practices. The first and most obvious is that the policies do not work. Renewal operations are used to drastically transform the tenure composition of neighborhoods, but it is questionable whether they reduce overall levels of segregation (Bolt et al., 2008). Moreover, there is no evidence that the mixing of different tenure types and income groups produces a cohesive community (Uitermark et al., 2007). But a more fundamental criticism of the government's policy is that these goals – mixing neighborhoods and balancing the housing stock – signal a move away from the just urbanism that had reached its zenith around 1980. The fears of rich people living in social housing and of poor people living in poor neighborhoods grow from the commodification of the housing market that segregates the stock along the lines of purchasing power. Social mixing was achieved in the 1980s as a by-product of a more general development towards just urbanism which equalized the access of different income groups.

As the government has made the reduction of social housing into an official policy goal, the housing shortage has disappeared from the political agenda. Even though the waiting time for a two bedroom apartment is up from two years in 1982 to ten years in 2008,[9] the very word "housing shortage" does not appear in the current policy vision of Amsterdam.

Not only do these policies lead to less equity, they also lead to citizen disengagement at the neighborhood and city levels. Whereas in the early 1980s urban renewal was oriented towards the neighborhood itself, it is now oriented primarily towards people from outside of the neighborhood. Housing corporations now press tenants in renewal projects to try their chances on the city's housing market rather then facilitating their participation in planning the neighborhood itself. In short, whereas urban renewal was previously instrumental for *improving* the condition of a neighborhood and *strengthening* ties among different groups of neighborhood residents, it is now used to *disperse* tenants and to *transform* the neighborhood from above. Amsterdam's contemporary neoliberal policies differentiate the population, individualize residents, and hand over the government's democratic responsibilities to actors – housing corporations – that are accountable neither to their tenants nor to the government.

Why?

One might ask: how did this happen? Why was the ideal of the just city abandoned so swiftly and so smoothly? The largest part of the answer to this question cannot be found at the local level. The ascendancy of neoliberalism at the national level in the Netherlands – itself something that should be understood as part of a global trend – was extremely consequential for those who prioritized – above all else – the use value of the city. But part of the answer can indeed be found at the local level. For what has become of the movements that had previously forced the government to design the city for people rather than for profit? Why did they not protest as they had done before?

Part of the reason, I would argue, is that the resident movement was so successful in penetrating the state that they lost the urge and capacity to promote active engagement; the resident movement has turned into an interest group (see Mayer, 2007). As movements integrated into the state, interdependencies among the different segments of the resident movement that emerged around the Nieuwmarkt grew weaker and dependence on the government grew stronger. The official organizations for resident support – the Tenant Association (*Huurdersvereniging*), the Agency for Housing Support (*Amsterdams Steunpunt Wonen*), the Housing Union (*Woonbond*), the tenant representatives on committees, community workers – in practice serve as consultants for individual tenants rather than as movement organizations that bring together different groups. There are still many residents who fiercely resist forced relocations and the attendant rent increases, but the organizations for resident support generally encourage these protesters to accept better deals rather than to create linkages with other protesters or challenge the very logic of the government's policies.

Amsterdam shows that the state may be a necessary vehicle for achieving justice, but the case also shows how the state can neutralize justice movements through selective incorporation and accommodation (Nicholls and Beaumont, 2004). Many of the institutions that are now cooperating with the government to privatize the housing stock used to be either grassroots organizations (tenant and community associations) or were part of civil society (housing associations, social work). It is ironic that the municipality's housing association which before legalized squats and turned them into social housing has since its privatization made a name for itself as a ruthless demolisher of social housing. As a true Brutus, it now turns against the movement that gave it its power. In retrospect, it appears that Amsterdam would have been far more resilient to gentrification pressures if it had focused less on the legal rights of an increasingly select legal category – regular tenants – and more on the rights of inhabitants, regardless of their form of tenure and their purchasing power, to participate in the urbanization process and to share in the city's scarce resources.

Conclusion: just a nice city

Few passengers will nowadays notice the monument on Nieuwmarkt station. Its incoherent parts are likely to merely reinforce the image of a poorly maintained metro station with graffitti, broken glass, and unmanicured edges. There is only one part of the whole ensemble that is not messy, ambivalent, and chaotic. This is the slogan on the platform that is stretched across nearly 20 meters. There it is, grafted in stone, the most fundamental element of any right to the city: "housing is a right, not a favor" (*wonen is geen gunst maar een recht*). The slogan represents a promise of the government; the promise to provide housing to all its residents regardless of their income, background, or merit. The letters are big and bright, but very few people notice them. When the monument was created, it symbolized the power of a residents' movement that had their ideas inscribed into the urban fabric and institutionalized into local organizations. The meaning that it conveys today is that a massive momentum can be reduced to an incoherent collage. The monument has been transformed from a sign of strength of the residents' movements to an *in memoriam* for the just city of Amsterdam. The case of Amsterdam shows that it is very difficult to work towards a just city but nearly impossible to sustain it.

While Amsterdam may no longer be a close approximation of the actually existing just city, it has not become a playground for hard-edged neoliberalism. The stock of social housing is still comparatively large and tenants enjoy a strong legal position. For international scholars, it makes sense to hold up Amsterdam as an example that proves to conservatives and neoliberals that a city can score well on a range of criteria when it combines a relatively comprehensive welfare system with progressive policies. But when we analyze the city historically rather than comparatively, Amsterdam's condition looks rather different. All the institutions that had previously decommodified the housing market and engaged residents now ease gentrification. Ironically, it was the residents' movement of the 1980s that invested these institutions with the power and resources necessary to impose their view upon the city. Neoliberalization proceeds so smoothly exactly because the gains of past social struggles are used to compensate the most direct victims of privatization and demolition.

By way of conclusion, I would like to flesh out how critical urban analysts could take on this responsibility. Scholarship has played a crucial role in both the tendential emergence of the just city and in its demise. In the 1970s and 1980s, academics and experts actively cooperated with resident groups and tried to help them to translate their demands and desires in concepts, figures, and drawings. For instance, students in architecture thought of new ways to renovate houses and sociologists attempted to unearth policy processes and to map the needs of residents and house seekers. But in the 1990s residents lost most of their academic support. Today, housing corporations and municipalities fund the bulk of research into cities and especially lower-class groups. Thus discourses and data on cities reflect the interests of entrepreneurial governments and corporations rather than those of residents. The idea that there are "too many" social houses and that promoting gentrification is the best way to improve "livability" goes virtually unchallenged in the large grey area between academe and the state (see also Slater, this volume). I think critical urban analysts – including those who do not subscribe to the ideal of the just city as I have sketched it here – do have a responsibility to improve reflexivity and to open up debate. The way to do this is to critically scrutinize dominant conceptualizations of the city and to show that alternative conceptualizations are possible. When notions such as "integration," "livability," and "differentiation" are measured and mapped as if they reflected an objective reality, then there is a need to challenge the discursive hegemony of the authorities and their mercenary experts. To show that the definition of these concepts reflects power relations is one crucial enterprise for critical urban analysts.

Next to deconstructing naturalized renderings of reality, critical scholars face the daunting but fascinating challenge to provide rigorous yet imaginative alternative conceptualizations of the city and its possible futures (Marcuse, this volume). Unfortunately, however, the allure of the state – a massive source of financing and prestige – draws many academics away both from science and grassroots mobilization. The alternative urban imagination now appears to flourish in the United States (e.g. Nicholls, 2003) where movements foster linkages that enable them to serve as a counter force to the state rather than as its extension. Under present conditions in Amsterdam, however, it is highly unlikely that residents will regain the momentum of the late 1970s and early 1980s. The heritage of the just city can be seen everywhere in Amsterdam, but the just city itself died with the momentum of the movement.

The heritage of the just urbanism that permeates the urban fabric is now considered an obstacle to the functioning of the housing market – once again, "market" and "housing" go together as an inseparable couplet. It is now the market rather than residents that needs to be freed from constraints and put in charge. To think of the just city under such conditions is frustrating but also necessary and stimulating. The full implementation of the right to the city may be a lost cause but it's worth fighting for.

Notes

1 It is difficult to say whether it is an original. It might be the case that some government officials have pulled it from the rubble to preserve a reminder of the houses that other government officials destroyed. It could also be the case that they commissioned someone to reproduce the wall and to write – in big brushes of white paint – the words that had motivated so many to stand up for their neighborhood.

2 The careful observer will find another quirky little monument above ground. It is made of stone and features a turtle that carries an ionic pillar on its shell. The symbolism is lost on me but fortunately we do find some text here. On one side of the pillar there is a poem of Jacob Israël de Haan on the nostalgia for Amsterdam of Jews who had migrated to Israel. On the other side there is, finally, a text that describes what happened: "Up to this point the old city pattern disappeared. Beyond this point the urban renewal of the neighborhood started. By way of commemoration, this memorial stone was erected in 1986."

3 Note that this is not the same as quality – it may be the case that houses are small or lack comfort, but I still think a city could be legitimately called just (though not necessarily pleasant) if it provides its limited or imperfect housing evenly across the population. The criterion for the just city is not the extent to which there is scarcity but how scarcity is distributed.

4 In fact, the realization of the just city as it is sketched here would not be desirable as such a city would probably have sacrificed too much on other qualities that make cities dynamic and exciting.

5 The residential areas that planners could construct without the interference of residents became planning disasters. The most famous example is the gigantic futuristic suburb in South East Amsterdam colloquially referred to as Bijlmer. But where residents were present and engaged, they managed to temper the modernist ambitions to write designer history and to focus instead on the needs of residents in the renewal neighborhoods.

6 This is, of course, an idealization – there were many things to criticize – but I think this is the type of idealization we need in order to imagine what a just city might actually look like. What should be idealized then, and elaborated through dialectical analysis, are the processes that empowered residents to make the city. What should be dissected and struggled against are the processes that give urban development over to the state and the market.

7 Tenants with regular contracts enjoy very strong legal protection: the property owners can only force them to relocate if they urgently need to have control over the house (for instance, to proceed with urban renewal) and only after they have offered alternative housing and a relocation fee.

8 There are many varieties of the *leefbaarheidsmonitor*. The most recent and comprehensive is online: http://www.leefbaarometer.nl (accessed March 14, 2009).

9 Among the most important reasons for the increase in waiting time are the shrinking of the social sector, the growing number of displacees with urgency status (and hence priority), and the virtual standstill of housing production.

References

Aalbers, M. (2010) The revanchist renewal of yesterday's city of tomorrow. *Antipode*, 42 (forthcoming).

Bolt, G., Kempen, R. van, and Ham, M. van (2008) Minority ethnic groups in the Dutch housing market: spatial segregation, relocation dynamics and housing policy. *Urban Studies*, 45(7), 1359–84.

Brenner, N. and Theodore, N. (2002) Cities and the geographies of "actually existing neoliberalism." *Antipode*, 34(3), 349–80.

Castells, M. (1983) *The City and the Grassroots*. London: Edward Arnold.

Dienst Wonen (2008) *Jan komt. Deel 2 van De Amsterdamse Volkshuisvesting, 1970–2005*. Amsterdam: Dienst Wonen.

Duyvendak, J. W. and Uitermark, J. (2005) De opbouwwerker als architect van de publieke sfeer. *Beleid & Maatschappij*, 32(2), 76–89.

Fainstein, S. (2000) New directions in planning theory. *Urban Affairs Review*, 35(4), 451–78.

Fainstein, S. (2005) Cities and diversity. Should we want it? Can we plan for it? *Urban Affairs Review*, 41(1), 3–19.

Fainstein, S. (2010) *The Just City*. Ithaca: Cornell University Press.

Gemeente Amsterdam (2008) *Woonvisie Amsterdam*. Amsterdam: Gemeente Amsterdam.

Gilderbloom, J. (2008) *Ideal City: New Perspectives for the 21st Century!* Online, available at http://www.hollandnow.org (accessed April 14, 2009).

Gilderbloom, J., Hanka, M., and Lasley, C. B. (2007). Amsterdam, the ideal city: planning and policy. Paper presented at Urban Justice and Sustainability, 22–5 August 2007, University of British Columbia, Vancouver, Canada.

Huisman, C. (2009) *Splitsen als onderdeel van overheidsgestuurde gentrification*. Amsterdam, unpublished paper.

Huisman, C. and Kelk, S. (2008) *A (very) rough guide to Amsterdam housing policy*. Online, available at housingamsterdam.org/po_inside/roughguide2008.doc.

Malpass, P. (1990) *Reshaping Housing Policy: Subsidies, Rents and Residualisation*. London: Routledge.

Mamadouh, V. (1992) *De stad in eigen hand*. Amsterdam: SUA.

Mayer, M. (2007) Contesting the neoliberalization of urban governance, in H. Leitner, J. Peck and E. S. Sheppard (eds) *Contesting Neoliberalism*. New York: Guilford, 90–115.

Nicholls, W. and Beaumont, J. (2004) The urbanization of justice movements. *Space & Polity*, 8(2), special issue.

Nicholls, W. J. (2003) Forging a 'new' organizational infrastructure for Los Angeles' progressive community. *International Journal of Urban and Regional Research*, 27(4), 881–96.

Pruijt, H. (1985) Cityvorming gekraakt. *Agora*, 1(4), 9–11.

Priemus, H. (1995) How to abolish social housing? The Dutch case. *International Journal of Urban and Regional Research*, 19(1), 145–55.

Purcell, M. (2002) Excavating Lefebvre: the right to the city and its urban politics of the inhabitant. *Geojournal*, 58(2–3), 99–108.

Soja, E. (1992) The stimulus of a little confusion: a contemporary comparison of Amsterdam and Los Angeles. In M. P. Smith, *After Modernism: Global Restructuring and the Changing Boundaries of City Life*. New Brunswick, NJ: Transaction Publishers.

Uitermark, J. (2005) The genesis and evolution of urban policy: a confrontation of regulationist and governmentality approaches. *Political Geography*, 23(2), 137–63.

Uitermark, J., Duyvendak, J. W., and Kleinhans, R. (2007) Gentrification as a governmental strategy. Social control and social cohesion in Hoogvliet, Rotterdam. *Environment and Planning A*, 39(1), 125–41.

13

A CRITICAL APPROACH TO SOLVING THE HOUSING PROBLEM

Peter Marcuse

How might critical theory deal with a problem such as the harrowing housing crisis in the United States today? Using the approach of critical theory, critical planning would attack such an issue in three steps: *expose, propose, politicize* (Marcuse, 2008, 179–91; 2010b, 13–16). *Expose* here means dealing with the immediate mortgage foreclosure crisis in the United States as part of a more generalized housing crisis (itself part of the broad economic crisis, in turn a part of the capitalist organization of the economy). It would show: 1) how housing is produced in accordance with the rules of the capitalist economic system; 2) how housing is regulated by the state to maximize profit; and 3) how housing is supported by manipulated ideological and cultural underpinnings – the three pillars of the crisis. *Propose* means setting forth the actions that are necessary to address the immediate problem today, seeing them always in the context of alternatives to these three pillars, examining current proposals for reform and exploring long-term possibilities for non-reformist reforms. Proposals would include, addressing each of the pillars: 1) market domination in housing through decommodification in production and distribution; 2) state regulation of housing through fully democratic governmental control; and 3) ideological clarity through widespread understanding of the social character of housing. *Politicize* then means showing what actions and what changes are immediately feasible and what are ultimately necessary to address fully the causes of the problem. A critical approach would end with seeking the means, the forces, the strategies, by which its proposals might be put into practice.

The argument

That there is a housing crisis in the United States is beyond doubt. Upwards of 4,000,000 households[1] are in danger of losing their homes through foreclosure of their mortgages, tenants are threatened from woefully inadequate maintenance of their units or eviction if their landlords default on their buildings mortgage, and nearly 13 million low-income persons pay more than half their monthly income for rent, live in severely substandard housing, or both (US HUD, May 25, 2010).

Underlying the argument here is the understanding provided by critical theory that the housing crisis, of which the subprime mortgage crisis is a part, is an inherent consequence of an economic system, broadly called capitalist, in which housing and land are treated as commodities, produced, sold, and managed for private profit, grounded in an economic system whose engine is the drive for increasing profits for some at the expense of others;[2] housing, to the extent needed for a full life, should become a public responsibility, with the for-profit private sector's being supportive only, restricted to where it can demonstrably assist in meeting public needs. By contrast, the public sector is disfavored and widely stigmatized for both materialistic and ideological reasons. The argument runs as follows:

The subprime mortgage crisis is not a result of greed or stupidity and it did not come about because the underlying free-market system for the provision of housing is not working; rather, the crisis occurs precisely because the system *is* working. The prevailing system and the consequent subprime mortgage crisis rest on three pillars:

- the commodification of almost all housing – its production, ownership, and management for profit;
- the consequent restriction of any governmental involvement which might restrict private profit;
- the propagated myth of homeownership, seeing ownership as an investment entitled to speculative profit rather than providing housing services to its occupant.

These three pillars need ultimately to be addressed. Until they are, intermediate steps can be proposed that will move in the direction of such fundamental action (see the discussion of critical alternatives, below), and reforms can be proposed which can be both effective immediately and open the door to more thorough approaches.[3]

The nature of the housing crisis

What is called the "subprime mortgage crisis" reflects a fundamental crisis in the housing system of the United States (Stone, 2006). Subprime mortgages are mortgages given to borrowers considered not eligible for a conventional mortgage at the prevailing interest rate on prevailing terms because their incomes or credit ratings or the equity in their property is inadequate. Instead, subprime mortgages carry a higher interest rate and are seen as having a greater risk of foreclosure for non-payment. The subprime mortgage crisis is not a crisis of liquidity in the mortgage market, or a failure of regulation, nor is it the same as the crisis of Fannie Mae and Freddie Mac, two large government-sponsored corporations active in the secondary mortgage market, which is a different crisis with which the subprime market crisis is often confused. It is rather the result of the inability of the housing market system to provide adequate and affordable housing for large numbers of Americans, and of the ideological commitment implicit in that system to private individual homeownership as the incarnation of the American Dream for the masses.

The subprime mortgage problem is part of a crisis in housing that has been part of the US housing landscape for a long time. It was officially recognized at least as far back as the Housing Act of 1937, whose objective was to provide "adequate housing within their means for all Americans." That promise was never fulfilled, and the history of US housing policy is replete with one effort after another to solve the problem while preserving the dominance of the private housing market (Marcuse and Dennis Keating, 2006).[4]

The obvious injustice in the results of such a system is clear. There is an absolute shortage of housing available at affordable costs to low-income families, 12.97 million renters have what HUD calls "worst case housing needs" (HUD, 2010), and 11 million home owners are in danger of foreclosure of their homes in 2010 (measured by arreagages in payments or actual foreclosure proceedings (Hart, 2010)).The foreclosure of homes marketed to families of limited income is only the most current excrescence of that on-going crisis.

The problem is accentuated at this time by the more general crisis caused by a surplus of capital looking for profitable investment opportunities, with investment in real estate, including subprime mortgages, offering an apparently reliable partial solution (Harvey, 2010). Thus, the pressing desire to expand the market beyond what it already was in the preceding real estate bubble to profit from even lower income home seekers. If there was a loss from the crisis in excess of $2–4 trillion, mostly from non-paying mortgages, that's some measure of the amount of the surplus capital floating around looking for investment sites.

Its timing has to do with the general economic crisis taking place today. The subprime mortgage crisis did not produce the general economic crisis; rather the exact opposite: the general crisis produced the subprime crisis. The logic is simple.[5] As the normal tendency continues, with producers seeking to maximize profit by holding down wages, and financialization continues to increase the disparity between the wealth at the top and bottom of the class structure, so the number of those who can afford housing at current market prices fails to rise – or diminishes – and does not provide a market for housing that is both affordable and returns an adequate profit for its producers. To make up for the shortfall in wages, the shortfall in financially effective demand, the producers of housing need to fund their market, to provide buyers the money that they do not have from wages but need in order to buy. Loans, secured by mortgages, are the answer. Speculating that land and housing prices will continuously rise, lenders make loans – provide subprime mortgages, assuming that the speculative increase in prices will ultimately permit their repayment. The more that is loaned, the more housing that can be produced and sold at a profit, so the incentive is to loan more and more. Without expanded lending, the housing supply will not grow and new profits will cease; the system will stagnate. But as the expanded lending outpaces increases in wages necessary to support the expected increases in prices, the loans cannot be repaid; they were "subprime" in the sense that ordinary lending criteria, without the speculation of increased incomes and prices, would not have warranted their issuance. Thus a subprime mortgage loan crisis.

Beneath this crisis lies something deeper. The underlying economic system is built on the drive for the steady accumulation of profit and the necessity of constant growth to provide that profit. That requires a constantly expanding market. Globalization of production and distribution is one answer; the markets in countries like China and India seem a fertile source of new demand. But some industries cannot enter markets abroad. Individual home builders, for instance, are largely confined to the domestic market; only the very largest can operate internationally. And speculative land owners holding property in the United States need to find a profitable use of that land in the United States. As the economic surplus that growth produces increases, the pressure to find new markets increases. Thus, as Lord Keynes would argue, the pressure to expand markets is constant and pervasive. But it is inherent in the system that profits grow by holding down wages, and thus the ability to pay for everything that is produced lags behind the ability to produce it. A surplus is produced that needs to find an outlet for its investment. The solution of globalization is not available to the large majority of home builders, nor to the owners of land within national borders. One possibility then is to let those needing housing borrow the money to pay for it, since they are not able to pay for it out of wages; that would be one solution, and was the one adopted. The development of the subprime housing market is one result: a whole new stratum of home buyers is created, the market for homes is increased dramatically, and as long as prices continue to rise knowledge of the fact that the increase is based on calls for buying by those that cannot afford to buy is repressed. Until prices start to fall. Then you have a crisis, as we have today.

The three pillars of the subprime mortgage crisis

Against the background, then, of a limited rise in wages and the quest for ever-increasing profits in the private housing industry, we need to examine the three pillars of the housing crisis that make up its specific form in the United States today:

1   The reliance on the private profit-oriented market for the provision of the overwhelming bulk of all housing.
2   The restricted role of government in either providing housing or regulating is private provision.
3   The myths of speculative home ownership which is the ideological underpinning of the first two pillars.

The first pillar: the private profit-oriented market

The private housing market system itself produces these crises in housing not because it is not working, but precisely because it is working. Housing is only provided to those who can pay enough for it to make a profit for its supplier. There is an obvious injustice in the results of such a system – today, there is not a single state in the United States in which an individual working full-time at the minimum wage can afford a two-bedroom apartment for his or her family (NLIHC, 2010), not to speak of buying a two-bedroom house. And this is a situation in which African–Americans, Hispanics, immigrants, and women suffer in grossly disproportionate numbers. When it then turns out that, as was predictable, buyers cannot repay loans they needed to be able to buy the housing they needed for themselves and their families – loans they were sold by a housing industry desperate to increase its profits by expanding its market – and foreclosure results, it appears as a credit crisis, rather than the crisis of the housing system it really is.

The first pillar of the crisis is thus the nature of housing development in America: It relies on the private for-profit sector to meet housing needs (Bratt et al., 1986). As a corollary, it relies on the second pillar, the restricted role of government.

The second pillar: the restricted role of government

Government action is welcomed by the private housing industry to the extent that it facilitates the construction, marketing, sale, and management of housing for profit, as by the provision of infrastructure, layout of streets, judicial enforcement of contracts, provision of police and fire services, technical research, and setting of common standards, etc. But as to the public provision of housing, government is required to be penurious to the point of starvation in the resources it provides to meet the true need for housing, one of life's necessities. The history of attempts to change the system by governmental action is rife with the lesson that piecemeal reforms can ameliorate, but don't solve, the problem. Grassroots groups, alarmed by one phase of the crisis or another, have pushed for reform. With only one significant exception – public housing – and even that one to a limited degree, every public program to enlarge the supply of affordable housing has relied on bribing the private housing industry to make its product more affordable. Those programs have systematically been underfunded, have never been made a matter of entitlement, and have always been conspicuously inefficient in terms of the amount of subsidy siphoned off by those involved in producing for profit. Besides the first pillar of the housing crisis, the reliance of the system on the private sector to meet housing needs, it is also penurious to the point of starvation in what government resources it makes available to meet the true need for housing.

It should be clear that suggesting an expanded role for government in the housing sector is not the same as saying that deregulation is the cause of the housing crisis. The government's role can go well beyond regulation, and with regulation itself the question of what is regulated, and for whose benefit, is key: simply calling for more regulation is not enough.

Deregulation, in the past 20 years, has certainly contributed to the present crisis, but "deregulation" is not quite the right word for the culprit. Dan Immergluck, in his excellent and detailed discussion of the development of the mortgage foreclosure crisis (Immergluck, 2009), presses two points, each essential to understanding the crisis and policy options to deal with it, but in some logical contradiction to each other.

One point is that the steady erosion of governmental supervision of mortgage transactions for the protection of the consumer (and, as sometimes suggested, as in the title of his legal book, the protection of "American's mortgage market") has permitted free-wheeling, high risk, unscrupulous dealing in that market, in situations where government has the power, and had exercised the power, to prevent such dealing but had deliberately declined to use it, in fact steadily reducing after 1990 the preventive role it had earlier reluctantly played.

The other point is that the government has always played, and continues to play, a constitutive role in that market, creating the legal and institutional structures without which the market could not act as it does, subsidizing various aspects of its operations. The conduct of users of housing continues to be thoroughly regulated; only that of the housing industry has been deregulated. Thus "deregulation" is not a withdrawal by government from the market, but a change in its role in that market.

The exact definition of what is and is not deregulation may sound like academic hair-splitting, but it has direct political consequences. For those whose primary concern is protecting homeowners from being foreclosed on, evicted, and perhaps left homeless, the key question is does governmental action help home owners as opposed to financial institutions, or does it support the rights of such institutions to foreclose and simply establish some guidelines for how and when that might be done? It is not a question of regulate or not, but regulate what, and for whose benefit. It is the same question that applies to other government actions which are not normally considered regulation: the granting of subsidies, the establishment of institutions, the operation of the judicial system – is paying sheriffs and giving them the power to evict not a form of "regulation" of the conduct of home owners?

The third pillar: the myths of speculative home ownership[6]

All efforts to address the housing crisis have also been colored by the officially promulgated fantasy of home ownership as the American Dream.[7] It is a powerful ideology that relies on two confusions and a myth. The first confusion is the widespread equation of home ownership with the single-family house on its own lot – a design concept that would puzzle the majority of the people living in cities in the industrialized world. The second confusion lies in the idea that home ownership is necessarily linked to the possibility of making a speculative profit on a rise in its price. More broadly, the confusion is linked to a misunderstanding of the possible range of tenure forms. The idea that security of tenure can only be achieved through conventional ownership of housing, security being identified with no landlord having the right to evict, ignores the fact that that right to evict can be limited in a whole variety of ways. It further ignores the fact that conventional home ownership does not in fact always provide security, as millions of households are finding out today. These are ideological problems. Most buyers accepting this ideology are unaware that there are other forms of tenure that can provide equal rights of occupancy, because ownership is in fact a complex bundle of rights, among which security of occupancy may or may not be provided, and to which the possibility of speculative profit or loss need not necessarily be linked.[8]

The governmental programs initiated in recognition of the political need to address the housing crisis in fact did nothing to challenge the first two of these pillars on which the crisis itself rested, and ideologically promoted the third. They promoted private home ownership, in homes supplied by the private market, not only for those who could with private means afford them, but also those whose wages and resources were financially inadequate to do so. One of these, the Community Reinvestment Act of 1977 required banks to allocate prescribed portions of their mortgage portfolios to lower income neighborhoods if they accepted deposits from residents in them. The programs had a progressive component: preventing discrimination in housing, including mortgage provision, because of race, and the red-lining of minority neighborhoods. The CRA has thus been accused by defenders of the real-estate industry of requiring banks to modify their normal handling of risk to satisfy the act, and thus in turn meant to make more risky loans than they wanted. Thus the effort to help low-income households in need of housing obtain it was blamed for the subprime mortgage crisis. However, the CRA explicitly expects banks to use conventional measures of risk in granting loans, and only a small fraction of the loans facing foreclosure have resulted from CRA-related loans; the majority came from loans pushed by banks and brokers simply concerned with making a profit from an even greater market, not with satisfying a housing need previously subject to racial discrimination.[9] So government policy massively promoted home buying by low-income households. As a result, many homes were in fact provided to families who could not afford them. As long as their price on the market went up, the expectation that the increase in price, speculative though it was, would ultimately make up for the earlier difficulty in making current payments prompted lenders to make loans; when prices started stabilizing or dropping, panic ensued, and so did foreclosures, and thus the present subprime mortgage crisis.

To be clear: it is not "the dream that created the crisis," as Joe Nocera's article in the *New York Times* was headlined. People don't innately want "home ownership." Ownership is a bundle of rights as to a particular object. People want one or another of the sticks in that bundle: single-family homes with a garden, security of tenure, right to exclude, right to modify, right to pass on to heirs. Many have been sold an untenable bill of goods about its economic advantages: John Taylor, the chief executive of the National Community Reinvestment Coalition,[10] for instance, is quoted as saying: "I think owning a home is the most common way for working people to join the middle class" (Nocera, 2010: B1). Mainly, he said, that was because of a home's appreciation, which gave people the opportunity for wealth-creation that would otherwise have remained out of reach.

This is really an astonishing statement, given that it is made just as the speculation that home prices always appreciate has brought on a major recession around most of the world. The wealth creation argument has in fact been effectively demolished, both logically and empirically; other investments are likely to do much better over time (Edel and Elliott, 1984), and what wealth may be created is more likely to be consumed than invested. Technically if you need dialysis and buy a dialysis machine, you have made an investment that counts as part of your wealth, but you're hardly able to use that wealth to generate profit for yourself or your family. A dialysis machine is not "wealth" in any meaningful sense for someone dependent on it. The controversy around Hernando de Soto's widely marketed idea that giving shack dwellers title to land on which they are squatting illegally will help eliminate poverty is widely discredited: the title is likely to be sold for money for other immediate needs, and the household has the worse housing for it.

Critical alternatives: surface reforms and non-reformist reforms

Proposals for reform are many and varied, and all hold elements of what needs to be done, but they almost always neglect examination of the three pillars of the crisis. They include proposals for mediation conferences between lenders and borowers to rewrite mortgages; stricter requirements for disclosure of terms and risks; capital reserve requirements for banks; more careful processing of foreclosures by banks; imposition of standardized credit requirements for mortgages; allowance of extended time to move for evictees; and similar.

The need for such reforms is hard to question; the most recent scandal has revealed that banks presenting affidavits as to facts to courts in mortgage proceedings had them signed by robo-signers, who have no knowledge of the facts whatsoever but simply sign one document after the other as they are bidden, often at the expense of hand cramps. Reforms of such practices are useful. Yet none of them addresses the pillars of the crisis, or even move in that direction. There are alternatives.

It's hard for me to write these words, but President Bush was right. Speaking on Wall Street just before the G20 meeting in November 2008, he said, "The crisis was not a failure of the free-market system, and the answer is not to try to reinvent that system" (Pear and Stolberg, 2008). Indeed. The crisis was not a failure of the system; it is how the system works. And the answer is not to reinvent the system, but to reject it and try something new.

What is the system which needs to be rejected? As to housing, it is both ideological and economic, and its name is the same in both: the supply of one of life's necessities through the private market, the provision of housing for profit and not for people. In more classical terms, the problem is the handling of housing for its exchange value rather than for its use value, that is, the commodification of housing (Bratt et al., 1986: 4–11).

Commodification of housing is *the* underlying problem. Commodification is the handling of housing not as one of life's necessities, something that provides shelter, protection, privacy, space for personal and family activities, but rather as something that is bought and sold and used to make money. Commodification is handling something that is a necessity of life and needed for its use value as something that is acquired for its exchange value, so it can be exchanged for profit, so that people can make money out of its sale, management, and financing. Clarity on these points is necessary. Every step that tends towards limiting the commodified character of housing, such as those described at the end of this article, is worth doing. Every step that limits the commodified character of housing contributes to solving the housing crisis.[11]

No immediate step is likely to bring about decommodification as such. However, we may evaluate alternate proposed steps by the extent to which they tend in this direction and support the ultimate removal of housing from the profit-oriented private sector.

Addressing the first pillar: the profit-orientation of housing

While the private profit-oriented sector is the key direct provider of housing for most people in the United States, government action is necessary in countless ways to support that activity: providing roads, sewage, water, zoning controls, mass transit, environmental standards. And it regulates what housing is provided in countless ways: building codes, health and safety codes, height limits, planning controls. Yet it also interferes very gingerly in regulating the profit aspect of the private provision. Rent regulation, for instance, is accepted in times of war or national emergency, or when the housing shortage reaches crisis proportions; but why only then? The logic, as accepted even by the New York Court of Appeals (1977), is that land values are socially created; at least to that extent, the profit from land ownership might well accrue to the social collectivity, acting through government, rather than the private sector.

Reforms that lead in this direction are clearly possible. Rent regulation is an obvious example: it can be a major help to those facing mortgage foreclosure and seeking an alternative in rental housing, and it can dampen the speculative inflation in housing costs across the market.[12] A speculative profits tax on sales goes in the same direction. The tax structure now in fact favors ownership and accentuates its profitability; the tax benefits provided to home owners are unwarranted economically and expand the private interest in profit-oriented development; they should be abandoned. Measures that reduce the profit element in housing should by systematically favored.

Addressing the second pillar: the limited role of government

The present foreclosure crisis has created a political climate in which there is widespread recognition that something is wrong and needs fixing. Seven hundred billion dollars in a bailout package for large financial institutions strikes most people as wrong, whereas helping people at risk of losing their homes seems right. The comparatively trivial allocation of $7 billion for neighborhood stabilization programs to help to deal with foreclosures[13] suggests there was an opening to consider something further. Regardless of the present political situation, the demand for a major increase in the level and principle of funding must remain a core of all demands for dealing with the housing crisis.

The attention should not be confined to the immediate foreclosure crisis, although it of course demands priority. The problem is not short-term; it is chronic – inherent in the system. As long as housing is provided only in response to "effective demand," that is, for those rich enough or highly enough paid to purchase it with a profit for the provider, governmental action will be necessary if the large numbers of those with "ineffective demand" but real need are to be decently housed. There are no legal, administrative, or procedural obstacles to such a reform; only a matter of securing the political power to achieve it.

The conclusion is radical, but very simple: until adequate incomes are guaranteed, providing adequate public financing to cover the gap between even regulated housing costs and the ability to pay is going to be permanent. Where that financing is to come from can be debated; measures such as the military budget and raising progressive income taxes are surely obvious possibilities; that the need will be ongoing is not debatable. When the power to achieve that reform is obtained, it will necessarily be based on a broad grassroots democratic social movement, which will necessarily transform, rather than merely reform, the government's role in housing and its political direction.

Addressing the third pillar: the ideology of speculative home ownership

The ideological problem lies in the belief in the goal of private single-family home "ownership" with the American Dream, visualized as a single-family home on a suburban lot, and the coupling of that belief with the conviction that the private market is the best way to achieve that goal. Underlying the widespread acceptance of the goal are some facts of life in the dominant housing system:

The beliefs on which the "American Dream" is based include:

- that rental tenure is insecure and always subject to the danger of eviction;
- that the only alternative to insecure rental is ownership in fee simple;
- that "ownership" in fee simple guarantees unrestricted use and secure occupancy and the ability to sell at a profit;
- that housing prices are steadily rising, and thus occupancy seems secure;
- that "ownership" is a safe way of accumulating assets for households;
- that the economic value of owning a home is one created by the owner's hard work and is proof of his (although perhaps as much her) personal achievement and moral worth;
- that substantial economic incentives for homeownership come through the mansion tax subsidy, the deduction from income taxes of mortgage interest and real property taxes, and the failure to tax imputed income, and these subsidies will always be there; and
- that the experience of any kind of supportive collective or communal ownership and residential facilities is minimal.

So the ideology is rooted in real-world experience, but a limited experience, more extremely limited in the United States than in many other countries. Knowledge of the way the housing system functions in the real world in fact contradicts the conclusions drawn from this limited experience. The beliefs on which the "Dream" is based are simply wrong, as both past (for example, Sclar et al., 1984), and present experience show.

Rental tenure could in fact be made at least as secure as "ownership" by appropriate lease provision and selection of appropriate landlords, usually, certainly at a large scale, nonprofits or government. And a wide variety of nonprofit and limited equity tenures is available: cooperative, condominium, limited equity co-ownership, mutual housing association, land trust, each of which combines various attributes in the bundle of rights that is "ownership."

Government policies supporting such tenures would be reforms that move in the direction of assuaging the effects of the myth of home ownership, as well as slowly undercutting the dominance of the private market in housing. They might thus move in the direction of shifting the understanding of housing as a symbol of private initiative to an appreciation of it as a social product and part of the social culture of a decent society.

Conclusion: a critical approach to housing

If the three pillars of the housing problem are exposed, their foundation becomes clear. It results from the simple fact that the overwhelming majority of housing, both units and services, are privately provided for profit, and given the level of payments required to produce that profit, major parts of the population are not paid enough to afford adequate housing, and will either pay a disproportionate part of their incomes for housing, neglecting food or clothing or health care or education, or go homeless. There are two answers to this problem.

One is a mild one: extend control over the level of profits that is permitted in the provision of housing. The tools for this purpose are at hand: rent control; anti-speculation and excess profits taxes; criminalization of discrimination and unfair practices; eviction controls and building code improvement and enforcement. Such measures are more than lipstick on a pig, but fall short of reshaping the animal: providing an alternative.

The second answer is a frontal attack on the myths supporting the three pillars that underlie the present (and past) crisis. Rental tenure could in fact be made at least as secure as ownership by appropriate lease provisions and selection of appropriate landlords, e.g. nonprofits or government.[14] And rental is not the only alternative to individual ownership. A wide variety of tenures is available: cooperative, condominium, limited-equity co-ownership, mutual housing association, land trust, each of which combines various attributes in the bundle of rights that is "ownership" (Davis, 2006). Perhaps we should develop a form of "non-speculative home ownership," or "private user ownership," to make it clear that "ownership" can exist, with full protection for the security of the private for its user, without the connection to marketization and the possibilities of speculative profits and losses.

Further, the mortgage foreclosure crisis is a multifaceted problem – for neighborhoods, a community development, as well as for individuals. Alternative forms of tenure to conventional individual private home ownership or profit-motivated rental should be expanded: collective forms of tenure such as community land trusts or mutual housing associations, or through a cooperative management arrangement, and, of course, public housing.

Public housing is generally thought of as multi-family housing, but it could be adapted for single-family homes to provide the security and individual control that "owners" seek.[15] There should be a wide range of experimentation with other forms of non-private–profit oriented ownership models. Many ideas are already on the table. Physical forms of housing can be varied; for instance, Dolores Hayden has argued from a feminist perspective that a non-sexist housing program would include the possibility of separate houses but common cooking and eating facilities, shared recreational space, and so forth (Hayden, 2002; Talen, 2009).

The balance between private for-profit ownership of housing and social ownership, private, nonprofit, and public, should be shifted dramatically in favor of the latter. Likewise, development and construction and management should shift to the public sector; there is plenty of good experience in each area.

Critical urban theory, with its probing historical analysis, examining both the material and the cultural origins of social phenomena, constantly holding up the possibility of alternatives to the actually existing, and calling out for the exploration in practice of the potentials of those alternatives, can be a major contributor to the solution of key urban problems such as those of housing. By addressing the three pillars of the housing crisis, juxtaposing to the commodification of housing the possibility of the social provision of housing outside of the profit-oriented market, juxtaposing to a business-dominated set of government policies the possibility of democratically controlled social policies, and promulgating an understanding of the misconceptions of home ownership and the vision of housing as a social good, critical urban theory can lay the foundation for what critical planning may hope to accomplish. It can expose the causes of the problem, propose reforms with immediate effect but pointing to real changes, and help frame politically the understanding of what is happening, what which reforms can do and what their limits are, so that movement in the direction of real solutions can be made more possible.

Notes

1 Estimate is for 2010: 2.9 million foreclosure notices filed, over one million homes repossessed, perhaps 250,000 foreclosures in abeyance because of paper-work scandals. See http://foreclosures.homemortgageforeclosures.com/2011/01/repossessed-homes-top-one-million-in-2010.

2 For a general account of the relationship of housing shortages and the functioning of the housing system to the structure of the capitalist economy, see Achtenberg and Marcuse (1986).

3 Space does not allow a detailed discussion of such possible immediate reforms, but a sketch of them may be found in my blog (Marcuse, 2010a: http://pmarcuse.wordpress.com).

4 See Marcuse and Dennis Keating (2006), which traces the history of successive governmental actions dealing with the housing crisis in the United States, including the suppressed alternatives that were not put on the policy table.

5 On the general economic crisis, see Wolff (2009), Harvey (2010) and the ongoing commentary of the editors of *Monthly Review*.
6 There is a substantial literature on the myths of home ownership, perhaps starting with Dean (1945) in the 1930s. Most recently, see http://www.washingtonpost.com/wp-dyn/content/article/2009/11/13/AR2009111302214_pf.html.
7 The approach has a long history, going back to the days of Jefferson and Hamilton, Herbert Hoover's commission on home ownership, FDR's moratorium on evictions and adoption of Federal mortgage insurance, the Section 235 program, Clinton's National Homeownership strategy, and so forth.
8 For a detailed discussion of ownership as a bundle of rights, see Marcuse, 1972. A discussion of some alternate forms of tenure may be found in Andrusz et al., 1996: 119–91.
9 For a detailed discussion, see Marcuse, 1979. For a summary of the debate and evidence that CRA loans were not a significant contributor to the foreclosure crisis, see Media Matters, "Media conservatives baselessly blame Community Reinvestment Act for foreclosure spike," September 30, 2008, http://mediamatters.org/research/200809300012.
10 A mixed coalition of grassroots-based nonprofits working in community development, working with banks and lending facilities to "increase the flow of private capital into traditionally underserved communities." See http://www.ncrc.org/about-us.
11 Whether the housing question can be "solved" under capitalism, or only ameliorated, is debatable; certainly Frederick Engels (1975 [1887]) thought its solution would have to await the arrival of socialism. However, he wrote at a time when the role of government in welfare provision was far less than it is today, and it is possible that housing as a sector, perhaps akin to education or policing or fire protection, might be largely removed from the market even within a capitalist framework. That discussion goes beyond the limits of this chapter.
12 Its impact can be seen in the recent sales fiasco of Stuyvesant Town in New York City. In a project that had regulated rents, a buyer paid $5.4 billion for the property, expecting to evict rent-regulated tenants and collect market-level rents. When the courts blocked that move, the value plummeted to an estimated $2.8 billion, and the buying entity went bankrupt.
13 http://www.housingwire.com/2010/09/08/hud-awards-another-1-billion-in-nsp-funding.
14 See the model lease drawn up for the Urban Institute by Peter Marcuse and Richard Clark (1973). The arrangements in the socialist states in the post-World War II period provide an example (Andrusz et al., 1996).
15 The Right to the City Alliance has produced a comprehensive current review of the admitted problems that plague much of public housing in the United States today, with sound proposals for effective solutions (Right to the City Alliance, 2010; see also Liss, this volume).

References

Achtenberg, E., and Marcuse, P. (1986) "The causes of the housing problem," in R. Bratt, C. Hartman, and A. Meyerson (eds) *Critical Perspectives on Housing*, Philadelphia: Temple University Press, 4–12.
Andrusz, G., Harloe, M., and Szelenyi, I. (eds) (1996) *Cities After Socialism: Urban and Regional Change and Conflict in Post-Socialist Societies*, London: Wiley-Blackwell, 119–91.
Bratt, R., Hartman, C., and Meyerson, A. (1986) *Critical Perspectives on Housing*, Philadelphia: Temple University Press.
Bratt, R., Stone, M., and Hartman, C. (2006) *A Right to Housing: Foundation for a New Social Agenda*, Philadelphia: Temple University Press.

Davis, J.E. (2006) *Shared Equity Homeownership: the Changing Landscape of Resale-Restricted, Owner-Occupied Housing*, Montclair, NJ: National Institute [online]. [Accessed April 15, 2011]. Available at http://www.nhi.org/pdf/SharedEquityHome.pdf.

Dean, J.P. (1945) *Home Ownership: Is it Sound?* New York: Harper & Row.

Edel, M. and Elliott, S. (1984) *Shaky Palaces: Homeownership and Social Mobility in Boston's Suburbanization*, New York: Columbia University Press.

Engels, F. (1975 [1887]) *The Housing Question*, Moscow: Progress Publishers.

Hart, T. (2010) "US home ownership rates falling as foreclosure crisis deepens" [online]. [Accessed April 15, 2011]. Available at http://personal moneystore. com/moneyblog/2010 /11/02/u-s-home-ownership-rates-foreclosure-crisis.

Harvey, D. (2010) *The Enigma of Capital*, London: Profile Books.

Hayden, D. (2002) *Redesigning the American Dream*, revised and expanded edition, New York: Norton.

HUD (United States Department of Housing and Urban Development) (2010) *Worst Case Housing Needs 2007: A Report to Congress*, press release 10–107, May 25, 2010 [online]. [Accessed April 15, 2011]. Available at http://www.ncsha.org/blog/hud-releases-worst-case-housing-needs-report and http://portal.hud.gov/portal/page/portal/HUD/press/press_releases_media_advisories/2010/HUD.

Immergluck, D. (2009) *Foreclosed: High Risk Lending, Deregulation, and the Undermining of America's Mortgage Market*, Ithaca, NY: Cornell University Press.

Marcuse, P. (1972) "The legal attributes of home ownership," *Working Paper*, 209–1–1, Washington, DC: The Urban Institute.

Marcuse, P. (1979) "The deceptive consensus on redlining definitions do matter," *Journal of the American Planning Association*, 45, 4, 549–56.

Marcuse, P. (2008) "An Interview with Peter Marcuse 2008," *Critical Planning*, Los Angeles: University of California, 15, summer, 179–91.

Marcuse, P. (2010a) "Towards a comprehensive housing policy," [online]. [Accessed April 15, 2011]. Available at http://pmarcuse.wordpress.com.

Marcuse, P. (2010b) "Changing times, changing planning: critical planning today," *Progressive Planning*, 182, Winter, 13–16.

Marcuse, P. and Clark, R. (1973) "Tenure and the housing system: the relationship and the potential for change," *Working Paper*, 209–8–4, Washington, DC: The Urban Institute.

Marcuse, P. and Dennis Keating, W. (2006) "The permanent housing crisis: the failures of conservatism and the limitations of liberalism," in R. Bratt, M. Stone, and C. Hartman, *A Right to Housing: Foundation for a New Social Agenda*, Philadelphia: Temple University Press, 139–62.

New York Court of Appeals (1977) *Penn Central Transportation Co. v. City of New York*, New York: New York Court of Appeals.

National Low Income Housing Coalition (NLIHC) (2010) *Out of Reach 2010 – June Update* [online]. [Accessed April 15, 2011]. Available at http://www.nlihc.org/oor/oor2010/introduction.pdf.

Nocera, J. (2010) "Wake-up time for a dream," *The New York Times*, June 12, 2010, New York: B1.

Pear, R. and Stolberg, S.G. (2008) "Bush speaks in defense of markets," *The New York Times*, November 14, 2008, New York: B1.

Right to the City Alliance (2010) *We Call these Projects Home* [online]. [Accessed April 15, 2011]. Available at http://www.wehavenoart.net/public/righttocitycolor4-10-10.pdf.

Sclar, E., Edel, M., and Luria, D. (1984) *Shaky Palaces: Homeownership and Social Mobility in Boston's Suburbanization*, New York: Columbia University Press.

Stone, M. (2006) "Pernicious problems of housing finance," in R. Bratt, M. Stone, and C. Hartman (eds), *A Right to Housing: Foundation for a New Social Agenda*, Philadelphia: Temple University Press, 82–104.

Talen, E. (2009) *Urban Design Reclaimed: Tools, Techniques and Strategies for Planners*, Washington, DC: Planners Press.

Wolff, R. (2009) *Capitalism Hits the Fan: The Global Economic Meltdown and What to Do About It*, Chicago: Interlink Publishing Group.

14

SOCIALIST CITIES, FOR PEOPLE OR FOR POWER?

Bruno Flierl in conversation with Peter Marcuse

The form and meaning of cities change historically with changes in the political and economic structures in which they are embedded. Both economic and political relationships are critical; changes in one sphere do not automatically lead to changes in the other. The absence of the market relationships that so widely determine the shape of capitalist cities is not a guarantee that cities free of those relationships will be democratic. Further, even within existing relationships of power, subcurrents shaped by varying internal ideological and external national and international relationships exert their influence. The history of Berlin over the past century is an extreme example of such changing influences, which can be traced in detail in the specifics of its built structure. Discussions between Bruno Flierl and Peter Marcuse date to the year of "turn" (Wende) in East Germany, 1989/1990, when Marcuse was teaching and conducting research in Weimar and in East Berlin. The dialogue among these friends has continued over the years, most recently at the conference on "The Right to the City" held at the Center for Metropolitan Studies, Berlin, in November 2008. This chapter documents some of the main elements of this ongoing conversation between two critical urbanists.

Opening remarks by Peter Marcuse

This book addresses one of the major obstacles to achieving a humane city for all: the role of the profit-driven market dominant in the capitalist economies of today. But the market in capitalist economies depends on the state for its operations, and the institutions of the state reinforce the social controls and relations of power that are an integral part of the capitalist economic system. What would a "city for people, not for profits," a humane city, look like? Most of the chapters in this book suggest it would be a city in which the profit-driven market is not the primary determinant of city form or city use.

Is eliminating the profit-driven market enough – even if it is based on an elimination of the economic relations that undergird and are fortified by that market, i.e. the relations of production and the drive for accumulation with which we are familiar? How about the effect of relations of power not dependent on the market? Relations of power existed before capitalism, as the study of history reveals. Cities were built with various relations of power before the capitalist market and capitalist production took their place. Cities like Vienna, Paris, indeed most European cities and many elsewhere, were built under feudal regimes and by various forms of monarchic, tribal, or hierarchical power. But such cities generally existed before the advent of capitalist industrialization. Do we have any experience of what the impact of relations of power might be on a city today, absent a profit-driven market, that is, absent capitalist relations?

Yes, we do. The cities of really existing socialism provide ample, but very inadequately studied, evidence of what a "city not for profit" might look like.[1] Were they "cities for people?" The question is an important one, for the overwhelming view today is that they were not, certainly not cities worth emulating as a whole, not cities that could serve as models for what we would aspire to today. Why not, if the profit motive is to blame for everything that's wrong in contemporary cities; why does abolishing the profit motive not produce ideal cities?

The question has direct implications for practice as well as for theory. Often the criticism of what the market has produced in cities is met by pointing at the cities of really existing socialism, by the retort, "But look what cities without markets look like; is that the alternative you want?" One answer has to do with the concept of markets: Could one not have a market not driven by profit, a so-called social market? That is a complicated question, not addressed here. When we speak of markets, we mean markets driven by the desire for profit in their production and distribution. But the other answer, which this dialogue does address, is that there are relations of power that need to be considered outside of the economic sphere, even if based on it, and relations of power can prevent the development of cities for people just as the profit-driven market can, although in different ways. This is why so many socialists insist on using the phrase "really existing socialism," and juxtapose it to "democratic socialism," to make the point that radically charging economic relations are a necessary but not a sufficient condition for creating a better world and better cities; changing (or eliminated) relations of power is necessary as well.

The question of power is important not only in the really existing socialist cities of our recent past, but also in today's cities in the capitalist countries. Power relations (again, largely but not exclusively based on economic relations) determine the extent of public space, of recreational opportunities, of access and mobility, of environmental quality, of the differential management, maintenance, and indeed availability of infrastructure. Nowhere is this more immediately visible than in architecture. Volumes have been written on the architecture of power; the concept is hardly a radical one. It is perhaps particularly evident in colonial cities, and certainly strikingly so in fascist building; historically it is indeed the leitmotif of formal architectural history before the seventeenth century. Palaces and cathedrals are pieces of that history, and reflect a power to which the market only indirectly relates.

Less examined, however, is precisely what the relationships between markets and power-driven development are. We have cathedrals of commerce and dominant skyscrapers, universities as dominant enclaves in the midst of slums, department stores built to express elevated social status, first- and second-class public railway cars, and class-conscious courtrooms and hospitals. Just how far will we get to cities for people if we simply eliminate the profit motive in their construction?

The cities of Eastern Europe provide an excellent case study to get at such questions with a minimum of (or perhaps only with different?) complications. They raise, to oversimplify a good bit, the question of the relationship between political democracy and economic equity. And of all cities, Berlin is probably the most accessible example: it is a city that has gone from strong absolutism to liberal democracy to fascism to, in one part, really existing socialism and, once there, back again, and in the other part to a neoliberal and globalized existence. Its architecture is exemplary of this history, isolating the manifestations of power from the manifestations of the profit-driven market in the visible, physical form of Berlin's buildings.

So, Bruno, how do you react to these thoughts about society and architecture – about architecture for people, for profit and/or for power – on the basis of your own knowledge and experience working in Berlin, which was for 40 years the capital of the GDR under really existing socialism, and since 1990 the capital of the FRG under the conditions of today's really existing capitalism?

Response by Bruno Flierl

History is always worth thinking about in the interest of making the future.

Indeed: the GDR – founded in 1949 – had a pattern of urban development that was economically oriented not by the profit motive but by the desire to meet human needs. Yet it was politically not free from state power over people's lives. Architecture, as the constructed environment of society, expressed this relation between people and power – as it has always been in history and everywhere in the world – in a specific East German manner.

I will try to analyze what happened in society, urban development, and architecture during the years of the GDR's existence and then after 1990 in the process of unifying the divided Germany – and especially the divided Berlin – inside the territory of a developed Federal Republic of Germany. I will end with the question of how to develop in the future human cities without domination – and without profit – and how to have an architecture for the people. I want to end later with a brief comment on what should be examined in future research.

Urban planning in the GDR, and with it the form of cities and architecture, developed on the basis of socialist relations of production, that is, it rested in the first instance on the instruments of production: from land to technical machinery to buildings allocated in accordance with policies that were intended to serve the interests of the human beings in their constructed environment, including houses, cities, the transformed landscape. The legal basis for this was the *Aufbaugesetz*, the Reconstruction Law of September 1950. That law included the *Grundsätze des Städtebaus* (the principles of urban planning), which became known as the *16 Grundsätze des Städtebaus* (the 16 principles of urban planning). They were initially focused on the reconstruction of the cities destroyed in the war, the so-called "Reconstruction-Cities." They were elaborated in 1960 in the *Grundsätze der Planung und Gestaltung sozialistischer Stadtzentren* (the principles of the planning and design of socialist city centers). Additions were made from time to time thereafter.

All of these state measures for the *Leitung und Planung* (the direction and planning), as it was then called, of the built and spatial development of cities were intended to be on the basis of socialist economic and political relations, in contrast to the profit-oriented housing, land, and building markets of capitalist societies. Their purpose was to make sure the built environment, housing, buildings, and built ensembles, would not have the character of commodities, in other words, would not be determined by their exchange value but by their use value, and on the basis of uniformly established prices. Since land, buildings, and living quarters weren't commodities, the typical capitalist market that determined their form and use did not exist, and therefore also nor did polarization, segregation, or a displacement of urban residents. The urban policies of the GDR were based on the social equality of all citizens. Thus the second of the Principles of City Construction held that "the purpose of urban development is the balanced satisfaction of human demands for work, housing, culture, and recreation." It was a rather idealistic, humanistic conception of how a "city for people" should be constructed.

And this way of framing these principles was quite different from the Athens Charter, whose basic guidelines had been conceived by the CIAM as early as 1933 and which was documented by Le Corbusier in the 1940s, but did not become generally known around the world until after World War II: as an appeal by architects and urban planners to the governments in countries around the globe to develop a city that would serve the functions of human life. The principles of urban planning in the GDR were, by contrast, a mandate issued by the state to architects and urban planners to build a city adapted to human needs on the way to socialism.

This rather idealistic approach to a non-capitalist form of urban development did not lead to the success its authors intended, for real reasons, both external and internal, that determined the development of the GDR more generally.

There was, first, the global Cold War between the capitalist and the social-ist countries, which had begun as early as 1947 and in which the GDR was entangled from its very founding in 1949. The GDR was the smaller and weaker of the two German states, dependent in everything – economically and politically – on the Soviet Union. It was integrated into the Eastern European system of military alliance, but was also firmly determined to stand its ground, especially against the West German Federal Republic, and its politics were fueled by the ambition to outperform West Germany even in matters that did not merit being pursued from the perspective of East Germany's own cause. In an international constellation of this sort – reinforced by the situation of the divided Germany, the two states separated by different societies but, despite all borders, united by media and the shared language – the GDR in general, and the urban development it pursued, stood only a limited chance.

Second, on its own territory, the GDR commanded only rather limited supplies of the material means required for lasting achievements. It always had what was necessary to secure, on average, a decent quality of life for its peo-ple, but nothing was available in abundance, there were occasional shortages, sometimes serious ones, on a more or less regular basis. To achieve normality always required massive efforts. In such circumstances, even the best urban planning had to fall short of its goals. Moreover, some socialist ideals often lacked a solid economic basis. For instance, the state, for reasons of social pol-icy, guaranteed for 40 years that apartment rents were held to approximately one East German Mark per square meter, without any consideration of the possibility that construction expenditures might be amortized through rents. The state served as a benefactor in a society that was not wealthy.

Dialogue

Peter Marcuse (PM): You say "for reasons of social policy." But for reasons of social policy one would not promise more than can be delivered, which is in effect what setting rents that low and promising all a comparatively high quality of housing meant. Might you not interpret the housing policy of the GDR as heavily influenced by the need to preserve the power of the state over its people against the subversive influence arising from the sight of greater prosperity in the West – in other words, putting the social at the service of the political, the maintenance of power?

Bruno Flierl (BF): I agree. And that brings me to the third reason that the social aspirations for a socialist society were not realized. The GDR never developed popular democratic self-determination, something that presupposes an open and public debate and public participation in decisions con-cerning the *res publica* in all social processes. The really existing socialism of the GDR – developed under the doctrinal influence of Soviet Stalinism and the leading state party of the Soviet Union, the CPSU – was a state socialism established by authoritarian means, not a democratic popular socialism of the sort envisioned also by socialists in the early years of the GDR, not a "people's democracy." The slogan, often popularized as an invitation to everyone to "contribute ideas, join the work, participate in government" usually remained an empty phrase. An undemocratic division of labor was more or less in effect: the leading state party, the Socialist Unity Party of Germany (SED), and its state did the thinking and governing, the people worked. Although it should be noted that there was a fundamental agreement that socialism was – or at least could become – the better society, better than capitalism. How much goodwill and ability remained unutilized or was rejected and thus lost!

PM: But wasn't there a tension between the kind of idealistic ambitions you described in the beginning, involved in the founding of the GDR and embodied, regarding urban development, in the 16 Principles, and the lack of democratic decision-making processes that you call the third reason for this failure to fulfill the ideals of socialism? When we were in the GDR in 1989–90, we encountered many people, some in quite important positions, who were quite critical of the lack of democracy and participation in urban planning decisions. Our sense was that they were indeed dedicated to building "cities for people," and aware that the regime was betraying some of its supposed ideals in the way it was going about things. But the critics did not feel they should go into outright opposition – "should not" rather than "could not," because they hoped the regime, and the basic structure of the society, was still at bottom tending in the direction of the original ideals. It was better to work within the system to bring those ideals to fruition, than to oppose the regime outright and implicitly the ideals on which it was based.

BF: You're right, and that situation already existed at the very beginning of urban policy in the GDR; the debate about the development of the city center in Berlin, which I want to discuss, is a classic example. And in general all of this could not in the long run come to a good end. And it didn't. After the Cold War between the superpowers had been brought to an end in 1988–9 because of an increasing fear for, and a rational focus on, survival, the division of Germany this Cold War had once created also became historically obsolete, at least in its existing form. The GDR might have stood a chance as a democratic socialist state, but only with a Soviet Union reformed into a democratic socialist state as a strong partner. Since that was not the course history took, the GDR was doomed.

Yet with the dissolution of the GDR into the capitalist Federal Republic of Germany, many things also no longer had a future that had been positive hallmarks of the GDR as a socialist society – not least among them an urban development that was not for profit.

PM: So what happened after the Wall came down? Could you see, from the change in direction from the policies of the GDR to the policies of the FRG, that is, from really existing socialist to really existing capitalist policies, the difference between cities whose development is not driven by market principles and cities whose development is? Or does the existence of the tendencies toward the accumulation and protection of power in both systems essentially erase the difference between them?

BF: I think the difference is very visible, but you can judge for yourself. Let me take the case of Berlin. As was to be expected, since 1990 – first with the monetary union between the two German states starting on June 30, then with their political union on October 3 – urban policies in the entire former GDR, both in the so-called New *Länder* and in East Berlin, underwent a rollback toward a profit-driven capitalist economy, including an almost complete privatization of socialized real estate, and toward an architectural and spatial reconstruction of the city in accordance with the functions and the image of the city before the GDR – the aim was to purge the East German past in practical and aesthetic terms from the newly appropriated cities. At the same time, the goal was to create, in each of the New States with its old cities, architectural signs that would symbolize the new leading political and economic institutions and impress upon the inhabitants of every town that they were now living in a new state: the Federal Republic of Germany.

Architecture, as the constructed environment of human life, is, in material and ideal terms, in practical and aesthetic terms, the product of human social and individual existence. It plays an immediate role as a concrete object in the life of people in a historically concrete society, but it also serves to signify and communicate meanings – that is, as a symbol. All constructive forces in all societies have always made use of these capacities of architecture. That is why societies and the people in them can be recognized in the environment they have constructed, unless subsequent societies have misused, destroyed, or altered it beyond recognition.

Berlin – until 1945 the capital of the German Empire and the Weimar Republic, then after 1949 in its Eastern part the capital of the GDR, and now since 1990 in its entire traditional territory the capital of the Federal Republic – is an open book, presenting a social, urbanistic, and architectural history full of contradictions.

Berlin as the capital of the GDR was defined by two primary architectural and urbanistic mandates (besides the need to rebuild, convert, and build production and scientific facilities and educational, pedagogical, health, and recreational institutions): a comprehensive state-subsidized program of residential construction in large urban areas, and the erection of buildings that would house the highest organs of the state and stage them in effective architecture. All of this was not-for-profit construction, to be paid for and used by the society as a whole, but popularized by political propaganda: both mass-housing construction and the special piece of architecture for the state. Yet the successes achieved in solving these challenges served not least also to hide the deficiencies and internal contradictions of GDR architecture and urban planning, e.g. the fact that, remarkable individual achievements notwithstanding, insufficient funds and technical means were available for a reconstruction and renovation of the pre-war residential building stock (of which Berlin, in particular, had plenty).

The largest and at the same time most representative residential construction project had been undertaken right at the beginning of the GDR's development: the creation of the grand East Berlin thoroughfare and boulevard called, between 1949 and 1960, Stalinallee, with apartments for 5,000 inhabitants from all social strata in eight-story buildings, each 150–200 meters long, along both sides of the street for altogether 1.5 kilometers (Figure 14.1).

The Stalinallee was the showpiece of Berlin's reconstruction program in the first half of the 1950s. It was considered a representative promise of future residential life in a socialist city. But it was too expensive, much too expensive to serve as a model for the future.

The construction along Stalinallee had not yet been finished when the first GDR architecture conference of 1955 passed a series of motions to industrialize residential construction that amounted to a radical paradigm shift. After a brief preparation period, from 1960 virtually all new

FIGURE 14.1 Stalinallee in Berlin; built 1952–7
Source: Bauinformation Berlin

residences were built industrial-style, in dry construction using precast concrete slabs. This was no doubt the more effective way, enabling builders to meet the targets defined by an ambitious program of social housing that called for low rents and politically mandated short deadlines – but it was more effective only in quantitative terms. The apartments, usually with balconies, in these wide residential blocks, were in most cases 11 stories tall and grouped in gigantic new neighborhoods. Most were located along the city's periphery, but some were also in the inner city. The apartments were acceptable in the sense that first and foremost everyone was to get *an* apartment before, later on, people would get *their own* apartments. But this focus of the residential construction program on meeting quantitative targets led to rather unsatisfactory architectural results: apartments in an industrial grid of residential blocks demonstrated the social equality of their tenants, but they also leveled individual differences. And despite their provision of all the social facilities necessary for people's lives, these neighborhoods sorely lacked urban quality and were both functionally and aesthetically much too monotonous. By contrast, the pre-war building stock in the inner city was left to decay. In the GDR's Berlin, paradigmatic examples include the industrially constructed peripheral residential area of Marzahn-Hellersdorf, with its 150,000 residents (Figure 14.2), and the inner city pre-war neighborhoods in the boroughs of Prenzlauer Berg and Friedrichshain.

In the reunited Berlin, new residential construction, but also the maintenance, renovation, and conversion of the existing post- and pre-war building stock, takes place primarily on a private basis, undertaken by commercial development companies that aim to make a profit and see their property appreciate; that leads to mercilessly increasing rents and to the displacement of disadvantaged social groups, which move to cheaper

FIGURE 14.2 Marzahn residential area in Berlin in the 1980s
Source: Archiv Stadtbüro Hunger, Berlin

but also poorer and usually lower quality neighborhoods – in short, to gentrification, as has happened everywhere in the world of capitalism. Those who have enough money buy themselves condominiums for their personal happiness – and these are primarily the city's new residents who have moved here from the western Federal Republic.

The new property owners from the old Federal Republic have a highly differentiated view of the value of GDR residential real estate: the historicist buildings along the former Stalinallee – today's Karl-Marx-Allee and Frankfurter Allee – have been declared landmark achievements in architectural and urbanistic terms, whereas the industrial-style modern residential building stock created by the GDR has been mercilessly devalued and vilified as *Platte* – short for *Plattenbau*, prefabricated concrete slab construction. All of this can only be understood once we see it in the contemporary valuation of heritage coupled with the ruthless quest for profit within today's residential market. It makes perfect sense that these two factors would lead to a preferential interest in a privately controlled appropriation of pre-war residential areas.

Besides residential construction, the second and very different challenge the GDR faced was the urbanistic and architectural *mise-en-scène* of the GDR's state power in Berlin's historic center. This called for highly effective signifiers representing the society as a whole not only to this society itself but also to outside observers, first and foremost in West Berlin. Even in the summer of 1950, a *Volkshaus* (People's House), a multi-functional building in the tradition of the labor movement of the late nineteenth century and the era of the November Revolution of 1918–19, was still being talked about for the so-called "central building of the capital." But then Walter Ulbricht, the leader of the SED,

FIGURE 14.3 Project for the East German governmental high-rise, 1951
Source: Bauakademie, in Bauwelt 1991, Heft 12, p. 612, Berlin

called for a *government high-rise* as a "central building" in the middle of the city's historic core, roughly where, before the devastations of the World War II bombing, the Prussian kings and the German emperors had had their *Schloss*, a castle the GDR, for political and ideological reasons, had no intention to rebuild. So instead of a *people's house*, a *state house*! (Figure 14.3).

This was the first architectonic expression in the GDR of what was already the intention of its political leadership: the establishment of a Stalinist *state socialist* system based on the Soviet model. This building – a tower rising to a height of 150 meters in the mold of Moscow's high-rises – was never built, first because the money wasn't there, then out of better insight into what Berlin, as the socialist capital of the GDR, would need. So, in the late 1960s, instead of a government high-rise, the city built the Alexanderplatz as a newly planned urban ensemble and, nearby, the 365-meter television tower, which became Berlin's landmark building, beloved in the East, hated in the West (Figure 14.4).

On the city's central historic site, however, the *Spreeinsel* – an island in the Spree river in the city's center, abutting Marx-Engels-Platz – the state built, in the first half of the 1970s, the *Palast der Republik* (Palace of the Republic), a mixed composite of *people's palace* and *state palace*. Although the palace included a plenary meeting room for the GDR *Volkskammer* (people's chamber) or parliament, it was a building that represented not state authority but cultural communication and was open and publicly accessible to anyone and therefore generally popular. The foreign ministry, the building of the *Staatsrat* (state council), and the seat of the Central Committee of the SED in the former *Reichsbank* (German central bank)

FIGURE 14.4 City center of the East German capital in Berlin, 1990
Source: SenBauWohn Berlin, in: Spreeinsel, Städtebau und Architektur, Bericht 16, 1992, page 2

building along the edges of Marx-Engels-Platz, those were the representative buildings of GDR state power – not the Palace of the Republic. It is remarkable that all other government institutions were housed not in new buildings but in older buildings erected in earlier stages of Berlin's development as a capital. The architectural *mise-en-scène* of the GDR's state power presents a picture marked by significant contradictions.

PM: That's a fascinating story. So the construction of the Palace of the Republic was a victory for the advocates of a democratic socialism in the GDR, over the pressure of the ruling party to build a symbol of its own power in the center of the city. These internal conflicts within the GDR aren't generally known. The idea that the seat of the national legislature might also be a building where cultural and recreational spaces were provided for popular performances, public restaurants, meeting rooms, etc., is hard to imagine in a capitalist society; the old-time *Rathauskeller* in medieval city halls might perhaps be the closest precedent? Even if access was restricted when the legislature was actually in session, the symbolism is striking.

What is the analogous development in the FRG today like?

BF: It's very different. You can see it in the handling of the location where the Palace of the Republic once stood, a controversy in which I was directly involved. Today's Federal Republic, which has, since 1991, taken its seat in Berlin as the new federal capital, pursues the reunification of all Germans with too much high-handedness to be interested in the internal contradictions of the GDR's development – it only cares for its own antagonism to the GDR in general. But interestingly enough, this antagonism is very differentiated. The FRG isn't afraid of using the former state council building, the seat of the GDR State Council headed by Walter Ulbricht and then by Erich Honecker, to house first, though only temporarily, the Chancellor's offices and now a training facility for the young cadres of capital, the so-called "European School of Management and Technology." But it also advocated from the very beginning the demolition not only of the GDR's foreign ministry building but also and most importantly of the Palace of the Republic, with the declared intention to rebuild on its site the old Berlin Schloss, a building that is simply indispensable if Berlin is to return to its "true old self," as the influential conservative journalist and pundit Jobst Wolf Siedler never tires of arguing. Of course, every historically conscious German knew after the end of the GDR that the Palace of the Republic, as a symbolic building of the GDR, could not simply become a symbolic building of a reunified Germany, even if it would be rededicated to alternative purposes – but the solution to the question of which new meaning would be created on this site should have been sought in a perspective turned not toward the past but toward the future. This attitude of "back to the era before the

GDR, before the division of Germany" instead of "forward into an era after the GDR, and so after the division of Germany," is exemplary of the failure of today's FRG to address the historical challenge of solving the contradictions of German history, and in particular Germany's most recent history, by dialectical means, by "sublation" (*Aufhebung*). Instead, it seeks to replace, especially in the city's historic center, the image of the most recent past with the image of a past that is long gone, to replace the image of the GDR's Palace of the Republic with the image of a Hohenzollern castle from the era of Prussia and the German Empire. As though it were a matter of images rather than of today's people, who have a vital interest first and foremost in their own future! When the German Federal Parliament, in 2002, voted to demolish the palace and to rebuild the much earlier castle, what it envisioned was the replacement of one image with another. The ultimate aim of

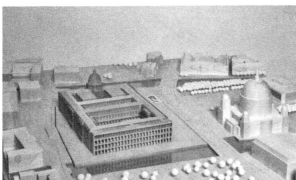

FIGURES 14.5 AND 14.6 Castle design, 2008
Source: Jürgen Prange

resurrecting the image of the castle was to efface the image of the palace and, with it, the memory of the palace and of the GDR more generally. The endeavor has been successful. The site on Mitte's Spreeinsel, where the Schloss once stood and the palace no longer stands, is now Berlin's *Ground Zero*. The architect Franco Stella has already presented a general design for the image of the old new castle, which is planned as a *Humboldt Forum* but still very undefined in practical and intellectual terms (Figures 14.5 and 14.6). But it is entirely unclear when this Schloss will be built, given the global financial and economic crisis, which is now being increasingly felt in Germany.

The Federal Republic made a rather felicitous choice when it chose the design by the architects Axel Schultes and Charlotte Frank for the new governmental forum in the Spreebogen area: a horizontally expansive ensemble of buildings, certainly monumental but of human dimensions, that incorporates the old Reichstag building with its cupola designed by Sir Norman Foster and bears the countenance of a democratically governed country (Figure 14.7).

PM: But aren't there also questions as to how democracy is furthered by this construction, what with the tight control of popular demonstrations within the *Bannmeile*, the rejection of the idea of an open forum between the chancellery and the administrative structure to the north of the Reichstag, the limited contact from the open dome down to the actual sessions of the legislature in the Reichstag, and so on?

BF: True. The government complex represents democracy more as an image than it is in reality.

In the new Berlin, the federal capital, the profit motive as a driving force in urban development, a characteristic feature of capitalist

FIGURE 14.7 Governmental quarter of the Federal Republic in Berlin. The old Reichstag and the new buildings near the Spree
Source: Bruno Flierl

FIGURES 14.8 AND 14.9 High-rises on Potsdamer Platz
Source: Bruno Flierl

societies, is manifest primarily in the architectural staging of the market economy in dazzling stores – e.g. those along Friedrichstraße – in high-rise construction, and in entire urban settings exclusively dedicated to shopping – especially on Potsdamer Platz and, in part not yet realized, on Alexanderplatz (Figures 14.8, 14.9, and 14.10).

So Berlin, with its various phases as a capital in the post-World War II era – first 40 years as the capital of the GDR in really existing socialism, and then what has now also already been almost 20 years as the capital of the Federal Republic in really existing capitalism – is a striking example of how a city has been shaped by the people and by power, the power of the state and the power of profits – under forms of democratic government or/and dictatorship.

PM: Well, what lessons do you draw from the experience of the divided and then unified Germany, the really existing socialist city and the really existing capitalist city? The answer may illuminate what is really the ultimate question: will we ever have a City for People?

BF: The struggle for a city not dominated by, or even entirely free of, the profit motive must be part and parcel of the struggle for a society not based on the profit motive. This city can only come into being in such a society. For the creation of an urban development that serves people's needs rather than the profit motive is based on the creation of a society that serves not the production of profits but people's needs.

The decisive question in this context is: in whose hands is the ownership of the means of production, and in whose interests are these means

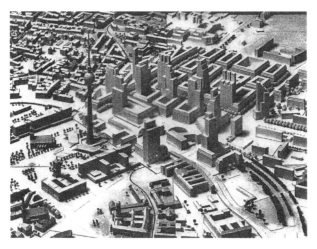

FIGURE 14.10 High-rises for the unrealized Alexanderplatz Project of architect Hans Kollhoff, 1993

Source: Uwe Rau, Das Alexanderhaus, Der Alexanderplatz, Jovis Verlag, Berlin, 1992, p. 86

deployed such that a city for people – and not for profit – can be produced and reproduced? But that is a question that concerns the society as a whole. It invites one ready answer: there is no way here without Marx, without his analysis of capital and its possible sublation (*Aufhebung*). Ideas, social aims, and moral principles may be perfectly correct, but they are ultimately ineffective as long as the necessary economic as well as political conditions are absent or insufficiently present – that is, democratic control over the ownership of the means of production that serve to produce and reproduce the city and, more expansively conceived, the entire populated earth. I believe that the ultimate goal must be the creation of a democratic society beyond the society of today's capitalism, which is based on the production of profits – a new society that transcends capitalism.

I think there are primarily two aspects to be considered in this context: First, such a new society – and the new city in it – will have to be different from the society of capitalism, but also different from the society of twentieth-century socialism. And the struggle against capitalism and the profit motive – both in the US and in Germany – but also against state socialism – as it continues to exist, in parts, in China – will have to be conducted in ways different from how it was conducted in the past century. For if the struggle against profit-motivated capitalism only renders it socially tolerable without ultimately daring to touch the private ownership of the means of production and, based on it, the private appropriation of the fruits of social production and the surplus product – if, hence, the exploitation of human labor, as the economic precondition of profit, continues – then the development of society and city – more or less tolerable or intolerable – remains at bottom a reform of capitalism in which the profit motive continues to reign. We saw in the twentieth century that, conversely, once the struggle for a democratic socialism and against state socialism, which had become intolerable, expanded into a struggle against the social ownership of the means of production, the abolition of the socialist society in its entirely was the inevitable consequence: by negligence or deliberately and, in any case, with support and praise from the capitalist antagonist. What we will need in the future is something new: not the old capitalism nor again any sort of new, renovated capitalism in which private ownership of the means of production and, hence, democratically mediated exploitation and profits persist; nor, on the other hand, a new or somehow renovated socialism with social ownership of the means of production under state-controlled planning and leadership and without democracy; but instead a society defined by democratic self-determination and self-regulation of its social production and reproduction in accordance with its own interests. This is the logical consequence of history, the realm of freedom: the production and reproduction of humans and humankind – according to humankind's own measure. It's the easy thing that is hard to do.

Second, the struggle for a new society and for the new city in it – more comprehensively conceived: for the new social–spatial forms of social habitation – must be thought and practiced in global dimensions and no longer in the dimensions of the national state nor even in the dimensions of this or that continent by itself. The theory and praxis of a "socialism" in one country or in a group of countries, which had emerged in the twentieth century with the socialist October Revolution in Russia in 1917 and the attempt to create a superior counter-society in confrontation with the international world of capitalism, can no longer be the way that, under the current and future conditions of global development, will lead to a new society and its new urban habitation in free and human self-determination and production. In this sense, the interconnections between *society*, *city*, and *world* must be conceived in new ways, theoretically and practically, to make interventions possible. The new society and its new urban habitation grow out of the struggle for a world as a whole that must be conducted everywhere in this world at once and by globally networked means, on a small as well as a large scale. This is a long process that will take persistence and patience. But that, of course, is precisely the new challenge.

What the city and the architecture of this new society of free production and self-determination will look like is not a question we need to discuss today. It will be, in practical and aesthetic terms, what the new society, fusing the global, the territorial, and the local with its individual concrete economic and social, political, and cultural needs and capabilities, will need and achieve: the constructed environment of a dynamically changing new society.

If these ideas will be read as utopian, that is fine by me. Utopias – as long as they contain a rational core, which I would maintain these ideas do – are the (as yet) impossible real or, in other words, the real that is (as yet) impossible because it is as yet unfeasible. They are provocations that invite us to discover and change the world. Those who consider only what is feasible today to be the really possible or possibly real outcome of development are ultimately stuck in one place. Instead, we need to recognize and foster the becoming-feasible of that which is really possible or, in other words, possibly real.

PM: To summarize: the experience of the GDR and its cities under really existing socialism and then under really existing capitalism reveals two different obstacles to the creation of cities for people. The first is the dominance of the profit motive; the second is the dominance of a government concerned with the maintenance of its own power. And you further argue that both of these problems can be solved only within societies as a whole, not just within cities, and they must be solved globally, and not just within one country or even system of countries.

Perhaps the slogan needs to be: Cities *and societies* for *and by* people, not for profit *or power*.

BF: I agree.

Note

1 Among the more critical examinations are Marcuse and Staufenbiel (1991).

References

Marcuse, P. and Staufenbiel, F. (eds) (1991) *Wohnen und Stadtpolitik im Umbruch: Perspektiven der Stadterneuerung nach 40 Jahren DDR*. Berlin: Akademie Verlag.

Selected texts by Bruno Flierl

Gebaute DDR. Über Stadtplaner, Architekten und die Macht. Berlin: Verlag für Bauwesen, 1998.
Berlin baut um – Wessen Stadt wird die Stadt? Berlin: Verlag für Bauwesen, 1998.
"Das alte Berliner Schloss in der neuen Hauptstadt Deutschlands – Realität und Metapher aufgehobener Geschichte?" *Die Alte Stadt*, 30, 4, 2003, pp. 349–70.

Translation assistance by Gerrit Jackson.

15

THE RIGHT TO THE CITY

From theory to grassroots alliance

Jon Liss

Over the past 30 years capital has "re-founded" itself by imposing neoliberal programs (see Leitner et al. 2007) linked with imperial expansion. This refounding was a response to a crisis of accumulation or declining profit rates. Components of neoliberalism have included privatization, aggressive attacks on unions, attacks on the "social" wage in general and women of color in particular. The dominant class response to the political and accumulation crisis of the early 1970s has now generated its own crisis with the 2008 and ongoing crash.

The ideas, institutions, and programs of the dominant class have figured crucially in the capitalist refounding project of the past 30 years. Their dominant *ideas*, most sharply visible in the US context, include the agenda of "getting government off the people's back," the need to stop tax-and-spend liberalism, and the iconic and mythic images of Ronald Reagan's welfare queen or today's gun-toting gangster, day laborer, etc. Importantly, the dominant class has successfully created a three-way interchange or dialogue between formal intellectuals (Friedman, Hayek) with organic intellectuals (Irving Kristol, Anne Coulter, or more recently Glenn Beck) and with masses of supporters (for example, the Tea Party). Furthermore, their ideas are developed, modified, tested, and multiplied by a range of *institutions* that propagate and implement neoliberalism, ranging from a number of think tanks like the Manhattan Institute (urban policy) to Fox News and the US Congress. *Programs* have included efforts to cut taxes on the wealthy or to slash welfare as we know it.

Up until the 2007 economic crisis, the neoliberal program could largely be classified as a smashing political success. However, the *ideology* of neoliberalism has achieved a high level of hegemony: it is, despite the 2008 economic crash, almost universally accepted by both dominant electoral parties in the United

States. These politics and policies were made dominant through the forging of an historic bloc that elects like-minded officials while also serving as a political tail wind that keeps things running the way they are and the way they "have always been." By expertly blending racism with appeals to capitalist mythology, Reagan and his followers manufactured an anti-New Deal majority that was tied to multinational industrial capital, the military, extractive industries, and white workers and outer suburbanites. Spatially, this "revanchist" (Smith 1996) regime was directly tied, in its formative decades, to the rise of exoburbs and outer suburbs. After the events of 9/11, the outer suburban spatial regime ran head-on into the limits of capital, its inability to compress time and space and heightened political contradictions, as masses of African–American and immigrant renters from urban areas bought homes in the predominantly white outer ring. In response to these contradictions, in its insatiable quest for profits, capital returned to the inner suburbs and city (Smith 2002). This round of post-9/11 gentrification fueled the creation of a new national formation – the Right to the City Alliance (2007). Three dozen urban/community-based organizations confederated to stem the tide of gentrification on working class communities of color. Who are these groups? From where have they come?

Recomposition of the working class

Right to the City (RTTC) Alliance member organizations are a political expression or response to the recomposition of the working class in the United States over the past 40 years. The urban poor who are represented by the RTTC Alliance are a product of:

1   The deindustrialization of the urban United States, heavy manufacturing jobs in auto industries, aeronautics, and steel moved overseas or, in some cases, to rural areas or outer suburban office parks. A concomitant reindustrialization kept total industrial employment constant numerically but shrinking in relation to the rest of the economy. Relevant to the rise of a new working class, in this period in particular, the United States experienced massive deindustrialization of sectors that had been at the heart of the economy and the main provider of stable employment for the working class. While initially these jobs were reserved for the white and male working class, over time through the social and anti-racist struggles of the 1960s and 1970s, these jobs became critical to the development of a stable African–American working and middle class in many urban areas. Thus, the post-1970 deindustrialization devastated inner city Los Angeles (Davis 1990), Detroit as well as New York and Chicago (Abu-Lughod 1999).

2   Flexible and unstable employment in the low-wage reindustrialized sectors (sweatshops), service sectors, public service and government jobs, or some form of state welfare dependence emerged as the primary bread-winning opportunities for working class people.

3   During this same period, there was a significant increase in immigration, due to both the liberalization of immigration policy in the 1960s and 1970s, as well as the deepening economic crises affecting working people in the Third World (the latter having been caused primarily by the creation of massive national debts through structural adjustment policies and war).
4   The disappearance of well-paid working-class jobs and the increase in unstable, low-wage jobs meant that women of color in particular were, more than ever before, forced to work double time – in their unpaid domestic labor in their own homes and in paid work, typically in low-wage service sector positions (in many cases, doing paid domestic work for other families).
5   The growth and urban concentration of FIRE sector (financial, insurance and real estate) jobs.

Through these changes, the US working class has been recomposed in its relation to sectors of capital. In terms of who does the work, the working class now consists to a far greater proportion than previously of immigrants, people of color, and women. Significantly, this recomposition has also created a more unstable, flexible, and poorly compensated working class that faces speed-up pressures, contingent work, varying degrees of citizenship or legalization, and growing bouts of unemployment and limited or no social benefits. In the wake of the 2008 economic crash, it is also important to note that unemployment has spiked to up to 30 percent for African–Americans and Latinos and that political attacks on immigrants combined with the failing economy have resulted, for the first time in decades, in a declining Latino immigrant population.

A central task for our period, then, is to figure out which are the key nodes in this reshaped political economy at which we must build strong, fighting mass organizations, and who are the key historical actors that can build unity and lead a movement for a right to the city. A key question, for example, is this: in the absence of well-paying and stable industrial work, which groups or people, organized on what basis, will prove catalytic in organizing resistance and developing a political alternative? What constellation of the recomposed working class – child care providers, taxi drivers, janitors, computer, or biotech workers (all of whom share the contingency of work and low/no benefits with other members of the new working class) – has the capacity to motor societal transformation?

In the United States, we face an uphill battle to achieve the key tasks of this period, as we fight against a dominant ideology that has achieved the level of "common sense" for most of society, labor laws that exclude and divide workers with little to protect or promote their rights, a historical trajectory that has left us with diminished social movements and organizations, and spatial divisions that isolate our organizations and movements.

Social reproduction: gender, market integration, and a new historical actor

Part of the dominant class response to the accumulation crisis of the early 1970s was to bring socially reproductive labor more fully into market conditions, or in other words, to move work that was not traditionally waged into the waged work world. This is work usually done by women involved in the social reproduction (through schooling, childcare, housekeeping, and so forth) of the next generation of workers. Capital continually looks to fill its insatiable need to expand by moving unwaged work to waged work. This has been a long protracted process that, combined with 20 years of massive immigration (particularly of women from the global South), has created hundreds of thousands of newly waged jobs. In New York State alone, Domestic Workers United claims over 200,000 women working as domestic workers. The movement of women into the labor force, particularly its most undervalued and superexploited sectors, expands the labor market and the centrality of women workers' struggles.

Furthermore, neoliberal restructuring drove a polarization of wealth and power and created a new demand for a whole range of domestic service and other services (see http://www.faireconomy.org/files/GD_10_Chairs_and_Charts.pdf). This emerging stratum of the working class is the lowest paid, works the longest hours and is in perennial crisis. In addition, immigration laws further segment the labor market creating a gray market for undocumented workers who have little legal protection under the law. At this intersection of race, class, and gender has emerged a newly important historical actor – working women of color – who are the largest social base of the New Working Class Organizations (NWCOs) that have arisen in the United States during the past two decades.

The past 25 years have seen an historic rise of community-based working class organizations (Mayer, this volume; Fine 2006). The decline of the new and old left (Elbaum 2002), the decline and self-limiting nature of the US labor movement, a massive wave of immigration from the global South (including many schooled in their native countries' popular movements), and a growing philanthropic sector at least partially influenced by the social movements of the previous decades, have created the political space, the unorganized social base, and potential resources for the rise of new working class organizations. Filling this void was a rising politicized generation of formally educated youth or recent college graduates of color who identified neighborhoods or working-class sectors to organize and began to build organizations. There are over 200 such organizations in the United States and over 40 affiliated with the national Right to the City Alliance (Fine 2006). RTTC-affiliated organizations include City Life/Vida Urbana in Boston, Community Voices Heard in New York, Miami Workers Center in Miami, and Causa Justa/Just Cause in San Francisco/Oakland.

I have been involved in this movement through my role as Executive Director of Tenants and Workers United (TWU) and Virginia New Majority, two NWCOs which have developed over the past 25 years in Northern Virginia (the inner and outer suburbs of Washington, DC). In the early 1980s, Arlandria, an inner suburban barrio/neighborhood in Northern Alexandria, became home for over 8,000 immigrants fleeing civil war, forced inscription, and economic destruction in El Salvador. This population was layered onto an existing African–American population with roots in Virginia's colonial plantation economy, and a small working class white population. By the mid-1980s, the residents of Arlandria reflected the changing local economy. They were employed as hotel housekeepers, janitors, cooks, and construction workers. The residents of Arlandria formed the militant activist core of TWU. Over the past 25 years, TWU has led multiracial/multinational struggles that include, among others: preventing the planned mass eviction of 8,000 Arlandria residents (1985–9); creating a 300-unit resident-owned housing cooperative (1990–6); fighting for language rights and living wages in hotels (1992–2000); winning $1.5 million in medical debt relief; and winning $400,000 in annual health care subsidies for home-based childcare providers (2000–4). Men of color have certainly been involved and have provided significant leadership, but it has consistently been immigrant and at times African–American women who have been the core of both formal and informal leadership. Elsewhere, in urban areas throughout the country, it has been women of color who have come together to drive the overwhelming majority of NWCOs. The political demands of the 40 organizations that are now members of the RTTC Alliance are centered around social reproduction, that is, around collective needs and wants associated with sustaining and raising working people. Many of our struggles are to preserve and expand collective (societal) support for social reproduction. This includes fights for affordable and public housing, high-performing schools as well as a range of social wages such as childcare subsidies and access to public and recreational space.

Organizing during the neoliberal era: pragmatism in unions and community organizing

For decades, the old-school Alinsky model has dominated community- and workplace-based organizing in the United States; it is time to formally declare its failure. The Alinsky model emphasizes a "non-ideological," pragmatic approach to organizing that is ill-equipped to winning power for oppressed people or transforming society. In *Rules for Radicals* (1971) and *Reveille for Radicals* (1969), Alinsky elaborated an approach that combined the militant tactics of the depression era Communist Party (and others) with a pragmatist orientation that was geared to "cutting deals" and gaining a seat at the negotiating table but not replacing the dominant race/class/gender power structure. It grew in the space created by the decline of the New Left, the rise of liberal foundations, and the purging of the left-affiliated militants from unions. Over time, Alinsky and his approach (institutionalized by the Industrial Areas Foundation) strongly influenced a whole generation of organizers, including Cesar Chavez and the United Farm Workers, the Service Employees International Union, and the Association of Communities Organized for Reform Now (ACORN). In terms of size and influence, from the 1980s until 2009, ACORN was the biggest and most influential community-based organization. Recently, internal contradictions related to the lack of democracy and transparency combined with its close ties with the Democratic Party created a crisis that has resulted in the dissolution of ACORN, including its 200 chapters and its millions of declared members.

At the same time, with few exceptions, the labor movement has not organized the most militant and dynamic sectors of the working class, and it has not adapted well to the formation of the New Working Class referenced above. Over 87 percent of the workforce in the United States is non-unionized. On the whole, the labor movement has not broken from a Gomperist relation to the dominant class (Fletcher and Gapasin 2008). This situation is derived from struggles and splits that occurred within the labor movement over a century ago, when Samuel Gompers created and led the American Federation of Labor (AFL) using a business union approach. Business unionism approaches worker organizing in terms of a narrow stratum of the working class and with the goal of negotiating a deal with capital based on narrow, exclusively workplace-related interests. In exchange for better pay and benefits, labor peace is promised. The vast majority of the workforce is excluded from such agreements. This type of regulation of labor has been a characteristic feature of Fordism; its heyday is generally considered to have run through the 1950s until about 1973. Historically, this approach has benefited white men over working people of color and women; it generally excluded wide swaths of the working class from the privileges of the unionized sectors. Some workers (such as farm and domestic laborers) were excluded by federal law, while others (African–American, Chicano, and immigrant workers) were excluded by political choice. Until very recently, organized labor ignored or was overtly hostile to the immigrant and women and African–American workers who work in the most expansive job-creating sectors of the economy. A number of authors have explored the limits of US working class organizations, the choices these organizations made, and the long-term historical impacts of such choices (Davis 1986; Arrighi 2009). The point here is that, as the internal composition (gender, race/nationality) of the working class changed, the labor movement did not respond; consequently, millions of working people (especially women and workers of color) were left to create their own organizations and to make their own history. It is in this void that new organizational forms have developed and struggled over the past few decades.

Organizations for the new class: emergence, approach, and critique

Over the past 20 years a new urban movement has been emerging in the growth of new working class organizations – such as Causa Justa/Just Cause (Oakland), Miami Workers Center, Tenants and Workers United (Virginia), Domestic Workers United, Alternatives for Community and Environment (Boston), and many others. These organizations' social base consists of oppressed-nationality women, African–Americans, and others forced into the low-wage labor market because of welfare "reform" and globalization-driven immigration.

These groups attempt to organize whole neighborhoods, cities, or sectors of the workforce in campaigns that raise demands against the state. Through direct action, conscious political education, and putting forth counter-hegemonic demands (that is, framing demands in ways that challenge the dominant class "common sense"), these organizations fight for affordable housing, an end to displacement in the face of intense housing privatization, recognition of the rights of domestic workers, and other marginal and informal workers, access to quality transportation for these new tiers of workers, and an end to the mass criminalization of youth of color.

Perhaps most uniquely, there is a conscious effort amongst these NWCOs to link local base-building work with work against the US empire by engaging members in struggles and solidarity actions against war, occupation, and financial control of the Third World, by developing a tier of leaders from the new working class that is highly conscious of the role the United States plays financially, politically, and militarily in the world, and by actively participating in national and international social forums and other international exchanges that build and fortify an internationalist understanding and approach to organizing. Initially, this new approach to organizing was race- and, later, gender-conscious in its critique of Alinskian organizing. Many have characterized the orientation of the Center for Third World Organizing, where many young organizers learned the skills of community organizing, as "Alinsky plus race consciousness." Over time, the critique deepened to include a challenge to the notion that organizers were neutral facilitators and to the shallow and inauthentic democracy that was practiced. Independently, dozens of organizations were founded and developed along new political lines. Almost universally, popular education has developed as a deeply ingrained pedagogy. Whereas pragmatic Alinskian organizing focuses leadership development on skills and approaches that are narrowly centered on the campaign at hand, NWCOs have sought to blend ideological development with nuts-and-bolts organizing skills. For NWCOs, this has meant dedicating significant resources (time, money, staff) to running ongoing leadership development programs. These programs generally use popular education pedagogy and actively draw connections and create an international context for decision making and strategic planning and activities. Nuts-and-bolts organizing skills are also integrated as part of leadership development. These skills include: understanding how to "house visit" or directly organize door-to-door; how to work with the media; and how to best frame and contextualize our messages. Importantly, at the molecular level of campaign development and implementation, our member leaders (distinguished from paid organizers who are also leaders) are deeply involved in all decision making and in the creation and running of our campaigns.

This form of organization is relatively new, however, and has many challenges. The leadership of NWCOs is primarily university educated, "middle class," and oppressed nationality, with relatively few advanced leaders directly from the new class. Struggling with variations of race–class–gender suicide, an extension of Amilcar Cabral's (1974) formulation of class suicide, is an ongoing effort. Gaps are often large between staff with formal education and political development versus the deep personal experiences of members/leaders. Cultural differences in terms of religious/spiritual beliefs or social practices are also areas where potential conflict can develop. For a white man organizing in Virginia's multinational working class, questions of race or gender privilege are constantly negotiated: what is the "mass line" or the "common sense" of the streets, and how does that jibe with historic understandings that predate immigrant members' arrival or experience? Financially, NWCOs are dependent on philanthropic foundations for the lion's share of our respective budgets. The downside of philanthropic funding is that it may come with strings attached – at minimum, it requires legal incorporation as a nonprofit, which entails various legal constraints, particularly regarding electoral activities. Additionally, because foundations generally prefer dealing with corporatist structures, the act of grant writing requires a relatively high level of formal education; and grants generally need to be submitted in English. All of this has impacts on the development of NWCOs. On the other hand, foundation funding has created a much stronger institutional base for organizing – a physical location, office equipment, and professional organizers. This has meant that, while most NWCOs aspire to being member-centered, our organizations are more typically organizer-centered with members having a strong say in campaign/program design and implementation, and in most cases, formal leadership through a board structure. Severe limits on the use and amount of funding available and the relative lack of dues or grassroots fundraising have combined to functionally limit NWCOs' ability to organize at a mass scale. Much of our sector has an "our neighborhood or our nationality"-centered view of the world that has left us with only a very limited experience in building and leading coalitions. As a sector, we have considerable expertise in developing politically sophisticated members, but to date we have had trouble translating a solid leadership core into mass organizations with powerful and mobilized bases. NWCOs have generally focused narrowly on organizing this new sector of the class and have limited experience with broader formations. The financial crash and the corresponding drop in foundation funding have left many of our sister organizations in financial duress.

Right to the city: further self-defining as a new urban movement

In 2007, 40 community-based organizations representing the ideological left of NWCOs, allied academics, and resource allies (Advancement Project, Florida Legal Services, the Data Center) met in Los Angeles and created the RTTC Alliance. It is important to note that the original call for the founding conference was a short and clear articulation of the political moment. Every organization that attended was in one way or another fighting aspects of gentrification. This ranged from the fight for public housing (Oakland) to the fight against foreclosures (Boston), to the fight for public space (New York). Some of the organizations had long histories of exchanges and bilateral cooperation; but most did not. This initial coming together was a step toward a collective jumping of scales for a maturing and rising sector of the working class. Most of these organizations, heretofore, had generally led campaigns and fought at local and occasionally state levels. Our 2007 coming together and agreeing to form the RTTC Alliance was the first step towards enunciating a collective vision for our cities and a launching pad for us to develop coordinated national demands and activities. In the subsequent three years, this has proven harder than we could have imagined. In part, we are struggling to overcome a decade of practice in which every organization functioned by itself and for itself. Second, a march of 200 people in a city is great for a local campaign against a local government, but eight or ten such marches, even if highly coordinated, would be fairly laughable for making demands on the federal government. Finally, post-2008, it has taken us some time to gain clarity regarding how we can both support the election of a president while also ruthlessly criticizing him and pushing for our much more radical vision. It has also proven difficult to claim political space, or at least a position at the national "political" table with other larger, less radical formations, such as unions, established networks, and intermediaries. There is an undeniable thoroughness and logic to our Right to the City urban/political analysis and critique of neoliberalism. These politics place us well beyond the policy debates of Washington DC-oriented social movement sectors. As we have attempted to raise national demands, we have been stuck, vacillating between a reformist, piecemeal, and ultimately short-sighted position, and demands that are sharp, clear, and presently unlikely to gain legislative support. In the summer of 2010, we built sufficient unity to launch a three-pronged effort in the context of a national campaign. One prong is a translocal effort for immigration "reform." It is translocal in the sense that the fights will be led locally with the hope of using strategic communications to have a national impact. This means linking local efforts to stop the use of police to aggressively enforce immigration laws with a national fight against the cutting edge racist and xenophobic laws of the State of Arizona (Senate Bill 1070). Another prong entails fighting for the enforcement of federal laws requiring the hiring of public housing residents in projects that are rehabilitating public housing. Finally, we are also doing longer-term groundwork

– research, analysis, leadership development – to better establish our vision of eco-justice in cities.

As these demands indicate, there is a gap between the radical ideological roots, local practices, and leadership development of the RTTC, and nationally or federally oriented demands that could generally be called reformist. Working through this tension is a major task for the Alliance: how do we balance the immediate material demands/needs of our base with an analysis and demand that is comprehensive and profoundly radical? How do we balance our need to build and maintain a strong core of the most oppressed while reaching out to and working in alliance with others such as organized labor and people of faith? Electoral work explicitly seeks to build a majority bloc of voters; yet many of our core members are denied voting rights (due to felon disenfranchisement or lack of immigration documentation) and have a more radical political agenda born of class/race/gender position and oppression. Has the election of Obama led to a new political moment?

The state: a new moment?

The past 30 years of neoliberalism rolling back, over, and out created a narrow, defensive mindset for most NWCOs; most organizations choose not to participate in elections. This was a reflection of a disenfranchised base as well as an ideological aversion to supporting either of the two dominant (bourgeois) parties. By the 2008 presidential elections much had changed – many of the early arriving immigrants and their children were now, after over 20 years, citizens eligible to vote. In many areas, particularly in the Southwest and Southeast of the United States, the combination of new immigrant voters with historic African–American or Chicano populations is creating a demographic majority of people of color. Of course, restrictions on citizenship and voting rights means a 20-year lag before a demographic majority can even potentially become an electoral majority. This can be seen in the majority that elected Obama: a prefiguration of a rising historic bloc, centered on a unified Black nation, with wide layers of immigrants and other people of color, unionists, a broad stratum of the cybertariat (Huws 2003) and new economy working class. On a day-to-day basis, New Working Class organizations have much in common. Our work is centered on organizing working class women of color in urban areas. Our demands are primarily directed to the state for social wages. Our approach is similar in that we organize campaigns in which our members lead direct actions while linking in with allies and utilizing strategic communications to move larger political blocs. Every member group of RTTC incorporates some layer of political/ideological training into its organizing work. This training reflects our agreement on organizing working class women of color as central to building power and creating demands that transform society on multiple levels. To generalize, RTTC groups are class, race, and gender conscious. We reflect an interesting mix of class-centered analysis that has integrated an understanding of the role that racism and patriarchy have played in shaping US society. In many ways our organizations are experimenting in small urban settings with a range of approaches and understandings. The RTTC Alliance provides political space to debate and sharpen our agreements, differences, and understandings.

An area where the organizations in RTTC Alliance have less in common is our analysis of the state. Those of us, including Virginia New Majority, who are stepping up our statewide organizing and are most involved in electoral organizing, believe that our strategic approach should draw from Poulantzas and create political space that neither builds a parallel state that leads to a complete replacement of the old with the new (creating rupture), nor simply elects new people to fill the existing state (new wine in the old bottle). Instead, we are looking to develop new structures and laws to create fissures that increasingly alter the class, race, and gender power disposition of the state. Examples of this may include efforts at democratizing the system – for instance, same-day voter registration or mail-in voting, ex-felon voter registration (still an arduous process in Virginia and elsewhere in the US South), or the implementation of participatory budgeting or zoning in municipal jurisdictions. Other such initiatives might work to eliminate structural obstacles that systematically disempower people of color such as statewide election of senators and non-proportional elections. Still others could seek to democratize the economy through taxes on financial transactions or community control over banks or other flows of capital.

New organizing approaches

Along with the above-mentioned aggressive, innovative forms of campaign work and organizing, many NWCOs are engaged more and more in electoral work. For NWCOs, electoral work presents the opportunity to push our strengths in organizing to a scale we have been unable to reach up until now.

In Virginia, we have launched Virginia New Majority (VNM) in an effort to build statewide political power. We are skipping scales and elevating our focus from mostly local targets to local and statewide targets. This is leading to a range of political choices and in some cases contradictions. Because electoral work in the United States requires that a candidate win a majority of votes cast, we were forced to reconceptualize our work in ways that allow us to reach and build unity with and politically move tens of thousands of people. In 2008 and 2009 we attempted to talk with over 100,000 households. This shift means that a VNM canvasser may only spend three minutes at the door, but she will knock on over 15 doors an hour. The impact is great, for example in 2008 Obama carried Virginia in the US presidential election. On the other hand, the connection and involvement of people who are convinced to vote are relatively shallow. Additionally, following voters has led us to a different spatial focus: this work has allowed us to organize in the outer suburbs that had proven nearly impossible to organizing in the standard door to door approach. Related to this, electoral organizing has proven to be more conducive to multinational/multiracial organizing in two important ways. First, a statewide focus allows us to organize in predominantly African–American Tidewater (Norfolk) and Richmond, while uniting with our organizing in the multinational areas of Northern Virginia. At a micro-neighborhood level, cultural, political, and language differences have proven difficult to overcome, but by moving large blocs of people we are creating a functional unity and are working to build ties between leaders from each region. Second, for over 20 years, TWU had focused on the lowest and most Latino/a strata of the working class. Inherent in this is a radical politics but also severe limits in moving our political demands beyond very specific issue campaigns. Effectively, VNM and electoral-centered work allows the building of a much broader bloc of voters in terms of nationality, strata of the working class, and geography. The flip-side is that a broader formation with looser political and personal ties has led to political activity that is primarily focused on electing candidates whose politics, while better than the opposition, are nowhere near as progressive or radical or even as aligned politically as our own. To cite a local example, in 2010 VNM supported candidates running for town council in Herndon, Virginia, who supported "diversity." Given the alternative, candidates who supported the persecution of undocumented immigrants, this was an important advance. Yet at the same time, the standard of diversity falls far short of the notion of local governments directly challenging the Westphalian nation-state's right to dictate immigration laws and policy (Purcell 2003). Negotiating this gap is a huge political challenge. The goal is to figure out how to move a shaky electoral bloc into an historic bloc that successfully challenges the dominant common sense and class/race/ gender forces.

This work, when led by NWCOs, can allow us to:

1   Develop counter-hegemonic demands, or at the very least, counter-hegemonic framings that we advance through issue-based or even candidate-based campaigns. While these campaigns are in some way assessed by a simple measure of success (for instance, winning the election), NWCOs must use their electoral efforts to challenge the underpinnings of neoliberalism and empire. In Virginia, going back to the rise of Jim Crow (post-slavery apartheid), candidates from both parties have run on a "make Virginia business-friendly" platform. Through candidate's forums and independent electoral work VNM is questioning this orientation by asking what a worker-friendly Virginia could look like.

2   Win concrete material demands that improve life for our social base, build a sense of movement for our social base and force resources to be moved from the war economy to the social wage (increasing the social wage, albeit on a small scale, is the hallmark demand of most NWCOs).

3   Advance our practice and theory through engaging broader mass forces in what is, for the most part, their principal form of political involvement (elections). Thus, those organizations who are organizing electorally (VNM, Miami Workers Center, Causa Justa/Just Cause among others) and our allies will be actively engaged in strategizing. This will force us to continue building our base but also actively to construct a historic bloc or ensemble of race and class forces; this is necessary for a new order not dominated by capital. This provides an opportunity for different organized sectors – unionists, teachers and students, NWCM activists, and others to work together in a coordinated manner.

4   Practice limited forms of governance and power. NWCOs, Alinsky-type organizations, and unions all have experience fighting targets and powerbrokers. NWCOs, who largely come out of a tradition of electoral abstinence, do not have experience with even limited forms of power at this scale. For a budding movement, it is crucial practice for different epoch in history when questions of radical and plural democracy, working-class power, and organized accountability will be real and concrete questions. In other words, can we run housing cooperatives, elect our leaders to city councils or to boards and commissions in a way which builds power, accountability, and capacity.

This political moment characterized by the electoral defeat of the most reactionary presidential candidates (McCain/Palin), a deep and protracted economic crisis, and an active and motivated reactionary base (exemplified by the Tea Party) demands that we further jump scales and contest for power (ideas and programs) at the national level. This is all the more difficult because our capacities and experience are as an emerging social movement predominantly local in target and impact. Jumping scales is, however, proving difficult, questions of focus, capacity, and ability to sacrifice longstanding local work to move jointly at a national level are being worked through at this moment. We have attempted to bridge this gap through the concept and practice of trans-local campaigning. Essentially, our hope is that local actions tied together through common framing can create an impact that is at higher scales (national or international). To date, measured by our notion of building power through the combination of ideas and institutions, the RTTCA or the social movement left have not had the institutional capacity to have significant impact.

We have far to go in our struggle to win the *right to the city*. To the extent that this volume deepens the dialogue between formal intellectuals and organic intellectuals tied to the NWCOs, we will have taken a giant step forward. Our theory is enriched by deep practice and deep theory is needed to move us beyond the economic, political, and environmental crises of today.

References

Abu-Lughod, J. (1999) *New York, Chicago, Los Angeles: America's Global Cities*. Minneapolis: University of Minnesota Press.
Alinsky, S. (1971) *Rules for Radicals*. New York: Random House.
Alinsky, S. (1969) *Reveille for Radicals*. New York: Random House.
Arrighi, G. (2009) *Adam Smith in Beijing*. New York: Verso.
Cabral, A. (1974) *Return to the Source*. New York: Monthly Review Press.
Davis, M. (1990) *City of Quartz*. New York: Vintage.
Davis, M. (1986) *Prisoners of the American Dream*. New York: Verso.
Elbaum, M. (2002) *Revolution in the Air*. New York: Verso.
Huws, U. (2003) *The Making of the Cybertariat*. New York: Monthly Review Press.
Fine, J. (2006) *Workers Centers – Organizing Communities at the Edge of the Dream*. Ithaca, NY: Cornell University Press.
Fletcher, B. and Gapasin, F. (2008) *Solidarity Divided*. Berkeley: University of California Press.
Leitner, H., Peck, J., and Sheppard, E. (eds) (2007) *Contesting Neoliberalism*. New York: Guilford Press.
Purcell, M. (2003) Citizenship and the right to the global city: reimagining the capitalist world order. *International Journal of Urban and Regional Research*, 27, 3, 564–90.
Smith, N. (2002) New globalism, new urbanism: gentrification as global urban strategy. *Antipode*, 34, 3, 427–50.
Smith, N. (1996) *The New Urban Frontier*. London: Routledge.
United for a fair economy: http://www.faireconomy.org/files/GD_10_Chairs_and_Charts.pdf (accessed on 1 October 2010).

16

WHAT IS TO BE DONE?

And who the hell is going to do it?

David Harvey with David Wachsmuth[1]

At times of crisis, the irrationality of capitalism becomes plain to see. Surplus capital and surplus labor exist side by side with seemingly no way to put them back together in the midst of immense suffering and unmet needs. But this suffering also provides opportunity, as the irrationality calls out for an alternative. And so in this chapter I want to ask two awkward questions about the current crisis: What is to be done? And who the hell is going to do it?

Those questions have a habit of colliding with each other. Lenin's famous question "What is to be done?" cannot be answered, to be sure, without some sense of who might do it and where. But a global anti-capitalist movement is unlikely to emerge without some animating vision of what is to be done and why. A double blockage exists: the lack of an alternative vision prevents the formation of an oppositional movement, while the absence of such a movement precludes the articulation of an alternative. How, then, can this blockage be transcended? Can we reframe the problem more dialectically?

Class struggle from the factory to the city

The "who" question might appear premature because, despite the current crisis, we are not presently in a revolutionary situation. But we can think about the different social formations that do exist right now, and consider how they might enter into political activism. Traditionally, the answer from the Left to "Who the hell is going to do it?" has been the proletariat. But the proletariat is an unsatisfactory answer, and it comes from an unsatisfactory understanding of class relations that tends both to reduce the question of production to factory labor and to privilege the process of production over that of social reproduction. The events of the last few years are a good opportunity to rethink some of this.

It is no accident that Marx's *Capital* contains no dedicated analysis of class until a little snippet at the very end of Volume 3 on the "three great social classes" of capitalist society (Marx 1982: 1026). Many readers are surprised to see that landlords are one of them, and wonder if that is a residual category or a continuing category. That surprise comes from a long-standing tendency on the Left to say that class is defined by industrial production. On the one hand, this tendency leads to rent and land value being treated as derivative categories of distribution rather than the central theoretical categories for integrating geography, space, and the relation to nature into the understanding of capitalism. On the other hand, it leads to a fixation on factory labor as the locus of "true" class consciousness and revolutionary class struggle. But this has always been too limited, if not misguided, particularly as it relates to the process of urbanization. Production and class appear quite different when you ask, "Who produces the city?" or, following Henri Lefebvre (1991), "Who produces space?"

Those working in the forests and fields, in the "informal sectors" of casual labor in the backstreet sweatshops, in the domestic services or in the service sector more generally, and the vast army of laborers employed in the production of space and of built environments or in the trenches (often literally) of urbanization cannot be treated as secondary actors. They work under different conditions (often of low-wage, temporary, and insecure labor in the case of construction and urbanization). Their mobility, spatial dispersal, and individualized conditions of employment may make it more difficult to construct class solidarities or set up collective forms of organization. Their political presence is more often marked by spontaneous riots and voluntarist uprisings (such as those that occurred in the Paris *banlieues* in recent times or the *piqueteros* (demonstrators) who erupted into action in Argentina after the country's financial collapse of 2001) rather than persistent organization. But they are fully conscious of their conditions of exploitation and are deeply alienated by their precarious existence and antagonistic to the often brutal policing of their daily lives by state power.

Now often referred to as "the precariat" (to emphasize the floating and unstable character of their employment and lifestyles), these workers have always accounted for a large segment of the total labor force, and they have always played a crucial role in the production of urbanization. In the advanced capitalist world they have become ever more prominent over the past thirty years because of changing labor relations imposed by neoliberal corporate restructuring and deindustrialization, and their political role has also become more prominent. But then again, many of the revolutionary movements in capitalism's history have been broadly urban rather than narrowly factory based. Even when there were key movements in the factories (the Flint strike in Michigan of the 1930s or the Turin workers councils of the 1920s), the organized support in the neighborhoods played a critical but usually uncelebrated role in the political action (the women's and unemployed support groups in Flint and the communal "houses of the people" in Turin).

These examples suggest that, more than simply questioning the association of factory production with class structure and consciousness, we must also broaden our class analysis beyond the point of production. Class reproduction, after all, is very much an urban phenomenon. Class consciousness is produced and articulated as much in the streets, bars, pubs, kitchens, chapels, community centers, and backyards of working-class neighborhoods as in the factories. The first two decrees of the Parisian communards in 1871 were, interestingly, the suspension of night work in the bakeries (a labor process question) and a moratorium on rental payments (an urban daily life question). The city, in other words, is as much a locus of class movements as is the factory.

This also has a deeper resonance, because the living space – the point of reproduction – has an underappreciated importance for the generation and distribution of surplus value. Consider, for example, that in January of 2008, Wall Street bonuses added up to $32 billion, just a fraction less than the total in 2007. This was a remarkable reward for crashing the world's financial system. But at that moment nearly two million households in the United States had been foreclosed upon and lost their homes. In Cleveland, it looked like a "financial Katrina" had hit the city. Abandoned and boarded-up houses dominated the landscape in poor, mainly black neighborhoods. In California, the streets of whole towns, like Stockton, were likewise lined with empty and abandoned houses, while in Florida and Las Vegas condominiums stood empty. Those who had been foreclosed upon had to find accommodation elsewhere: tent cities began to form in California and Florida. Elsewhere, families either doubled up with friends and relatives or turned cramped motel rooms into instant homes.

At the top, $32 billion is accumulated, and at the bottom two million people lose their houses in what has been described as one of the biggest asset losses of all time for the African–American marginalized population. The losses of those at the bottom of the social pyramid roughly matched the extraordinary gains of the financiers at the top. Maybe we should think about the connection between these two facts, and analyze them as a "class event." Value is stolen from one segment of the population and accumulated by another. Isn't this a classic case of accumulation by dispossession (Harvey 2003)? Lenin, Hilferding, and Luxemburg all recognized at the beginning of the twentieth century that finance had become a prominent means of predation, fraud, and thievery; since the 1970s its importance in this regard has greatly increased. Again and again, vulnerable populations suffer massive losses – losses that have a way of emerging among the capitalist class as a massive accumulation of wealth.

So it is not only through production that the dynamics of class operate. Marx and Engels recognized this in the Communist Manifesto, where they say, "No sooner is the exploitation of the laborer by the manufacturer ... at an end ... than he is set upon by the other portions of the bourgeoisie, the landlord, the shopkeeper, the pawnbroker, etc." (Marx and Engels 2008: 44). There is a dynamic of exploitation within the process of social reproduction, which also has to be incorporated into how we understand class relations. The class relations at the point of reproduction are particularly focused on the relation of the workers to the merchants and landlords and other social classes that extract wealth from the workers, who come as it were ready-made with their money to be taken away from them by exploitative practices in the living place.

We often have difficulty pulling together these two forms of exploitation – in the process of production and the process of reproduction – and seeing them as a unity despite their differences. Until we can see the unity as well as the difference, we will not have a clear idea of the "who." In other words, if we are to advance our politics, we have to broaden and reconfigure the notion of class upon which we will base the notion of class struggle. In Marx's terms, we need to consider not just the proletariat but also the lumpenproletariat, whom he so frequently chastised and disliked. In contemporary terms, this means the urban precariat. Because class struggle in and around the urban is as important as class struggle in and around the factory. They are different loci of struggle, and they have a different dynamic, but they need to be unified. It is remarkable how difficult it seems to have been for the conventional Left to recognize the unity within that difference – the unity that begins to clarify the "who."

Crisis tendencies, financialization, and neoliberalization

Now this leads into the "what" – Lenin's question of what is to be done. There is no shortage of answers; we are in a crisis and the crisis has elicited a range of responses. But we need to understand the crisis in order to understand which responses are appropriate. So, first of all, we need a thorough account of where the current crisis came from and how it evolved. Capitalism never overcomes its crisis tendencies; it simply displaces them, in space or in time (Harvey 2006). And in many ways the roots of this particular crisis can be found in the crisis of the 1970s and particularly in the way in which that previous crisis was resolved.

There are two dimensions to the crisis of the 1970s that need to be highlighted: the labor problem and the monopolization problem. By the end of the 1960s, capital needed to destroy the power of organized labor, which was capturing too large a share of the surplus (Armstrong et al. 1991). Capital accomplished this through a politics of wage repression; since the 1970s, North America and Europe have generally seen stagnant or falling real wages. There were a number of ways to achieve that. One was to encourage immigration. The Immigration and Nationality Act of 1965, which abolished national-origin quotas, allowed US capital access to the global surplus population (before that only Europeans and Caucasians were privileged). In the late 1960s the French government was subsidizing the import of labor from North Africa, the Germans were hauling in the Turks, the Swedes were bringing in the Yugoslavs, and the British were drawing upon inhabitants of their past empire.

Another way was to seek out labor-saving technologies, such as robotization in automobile manufacture, which created unemployment. If that failed then there were people like Ronald Reagan, Margaret Thatcher, and General Augusto Pinochet waiting in the wings, armed with neoliberal doctrine, prepared to use state power to crush organized labor. Pinochet and the Brazilian and Argentinian generals did so with military might, while both Reagan and Thatcher orchestrated confrontations with big labor, either directly in the case of Reagan's showdown with the air traffic controllers and Thatcher's fierce fight with the miners and the print unions, or indirectly through the creation of unemployment.

Capital also had the option to go where the surplus labor was. Rural women of the global South were incorporated into the workforce everywhere, from Barbados to Bangladesh, from Ciudad Juarez to Dongguan. The result was an increasing feminization of the proletariat, the destruction of "traditional" peasant systems of self-sufficient production, and the feminization of poverty worldwide. Awash with surplus capital, US-based corporations actually began to offshore production in the mid-1960s, but this movement only gathered steam a decade later, accompanied by low-cost shipping made possible through containerization, after which point capital now had access to the whole world's low-cost labor supplies.

So, whereas in the late 1960s and 1970s the labor issue was a key problem for capitalists seeking to maintain and expand their class power, by the middle of the 1980s that problem had essentially been solved. It is clear at this moment that the problem for capital is not excessive power of labor, and so the current crisis cannot be directly attributed to a profit squeeze on capital by overly empowered labor.

The second problem that existed at the end of the 1960s was excessive monopolization among capitalists. The solution to this problem was to increase competition in the economy, partly through globalization and partly through financialization. And this solution was successful, enough so that by the middle of the 1980s excessive competition started to put downward pressure on prices and hence profit rates. The result was a peculiar structure of low profits and low wages – low wages because the labor problem was solved through smashing working-class power; and low profits because the monopolization problem was solved through globalization and financialization. This was what determined the form of subsequent crises. Because now the capitalist class was confronting a serious problem, which was: where can they invest their money and secure an acceptable rate of return? Low profits implied a low rate of return in production, so capitalists had to find different outlets for their surpluses. Thus, from the 1980s onwards, they began to invest in assets rather than in production. Why invest in low-profit production when you can borrow in Japan at a zero rate of interest and invest in London at seven percent while hedging your bets on a possible deleterious shift in the yen–sterling exchange rate?

Assets come in various forms, from stocks, commodity futures, and financial instruments to artworks and property. But one thing that distinguishes asset markets from ordinary commodity markets is that the former have a Ponzi-like character even without the Bernie Madoffs of this world explicitly organizing it so. The more that people invest in property, the more property prices go up; and the more property prices go up, the more attractive it seems to invest in property. The same is true for stocks. And starting in the 1980s the capitalist class in general was investing its surpluses not in productive activities but in assets.

Low profits helped drive surpluses into assets, but low wages for the working class were also implicated, because the only way to ensure that working people generate effective demand in the market despite stagnant wages was to encourage them to go into debt. That is, the gap between what labor was earning and what it could spend was covered by the rise of the credit card industry and increasing indebtedness. In the US in 1980 the average household owed around $40,000 (in constant dollars) but now it's about $130,000 for every household, including mortgages. Household debt sky-rocketed, but this required that financial institutions both support and promote the debts of working people whose earnings were not increasing. This started with the steadily employed population, but by the late 1990s it had to go further because that market was exhausted. The market had to be extended to those with lower incomes. Political pressure was put on financial institutions like Fannie Mae and Freddie Mac to loosen the credit strings for everyone. Financial institutions, awash with credit, began to debt-finance people who had no steady income. If that had not happened, then who would have bought all the new houses and condominiums the debt-financed property developers were building? The demand problem was temporarily bridged with respect to housing by debt-financing the developers as well as the buyers. The financial institutions collectively controlled both the supply of, and demand for, housing.

Now the crisis tendency of this particular configuration has erupted. But in fact there have been hundreds of financial crises around the world since 1973, compared to very few between 1945 and 1973; and several of these have been property- or urban-development led. The first full-scale global crisis of capitalism in the post-Second World War era began in spring 1973, a full six months before the Arab oil embargo spiked oil prices. It originated in a global property market crash that brought down several banks and drastically affected not only the finances of municipal governments (such as that of New York City, which went technically bankrupt in 1975 before ultimately being bailed out) but also state finances more generally. The Japanese boom of the 1980s ended with a collapse of the stock market and plunging land prices (still ongoing). The Swedish banking system had to be nationalized in 1992 in the midst of a Nordic crisis that also affected Norway and Finland, caused by excesses in the property markets. One of the triggers for the collapse in east and south-east Asia in 1997–8 was excessive urban development, fuelled by an inflow of foreign speculative capital, in Thailand, Hong Kong, Indonesia, South Korea, and the Philippines. And the long-drawn-out commercial-property-led savings and loan crisis of 1984–92 in the United States saw more than 1,400 savings and loan companies and 1,860 banks go belly-up at the cost of some $2 trillion to US taxpayers. For the post-1973 era, there is, therefore, nothing unprecedented, apart from its size and scope, about the current collapse. Nor is their anything unusual about its rootedness in urban development and property markets.

In the current crisis, as with its smaller and more localized predecessors over the past 40 years, the problem is not fundamentally one of excessive returns to labor, as it was in the 1970s. The problem this time is more like the 1930s: underconsumption, or a lack of effective demand in the market. Capitalists are operating in a low-wage, low-profit economy, and they cannot find enough buyers for the goods they are producing, even with massive recourse to consumer debt. Despite the financial troubles, the main problem lies in the fact that capital is too powerful and labor too weak, rather than the other way around.

How do you get out of this kind of crisis? The classic answer from the 1930s was Keynesianism, and right now you could say that we are in a "Keynesian episode," whether we like it or not. Keynesianism seems to contradict neoliberal rhetoric, but neoliberalization never practices what it preaches. For all the rhetorical commitment to a balanced budget, the whole of the neoliberal era has been characterized by recurrent Keynesian episodes. The major Keynesian episode in the 1980s was Ronald Reagan's massive, deficit-financed expansion of the defense budget. It was a form of military Keynesianism. The George W. Bush administration combined deficit-financed military Keynesianism with a kind of reverse class Keynesianism – restructuring the tax code to privilege the upper classes. These Keynesian episodes get to the heart of the neoliberalization project: the consolidation, recuperation, and expansion of capitalist class power (Harvey 2005).

One of the key elements of the neoliberal expansion of capitalist class power has been financialization. From the IMF bailout of the Mexican debt crisis in 1982 onwards, the actual practices of neoliberalism (as opposed to its utopian theory) always entailed blatant support for finance capital and capitalist élites (usually on the grounds that financial institutions must be protected at all costs and that it is the duty of state power to create a good business climate for solid profiteering). The present Keynesian episode is a continuation of that neoliberal practice, but this time the practice is delegitimizing the standard neoliberal rhetoric. As the state steps in to bail out the financiers, it has become clear to all that state and capital are more tightly intertwined than ever, both institutionally and personally. The ruling class, rather than the political class that acts as its surrogate, is now actually seen to rule. The neoliberal rhetoric now seems hollow, but even though the people are being hurt, they do not know quite how to interpret it. We have to come up with an interpretation of the crisis that stresses the need for a transformation of the entire economy. In other words, if we are now witnessing a return of a repressed Keynesian moment, but one that is oriented to bailing out the upper classes, then how can we redirect it in a socialist direction?

The Keynesian moment and the state–finance nexus

Despite the fact that there is often a substantial conflict between Keynesian thinking and Marxian thinking, my argument is that if we are in a Keynesian moment then we need to make use of it politically. Keynes himself took the view that the re-establishment of effective demand in the economy depended upon the empowerment of the working class as consumers in the market, which meant full employment. And the way to full employment, he argued, was through the reduction of working time. Even though there is a lot of discussion of Keynesianism in the press right now, nobody talks about this. But we could implement this proposal by redirecting spending away from the banks and other financial institutions and towards guaranteed minimum incomes, empowerment of workers in negotiating procedures, and legislation on the length of the working day. If we started to push Keynesianism into these areas, then we would also be establishing a basis for a different kind of politics.

But in order for that to happen, we have to deal with one of the most difficult aspects of the current situation. Margaret Thatcher always said that what she was really trying to do was not simply to change the economy, but to change the soul of the people. And to some extent she succeeded! Most people "think neoliberal" whether they like it or not. And this is dramatically evident in the current crisis, despite the evident hollowness of neoliberal rhetoric. As of now, faith in the underlying presumptions of free market ideology has not eroded too much. Those foreclosed upon in the United States (so preliminary surveys tell us) typically blame themselves for their failure (sometimes through bad luck) to live up to the personal responsibilities of homeownership. While there is anger at bankers' duplicity and populist outrage over their bonuses, there is very little hint that the people being foreclosed upon think of this as a systemic problem that has to be addressed through a systemic reform of the capitalist system. Which explains why the millions of people who have been foreclosed upon have not coalesced into a political movement. They've just disappeared. But if they are victims of a class event, it should be possible to change how they understand the situation and do something different with it.

So politically it comes back to the "who." Would the millions of people who lost their homes constitute a systemic force for political change? You would think so, but they do not. How do we change this? We are starting to see small movements around the occupation of abandoned housing, and the assertion of a right to return on the part of foreclosed families, to repossess what has been dispossessed (Rameau 2008). Until those movements grow, we won't have the "who." But until we can say what has to be done, we won't have the "who" either. So it is vital that we recognize that this is a Keynesian moment, and recognize that perhaps the best we can do right now is to redirect that Keynesianism in such a way that it benefits the mass of the people rather than continue to centralize capitalist class power.

The leading hedge-fund managers in New York pulled in personal remuneration of $250 million each in 2005, while in 2006 the top manager made $1.7 billion and in 2007, which was a disastrous year in global finance, five of them earned around $3 billion apiece. So if you think that the capitalist class is in trouble or losing its power, think again. They are more centralized than ever. And the banks that have survived the crisis are more powerful than ever. Marx and Engels (2008) advocated the centralization of the means of credit in the hands of the state. Of course, they thought that should occur under a dictatorship of the proletariat. What we're actually now moving into is a dictatorship of the world's central bankers over the global economy.

Within the state apparatus we can distinguish a "state-finance nexus." This describes a confluence of state and financial power that confounds the analytic tendency to see state and capital as clearly separable from each other. This does not mean that state and capital constitute an identity, but that there are structures of governance (such as central banks and treasury departments) where the state management of capital creation and monetary flows becomes integral to, rather than separable from, the circulation of capital. The reverse relation also holds as taxes or borrowings flow into the coffers of the state and as state functions also become monetized, commodified, and ultimately privatized.

Marx (1976) identified this as the "bankocracy," and we saw it in operation in the United States in September 2008, when a few Treasury officials and bankers including the Treasury Secretary, who was a past president of Goldman Sachs, and the present CEO of Goldman, emerged from a conference room with a three-page document demanding a $700 billion bail-out of the banking system while threatening Armageddon in the markets. It seemed like Wall Street had launched a financial coup against the government and the people of the United States. A few weeks later, with caveats here and there and a lot of rhetoric, Congress and then President George Bush caved in and the money was sent flooding off, without any controls whatsoever, to all those financial institutions deemed "too big to fail." The state-finance nexus got its $700 billion. This represents an emerging class configuration which has enormous power, and which it is very difficult to imagine how to confront. During the days of panic in September 2008, the President and Vice President of the United States disappeared, and it was the Secretary of the Treasury and the Chair of the Federal Reserve who made it clear that they were in charge.

Now if the state–finance nexus is in control and managing this Keynesian moment, it has considerable backing. In the United States, as Mark Twain said at the end of the nineteenth century, the Congress is always the best Congress money can buy. And the state–finance nexus is supported by the Party of Wall Street, which actually holds power in Washington. The Party of Wall Street draws its membership from the Democratic Party and the Republican Party. There is a right wing of the Republican Party that is against them and there is a left wing of the Democratic Party that is against them, but the Party of Wall

Street governs. And so now the central bank, the Treasury department and the Party of Wall Street hold the reins of government.

The spiral of opposition and mobilization

There are the beginnings of an agitation against the state–finance nexus, which is not class based but populist. We cannot afford to reject it for that reason, though; we need to try to take the populist anger over preference given to bankers and turn it in a more class-based direction. Since throughout the world we are not in a revolutionary moment – with possible exceptions in Latin America and China – we do not currently have the option of rejecting Keynesianism. The only option is to ask what kind of Keynesianism it should be, and to whose benefit should it be mobilized. And, as Keynes argued in the 1930, perhaps this is the only way to save capitalism.

Now this would not be the first time that the Left has saved capitalism, and we may not want to do it. But the costs of not saving it right now are too steep. Members of the capitalist class have suffered from the crisis, but the people who are really suffering are those on the margins. There are stories coming out Haiti suggesting that malnutrition is escalating and deaths by starvation are on the rise. Why? Because the remittances sent to Haiti from the United States have fallen off. Haitians receiving perhaps $100 a month from a relative working as a domestic worker in New York City are now only receiving $25, because the relative has lost her job. And that $100 a month was the difference between life and death. So there is nothing good about saying, "let the system crash." Because the wealthy have prepared their arks, and they can float above the flood all too easily. The people who are going to be drowned are those on the margins. It is false to say that people in the informal economy in Mumbai or Haiti or elsewhere have nothing to lose. That is not the case; they are vulnerable too. And we need to construct a politics that recognizes that.

So the question of what is to be done is nowhere near as dramatic as we might like, and it is tightly tied together with the fact that the "who" doesn't yet have the vision to push Keynesianism in a more socialist direction, to push Keynesianism towards a class perspective different from that which is being articulated via the Party of Wall Street, via a global capitalist class that is prepared to crash the system in order to preserve its power. That is the problem to which we have to collectively respond, and it does us no good to imagine that there is a vanguard of the proletariat that is going to lead us out of this mess. Our response is going to have to be built through coalitions. Coalitions between the work place and the living space, coalitions which stretch across a whole set of differences but at the same time understand the unity that potentially exists within all that difference.

The relation between the vision of what is to be done and why, and the formation of a political movement across particular places to do it, has to be turned into a spiral. Each has to reinforce the other if anything is actually to get done. Otherwise potential opposition will be forever locked down into a closed circle that frustrates all prospects for constructive change, leaving us vulnerable to perpetual future crises of capitalism, with increasingly deadly results. It must be clear by now that capitalism will never fall on its own. It will have to be pushed. The accumulation of capital will never cease. It will have to be stopped. The capitalist class will never willingly surrender its power. It will have to be dispossessed. To do what has to be done will take tenacity and determination, patience, and cunning, along with fierce political commitments born out of moral outrage at what exploitative compound growth is doing to all facets of life, human and otherwise, on planet earth. Political mobilizations sufficient to such a task have occurred in the past. They can and will surely come again. We are, I think, past due.

Note

1 This text is based on a public lecture given by David Harvey at a conference on "Class in Crisis" organized by the Rosa Luxemburg Stiftung in Berlin, June 19–20, 2009. It has been edited extensively by David Wachsmuth building on the original lecture transcript as well as on the recently published book by David Harvey, *Enigma of Capital* (2010).

References

Armstrong, Philip, Andrew Glyn, and John Harrison. 1991. *Capitalism Since 1945.* Oxford and Cambridge, MA: Blackwell.

Harvey, David. 2003. *The New Imperialism.* Oxford: Oxford University Press.

—— 2005. *A Brief History of Neoliberalism.* Oxford: Oxford University Press.

—— 2006. *The Limits to Capital.* London and New York: Verso.

—— 2010. *The Enigma of Capital and the Crises of Capitalism.* Oxford: Oxford University Press.

Lefebvre, Henri. 1991. *The Production of Space.* Translated by Donald Nicholson-Smith. Cambridge, MA: Blackwell.

Marx, Karl. 1976. *Capital: A Critique of Political Economy, Volume 1.* Translated by Ben Fowkes. London: Penguin.

—— 1982. *Capital: A Critique of Political Economy, Volume 3.* Translated by David Fernbach. London: Penguin.

Marx, Karl and Frederick Engels. 2008. *The Communist Manifesto.* Introduction by David Harvey. London: Pluto Press.

Rameau, Max. 2008. *Take Back the Land: Land, Gentrification and the Umoja Village Shantytown.* Miami: Nia Interactive Press.

AFTERWORD

Peter Marcuse

"Light verse"

When it comes to the Right to the City,
Don't get mired just in some nitty-gritty,
   Maybe break for a ditty,
   Even if it isn't so witty,
Making it boring would be a real pity.

You need to understand class,
If you don't want to fall on your ass;
   It isn't so easy,
   But if you get queasy,
And fudge it, you'll lose it, alas.

If to critical theory you've aspired,
But in abstractions have gotten yourself mired,
   Link your theory with action,
   Help theory get traction,
You'll get clearer, be useful – and tired.

INDEX

Note: Page numbers followed by 'f' refer to figures and followed by 'n' refer to notes.

Abu-Lughod, Lila 108–9, 110, 113, 251
abu-Shcheita, Ali 163, 164
Achtenberg, Emily 190, 193
actor–network theory 119–20, 126, 127–8, 130; and assemblages 120–4
Adorno, Theodor 13, 14, 15–16, 17, 25, 40n, 92, 96, 99
Aesthetic Theory 96
African–Americans 26, 219, 251, 252, 254, 255, 266
agency, cultural politics of 107–10
Alinsky, Saul 254, 255, 256
All That is Solid Melts into Air 88
Alsayyad, Nezar 79, 129, 159
American Dream 221, 225
Americanism + Fordism = counterrevolution 92–3
Amsterdam: decommodification and equity in housing 203–4; democratization in 204–5; emergence as a just city 199, 202–6; erosion of just city 198–9, 202–6; housing construction 203, 206; Jewish residents of 197, 198; Nieuwmarkt subway station monument 197–8, 211; recommodification of housing 206–11; residents' movement in 203, 204–5, 205–6, 210–11, 212; social housing in 198, 198f, 200, 205f, 206–8, 209–10, 211–12; squatting movement 202–3; today's city 211–13; transfer of housing associations into housing corporations 207, 211
Anderson, Perry 88, 91, 95

anti-globalization movements 68, 69, 81–2n
architecture: of FRG 237, 242–6; of modernism 90, 91; new metropolitan 54; of power 233; relationship with the economic 96; urban planning and revolution 88, 89, 90, 93, 95; and urban planning of GDR 233–4, 237–9, 240–2
"Architecture or Revolution?" 90
Argentina 265
articulation 157–8, 159; and radicalization of Bedouin Arabs 160–6
assemblage: actor–networks and 120–4; articulations of assemblage analysis and political economy 124–7; "assemblage urbanism" 119, 124, 127, 128, 130, 132–4; and critical urban theory 122–3, 130, 132–4; as an ontology 119–20, 125t, 126–7; problems with 127–30
assets, capitalist investment in 268–9
Association of Communities Organized for Reform Now (ACORN) 70, 255
al-Athamin, Atiya 162
Athens Charter 92, 93, 234
autogestion 6–7, 59

Badiou, Alain 89, 94, 96, 99
Banham, Reyner 94
bank affidavit scandal 223
bank bailouts 70, 224, 272
bankers bonuses 266, 271
banking, alternative models of 107
banking crisis 1984–92 269–70
Bannerji, Himani 94, 111
Baumohl, Jim 189
Bayat, Asef 152

Bedouin Arabs: articulation and radicalization of 160–4; autonomous politics 164–6; Beersheba mosque 156–7; "gray spaces" of 154–7; land disputes with Israelis 154, 156, 161; Managing Authority for the Advancement of the Bedouins (MAAB) 165; memory building 162–4; Regional Council of the Unrecognized Villages (RCUV) 164, 165–6; *sumood* 161–2; village name dispute with Israelis 162, 165–6; Wadi al-Na'am mosque rebuild 150, 151f, 166; women in Egypt 108–9
Beersheba mosque 156–7
Bender, Thomas 119, 121–2, 125, 127, 128, 133
Benjamin, Walter 12, 20, 55, 87, 88, 89, 93, 97, 98, 99
Berlin: Alexanderplatz 241, 246; architectural and urbanistic mandates of GDR for 237–9, 240–2; "creative city" 143–7; culture industry workers in 143–5, 146–7; FRG and state buildings in 237, 242–6; gentrification 145–7, 240; housing 235, 238–40; Marzahn-Hellersdorf 239, 239f; Media Spree project 70, 71, 72, 147; Palace of the Republic 241–2, 243, 244; plans for a castle 243–4, 243f; Stalinalle 238, 238f, 240; Wall 32
Berman, Marshall 88
"big D" Development 103, 104, 108, 114n
The Birth of Biopolitics 91
Bokker, Eli 156
Boston 177, 178
Boyd, Michelle 181
Braconi, Frank 179, 180, 186, 187
Brazil 35, 73, 268
Brenner, Neil 2, 19, 55, 81n, 119, 131, 134n, 147, 158, 159, 202
Breton, André 88
Brixton riots 44
Buck-Morss, Susan 20, 88, 89, 93, 97
Bugeaud, Thomas R. 87
Burke, Edmund 90
Bush, George W. 223, 270, 272
business unionism 255
Butler, Tim 171

Cabral, Amilcar 257
Callinicos, Alex 12, 17
Capital 18, 95, 265
capitalism: "accumulation by dispossession" 3, 105, 106, 133, 266; cities as sites of capitalist accumulation 1–2; class struggles 66, 92, 147, 264–7; crises of 7–8, 27–9, 267–70; goal of right to city and rejection of prevailing systems of 37–9; production of urban space and role in accumulation of 104; spiral of opposition and mobilization against 271, 273–4; state-finance nexus of 271–3
Castells, Manuel 3, 45, 60n, 81n, 97, 117, 122, 202
center and periphery 56, 57, 104–5, 106
Center for Metropolitan Studies Berlin, Conference 2008 5, 231–49
Center for Third World Organizing 256
centrality, urban 47–8; displacement and exclusion from 57; new forms of 50, 53, 55
Changer la vie, changer la ville 89
Charter of Athens 92, 93, 234
Charter of Rights and Duties 73
charters and covenants 63, 73–4, 75
Chicago School 11, 117, 119
Cities of Tomorrow 90
class reproduction 266–7
class struggle 66, 92, 147, 264–7
"co-revolutionary movement" 30–1
colonialism, urban 157–60; and gray spacing of Bedouin Arabs 154–7
Comment is Free (The Guardian) 173, 175
commodification 2, 3, 6, 9n; of cultural forms 143; decommodification and recommodification in Amsterdam 203–4, 206–11; and decommodification of housing 183, 190–1, 193n, 203–4, 209, 215, 216, 223, 227; of the urban 4, 55–6
Communist Manifesto 266
community organizing: in neoliberal era 254–5; new urban movements 256–7
Community Reinvestment Act (CRA) 1977 221
concrete utopia 48–9, 56, 57–9
The Condition of the Working Class in England in 1844 46, 86–7
Considerations on Western Marxism 95
covenants and charters 63, 73–4, 75
"creative cities" 76, 105, 142–8
creative class, theory of 54, 78, 89, 94; appropriation for justification of neoliberal urban policies 72, 76–7, 147–8; claims of correlations between creative class concentrations and regional

growth in high technology sectors
142, 145; and "creative cities" 142–8;
cultural strategies and role in economic
regeneration of old industrial regions 143,
144; culture industry workers in Berlin
143–5, 146–7; and "dealer class" 139,
140, 141, 148; deconstruction of 139–42,
148; and membership of "political class"
141; Peck's critique of 138–9; problems
with delimiting types of creative activity
139–41
crises of capitalism 7–8, 27–9, 267–70
"crisis of the city" 42–3
critical development studies 103, 104–7,
108, 109
Critical Planning 37, 215
critical reflexivity 111
critical social theory 12, 13–14
critical theory: and critique 13–14;
emphasizes disjuncture between actual
and possible 17–18; entails a critique of
instrumental reason 16–17; is reflexive
16; is theory 15–16; key propositions
of 14–18; and solutions to right to the
city 36–7; and urbanization question
18–22, 58
critical urban theory 11–12, 18–22;
addressing problem of US housing
crisis through 215, 222–7; contribution
of assemblage to 122–3, 130, 132–4;
and contribution to right to the city
25, 26, 29, 33, 36–7, 39; and Marxist
urban theory 96; need for 3–5; need
to account for new political geography
of "gray spaces" 152, 157; and need to
open up debate on the just city 212;
and planning theory 102, 105, 108;
research agendas 117–20, 190; urban
colonialism and new 157–60
critique 12, 19; and critical social theory
13–14
Critique of Everyday Life 93, 98
Croatia 71–2
cultural terms, analysis of right to the city
in 32
culture industry 142–3; in Berlin 143–5,
146–7; *see also* creative class, theory of
Cunningham, David 98
Curran, Winifred 188

The Dark Side of the Nation 94
Davidson, Mark 188

Davis, Mike 88, 99, 154, 255
de Certeau, Michel 109
de Soto, Hernando 222
De Sousa Santos 80
"dealer class" 139, 140, 141, 148
Debord, Guy 97, 98
Debray, Régis 93
debt 269, 270; third world 107
DeFilippis, James 190
deindustrialization 251
democracy: grassroots 6–7; and just city
201, 204–5
deprived and discontented 7, 112; and right
to the city 30–1, 32, 33, 34, 35–6, 39
Derrida, Jacques 92, 94
Desai, Ashwin 25
Dialectic of Enlightenment 92
The Dialectics of Seeing 93
difference, urban 48, 49
discontented: *see* deprived and discontented
displacement: "accumulation by
dispossession" 3, 105, 106, 133, 266;
alternatives to 188–92; and arguments
of low working class mobility in areas
of gentrification 180–2, 183, 186–7,
188; in Boston 177, 178; of "creative
industry" in Berlin 145, 146–7; defining
173; direct chain 185, 187, 188; direct
last-resident 185–6, 187, 188; of elderly
178–9; and exclusion from centrality
57; exclusionary 185, 186, 188; four
types of 185–6; and gentrification 54–5,
145–7, 183, 184–8; indirect 187–8;
industrial 188; injustice of 189; of a
New York tenant 171; pressure 185,
188; as a result of gentrification of
London 174–7; in Shanghai 193n; of
South African peasants 106
Displacement: How to Fight It 173, 183
"Does Gentrification Harm the Poor?" 177
domestic workers 253, 256
Dreamworld and Catastrophe 88
Duany, Andres 188
Dutschke, Rudi 39

Economist Intelligence Unit 1
Egypt 108–9
emotional group-based phenomena to
channel discontent 33
Engels, Friedrich 2, 36, 46, 86–7, 266, 272
Enlightenment 13, 92
Enlightenment Against Empire 92

equity in a just city 200, 201, 203–4
European Charter to Secure Human Rights in the City 73
everyday life, concept of 97–8

Fainstein, Susan 37, 64, 65, 199, 200, 201, 206
Fannie Mae 217, 269
Fanon, Frantz 104
Farías, Ignacio 119, 121, 122, 123, 124, 125, 127, 130
Fast Cars, Clean Bodies 98
Federal Republic of Germany: housing in Berlin 239–40; response to global financial crisis 141; state buildings in Berlin 237, 242–6; and transition from socialism of GDR 237; urban social movements 69, 70, 71, 72, 82n, 147
feminism, transnational 111–14
feminization of poverty 268
financialization 168, 270, 271–3
Flierl, Bruno 233, 248
Florida, Richard 54, 89, 129, 138, 139, 140, 141, 142, 144, 145, 147, 148
Fordism: + Americanism = counterrevolution 92–3; crisis of 65–6; labor regulation 255
Foucault, Michel 91
France: urban planning 87; urbanization process 42–3
Frank, Charlotte 244
Frankfurt School 12, 13, 14, 15, 16–17, 17–18, 89, 93, 96, 107–8
Fraser, Nancy 19, 111, 112
Freddie Mac 217, 269
Freeman, Lance 179, 180, 181, 182, 183, 186, 187
Fried, Marc 179
Friedemann, John 6, 57, 58
Fukuyama, Francis 105

G8 protests 75
García-Herrera, Luz 179
gentrification: and abandonment 184–5; alternatives to 188–92; in Berlin 145–7, 240; commercial 187–8; defining 173, 192n; and displacement 54–5, 145–7, 183, 184–8; of ghettos 160, 181; Hamnett on 173–7; in London 172, 173–7; mobility rates of working-classes after neighborhood 180–2, 183, 186–7, 188; "positive" arguments for

172–3, 177–83; post 9/11 251; rejecting celebration of 189–90; Ruth Glass on 171–2; struggles against 68, 71–2, 258
"Gentrification: Not Ousting the Poor?" 183
German Democratic Republic: architectural and urbanistic mandates for Berlin 233–4, 236, 237–9, 240–2; Reconstruction Law 1950 234; socialist cities of 233–7, 248; state housing 235, 238
ghettos 160, 181
Gilderbloom, John 199
Glasgow 143
Glass, Ruth 171–2, 173, 175
global financial crisis 20, 26–7, 272; background to 267–70; bank bailouts 70, 224, 272; bankers' bonuses 266, 271; as a crisis of capitalism 28–9; establishment's response to 29; German state response to 141; politicization of urban movements after 69–71; providing an alternative to capitalism after 107, 264–7, 271, 273–4; public reactions to 8; right to the city in context of 69–70; state-finance nexus 271–3; US unemployment after 252
globalism 105, 107
globalization 53, 80, 218, 256, 268; anti-globalization movements 68, 69, 81–2n; critique of actually-existing-globalization 105, 107, 113; relationship between planning, imperialism and 104–7
Goldman Sachs 26, 29, 272
Gompers, Samuel 255
Good City Form 86
Goonewardena, Kanishka 111, 112, 157
governmentality 91, 159
Graham, Stephen 119, 121, 124, 125, 126
Gramsci, Antonio 86, 92, 99, 157, 159
"grassroots democracy" 6–7
"gray space" 150, 152–4; of Bedouin Arabs 154–7; and links with *sumood* 161; and urban colonialism 157–60
Great Depression 27, 189–90
"green capitalism" 105
Greenspan, Alan 29
"Grieving for a Lost Home" 179
The Guardian 173, 175

Habermas, Jürgen 13, 14, 16, 17, 19
Habitat International Coalition (HIC) 73, 74, 75

Hackworth, Jason 172, 192n
Haiti 273
Hall, Peter 90
Hammersley, Martin 177
Hamnett, Chris 173–7, 187–8, 192n
Hart, Gillian 103, 106, 107, 111, 113, 114n, 159
Hartman, Chester 172, 173, 183, 185, 187
Hartz reforms 69, 81n, 144
Harvey, David 2–3, 4, 6, 8, 9, 20, 30, 35, 38, 40n, 58, 65, 68, 77, 79, 95, 96, 97, 98, 104, 105, 117, 133, 152, 159, 189, 217, 227n, 266, 267, 270
Haussmann, Georges-Eugène 87
Hayden, Dolores 226
Hayek, Friedrich von 90, 105
hegemony 86, 159, 160
Herema, Tjeerd 207–8
"hidden transcripts" 109, 110
Hitchcock, Henry Russell 92
Horkheimer, Max 13, 14, 17
housing: in Berlin 235, 238–40; commodification and decommodification of 183, 190–1, 193n, 203–4, 209, 215, 216, 223, 227; informal Mumbai 128–9; policy in Great Depression 189–90; *see also* housing crisis in United States; housing in Amsterdam
Housing Act 1937 217
Housing Act 1969 173–4
housing crisis in United States 215–30; bank affidavit scandal 223; and Community Reinvestment Act 221; critical alternatives to 215, 222–7; Critical Planning approach to 215; and foreclosures 217, 226, 266, 271; and myths of speculative home ownership 221–2, 225; nature of 216–18; private profit-oriented market 219, 223–4; and problem of commodification of housing 223; proposals for surface reforms 222–3; rent regulation 223–4, 226, 228n; and reoccupation of abandoned housing 271; restricted role of government 219–20, 224; subprime mortgage crisis 216, 218–22, 269; and types of tenure 221, 225, 226
housing in Amsterdam: construction 203, 206; decommodification 203–4; and livability 209, 212; recommodification 206–11; social housing 198, 198f, 200, 203, 205f, 206–8, 209–10, 211–12; tenure types in Netherlands 207, 209;

transfer of housing associations into housing corporations 207, 211
Housing Studies 190
Hurricane Katrina 37

identity, transformations of 157–60; politics of Bedouin Arabs 164–6; radicalization of Bedouin Arabs 160–4
Immergluck, Dan 220
immigrant voters 259
immigrant workers 69, 81n, 219, 251, 252, 253
immigration 252, 256, 259, 267
imperialism, planning and globalization 104–7
Industrial Revolution 46
"infrapolitics" 109, 110
The International Style 92
Israel: and dealings with RCUV 165–6; and gray spacing of Bedouin Arabs 154–7, 158, 165; land disputes with Bedouin Arabs 154, 156, 161; Managing Authority for the Advancement of the Bedouins (MAAB) 165; policy on Beersheba mosque 156–7; village name dispute with Bedouin Arabs 162, 165–6
Italy 44, 69

Jacobs, Jane 2, 94, 158
Jameson, Fredric 91, 96, 99
Jencks, Charles 92
Johnson, Philip 92
just city 199–202; ascendency of Amsterdam as a 199, 202–6; and demand for full implementation for right to the city 201–2; democracy in 201, 204–5; equity in 200, 201, 203–4; erosion in Amsterdam of a 198–9, 209–11; role of scholarship in rise and fall of 212

Katz, Cindi 106
Keating, Dennis 217, 227
Keynes, John Maynard 218
Keynesianism 66, 68, 77, 88, 90, 95, 270, 271–3; moving in a more socialist direction 273
Kipfer, Stefan 46, 48, 55, 60n, 112, 158, 159, 160
Kopp, Anatole 89

La production de l'espace 49
La révolution urbaine (The urban revolution) 45, 49
labor unions 29, 69, 70; crushing of power of 267–8; organizing in neoliberal era 254–5
Laclau, Ernesto 157, 158
The Language of Postmodern Architecture 92
Late Capitalism 96
Latin America 44, 79, 129, 273
Latour, Bruno 119, 120, 121, 125, 127, 130, 134n
Le Corbusier 88, 90
Le droit à la ville (The right to the city) 45
La Guerre des Rues et des Maisons 87
Learning from Las Vegas 89, 91, 92, 95
Lefebvre, Henri 2, 3, 6–7, 12, 21, 29–30, 35, 37, 43, 45, 46, 47, 49, 51, 53, 55–6, 57, 58, 59, 71–3, 86, 90, 93, 94, 95, 96, 97, 98, 99, 102, 131, 132, 133, 134, 159
Lenin, Vladimir 90, 96, 97, 264, 266, 267
Li, Tania 106
"Light Verse" 275
Limits to Capital 96
local, the 58, 69
London, gentrification of 172, 173–7
Luhmann, Niklas 14
Lynch, Kevin 86

Managing Authority for the Advancement of the Bedouins (MAAB) 165
Manchester 2, 86–7, 143
Mandel, Ernest 96
Marcuse, Herbert 13, 14, 15, 18, 30, 131
Marcuse, Peter 5, 6, 31, 57, 75–6, 102, 105, 111, 112, 130, 160, 184–6, 190, 191–2, 217, 275
Marris, Peter 189
Marvin, Simon 119, 121, 125, 126
Marx, Karl 12, 13, 18, 36, 95, 97, 134, 265, 266, 267, 272
Marxism 13, 14, 97–8, 99
Marxist urban theory = excrescence of capital 95–6, 97
Massumi, Brian 121
material interests, analysis of right to the city in terms of 31–2
materiality 122–3, 128–9
Mayer, Margit 6, 60n, 66, 67, 68, 82n, 158, 210

McFarlane, Colin 119, 121, 122, 123, 124, 125, 127, 128, 129, 130, 131
McKinnish, Terra 182–3
Media Spree project 70, 71, 72, 147
mediation, urban 46–7, 95
memory building 162–4
metabolism, concept of 125, 126
"Metropolis and Mental Life" 98
Mexican debt crisis 1982 270
migrant workers, informal 80, 253
Mitscherlich, Alexander 65
modernism 92, 93, 202; modernism = Breton + Corbusier + Lenin 88–9; modernization = modernism – revolution 90–1
modernization 92, 93, 94; modernization = modernism – revolution 90–1
monopolization problem 268
Mouffe, Chantal 157, 158
multiculturalism 94, 112
Mumbai 123, 128–9
Muthu, Sankar 92
My Poznanciacy 73

Nagar, Richa 112
National Community Reinvestment Coalition 222
Negri, Tony 99, 159
neocolonial binaries 105
neoliberalism 55, 142, 250–1, 270, 271; appropriation of creative class theory 72, 76–7, 147–8; ascendancy in Netherlands 209–10, 212; and development of urban social movements 64, 66–9; impeding mobilization for social change 77, 78, 80
networks, city 121–2
"new metropolitan mainstream" 54–5
New Working Class Organizations (NWCOs) 253–4, 256–7; areas of similarity and difference amongst 259–60; creation of RTTC Alliance 258–9; funding 257; new organizing approaches 260–2
New York City 171, 184
New York City Housing and Vacancy Survey (NYCHVS) 179, 180
New York Times 222
Newman, Kathe 171, 179–80, 181–2, 187
Nieuwmarkt subway station 197–8, 211
Nocera, Joe 222

Non-Aligned Movement 107
non-governmental organizations (NGOs):
    campaigning for formal recognition of
    right to the city 73–5; of limited help to
    movements in global South 78–9
"Not in Our Name" manifesto 71, 72, 82n

Obama, Barack 25–6, 259, 260
One-Dimensional Man 14, 18
Ordinary Cities 105
Orientalism 105
Osborne, Peter 97

Palace of the Republic, Berlin 241–2, 243,
    244
Paris 20, 44, 45, 55, 87, 127, 232;
    Commune 25, 43, 89, 266; May 1968
    27, 28, 43, 52, 89
Park, Robert 35
Passagen-Werk 12, 97
Peck, Jamie 20, 54, 105, 138–9, 148, 172,
    189
periphery and center 56, 57, 104–5, 106
Philosophizing the Everyday 97
Pinochet, Augusto 268
Pithouse, Richard 79
The Planet of Slums 88
planning theory 102–16; benefits of
    encompassing a perspective on critique
    103; catalyzing collective critical
    consciousness among individual
    groups 111–14; and complicity with
    neoliberal urbanism 110; postmodernist
    111–12; relationship to imperialism
    and globalization 104–7; resistance and
    cultural politics of agency 107–10
Playing with Fire 112
political economy: and articulating
    assemblage thought 124–7; characteristics
    of a colonizing urban 158; critique of
    13–14; urban political economy = capital
    + city – politics 96–8
politics of recognition and redistribution
    111, 113
The Politics of Time 97
Popper, Karl 14
postcolonialism 105–6
*Postmodernism, or, The Cultural Logic of Late
    Capitalism* 96
postmodernism 91; planning theory 111–12;
    postmodernism = revolutionary reaction
    93–5

Postone, Moishe 12, 13, 14, 17, 20, 131
poverty, feminization of 268
presidential election 2008 25–6, 259, 260
Principles of Urban Planning, 16 234
The Production of Space 94
public–private partnerships 67, 88

racism 25–6, 33, 251
radical urban theory 89, 90, 94, 95, 98, 99
radicalization of Bedouin Arabs 160–4
Randolph, Bill 174
Reagan, Ronald 250, 251, 268, 270
Reconstruction Law 1950 234
reflexivity, critical 16, 19–20, 111, 113
Regional Council of the Unrecognized
    Villages (RCUV) 164, 165–6
"relational comparison" 106, 111, 113
rent: in Amsterdam 203, 206–7; control in
    GDR 235; cost of renting in US 216;
    increases 171, 174, 185, 187; regulation
    223–4, 226, 228n
rent-gap theory 174, 187, 193n
research agendas 117–20, 190
residents' movement in Amsterdam 203,
    204–5, 205–6, 210–11, 212
resistance, subaltern 107–10
Reveille for Radicals 254
al-Rifa'iya, Hussein 150, 151f
"right to centrality" 46–7
"right to difference" 49
"right to space" 49, 53
The Right to the City 58
"right to the city": analysis in cultural
    terms 32; analysis in terms of material
    interests 31–2; as appropriation 71–3;
    in context of global financial crisis 59,
    69–70; context today 25–7; critical
    urban theory and contribution to 25,
    26, 29, 33, 36–7, 39; demanding full
    implementation of 201–2; formal
    recognition 73–7; future possibilities
    59; a global 77–81; goal of 37–9;
    history of 27–9; Lefebvre's definition
    29–30, 43, 98, 159; "Light Verse" 275;
    meanings of 69–71; new importance
    and content 6, 42, 58–9, 159–60;
    right to consume and right to produce
    36; and struggles for city 44–5; urban
    social movements. *see* urban social
    movements; what city? 35–6; what
    right? 34–5; whose right? 30–4; world
    charter for 63, 73, 74

Right to the City (RTTC) Alliance 70, 72, 251, 253, 259; centered around social reproduction 253–4; creation of 258–9; NWCOs affiliated to 253; organizing in neoliberal era 254–5; response to recomposition of working class 251–2
The Rise of the Creative Class 89
Roberts, John 97
Robinson, David 187
Robinson, Jennifer 19, 105–6, 107, 160
Ross, Kristin 98
Roy, Ananya 54, 79, 102, 103, 105, 113, 118, 129, 132, 134, 154, 157, 158, 159, 160
Ruge, Arnold 97
Rules for Radicals 254
Russian Revolution 27, 32, 248

Said, Edward 105
Sandercock, Leonie 89, 90, 92, 111
Sanders, Bernie 29
Sangtin Writers 112
Sassen, Saskia 53, 57, 118, 121, 125, 126, 134n, 192n
savings and loans crisis 269–70
Sayer, Andrew 12, 119, 128, 133, 134n
Schaeffer, Jan 202–3
Schultes, Axel 244
Scott, James 90, 92, 108, 109, 142
Second International 13, 14
Seeing Like a State 90–1
Segal, Steven 189
self-management 6, 59
Shanghai 193n
signification, process of 52
Simmel, George 45, 98
Simone, Abdou 157, 159, 160
Situationists 89, 95
Smith, Neil 2, 54, 88, 96, 104, 174, 175, 189, 190, 193n, 251
Social Centers 69
social exclusion 44, 67, 68, 70
Social Justice and the City 97
social reproduction 66, 253–4, 266–7
Social Urban Forum (SUF) 75
social wage 250, 261
socialism, cities of really existing 2, 232–3; GDR 233–4; reasons for lack of success in GDR 234–7, 248; and transition back to capitalism in GDR 237
socialist revolution = urban revolution 98–9

Soja, Ed 4, 5, 12, 19, 50, 117, 118, 130, 199
South Africa 79, 106
space = politics 86–8; *see also* urban space
Splintering Urbanism 126
squatting movement, Amsterdam 202–3
state-finance nexus 271–3; populist agitation against 273–4
Stella, Franco 244
subprime mortgage crisis: background to 216–18, 269; pillars of 218–22; *see also* housing crisis in United States
sumood 161–2
Swyngedouw, Erik 125, 126

Taiwan 106
Taylor, John 222
Tenants and Workers United (TWU) 254, 256, 261
Thatcher, Margaret 268, 271
"the city of heart's desire" 35–6, 80
"The Concept of Metropolis" 99
"The Gathering of the Distressed" 32
The Theory of Communicative Action 14
theory/practice problem 17, 18, 25, 57–8
Therborn, Göran 12, 13, 17
There Goes the 'Hood 179, 180–1
A Thousand Plateaus 121
Tickell, Adam 172, 189
Time magazine 183
tourism 76, 77, 78
Towards a New Architecture 90
Towards Cosmopolis 89, 90, 91
Town and Revolution 89
"Traditional and critical theory" 14

Ulbricht, Walter 240
UN – Habitat International Coalition (HIC) 73, 74, 75
unemployment 26, 36, 252, 267–8
UNESCO 73, 74
uneven development theory 96, 104, 133
urban growth, new ideology of: *see* creative class, theory of
urban planning 88, 89, 90, 93; architecture and revolution 88, 89, 90, 93, 95; and architecture in GDR 233–4, 236, 237–9, 240–2; Critical Planning 37, 215; in France 42–3, 87; "hypocritical" 87; of modernism 90, 91, 92; postmodern contribution to 94; production of urban space, accumulation of capital and 104;

rejection in Amsterdam of modernist
202; *see also* planning theory
urban political economy = capital + city –
politics 96–8
The Urban Question 97
"urban renaissance" 53–4
The Urban Revolution 90, 96, 98, 99
urban social movements 7, 38–9, 44, 45,
53; in Amsterdam 199, 202–3, 204–5,
205–6, 210–11, 212; and co-option
into neoliberal urban models 72, 76–7;
in a co-revolutionary movement
30–1; coalitions of 70–1, 72, 75,
76; comparing North American and
European 65–6; and crisis of Fordism
65–6; efforts for formal recognition
of "right to city" 73–7; fragmentation
of 67–8; in FRG 69, 70, 71, 72,
82n, 147; future of 8–9; in global
North 72–3, 77–8, 79–81; in global
South 72–3, 78–9, 79–81; historical
development of 65–9; invoking right
to city as appropriation 71–3; against
the neoliberal city 68–9; and organizing
on a global scale 79; politicization
following global financial crisis 69–71;
right to the city as appropriation
71–3; role of human dignity in 79–80;
transformation of relations between
state and 66–7; *see also* Right to the
City (RTTC) Alliance
urban space: appropriation and domination
of 56; commodification of 2, 3, 4,
55–6; privatization of public 57, 70, 78;
production of 49–53, 93, 96, 104; space
= politics 86–8
Urban Studies 174, 190
urbanization: and centrality 47–8; complete
45–6; and concept of urban 46–9;
"crisis of the city" 42–3; critical theory
and 18–22; and difference 48; in France
42–3; in global South 58; and mediation
46–7; and new centralities 55;
relationship to dynamics of capital 96;

research agendas 117–18; and urbanity
52–3; of the world 12, 20–1, 68, 132–3
USA Today 180
utopias 36, 38, 93, 97, 111, 248; concrete
48–9, 56, 57–9

Venturi, Robert 89, 94
Vietnam 27, 107
Vigdor, Jacob 177–9, 181, 182, 183
Virginia New Majority 254, 260, 261

Wadi al-Na'am mosque rebuild 150, 151f,
166
wages: demand for social 250, 261; stagnant
269
Waquant, Loic 104
Watson, Vanessa 160
Watt, Paul 176
We Are the Poors 25
welfare, dismantling of 68, 69, 250
Whitelegg, Drew 187–8
The Will to Improve 106
Wirth, Louis 46
Wittgenstein, Ludwig 184
women of color 252, 253, 254, 255, 259,
268
workers centers 69
working class: labor union and community
organizing 254–5; organizations for the
new 256–7; recomposition of 251–2;
social reproduction 253–4; *see also*
New Working Class Organizations
(NWCOs)
World Bank 69, 75, 129
World Charter on the Right to the City 73, 74
World Social Forum 32, 34, 37, 73, 82n
World Trade Organization 69, 75
World Urban Forum (WUF) 73, 75–6
Wyly, Elvin 171, 172, 177, 179–80, 181–2,
187

al-Ziadnah, Saleh 154
Žižek, Slavoj 33, 99

Lightning Source UK Ltd.
Milton Keynes UK
UKOW06f1121060315

247399UK00004B/78/P